ENGLAND: A CLASS
OF ITS OWN

ENGLAND: A CLASS OF ITS OWN

An Outsider's View

DETLEV PILTZ

BLOOMSBURY CONTINUUM
LONDON · OXFORD · NEW YORK · NEW DELHI · SYDNEY

BLOOMSBURY CONTINUUM
Bloomsbury Publishing Plc
50 Bedford Square, London, WC1B 3DP, UK
29 Earlsfort Terrace, Dublin 2, Ireland

BLOOMSBURY, BLOOMSBURY CONTINUUM and the Diana logo are trademarks
of Bloomsbury Publishing Plc

First published in Great Britain 2022

A catalogue record for this book is available from the British Library

Library of Congress Cataloguing-in-Publication data has been applied for

ISBN: HB: 978-1-4729-9304-5; eBook: 978-1-4729-9303-8; ePDF: 978-1-4729-9302-1

2 4 6 8 10 9 7 5 3 1

Typeset by Deanta Global Publishing Services, Chennai, India
Printed and bound in Great Britain by CPI Group (UK) Ltd, Croydon CR0 4YY

To find out more about our authors and books visit www.bloomsbury.com
and sign up for our newsletters

Contents

Foreword and Acknowledgements

Englishness is a peculiar beast. The natives use the term straightfor-wardly, with the ease of familiarity. If asked to explain it, their initial response tends to be a rather protracted '*W–e–e–e–ll*', followed by quite a long pause. Englishness is rather like the unicorn – a creature whose appearance is known to all, but which no-one has ever seen or touched: it has a presence, yet at the same time is elusive. Perhaps it is knowing that the desire for a precise definition of Englishness can never be realized that makes the craving for it so insatiable. To eat from the tree of Englishness is to be forever in its thrall and, having partaken, the author is no exception.

A prominent feature of Englishness is class – not in the mean-ing of excellence (although this is often encountered in England), but in its social sense, signifying the division of society into various groups. Class embodies differences between people, and in England has both tangible and intangible dimensions. In the former case, class is openly discussed as something defined by occupation, income and wealth, and education: the hard class markers. The intangible aspect is not aired in public and is a subject almost shamefacedly concealed, denied and glossed over. It finds expression in the soft class markers. These have something mysterious about them, even more so today than in the past, because class differences are regarded as unseemly. Nevertheless, they exist, although they are not always easy to detect. Having hair does not reveal which class you belong to, but how you wear it most definitely does. Being a dog-owner does not indicate your class, but the breed you choose speaks volumes. Owning a car is not a class statement, but how often you wash it is. Going on holiday has nothing to do with class, but what you do when you get there certainly has.

The English know about class. Otherwise why would the phrase 'It depends on your class' be heard so much? Class is even harder to pin down than Englishness because, while Englishness is acknowledged and admired by many, class is to some extent 'off limits' and widely condemned – surely a good reason for bringing it out in the open, without value judgement.

This book attempts to provide a snapshot in words of the English class system – not only from its best side, but 'warts and all', as Oliver Cromwell might say. There are occasions when distorting impressions to the point of caricature cannot entirely be avoided. But is that not quintessentially English, given the great and grand tradition of caricature in England? Has the author come any closer to understanding Englishness and its hallmark, class, in the course of writing this book? Perhaps. At any rate, he is even more fascinated by England than before, and has not escaped the biographer's fate of falling in love with his subject.

My first and overwhelming thanks must go to the wonderland that is England and its wonderful, wonderment-inducing and sometimes wondrously wacky people. To study them makes it virtually impossible not to become an anglophile. My second thank-you goes to all those who have opened my eyes to Englishness and class when I was unseeing, or who have corrected my misconceptions. For their keen-sighted reading of the manuscript I thank Hans-Wolfgang Arndt, Robert Colls, Richard Jenkyns, Geoff Sammon, David Walker and Alexander Piltz. Special thanks go to my publisher Robin Baird-Smith for his confidence in this book, to Jamie Birkett for his great skill and attention to detail and also to Sarah Jones for project editing the book through to publication. Any mistakes and inaccuracies contained in this book are of course my own, especially where they are there by design.

Autumn 2021, Detlev Piltz

Introduction

Class does not matter in England – say some. England is divided by class – say others. The classes struggle against each other – say some. The classes live in harmony – say others. And so it has continued since time immemorial. Quotations from a stroll through 240 years of English history say it best.

I will back the masses against the classes.

Prime Minister William Ewart Gladstone, 1886

There is no change which is more marked in our country than the continual and rapid effacement of class differences.

(Later) Prime Minister Winston Churchill, 1940

England is the most class-ridden country under the sun.

Novelist George Orwell, 1941

The class war is over.

Prime Minister Harold Macmillan, 1959

Margaret Thatcher is fighting for her class, I am here fighting for my class.

President of the National Union
of Mineworkers (NUM) Arthur Scargill, 1984

I want to get totally rid of class distinction.

Prime Minister Margaret Thatcher, 1985

We are all middle class now.

Deputy Prime Minister John Prescott, 1997

A child's social class background at birth is still the best predictor of how well he or she will do at school and later on in life.

Prime Minister Gordon Brown, 2008

The sharp-elbowed middle classes – like me and my wife.

Prime Minister David Cameron, 2010

It is virtually impossible to open a newspaper today without headlines such as 'Britain's obsession with class is defeated' on the one hand, or 'Classless Britain is a myth' on the other leaping out at you from the page – not infrequently in the same publication. Who should we believe? The politicians, the scientists, the media?

Class exists. The very fact that the Great British Class Survey was conducted in 2013 by the BBC, together with the huge response it generated, demonstrates that classes are real. What has changed is their weight and their markers. Class is not talked about in public, but is played down or even denied altogether. Class is the elephant in the room. The traditional, hard markers of occupation, income, wealth and education or title are no longer reliable in isolation and only signify social class in conjunction with other, soft markers such as accent, language usage and behaviour. Although this has always been the case, the weight of hard class markers has steadily declined, while soft class markers have gained in importance. All the more reason to look at them more closely.

The first part of this book lays the foundations. In view of the English reticence to speak about class and widespread tendency to deny its very existence, a number of things must be brought out in the open. Why is the phrase 'It depends on your class' heard so often? Class or something like it must exist, together with the accompanying social framework. The focus of class is on differences between people. But which ones? This section therefore deals with inequality, the definition of class, the traditional class markers and the age-old division of society into working, upper and middle classes, and possibly an underclass as well. It also explores the implications for people of belonging to a class. The fear of class and a class society leads to the phenomenon of class denial, which is expressed not only by flatly rejecting the notion, but also in language, dress and behaviour. For politicians and their parties to gain and retain power, they rely on the votes of people from all classes. Class and politics are therefore inextricably linked.

Part two of the book is devoted to what are termed the soft class markers. They stand alongside the hard class markers (occupation, income, education) that dominate the official studies and statistics on class. Unlike the latter, they are not quantifiable, but they are no less visible and may these days even be more important. The standards by which people measure the soft class markers of their fellow human beings are not written down anywhere, but are soft and silent (Chapter 9). These soft class markers include virtually all the characteristics and activities through which people achieve self-realization, their language (including accent and terminology), manners, attitudes, dress, leisure activities, furniture and even their gardens and pets.

The third part of the book discusses the question of whether a person's class is unalterable, and contemplates the possibility of a classless society or at least class-free zones. While classes persist, all individuals will be born into one, their class of origin; many will remain in it for their entire lives, although some will switch. Like all rules, those governing class can be broken. Whereas the English don't really care what others think of them or their class system, foreigners find the latter both intriguing and astonishing.

Part four celebrates the England that exists beyond class boundaries and ventures a classless look to the future.

This book is not a wish list or a moral treatise, nor is it a recipe book for a better world or a guide to etiquette. The intention here is to reflect what is, rather than what could or should be.

We have not aimed to be politically correct. Far from it. Political correctness does too much to bury the subject of class. Concealing class deepens class distinctions by impeding class awareness. This is extremely unfair. Here, as so often, political correctness serves neither justice nor fairness. PC was once thought to protect the weak and minorities from insult and oppression, but all too frequently it disguises the pursuit of selfish, far-from-righteous interests by suppressing truth and dissenting opinions under the cloak of morality. Why not call a spade a spade?

Around 200 years ago a comedy entitled *Scherz, Satire, Ironie und tiefere Bedeutung* was published in Germany. Its title in English, 'Jest, Satire, Irony and Deeper Significance', could serve as a strapline for this book, which endeavours to bring together class-related facts, opinions, insinuations, truths, assumptions, theories, science and silliness. In 1895 Oscar Wilde's famous comedy *The Importance of Being Earnest* was performed for the first time in London. Its title is a second motto for this book if you put in a 'not' between 'of' and 'being': not being earnest being a fundamental rule of Englishness.

This book begins with quotations, ends with one, and is packed with them in between. Quoting others is an English virtue or an English vice, depending on your point of view. We prefer the former. Class in England has prompted such outstanding writings that not to quote from them would be to squander riches.

Part I

About Class

1

'It depends on your class'

England is the most class-ridden country under the sun.

George Orwell, *The Lion and the*
Unicorn (1941)

ENGLAND

It is a peculiarity of England that no-one appears to know exactly which geographical area is actually meant, not even the English themselves, which led George Orwell to observe: 'We call our islands by no less than six different names: England, Britain, Great Britain, the British Isles, the United Kingdom and, in very exalted moments, Albion.'[1] George Mikes said: 'When people say England, they sometimes mean Great Britain, sometimes the United Kingdom, sometimes the British Isles – but never England.'[2] This may be a little overdone, but perhaps is not too far from the truth. Prime Minister H. H. Asquith's tombstone in the graveyard in Abingdon Oxfordshire reads:

Earl of Oxford and Asquith

Prime Minister of England April 1908 to December 1916

'England' here is clearly an understatement. Nearly every author writing about England, the United Kingdom or a part thereof has therefore felt it necessary to explain exactly which entity he is concerned with. The 'official' classification is (or rather seems to be) the following:

The 'British Isles' comprise Great Britain, (the whole of) Ireland, the Isle of Man, the Hebrides, the Orkney Islands, the Shetland Islands, the Scilly Isles and the Channel Islands.

'Great Britain' refers to England, Scotland and Wales as created in 1707.

The 'United Kingdom' and 'Britain' refer to Great Britain (as defined above) and Northern Ireland as established in 1921.

'Albion' (rather archaically) denotes Britain *or* England.

'England' is the central and southern part of Britain as opposed to Scotland, Wales and Northern Ireland.

We are dealing here with England (the part) and the English, and hope to be forgiven if we use the terms English or British incorrectly. Those residents of other parts of the British Isles who recognize themselves in our comments, despite their restriction to England, should feel free to do so.

Statistically speaking, England as a country is unremarkable. It occupies 130,395 km^2 – not much compared to giants such as the USA with 9,826,675 km^2, China with 9,571,302 km^2 and Australia with 7,602,024 km^2, or even its European neighbours such as France with 674,843 km^2, Spain with 504,645 km^2 and Germany with 357,340 km^2, but a lot compared to the 254 other states with a smaller land mass. It is inhabited by 54.3 million people, compared to 66.3 million in France, 82 million in Germany, 143.6 million in Russia and 317.2 million in America. The majority of the population lives in cities with more than 100,000 residents, the remainder in smaller towns and in the country. The gross domestic product is US$2,600 billion, compared to US$3,800 billion in Germany. There are no exceptionally high mountains: the tallest, Scafell Pike in Cumbria, has a height of 3,209 feet. The Thames, England's second longest river (after the Severn), is 215 miles long, and in Wast Water in the Lake District, the country's deepest lake, you can dive down to a depth of 258 feet. The weather is neither particularly good nor particularly bad, with an average temperature of 10°C, maximum temperatures in summer of 32°C and minimum temperatures in winter of −10°C. There is not a single natural feature in the country that ranks anywhere as the world's highest, longest, deepest, largest, hottest or coldest. Everything seems most average. Really?

ENGLISHNESS

This country is a blessed nation.
The British are special.
The world knows it.
In our innermost thoughts, we know it.
This is the greatest nation on earth.

Prime Minister Tony Blair, farewell speech, 10 May 2007

Britain is the greatest country in the world.

Prime Minister Clement Attlee, *As It Happened*
(autobiography, 1954)

I find England so overwhelmingly the best country in the world that it is really bad form to say how much.

Godfrey Smith, *The English Companion* (1996)

England is English. There is nothing new or original about that statement. Generations of Englishmen and foreigners have tried to reveal the Englishness of England, to define the English or national character. And many have written, and are still writing, books of varying thickness and quality about it:[3] some factual and scientific, others humorous; some admiring, others critical of the country's deficiencies; many mourning the loss of Englishness – but all fascinated by and passionate about their subject. No other people on earth appears to have inspired so many portraits from such differing viewpoints as England and the English. The search for Englishness, the English character or a national identity resembles the quest for the Holy Grail. It never ends.

8

Many things that make England unique are easily visible. An Englishman unaware he was coming home would know immediately that he was in England, whether he was crossing the English Channel by ship and approaching the cliffs of the south coast or driving away from the Channel Tunnel or flying into London. A glance at the landscape would suffice. As George Orwell put it:

> When you come back to England from any foreign country, you have immediately a sensation of breathing a different air. Even in the first few minutes dozens of small things conspire to give you this feeling. The beer is bitterer, the coins are heavier, the grass is greener, the advertisements are more blatant. The crowds in the big towns with their mild knobby faces, their bad teeth and gentle manners are different from a European crowd.[4]

However, the fascination goes beyond these outer signs. Is there an English national character or a national identity, to use the more modern term? Are there character traits possessed only by Englishmen, or that are especially pronounced in the English? Or are there traits that most other people have but the English do not? And if such peculiarities do exist, why have they occurred in England of all places? Why are the English of all people the way they are? Does the reason lie in an accident of geography, of the island location, or in the weather of the British Isles, as Harry Mount describes in his book *How England Made the English*? It is no coincidence that the English like to be called the island race. Are the effects still being felt of the 400-year rule by the Romans, the Anglo-Saxon settlement from the fourth century onwards, the invasion by the Vikings, or the Norman Conquest in 1066? Or the abolition of Roman Catholicism in favour of Protestantism in 1531? Are we in our search detecting consequences of the British Empire, which lost the American colonies in 1776 but nonetheless ruled one-quarter of the world for some 200 years, the empire on which the sun never set? Or is it the other way round: can only a race with a quite exceptional character build up and maintain such an empire? And what was the influence of the two world wars and the loss of the empire following the Second World War?

Although impossible to define, Englishness can still be experienced and described. There are hundreds or maybe more small characteristics and differences compared to other races that make the Englishness of England what it is. Many observers have compiled lists, whose individual points, like the dots of colour of an impressionist painting, are intended to give a picture of Englishness when combined to form a whole. Most famous among them are George Orwell,[5] John Betjeman[6] and T. S. Eliot,[7] who are all quoted along with many others by Peter Mandler.[8] Jeremy Paxman, who after George Orwell has perhaps delved deepest into the traits of Englishness,[9] undertook to do the same:[10]

> Off the top of my head, mine would include 'I know my rights', village cricket and Elgar, Do-It-Yourself, punk, street fashion, irony, vigorous politics, brass bands, Shakespeare, Cumberland sausages, double-decker buses, Vaughan Williams, Donne and Dickens, twitching net curtains, breast-obsession, quizzes and crosswords, country churches, dry-stone walls, gardening, Christopher Wren and *Monty Python*, easy-going Church of England vicars, the Beatles, bad hotels and good beer, church bells, Constable and Piper, finding foreigners funny, David Hare and William Cobbett, drinking to excess, Women's Institutes, fish and chips, curry, Christmas Eve at King's College, Cambridge, indifference to food, civility and crude language, fell-running, ugly caravan sites on beautiful clifftops, crumpets, Bentleys and Reliant Robins, and so on.

Tony Blair's list was shorter but equally impressive:

> There's still no place on earth that has our combination of qualities. Our creativity, our determination, our courage, our sense of fairness . . . Foreigners will continue to ask: Why does such a small

country produce so many great actors, singers, authors, architects? Why is there such a concentration of ground-breaking scientists, inventors, thinkers? The answer I think is that there is still something called the British genius – a collection of qualities deep in our character.[11]

Anthropologist Kate Fox takes a more dynamic approach in listing the defining characteristics of Englishness.[12] She maps these characteristics as a system with a core – 'social dis-ease' – surrounded by three clusters: reflexes, outlooks and values. The reflexes include humour, moderation and hypocrisy. The outlooks cover empiricism, Eeyorishness and class consciousness; and the values are fair play, courtesy and modesty. These characteristics are neither ranked nor placed side by side. Instead they are interconnected and influence each other, a breathing, interdependent system.

INDIVIDUALISM, HYPOCRISY, BELONGING, HUMOUR

Of the many traits of Englishness there are four without which the English preoccupation with class would hardly be conceivable: individualism, hypocrisy, belonging and humour. A prerequisite of class is that people are different – individuals and not simply clones. Individualism is deeply ingrained in the English. A. H. Halsey put it thus:

> Most fundamentally, British culture is deeply individualistic. It is no accident that Hume and Locke are its philosophers rather than Hegel or Marx. The deeply embedded cultural assumption is that ultimate values are individual, that society is in no sense superior to the sum of the people who make it up; that collectivism can only be instrumental and that the state is best when minimal. Not that ordinary British men and women or their politicians have ever had much taste for such abstractions: it is just that individualism is built into 'custom and practice', into local workplaces and

community organizations, into all commonsensical explanations of why people do what they do.[13]

An equally interesting aspect of the English character with regard to class could be summed up by the words contradiction or paradox. The English are able effortlessly to reconcile character traits that most other races would regard as completely incompatible. The national term for this is hypocrisy, which is highlighted as a defining characteristic of Englishness not only by foreigners but also by the English themselves. The best example is probably money and the taboo on talking about that most sordid of subjects. Of course, the English are just as interested in money as anyone else, and prefer living in the lap of luxury to life on a shoestring. Not for nothing is England called a 'nation of shopkeepers', an expression often ascribed to Napoleon but actually coined in a non-pejorative sense in *The Wealth of Nations* (1776) by Adam Smith. Be that as it may, mentioning money is a no-no while making and having it are taken for granted. For the upper echelons, talking about money is even deemed vulgar or common, although they also undoubtedly owe their position to their money or the money of their ancestors.

Another example from history is the British Empire. It is truly astonishing that someone could become famous for making the following utterance: 'We [the English] seem, as it were, to have conquered and peopled half the world in a fit of absence of mind.'[14] Surely it is much likelier that the biggest empire humanity has ever seen was created in anything but a state of absent-mindedness, but took intelligent planning – although naturally not in the sense of a master plan for the next 200 years, but a constant, step-by-step approach when an opportunity for further expansion arose. Even more surprisingly, this empire was created and governed while the attitude of most intellectuals (both left- and right-leaning) was against it. They regarded the British Empire with a sort of amused detachment, made jokes about Kipling's White Man's Burden and 'Rule Britannia', sneered about Anglo-Indian colonels and generally claimed to be outside the 'empire racket'. Empire bashing was a favourite sport even before the empire was over. At the same time, virtually none of these anti-imperialists lifted a finger against the empire; instead, on the contrary, they were perfectly ready to accept and enjoy the products of empire and the other benefits the empire brought with it. Their own morality and their own souls could only be saved by sneering at the people who held the empire together.[15]

With the third example of hypocrisy we are already entering the realm of class. A large majority of all Englishmen are against people being vested with privileges simply by birth. They regard this as unfair, unjust and a breach of the principle that 'all men are equal'. But a similar proportion feel most honoured if a duke opens their fête or flower show or becomes the president of their club; likewise, most people consider the hereditary monarchy – the ultimate embodiment of privilege derived from birth – to be a good form of government, even though the monarch is little more than a figurehead.

The third factor when it comes to understanding the English class system is the desire shared by virtually all Englishmen to belong to a group. One way is a unique culture of clubs and societies. Belonging to a group also means excluding those who are not members, and this too is a prominent feature of Englishness. Such clubs also represent the class to which one belongs or with which one identifies oneself.

The fourth major component is humour, which is a typical, if not the archetypal, characteristic of the English. It comes in many shapes and forms, from irony to understatement, self-deprecation, wordplay, self-mockery, parody, wit, satire, teasing, banter, sarcasm, comedy, etc. If an Englishman were asked to complete the following list of national word associations – American money, French food and drink, Italian way of life, German efficiency, Russian soul – with a British attribute, nine times out of ten he would insert the word 'humour'. On the rare occasions on which the English speak about their class system, their favourite ploy is to make fun of it. The lower class laughs at the upper, the upper class mocks the lower – invariably accompanied by the quip that the whole thing is a bit of a joke: if it were actually meant seriously, only a large dose of humour would save the day.

A further aspect of Englishness spotted by perspicacious observers is that an Englishman is not aware of his Englishness, nor is he interested in probing it too deeply. The historian and author John Julius Norwich summed it up: 'What is quintessentially English is not bothering about it.' Accordingly, a quintessential Englishman would not write a book about Englishness and class. How wonderful then that Englishness also includes a willingness to break rules!

CLASS

Whether Englishman or foreigner, anyone describing England has always, alongside the many traits constituting Englishness, referred to class and its many derivations: class system, class war, class rules, class consciousness, class distinctions, class society, lower, middle and upper class, underclass, etc. Likewise, anyone visiting England today will inevitably at some point be confronted with class as a particular feature of Englishness. 'It depends on your class' is an answer likely to be received to any number of questions:

Why do some people address everyone as 'love' or 'darling' or 'dear', although they don't know each other?

Why do some people say 'napkin' and others 'serviette', some 'loo' others 'toilet', some 'pudding' others 'afters'?

Why do some people introduce themselves with 'How do you do? I'm George Hamilton', others with 'Hello, I'm George. Nice to meet you.'?

Why do some children call their parents 'Mummy and Daddy', others 'Mam and Dad', and some speak of their parents as 'my father, my mother', others of 'my dad, my mum'?

Why do some people call their midday meal 'lunch', others 'dinner', or some call their evening meal 'supper', while others call it 'tea'?

A catalogue like the one above that confines itself to vocabulary and pronunciation can be drawn up for virtually every area of human life, such as variations in dress, in hairstyle, in home furnishings, leisure activities, etc. Class is essentially about differences – differences between people. Why do these disparities exist? Ever so often the answer is: 'It depends on your class' or 'That depends on one's class.'

The natural response is to ask what class means. Which classes are there, and how is class expressed? The reply is generally rather hesitant, convoluted, and guaranteed to start up an interesting conversation. If this leads to curiosity and a desire to research the subject, the result might be similar to what you will find in this book.

Class has evolved in England as an elephant in the room. The word was once on the brink of extinction (in politics at least). The concept itself also has other names, and there is a plethora of related terms and social phenomena that describe class or refer to it: status, rank, ranking, position, background, gentleman, privilege, establishment, elite, meritocracy, aristocracy, high society, oligarchy, upper class, snobbery, social mobility, manners, estates, social hierarchy, middle class, working class, old money, *nouveau riche*, ruling class, chavs, proletariat, underclass, arrogance, standing, lifestyle, precariat, celebrity, identity, classless society, class envy, class war, anarchy – all of which disprove those who love to talk about Britain today as a classless society or who regard class as a social dinosaur.

One thing we will not encounter is the so-called English class *system*. A system is distinguished by rules, consistency, methodology, reproducibility and recognizability. English class rules do not represent a system in this sense. In fact, quite the opposite: the English class 'system' is a mishmash of characteristics and behavioural patterns, rules and exceptions, confusions, vaguenesses and contradictions.

The starting point is equality or rather inequality among human individuals.

2

Equality and Meritocracy

When everyone is somebodee, then no one's anybody.

W. S. Gilbert, *The Gondoliers* (1889)

Equality may perhaps be a right, but no power on earth can ever turn it into a fact.

Honoré de Balzac, *La Duchesse de Langeais* (1834)

For as long as records have existed, equality and inequality have been key concepts of human societies. The saying 'all men are equal' has permeated religious, political and social traditions in Western societies at least for more than 2,000 years. As a statement of fact, 'all men are equal' is of course nonsense. The opposite is the case: all men are unequal. No one person is the same as the next. People famously attach the greatest of importance to their individuality: 'I am different from everyone else.' To be told you are the same as all others is universally understood as an insult. Men and women are not alike, otherwise there would be no human race. Genetic endowment, including height, weight, appearance, skin colour, intelligence, musicality and sporting talent, as well as the circumstances into which one is born, including native land, home town, wealth, parental income and education, etc., are determinants of inequality, not equality. They create disparities in income, wealth, education, employment, influence and status. Every one of the 100-metre finalists at the 2012 Olympics in London was not only black but a descendant of West Africans, and all from families who had once been slaves. It's pretty much been that way ever since Jesse Owens competed in Berlin in 1936. In most ethnic groups poor students perform about 20 per cent worse than the average. The one exception is children of Chinese heritage: 90 per cent of poor Chinese children get five good GCSEs and beat every other demographic irrespective of social class;[1] the young Chinese are the best pupils in Great Britain.[2] Can all this be a coincidence? Whether a society should eradicate or compensate for these inequalities, and to what extent that is possible if desired, is quite a different matter (see Chapter 29).

WHICH EQUALITY?
In England, equality was for centuries chiefly understood to mean equal political rights – who can hold political office, and who decides on the holders: in sum, active and passive suffrage. Up to 1832 only male owners of property worth a certain sum were entitled to vote. Following the 1832 Reform Act, voting rights were extended to adult males who owned or rented propertied land of a certain value, thus granting the right to vote to one in seven adult males. Although the franchise was subsequently expanded in 1867 and 1884, it continued to be restricted by a minimum property requirement, and women still had no vote. Only with the 1918 Representation of the People Act were all men over 21 given the vote without property restrictions. Yet women had to be over 30 to vote and were still subject to minimum property qualifications. It was not until 1928 and the introduction of the so-called 'flapper' vote that all women over 21 were granted suffrage whatever their financial circumstances in the same way as men to complete the political equality of the sexes. In 1969 the voting age was lowered to 18. Today, regardless of their individual characteristics and circumstances, all people have the right to vote and are eligible to hold political positions.

Many other inequalities have been dismantled over recent centuries. Slavery, servitude and forced labour have been abolished, at least in Western countries. As far as basic living standards are concerned, a worker in the twenty-first century is in many respects better off than was a nineteenth-century duke. Nowadays, the ways in which the existential needs of both dukes and workers are met are fundamentally identical. In England all citizens enjoy the same medical care and are provided with food, clothing and a roof over their heads in time of need. Many key constituents of modern life benefit the population absolutely equally and regardless of material status. Just about everyone can receive the same television and radio programmes, read the same newspapers and books and have the same access to the internet. Nearly everyone has a car and most people can go on holiday. Sufficient clothing of every kind is available to all. Overall, the past 150 years have seen a tremendous levelling-out of living conditions from the bottom up.

One remaining area of inequality is that of people's wealth and income. Following the French economist Thomas Piketty's *Capital in the Twenty-First Century* (2014),[3] it is impossible to open a newspaper or switch on the radio or television without encountering a discussion about inequality. Previously unknown terms such as 'Gini coefficient' and 'wealth and income distribution' have become almost commonplace. For the United Kingdom the latest figures are as follows: the Gini coefficient (0 = perfect equality, 1 = perfect inequality) for income is 0.32, and for wealth 0.68. As bald figures, these numbers tell us very little. They do not become meaningful until compared to other countries' values, when they answer the question of which nations are more or less equal than Britain. In the USA the corresponding indicators are 0.4/0.85 (therefore the distribution of income and wealth is more unequal in the USA than in Britain), compared to 0.3/0.77 in Germany, 0.32/0.70 in France. The top 10 per cent of earners in the UK account for 28 per cent of the total national income after tax, compared with the US (30 per cent), Germany (23.5 per cent) and France (25.3 per cent). The share of the top 10 per cent in assets in the UK is 47 per cent, in the US 78 per cent, Germany 59 per cent and France 50 per cent (if you believe statistics).

THE TRAGEDY OF MERITOCRACY

Ironically or tragically, such inequalities have resulted (not solely, but at least in part) from the achievement of recent years that was intended to put an end to class-related inequality: meritocracy. Meritocracy is a society or social system or organization in which people achieve power, positions, status and money because of their personal abilities and not because of their family background, money, connections or social position. The German word *Leistungsgesellschaft* (literally: achievement-oriented society) hits it on the head.

Meritocracy embodies equality of opportunity. Equal opportunity found its first concrete expression in the American Revolution of 1776, in a proclamation immortalized in the US Declaration of Independence: 'All men are created equal' also meant having access to the full range of possibilities offered by human existence, including power and wealth, which had only been attainable until then by birth. As the physician and historian David Ramsey put it in his oration on the advantages of American independence (1778): 'All offices lie open to men of merit of whatever rank or condition. Even the reins of state may be held by the son of the poorest man, if he is possessed of abilities that are equal to this important station.' In his autobiography, Thomas Jefferson explained that his life had been directed towards creating 'an opening for the aristocracy of virtue and talent', to replace the old aristocracy of privilege and, in many cases, brute stupidity. This has become reality in present-day England. Graduates applying to join the UK Civil Service must complete a completely meritocratic process, beginning with anonymous rounds of psychometric and intelligence tests. If they pass these successfully they will be invited to spend a day at an assessment centre in Westminster and get a brochure in which is written: 'Fair and open recruitment is fundamental to us and underlies every part of the Fast Stream Assessment Centre process. We will assess you solely on the basis of your performance in the exercises and interview.'

However, there is also a snag, one that did not escape the early observer of America, Alexis de Tocqueville, in his *Democracy in America* (1835). In a chapter entitled 'Why the Americans are Often so Restless in the Midst of Their Prosperity', he sketched an enduring analysis of the relationship between dissatisfaction and high expectation, between envy and equality:

> When all the prerogatives of birth and fortune have been abolished, when every profession is open to everyone, an ambitious man may think it is easy to launch himself on a great career and feel that he has been called to no common destiny. But this is a delusion which experience quickly corrects. When inequality is the general rule in society, the greatest inequalities attract no attention. But when everything is more or less level, the slightest variation is haunting inhabitants of democracies in the midst of abundance and for that disgust with life sometimes gripping them even in calm and easy circumstances. In France, we are worried about the increasing rate of suicides. In America, suicide is rare, but I am told that madness is commoner than anywhere else.

The question is inescapable: if it is only personal achievement that should lead on to glory and wealth, then what of those who do not achieve that? Are they to blame for not being successful?

The capabilities, virtues and talents that people possess are not actually the same, but differ widely. The outcome of equal opportunity is therefore always inequality, because people are different, and some are better at reaching set goals than others. This was the case in Germany in 1948, when each citizen was given the sum of 60 deutschmarks after the currency reform. Some blew the lot within days; others used it to found a fortune.

The British sociologist Michael Young, who penned the Labour Party's 1945 manifesto, achieved fame in this connection with his book, *The Rise of the Meritocracy* (1958), a term he also coined. The title of the book is misunderstood by many who have not read it. It is a satire, concerned less with the advance of the meritocrats than with the misery of the majority of losers in the battle for power and wealth.

> In the old days, no class was homogeneous in brains: clever members of the upper classes had as much in common with clever members of the lower classes as they did with stupid members of their own. Now that people are classified by ability, the gap between the classes has inevitably become wider. The upper classes are, on the one hand, no longer weakened by self-doubt and self-criticism. Today the eminent know that success is just reward for their own capacity, for their own efforts, and for their own undeniable achievement. They deserve to belong to a superior class. They know, too, that not only are they of higher calibre to start with, but that a first-class education has been built upon their native gifts.
>
> What can they have in common with people whose education stopped at sixteen or seventeen, leaving them with the merest smattering of dog-science? How can they carry on a two-sided conversation with the lower classes when they speak another, richer and more exact language? Today, the elite know that, except for a grave error in administration, which should at once be corrected if brought to light, their social inferiors are inferiors in other ways as well – that is, in the two vital qualities, of intelligence and education, which are given pride of place in the more consistent value system of the twenty-first century.

And as a corollary:

> As for the lower classes, their situation is different too. Today all persons, however humble, know they have had every chance. They are tested again and again. If on one occasion they are off-colour, they have a second, a third, and fourth opportunity to demonstrate their ability. But if they have been labelled 'dunce' repeatedly they cannot any longer pretend; their image of themselves is more nearly a true, unflattering, reflection. Are they not bound to recognize

that they have an inferior status – not as in the past because they were denied opportunity; but because they are inferior? For the first time in human history the inferior man has no ready buttress for his self-regard.

In Ferdinand Mount's judgement, Young 'was out to show . . . that in a society where all the top places are awarded on merit the losers have no hiding place and no excuse.'[4] To the injury of poverty, a meritocratic system adds the insult of shame.[5] What Young wrote and indeed predicted some 60 years ago did not just remain a theory. Naturally, no Englishman who has made it to the top would be openly dismissive of those who have not. But the Russian businessman Mikhail Khodorkovsky, one of the so-called oligarchs, who became rich after the collapse of Communism, did not beat about the bush:

> If a man is not an oligarch, something is not right with him. It means for some reason he was unable to become an oligarch. Everyone had the same starting conditions, everyone could have done it. If a man didn't do it, it means there are some sorts of problems with him.[6]

He paid a heavy price however, spending ten years (until 2013) in a Russian prison.

Meritocracy is often seen as the antithesis of elitism in the sense that it supersedes the latter. This is correct if someone belongs to the elite solely on the basis of their family, their background or hierarchy, without having achieved anything themselves. It is incorrect if the elite status derives from ability. Meritocracy is nothing other than an elitism based on competence, and the purer the meritocracy gets, the more elitist it becomes. The way in which players in the England football team or English participants in the Olympic Games are chosen is meritocratic because only the best footballers and athletes are included. Background and connections do not count. At the same time, this selection is highly elitist. Those chosen are the best and therefore the winners. For each individual selected, countless others are not; they are the losers. It cannot be emphasized enough that meritocracy or a society based on achievement rules out equality. If only the best rise to the top, there will always be losers, and the losers will always be in the majority. This can be described as the tragedy of meritocracy: fair maybe, but nonetheless cruel.

The disparity of treatment between the winners and the rest is magnified by a phenomenon familiar from Greek history which modern sociologists call the 'winner-takes-all society'.[7] In the ancient Olympic Games, only the victor mattered; all the others were losers, even the runner-up. The winner alone was crowned with a wreath in the arena and honoured in his native city with money, honorary citizenship and a grand burial. Some aspects of life in modern societies are still similarly black-and-white. Take the English electoral system, for example. The candidate who is elected the MP for their constituency by a majority of just one vote receives the sole authority and salary of a member of parliament for that ward. All the other contenders go completely by the board.

The same thing happens in economic life too. Someone who is the first to invent something is granted a patent and can earn a lot of money; the person who comes along two days later does not obtain a patent.

However, there is a widespread perception that rewards should be tiered according to competence and performance. Someone with a rating of 100 should receive the highest reward; the reward for a score of 99 should be 1 per cent lower, while a performance of 90 should be rewarded on a level 10 per cent below that of the top performer. In real life, however, this is not the case either. Consider the winner of a tennis tournament who shades the match with just five or ten superior shots, say, or someone who wins a 100 metres or downhill ski race by being a few hundredths of a second faster than the runner-up. They are only a fraction better than the competitors beaten into second place, and probably only negligibly better than those in third, fourth and fifth place. However, the reward the winner receives is not just marginally higher than that of the others, but can possibly be twice as much. As a rule, the winner of a piano, violin or other music competition is only infinitesimally superior to their fellow-contestants, who have probably worked and practised just as hard, but only the first-placed performer can hope to become famous and maybe even rich; of the others, usually nothing further is heard. The situation is no different for careerists in the corporate world. The candidate who emerges victorious from the contest to become the company's CEO may have been only 1 per cent better than their rivals, yet as supremo they wield greater power and earn more money than the other board members.

This depressing consequence of the meritocracy concept for the losers has not gone unnoticed by more recent political commentators.[8] But not even they have so far thought of a remedy. Help may be at hand. The University of California under the presidency of Janet Napolitano instructs professors not to use expressions such as 'America is the land of opportunity' or 'I believe the most qualified person should get the job' or 'Everyone can succeed in this society, if they work hard enough' (to name but a few entries on the lengthy list). Why? Because these sentences are deemed to be 'microaggressions – considered examples of subconscious racism' and to promote the 'myth of meritocracy'. They imply that those who do not succeed have only themselves to blame.[9]

EDUCATION

One inequality that is particularly marked in Britain and an eternal bone of contention is the following: in England a disproportionately high number of top leadership positions across society are held by former pupils of independent schools (fee-paying, private or public schools) and Oxbridge alumni (graduates from Oxford or Cambridge universities). According to related figures published by the Social Mobility and Child Poverty Commission:[10]

About 7 per cent of pupils attend independent schools. But they provide 71 per cent of senior judges, 62 per cent of senior armed forces officers, 55 per cent of permanent secretaries, 53 per cent of senior diplomats, 50 per cent of members of the House of Lords, 45 per cent of public body chairs, 44 per cent of the *Sunday Times*

Rich List, 43 per cent of newspaper columnists, 36 per cent of the Cabinet, 35 per cent of the national rugby team, 33 per cent of MPs, 33 per cent of the England cricket team, 26 per cent of BBC executives and 22 per cent of the Shadow Cabinet.

Less than 1 per cent of the adult population have graduated from Oxbridge. But Oxbridge graduates provide 75 per cent of senior judges, 59 per cent of the Cabinet, 57 per cent of permanent secretaries, 50 per cent of diplomats, 47 per cent of newspaper columnists, 44 per cent of public body chairs, 38 per cent of members of the House of Lords, 33 per cent of BBC executives, 33 per cent of the Shadow Cabinet, 24 per cent of MPs and 12 per cent of the *Sunday Times* Rich List.

These figures are not necessarily representative of the present day. Because senior positions are not usually obtained until between the ages of 40 and 60, they depict the educational trends of 20 to 40 years ago. The report acknowledges this, and finds patchy evidence for more diversity. Actually, many things have changed here recently. This applies to nearly all the professions mentioned, and business in particular. In 1995, 2005 and 2015, of the hundred largest British companies' CEOs, 42, 27 and 23 had, respectively, been to Oxbridge. In 1995, three-quarters of the 100 largest British companies' heads had attended public schools. The figure was still over half in 2005, and just under one-third in 2015.[11] But overall the future leaders who are being educated at present still appear to be from a narrow range of social backgrounds. The Commission considers this to be a violation of the principle of equality.

What is regularly forgotten in this report, as in other similar comments on the subject, is the principle of meritocracy, which the same people hold in equally high regard: only the best should rise to the top. Could it be that the former pupils of independent schools and Oxbridge alumni are better than many of their rivals from other schools and universities? And if that is so, should they be discriminated against for that reason? Let us take top journalists as an example. The complaint is that nearly half of them come from privileged backgrounds, and are therefore unable to evaluate other people's circumstances properly because of their own limited experience. It is a fact that around 50 per cent of leading journalists come from intellectually-minded families and hold university degrees, particularly from Oxbridge. Owen Jones bemoans this preponderance.[12] On the other hand, where are top-notch articles to come from? Writing is no easy task and, without an intellectually challenging education, the chances of finding a good author are slim. Owen Jones himself also has a middle-class background and studied at Oxford; furthermore, he is one of the leading journalists from this class. Virtually all the *Guardian's* top writers have been educated at prestigious universities (see Chapter 7). The career of Julie Burchill, who was born into a working-class family and did not attend university, but nevertheless wrote for *The Times*, the *Observer*, the *Spectator* and other newspapers and magazines and has written bestselling novels and made television documentaries, is a shining exception.

Unpaid internships have been identified as a modern expression of class difference.

> They have become a pillar of the modern British class system, discriminating on the basis of wealth rather than talent. The system acts as a filter for entire professions, helping to transform them into closed shops for the über-privileged. Not only are they exploitative, they effectively allow the children of the well-to-do to buy up positions in the upper echelons of British society.[13]

Some MPs have called for a ban on unpaid internships, which they say unfairly penalize working-class young people who cannot spend long periods of time working for free.[14]

EXPLOITATION OF EQUALITY

These days, the greatest problem with the equality/inequality debate results from the fact that – despite assurances to the contrary – the subject is not approached with any degree of scientific objectivity or detachment. Instead, more often than not, it is emotionally and ideologically charged and unscrupulously exploited by interested parties – in particular politicians seeking to impress voters and companies hoping to boost sales, and there is virtually no opinion that has not been voiced on the issue, as exemplified by the following selection from leading lights in the worlds of politics, economics, science, etc., including Thomas Piketty, Martin Wolf, Greg Mankiw and Christine Lagarde.

Return on capital usually exceeds economic growth, resulting in an automatic increase in inequality. The proportion of income and wealth going to the richest 1 per cent has reached a historic high.

Inequality is in the nature of capitalism – those with a low IQ are ill-equipped to compete for its spoils.

Smarter parents are more likely to have smart children, and in turn this can lead to high incomes.

Economic inequality strengthens economic growth.

Economic inequality hampers economic growth.

Inequality is just when it results from intelligent industriousness.

Equal opportunity (to compete in the markets) matters.

Equality of outcome matters, to everybody what he needs.

Addressing high and growing inequality is critical to promote strong and sustained growth.

Contrary to conventional wisdom the benefits of higher income are trickling up not down.

Only inequality guarantees that people work hard to get to the top and thus promote economic growth.

Getting equality is easy by producing common misery with disastrous results known from communist states.

History shows that a too big wealth gap between the wealthiest and the poorest usually ends in one of three ways – either higher taxes, revolution or war.

Societies with pronounced inequality are more affected by social tensions and acts of violence than societies in which incomes are fairly similar.

The doctrine of equality diverts people from doing what they like to do and know to do and thus contributes to the moral disorientation and shallowness of our time.

For all these statements there are as many arguments against as for. Many are concerned not with truth, but with victory in the political struggle – which usually means quite the opposite. Take the OECD report, *In It Together: Why less inequality benefits all*, published in May 2015. The OECD General Secretary José Angel Gurria summed up the ground-breaking result of his organization's research as follows: 'High inequality harms economic growth.' The study itself, however, reaches the conclusion that there is no consensus on the link between inequality and growth – either in terms of sign or strength. Equally arbitrary is the OECD assertion that growth in Germany between 1990 and 2010 could have been 6 per cent higher (32 per cent instead of 26 per cent) if income inequality had remained at the 1985 level and not increased.

The Oxfam reports which are published each year to coincide with the annual World Economic Forum in Davos, are another case in point. According to the 2016 report's headline, the 62 richest individuals on earth own as much as the poorest half of the world's population, some 3.5 billion people, put together. In the five years preceding the report's publication, the richest individuals have got 44 per cent richer, while the poor have become 41 per cent poorer. The 2017 report states that the number of people owning the same wealth as the bottom half of humanity has fallen to just eight. As a result, Oxfam calls for greater wealth redistribution and higher taxes on the rich. A number of economists had already berated Oxfam's 2015 wealth and poverty analysis as 'dodgy' or 'crazy'. Ryan Bourne of the London Institute of Economic Affairs speaks of a 'nonsensical report'. The Oxfam researcher Nick Galasso himself admits that the net-wealth method used by Oxfam is 'a totally imperfect measure'. The same applies to statements along the lines of 'With just 1 per cent of the wealth of the richest 100 people in the world, X number of starving children could be fed/sent to school/cured of disease'. That may be arithmetically correct. But why does no-one ask how many children could receive food, education or medical care with the money it costs to buy a fighter plane or fund the war in Syria, or with the sums spent on the Davos conferences, the luxury goods acquired by China's new rich or the Oscars awards ceremony – or (best of all) with the money that football clubs pay for just one player or that top footballers earn? In August 2017 the French club Paris Saint-Germain signed the Brazilian Neymar for an inconceivable €222 million. All told, these would add up to many billions of pounds.

Is entertainment more important than relieving suffering? The authors of the Oxfam reports and similar studies may well care deeply about human justice and welfare (as well as the money and reputation they can earn themselves from their work), but all their endeavours are essentially based on Robin Hood's famous motto: 'Take from the rich to give to the poor.' This is not something they need feel ashamed of: this principle has been, and still is, a starting point for many revolutions, and is contained in the manifestos of many political parties, as well as in the minds of many academics and writers. Some great things have been achieved by humanity in its pursuit. However, what we have here is really class warfare disguised as science. Would it not be more honest to say so?

Even after many inequalities have been eradicated, the appeal to popular equality remains essential for modern democratic politicians in order to win votes – and in a democracy, votes are the means to power, which is the objective of all politics. In a modern democracy there is no such thing as a party manifesto without the aim of equality. Politicians know that voters love equality and detest inequality, which is why they promise equality, undertake to fight inequality and espouse politics that are 'not for the few but for the many'. Every prime minister has spoken these words in office or on their way there, including Boris Johnson with his mantra of 'levelling up'. And naturally every opposition politician does likewise, as seen most recently when Jeremy Corbyn promised 'a Britain for the many, not the few.' It is rather amusing to think of both Tory and Labour leaders using exactly the same slogan, but this clearly demonstrates that all high-ranking politicians view the electorate in the same way.

Politicians are not the only ones to celebrate equality. Companies wishing to sell their products happily do so by promising people the earth (but only if they buy their product), in the full knowledge that they are lying. A plain-looking woman will not become stunning, no matter how many times she applies a beauty lotion, and an unattractive, puny male cannot be turned into an Adonis. Sociologists, psychologists and authors are keen to jump on the bandwagon. The much-vaunted notion of the 'wisdom of the crowd' suggests that all people are equally intelligent or at least have one particular gift, and therefore 'can achieve anything'. The authors know this to be untrue and are aware that many, if not the majority, of people will live their whole lives without any chance of reaching the top due to insufficient intelligence or talent when up against others. The former mayor of London, Boris Johnson, was more candid. In his lecture in memory of Margaret Thatcher in November 2013, he reached for the cereal packet in an allusion to people's intelligence:

Like it or not, the free market economy is the only show in town. Britain is competing in an increasingly impatient and globalized economy, in which the competition is getting ever stiffer. No one can ignore the harshness of that competition, or the inequality that it inevitably accentuates; and I am afraid that violent economic centrifuge is operating on human beings who are already very far from equal in raw ability, if not spiritual worth.

Whatever you may think of the value of IQ tests, it is surely relevant to a conversation about equality that as many as 16 per cent of our species have an IQ below 85, while about 2 per cent have an IQ above 130. The harder you shake the pack, the easier it will be for some cornflakes to get to the top.

The remarks provoked outrage – not from the underdogs, but from those who, when the cornflakes were shaken, had risen to the top: the Establishment, the intelligentsia and politicians from all parties.

DO I SAY WHAT I THINK?

The self-interested and ambivalent attitude of politicians and business towards class is shared by virtually everyone else as well. Just about every survey reveals that people consider equality to be an outstanding and important aim of society. This statement is given near-total approval. Being in favour of equality is 'what one does' to be politically correct. In law, the English have actually attained equality.[15] In their private lives, the English are likewise in favour of equality, but only in one direction. As George Mikes summarized: 'Equality means that you are just as good as the next man but the next man is not half as good as you are.'[16] A prime example of this attitude is described by George Walden:

> All parents favour equal opportunity. It is just that, when it comes to their children, the principle ceases to apply. For parents to believe that other people's children are equal to their own would go against the laws of nature. What they want for them is *unequal* opportunity . . . In higher education, the same unprincipled approach applies. The theory is that access should be equal to equal universities, yet no one who can afford it wants any such thing: they want privileged access to universities that are far from equal. The greater the distance between poor and excellent institutions, the more parents strive to secure places for their children in the good ones and to avoid the bad.[17]

This observation is far from purely theoretical. The English media have a field day when people who publicly propagate the ideal of equality of education send their own children to private schools or selective state schools or particularly famous state schools, as politicians are wont to do. Prime Minister Tony Blair sent his children halfway across London to a grant-maintained, quasi-selective school of the kind Labour insisted was divisive. The allegations of hypocrisy he countered by saying that he 'refused to impose political correctness on his children' – in George Walden's eyes 'the most shameful thing he has said or done'.[18] The left-wing Labour politician Harriet Harman sent her son to a grant-maintained grammar school even though Labour Party policy was opposed to selection in schools. Labour MP Diane Abbott has been branded a 'total sell-out' for sending her son to private school. Her justification was that 'I knew what can happen to my son if he was sent to the wrong school and got in with the wrong crowd.' The Labour cabinet member and good friend of Tony Blair, Lord Chancellor Falconer, sent his four children to private schools, as did the minister Paul Boateng his son, as well as Baroness Symons and Education Secretary Ruth Kelly. Critics of public schools from other spheres are at it too. The journalistic doyenne of the left, Polly Toynbee, had two of her three children educated at fee-paying schools. What motivates such behaviour is obvious. Self-interest clearly trumps political stance – or, to put it another way, 'As a politician or a journalist, I am against private schools, but I am not stupid.' Such behaviour becomes more understandable when even the Labour Education Secretary Estelle Morris, in a statement in 2002, had no qualms about saying, 'Some schools I wouldn't touch with a barge pole' – by which she meant state schools.

Whether the desire for economic inequality to be curbed or eradicated reiterated in every survey actually reflects people's beliefs is also questionable. Politicians have it in their power if not to dismantle economic class barriers or economic inequality entirely, then at least to provide a more level playing field, by taking wealth and earnings from the rich minority and giving it to the poorer masses through high taxes for the rich and high welfare benefits for the poor. And indeed this did happen in England (and in the United Kingdom generally) for many years after the Second World War. Before Margaret Thatcher took office in 1979, the highest rates of income tax ran at 98 per cent, compared to 45 per cent today. However, the obvious conclusion that all a politician needs to do to secure the most votes is to take an especially high amount from the rich and give prodigiously to the poor is empirically refuted – on the one hand, by Margaret Thatcher, who oversaw massive tax cuts and was still re-elected twice, and on the other by the findings of politologists and sociologists that people in lower-income groups are not over-ridingly concerned with dispossessing those in the top income bracket. Inequality evidently troubles them less than is widely assumed. What does matter to them is being better off year on year and feeling well-treated compared to others in the same income group. The ultra-high earners are so far removed that they are no longer construed as a threat. Those at the bottom realize that if the rich are entirely dispossessed, there will be 'no-one to pull the cart', and that wiping out the elite would ultimately be detrimental to the population as a whole. Clearly, the formula for reconciling economic class differences by means of levelling down, whereby it's the same for everyone, but everyone has it equally bad, is not compatible with human nature in the long term. Consequently, politicians have no interest in eliminating economic class divisions 'at any cost'. For the communist states that tried it and in some cases made it reality, this was finally their downfall.

We can conclude that class and equality are irreconcilable: class is the enemy of equality. If all men really were equal, there would be no such thing as class. Class is about difference. Only if all men were cloned and had the same income and behaved identically would class cease to exist. Belonging to a class also means being different from others who belong to another class.

3

What is Class?

Class is something beneath your clothes, under your skin, in your reflexes, in your psyche, at the very core of your being.

Annette Kuhn, *Family Secrets: Acts of*
memory and imagination (1995)

Class. The English pox.

Godfrey Smith, *The English Companion* (1996)

Is class a disease, and an unpleasant one at that, as suggested by G. Smith (above), or the greatest pest ever invented, as observed by Deborah, Duchess of Devonshire (see Chapter 7)? Many modern commentators share the first view and call for it to be eradicated. Others see class as a necessary evil. They are backed up by history. All known human societies have organized themselves in groups with certain things in common and identified people as belonging to such groups, as James Nelson rightly noted in 1753: 'Every nation has its custom of dividing people into classes.' That is still the case today. The criteria were, and remain, among others, wealth, income, occupation, descent, educational level, and who your friends are.[1]

And the English are no different. They know that classes exist in their society, and to which class they and others belong; similarly, they are aware of the related consequences for themselves and their family. At the same time, however, they find class embarrassing and are not willing to talk publicly about either their own class or that of other people, far less to knock it. But is class also the great unknown? How do the English define class? What do they mean by it?

A precise, one-size-fits-all definition of class has so far proved elusive. The word itself is not very illuminating: 'class' comes from the Latin *classis*, denoting a class, division, army or fleet. The meaning of a division of society according to status dates from 1772. The general, modern sense of a number of persons or things regarded as forming a group by reason of common attributes is too broad to serve as a definition of social class. Defining class can easily pose a problem reminiscent of Saint Augustine's struggle to define time: as long as no-one asks, we know what it is. Others attempting to characterize class react as the US Supreme Court Justice Potter Stewart famously did when asked to define pornography: 'I know it when I see it.'

What makes it so difficult to pin class down is the word's use for distinct concepts relating to human traits and behaviour that in practice very often overlap. One is the individual's economic status, their occupation, income and wealth. The other is the intangible sphere of appearance, accent, language, deportment, manners, leisure activities, culture, etc. While national classifications tend to focus exclusively on the economic aspect, in reality the intangible element carries greater weight. In a nutshell, class is a combination of money and culture.

HISTORY

Specifically in England there has for many centuries been 'a great deal of consciousness of class as social description and social identity'.[2] The English perception of class during the last four centuries (as articulated in terminology that included ranks, orders, degrees, stations, condition, estates, sorts and occasionally sets) was threefold.

The first was the hierarchical model. England's social structure was, as the historian David Cannadine puts it, 'providentially ordained, hierarchically ordered and organically connected'. Society was structured in tiers, with the monarch, aristocrats, courtiers, heralds, lawyers, clergy and scholars – those who enjoyed prestige and wielded power – at the top. Under them lived the majority of the population as peasants, craftsmen, etc. It was a chain that extended from the titled nobility, baronets, knights, esquires, gentlemen, leading citizens and professionals, yeomen, husbandmen and artisans, right down to cottagers, labourers, servants and paupers. This was the natural order of things and was divinely sanctioned by the grace of God, and could therefore not be changed by human will alone, as C. F. Alexander and Charles Dickens put it:

The rich man in his castle,   *O let us love our occupations,*
The poor man at his gate,   *Bless the squire and his relations,*
God made them, high or lowly,   *Live upon our daily rations,*
And ordered their estate.[3]   *And always know our proper stations.*[4]

One of the great defenders of the hierarchical model was Edmund Burke. In his *Reflections on the Revolution in France*, written in 1790, he expounded: 'Nobility is a graceful ornament to the civil order. It is the Corinthian capital of polished society.' And hierarchy, station and degree were the 'unalterable relations which providence has ordained'. The 'principles of natural subordination' were to be observed. This fabric of society was threatened by the 'mob' and 'the swinish multitude'.

Despite many refinements, this hierarchical model had shortcomings, and a parallel notion emerged alongside it of society divided into three groups. The triadic or tripartite model perceived an upper class (higher-class or land-owning sort), a middle class (middle or middling sort), and a lower class (poorest or labouring sort). This became more and more the predominant view. Adam Smith in his *Wealth of Nations* (1776) suggested that society was fundamentally divided into landowners, businessmen and labourers because they drew their different incomes – rent, profits and wages respectively – from their different relationship to the means of production. These were the 'the three great original and constituent orders of our modern society'.

Alongside these two ideas of an organic hierarchy on the one hand and a tripartite division into upper, middle and lower strata on the other, there existed a concurrent view of society in simple terms of 'them' and 'us', or the 'haves' and the 'have-nots'. This dichotomous or binary model was already clear to Thomas Paine in 1791 when he published *The Rights of Man*, his riposte to Edmund Burke. Paine saw society as polarized between a corrupt, extravagant, ruling establishment and a cowed and oppressed majority: 'There are two classes of man in the nation, those who pay taxes and those who receive and live upon taxes.' He dismissed hereditary hierarchy and nobility as 'dishonourable rank', and thought titles marked 'a sort of foppery in the human character which degrades it'. The vocabulary used at the time to describe this vision of society is still worth recording today because many of the terms are still current.

them	us
patricians	plebeians, plebs
high	low
the few	the many
superior	inferior
polite	common
learned	ignorant
rich	poor
nobility	commoner, baseborn
'laced waistcoats'	leather aprons
those who use the hands of others	those who use their own hands
the oppressors	the oppressed
the nobility and gentry	the low life
extreme riches	extreme poverty
those with property	those without property
the educated	the uneducated
the upper classes	the mob

The polarized analysis was most famously put about by William Cobbett during the 1800s. On the one side was 'old corruption' or 'the thing' or just 'it': 'that parasitic amalgam of aristocracy and government, placement and jobbery, finance and debt, the church and the law, the East India Company and the Bank of England' (what is today called the Establishment). On the other was 'not the mob, the rabble, the scum, the swinish multitude', but rather the 'labouring classes', or 'working classes', or 'working people', or 'the people', from whom 'the real strength and all the resources' of the country 'had ever sprung and ever must spring'. For Cobbett, these two parties were locked in perpetual conflict: 'an insurrection of talents and courage, an industry against birth and rank'. Nobility was understood as 'no ability'.

Then, in 1848, along came Karl Marx and Friedrich Engels with their *Communist Manifesto*. Marx's basic idea was that there were two social classes: the owners of the means of production (landowners who drew their unearned income from their estates as rents and bourgeois capitalists who obtained their earned income from the businesses in the form of profits) and the proletariat, who did not own the means of production and made their money by selling their labour to the employers in exchange for weekly wages – as he saw it the exploiters and the exploited: 'Society as a whole is more and more splitting up into two great hostile camps, into two great classes directly facing each other: Bourgeoisie and Proletariat.' However, Marx recognized that there were other groups which, while not owning the means of production, were not being exploited to the same degree as the proletariat, which he called the petty bourgeoisie and middle class.

Matthew Arnold became famous with his division of society into three great classes: Barbarians, Philistines and Populace.[5] The Barbarians were the aristocrats, a caste distinguished by their panache, free indulgence of passion, love of field sports, politeness, good looks and belief in individualism, liberty and doing as one likes, detached from the rest of the world. The Philistines were the middle class: with their mundane wisdom and interest in commerce and industrialization, they are the Empire builders, inclined to progress and prosperity but lacking in aesthetic values. According to Arnold, these could however be acquired by discarding their materialism and embracing the virtues of the ancient Greeks. The Populace was the working class: exploited by the two other classes, 'raw and half-developed', according to Arnold, because of poverty and disease. Together with the Barbarians, the Populace was beyond redemption.[6] The term Barbarians was picked up again by Tim Glencross in his 2014 novel of the same name, which depicts the New Labour/Blairite Islington aristocracy around 2008.

Towards the end of the nineteenth century, Liberal as well as Conservative politicians favoured the view of Britain's society as divided between 'them' and 'us', as did Prime Ministers William Gladstone and Lord Salisbury, although both had earlier personally championed the traditional hierarchy. The former declared he would 'back the masses against the classes' and fight a general election on the issue of 'peers versus people'. By class Gladstone meant 'station, title, wealth, social influence, the professions'. Much the same understanding was shared by the then Chancellor of the Exchequer Lloyd George who, in the fight for the People's Budget in 1909, denounced the peers in the House of Lords as a body of '500 men chosen randomly from among the ranks of the unemployed' and contrasted them with the 'millions of people who are engaged in the industry which makes the wealth of the country' – idle parasites versus virtuous producers.

The last Englishman to identify only two social strata was the miners' leader Arthur Scargill: 'There are only two classes in Britain. The ruling class which owns and controls the means of production, and the working class which provides the labour. There is no such thing as a middle class.'[7]

MODERN CLASSIFICATIONS

The definition of the classes became more precise with the Registrar General's classification for the 1911 census, which derived social class from occupation as follows:

I. professional occupations
II. intermediate occupations
III. skilled occupations
IV. partly skilled occupations
V. unskilled occupations

Among private classifications, produced for purposes of market research, the one created by the National Readership Survey in the 1960s has become very popular and is still in frequent use today:

A. *Upper middle class:* Successful business persons (e.g. self-employed, manager/executive of large enterprise); higher professionals (e.g. bishop, surgeon/specialist, barrister, accountant); senior civil servants (above principal) and local government officers (e.g. chief, treasurer, town clerk).
B. *Middle class:* Senior, but not the very top, people in same areas as A.
C1. *Lower middle class:* Small trades people, non-manual, routine administrative, supervisory and clerical (sometimes referred to as 'white-collar' workers).
C2. *Skilled working class*
D. *Semi-skilled and unskilled working class*
E. *Those at the lowest levels of subsistence:* Including OAPs, those on social security because of sickness or unemployment, and casual workers.

Whereas armed forces personnel are excluded by the Registrar General, they are included in this classification and allocated according to rank as follows: lieutenant colonel and above, A; captains and majors, B; sergeants-major, warrant officers and lieutenants, C1; corporals, lance corporals and privates, C2.

In 2001 the UK Office for National Statistic (ONS) produced a new stratification, based on a class scheme developed by John Goldthorpe, known as the National Statistics Socio-Economic Classification (NS-SEC):

1. Higher managerial, administrative and professional occupations
2. Lower managerial, administrative and professional occupations

3. Intermediate occupations (e.g. clerks, secretaries, computer operators)
4. Small employers and own account-workers
5. Lower supervisory and technical occupations
6. Semi-routine occupations (e.g. cooks, bus drivers, hair-dressers, shop assistants)
7. Routine occupations (e.g. waiters, cleaners, couriers)
8. Long-term unemployed

This scheme does not recognize an upper or capitalist class. This results from classifying people by their occupation rather than by their wealth, and so company directors are placed in class 1.

The most recent classification study in this field, based on a framework devised by Pierre Bourdieu in 1984, was executed in 2011 by professors of sociology Mike Savage and Fiona Devine along with other academics, and published in April 2013 as the BBC's *Great British Class Survey*.[8] Occupation was dismissed as the sole criterion for belonging to a particular class and replaced by three 'capitals' as follows:

1. *Economic capital*: wealth and income, measured in terms of household income, household savings, property value
2. *Cultural capital*: the ability to appreciate and engage with cultural goods and credentials institutionalized through educational success, measured in terms of the amount and type of cultural interest and activities
3. *Social capital*: contacts and connections which allow people to draw on their social networks, measured in terms of quantity and social status of friends, family and personal and business contacts.

The results are summarized in the following table:

	% of population	Description	Occupations	Household income (£)	Household savings (£)	House value (£)
Elite	6	very high economic capital (especially savings), high social capital, very high highbrow cultural capital	chief executive officers, IT and telecommunications directors, marketing and sales directors, barristers and judges, financial managers, dental practitioners, advertising and public relations directors	89K	142K	325K
Established middle class	25	high economic capital, high status of mean contacts, high highbrow and emerging cultural capital	electrical engineers, occupational therapists, midwives, environmental professionals, police officers, quality assurance and regulatory professionals, town planning officials, special needs teaching professionals	47K	26K	176K
Technical middle class	6	high economic capital, very high mean social contacts, but relatively few contacts reported, moderate cultural capital	medical radiographers, aircraft pilots, pharmacists, higher education teachers, natural and social science professionals, physical scientists, senior professionals in education establishments, business, research, and admin positions	37K	66K	163K
New affluent workers	15	moderately good economic capital, moderately poor mean score of social contacts, though high range, moderate highbrow but good emerging cultural capital	electricians and electrical fitters, postal workers, retail cashiers and checkout operatives, plumbers and heating and ventilation engineers, sales and retail assistants, housing officers, kitchen and catering assistants, quality assurance technicians	29K	5K	129K
Traditional working class	14	moderately poor economic capital, though with reasonable house price, few social contacts, low highbrow and emerging cultural capital	medical secretaries, legal secretaries, electrical and electronic technicians, care workers, cleaners, van drivers, electricians, residential, day, and domiciliary care	13K	10K	127K
Emergent service workers	19	moderately poor economic capital, though with reasonable household income, moderate social contacts, high emerging (but low highbrow) cultural capital	bar staff, chefs, nursing auxiliaries and assistants, assemblers and routine operatives, care workers, elementary storage occupations, customer service occupations, musicians	21K	1K	18K
Precariat	1	poor economic capital, and the lowest scores on every other criterion	cleaners, van drivers, care workers	8K	1K	27K

42

This classification has a number of advantages over its predecessors, in particular a more detailed breakdown of occupations into classes and the inclusion of cultural and social capital (in addition to economic status). However, the threshold figures for income, savings and house value seem too low to qualify as elite, which explains why the figure of 6 per cent of the population appears too high. Very probably, the figures would be more appropriate if doubled, which would reduce the elite to 1 per cent of the population.

The official classifications according to occupation, income and assets are indispensable, and helpful for political and business purposes. But the peculiarities and absurdities of these divisions have been pointed out many times.[9] In particular, grouping people exclusively on the basis of their job can be seriously distorting. A peer who works for a living, be it as a stockbroker, lawyer, photographer, art dealer, scientist, policeman or skilled craftsman, is pigeonholed by this method according to his professional qualifications. By society, however, he is measured by his title and therefore remains upper-class. Above all, as every Englishman knows, there is more to class than just your occupation, wealth and earnings. To some extent class even transcends these. The impoverished child of an earl with all the class markers of their elevated station is upper-class and not working-class. And the working-class individual who, through good fortune or skill, has become rich but has none of the other markers of the upper class is not a member of it.

SELF-PERCEPTION

I was born into what you might describe as the lower-upper-middle class.

George Orwell, *The Road to Wigan Pier* (1937)

Given the choice, the English prefer not to talk about class at all, and especially not about their own. They try to dodge the issue by querying its existence or importance, or denying that it actually matters to them. If they subsequently do answer, the results are astonishing.

In the GBCS survey, only just under a third (32 per cent) regarded themselves as belonging to a social class: two-thirds considered they did not.

This result says more about the reluctance of the English to talk about their class than about where they actually see themselves in the class system. As anyone will find by questioning friends and acquaintances, almost all Englishmen and -women have a very clear picture of where they stand in class terms. That Tony Blair and David Cameron know they are upper-class goes without saying. However, they prefer not to say so, at least not in public. And if a (genuine) answer is obtained, people tend to stick to one of the two categories middle- or working-class. The likelihood of anyone stating they are upper-class can be discounted – next to no-one says that. What remains is the great divide in self-perception between working- and middle-class.

Conclusions differ in this respect. In some cases it is reported that, since 1955, the proportion of the population who identify themselves as working-class has remained nearly constant at around 60 per cent. In 2011, according to the results of the GBCS survey, 62 per cent of the population saw themselves as working-class and only 35 per cent as middle-class. This result is astonishing. Many observers would rather have expected the number of people identifying as working class to have gone down in recent decades, with an increase in the number of those classifying themselves as middle-class. This expectation is borne out by other findings indicating that around 70 per cent count themselves as middle-class and around 30 per cent as working-class.[10] These variances can probably be explained by inconsistent definitions and/or different formulations of the underlying questions.

STATUS

Class is not the same thing as status. Status (or standing) means one's value and importance in the eyes of the world, the honour or prestige which people attach to a person – their reputation and good name. Status to some extent refers to how a person is viewed from the outside, the way they appear to others. Hence, there are high-status or low-status occupations and high-status or low-status positions in society. The consequences of high status for the holder are usually positive: prosperity, freedom, time, comfort and – probably most important of all – the feeling of being appreciated. This explains why so many yearn for status and are so unhappy if they do not achieve it or – even worse – if they lose it once attained. Although status and class differ, the relationship between them is close.[11] If status is not acquired by birth, as in the case of hereditary titles in particular, it can be gained through accomplishments that society regards highly. This is reflected in the shift in perception of what constitutes a high-status occupation.[12] In ancient Sparta, it was the tough, aggressive, physically fit and highly trained warrior; in medieval Western Europe, the monk in his monastery; then, for around 400 years until 1500, it was the noble knight; in nineteenth-century England it was the (landed) gentleman; Amazonian Indians prized the tribesman who had killed a jaguar. In modern, democratic societies status largely mirrors the material wealth a person has accumulated (Bill Gates, Warren Buffett) – although not exclusively. Status may also accrue to members of the professions, media celebrities such as sporting heroes and television stars, as well as politicians. Status can lead to class. Take the typical example of a nineteenth-century family's rise through craftsmanship to wealth: its sons are educated in schools; a factory is built that enjoys national renown; the family's grandsons go to Oxford or Cambridge Universities; an international corporation is created. Equally, class can hold the key to status, as clearly illustrated by the duke's son who continues to enjoy status even if he is stupid, lazy and feckless – at least for a while. As a rule, status follows class, but the relationship is anything but rigid. Instead, there also exist very different status levels within the classes (see Chapter 4).

THE ESTABLISHMENT

The upper class is not to be confused with the Establishment. The latter is much bigger. Not all the upper class belong to the Establishment, and far from every Establishment figure is upper-class. The expression is, as Jeremy Paxman put it, 'a harlot of a word, convenient, pliant, available for a thousand meaningless applications"[13] – but nevertheless useful, and is experiencing a revival, which some sociological experts find unfortunate.[14] The term was coined by the historian A. J. P. Taylor, and taken up by the journalist Henry Fairlie in 1955. It was intensively discussed in Hugh Thomas's *The Establishment – A Symposium* (1959) and from then on was used in almost every book and article that dealt with the people 'who run England or rather the UK or who at least wielded substantial influence in this country'.[15]

Formulating a universally accepted definition of the term has so far proved elusive. What is clear is that it refers to a group of people who have certain things in common. It is easier to say what the establishment isn't than what it is. It is not an organization with a more or less fixed constitution and members that one can leave or be barred from. And it is certainly not a formal or informal secret society or a particularly exclusive club, like Bilderberg or the Trilateral Commission, nor is it a freemasons' lodge or gentlemen's club. The historian Peter Hennessy gives the following definition:

> Establishment is a phantom army of the great and good who fill positions in public, cultural and intellectual life exercising a special kind of subtle, supple, concealed soft power within our institutions and our society. Its members can set the tone, influence the direction of public policy and exert considerable sway over future appointments to the professions within which they have risen.[16]

Owen Jones suggests that the establishment comprises groups of mostly unelected and unaccountable people who really do rule the roost not simply through their shared wealth and power, but because of the ideas and mentalities that govern the way they behave. These groups 'protect their position in a democracy where almost the entire adult population has the right to vote'. 'As well as by a shared mentality the Establishment is cemented by financial links and a "revolving door" culture: that is, powerful individuals, gliding between the political corporate and media worlds.' Among these Jones counts politicians, media barons, the police, business tycoons and bankers.

To these must be added the monarch and her family, professions like the law and the Civil Service, the House of Lords, the Royal Society, the British Academy, the learned societies generally, the scientific and engineering institutes, the great medical colleges, the leaders of the army, as well as the intelligence and security services, as put forward by Peter Hennessy. The longstanding view of the Establishment as an old-boy network of former public schoolboys and Oxbridge graduates who know each other and scratch each other's backs is almost certainly now outdated. Equally mistaken is the opinion that there is no such thing as the Establishment.

An essential characteristic of the Establishment is the unspoken solidarity within its ranks, similar to that also found in other groups. Preferential status is given to members of one's own group, and non-members are admitted only if they are so clearly superior to the members of their own group that their rise to join the Establishment is only a matter of time. Without exception, the Establishment is made up of 'those who have made it', who have arrived at the pinnacle of their profession or field, be they distinguished politicians, exceptional artists, blue-chip entrepreneurs, top lawyers, pre-eminent physicians or other leading lights. Incidentally, this solidarity does not stop at national boundaries: despite conflicting interests, high-level representatives of different countries often get on well personally because they recognize that their opposite number has also 'made it'. 'We are the best. We are the chosen ones,' they mutually concur. When he was Prime Minister, therefore, Tony Blair had no problem in spending his 2004 summer holiday in the villa belonging to the Italian Prime Minister Silvio Berlusconi in Sardinia. Heads of government are united by a common bond.

Another factor that makes it so difficult to define the Establishment and identify the people who belong to it is the phenomenon, alongside class denial, of Establishment denial. Because the associations of the word Establishment have only ever been pejorative, no-one wants to be subsumed under its umbrella, least of all those who undoubtedly belong to it. We shall return to this aspect later.

Historically, the Establishment has been fiercely attacked, particularly on moral grounds. The people behind the attacks have a problem: virtually all the Establishment's critics either come from it themselves or from concomitant social circles. They are hardly ever from the working class. This is not surprising, since criticism of the Establishment requires an insight into its ways that only members or close associates may possess. That excludes the working class. If their attacks bring them success so that they acquire power or money or wealth as a result, then the critics automatically become part of the Establishment themselves. The revolutionary who deposes the current head of state and takes over his role is Establishment. The young journalist who attacks the Establishment and consequently becomes famous and rich is himself Establishment.

An example of this is the career of Jeremy Paxman, one of the most perceptive and astute observers of England and Great Britain since George Orwell.[17] Born in 1950, he recalls in the foreword to *Friends in High Places*, which was published in 1991, his schooldays in Malvern and his studies at Cambridge, and notes that 'several of my contemporaries have subsequently translated their student political careers into lives as MPs of various parties.' This strengthened his resolve to become a journalist from the mid-1970s onwards. In this critical book about the Establishment he writes, 'It was something of a shock to hear one-time contemporaries destined to eke out their lives on the backbenches maintaining that, because of the power of the mass media, one had become part of "the Establishment" oneself. I hope not.'

He hoped in vain. In the media world and as a journalist, Jeremy Paxman's membership of the Establishment is beyond question. For 25 years, from 1989 to 2015, Paxman presented BBC 2's *Newsnight*, and he is the incumbent question master of *University Challenge*, a role he assumed in 1994. He has written a number of intelligent books, and his annual earnings have at times exceeded a million pounds. His brother is a former British ambassador to Mexico and Spain. All his accomplishments have been earned fairly and on merit.

The transformation from rebel to establishment figure is the fate of many a high achiever. A case in point is David Bowie. Like many an ageing rocker, after a rebellious youth, he found himself seen as part of the Establishment he had spent his life wrong-footing – and not just part, but a very pillar of it. Even the youngest and most scathing critics of the establishment such as Russell Brand and Owen Jones have in the meantime joined its ranks, partly due to the plaudits their criticism of it have earned them in the media world.

Sometimes the chattering classes are equated with the Establishment. That is incorrect. However, they do overlap. According to contemporary thinking, pundits and political commentators use the term 'chattering classes' pejoratively to describe a group of the metropolitan middle class, especially those with political, media and academic connections. These well-educated, upper-middle or upper-class individuals enjoy discussing political culture and social matters and express opinions on a lot of subjects, mostly with a liberal tendency. The derogatory tag comes from the presumption that the chattering classes talk a lot about social injustice, disaster relief, Third World aid and all the other fashionable causes, but do next to nothing to help. They are seen as all talk and little action.

The idea of an informal network of powerful individuals, acting in mutual solidarity with the aim of defending their own privileged status, is far from new. More than 200 years earlier, William Cobbett had recognized that on the one side was 'old corruption', 'the thing' or just 'it', a parasitic amalgam of aristocracy and government, placemen and jobbery, finance and debt, the church and the law, the East Indian Company and the Bank of England'. Only the name Establishment is recent, as well as the social backdrop, of course.

THE ELITE

Roughly until the time of the Second World War the term 'elite' referred to the people who exercised the power and ruled the country. It was essentially synonymous with the ruling or governing classes or upper classes. Nowadays the expression is more neutral and broader and designates members of quite disparate groups of people that are thought to be 'the best' in their field, hence phrases such as the power elite, cultural elite, elite soldiers, elite footballers, elite surgeons, elite journalists, elite physicists or scientists, fashion elites and so on. In this sense people of any class can be elite. The working-class private may very well be an elite soldier.

The use of elite as a class-related term has undergone a shift in meaning. Traditionally, the old-style elite that ruled England was on the whole viewed positively, in some cases revered; it was looked up to and at least respected, with the result that the word's connotations tended to be positive. That has changed. In contemporary usage, the word has become rather pejorative. Elites are 'people with unearned privileges who keep honest folks from getting a fair shake'.[18] But not across the board, since today there are 'acceptable' and 'banned' elites. Elite athletes and a sporting elite, elite surgeons or elite pilots are acceptable, and England is proud of its elite soldiers. Banned elites are political, especially power elites. This category also includes ruling elites, business elites, literary, intellectual and taste elites.

Despite acceptance of the aforementioned special elites, the terms elite, elitist and elitism have become dirty words. Anti-elitism is a must, as is elite denial (Chapter 7). Regrettably, many anti-elitists are insincere. When their own interests are involved, those who help or serve them cannot be elite enough in their training or expertise. The anti-elitist naturally wishes to be operated on by an elite surgeon, or flown to their holiday destination by an elite pilot, defended by an elite soldier and advised by an elite tax expert who can help save them tax.

It is a similar story when it comes to the money earned by the elites. The salaries of chief executives are often held to be unconscionable. No such criticism is heard about the higher earnings of pop stars, actors and top athletes, though none of these is responsible for the jobs and investments that a CEO is. The ambivalence towards elites mirrors an equally ambiguous attitude towards others' wealth. There are good and bad kinds of wealth. It is good to be rich if you are a footballer, an actor, a TV anchorman, a writer (one thinks of *Harry Potter* author J. K. Rowling), a lottery winner or even the inheritor of

old money (or a country pile). Bad is the wealth of mid-size entrepreneurs or CEOs of major corporations, although the latter control
the material destiny of employees, suppliers and shareholders and are
vital for society as a whole, whereas those in the first group act only
for themselves; if they were to disappear tomorrow, society would
not suffer.

CELEBRITIES

A particular class of people that has only emerged in the modern,
media age is the celebrity:[19] someone who is famous for being well
known and well known for being famous, generally having found
fame and fortune in the entertainment and sports industries. A
common feature of celebrity life stories is the rags-to-riches trajectory or the meteoric rise to fame. They highlight that upward social
mobility based on one's own talent, skill and luck is attainable by
all. Prime examples of this kind of celebrity – alongside chef Jamie
Oliver, media-star Katie Price and the singer Adele – are the footballer David Beckham and his wife, former Spice Girl Victoria.
They have become one of the most famous and richest couples in
the country, imbuing their life with all the trappings of charisma
and glamour.

The popularization of television has also heralded the advent of
the TV personality, an individual seen at fairly regular intervals on
air, not just in their official role but, crucially, popping up in other
places too. As well as the stars of soap operas, this group includes
talk show hosts, quiz masters, sports presenters and even news-
readers and weather forecasters, whose job is only to read out texts
written by others from an autocue. The mere fact that their faces are
omnipresent lends them the status of stars. They are recognized by
millions of people and frequently stopped in the street. There lies
their strength: as long as they 'reign supreme', i.e. keep appearing
on television, they form part of the Establishment despite not being
upper-class. Although their position is insecure, being dependent
on public taste and the balance of power in broadcasting companies,
and most of them return to obscurity once they vanish from the

screen, they are treated on a par with politicians, business leaders, scientists, artists and successful sportsmen. They are booked to open supermarkets, for gala evenings, party conventions and after-dinner speeches, and to lead discussions (even without knowledge of the subject). Some of them have cashed in on their celebrity by founding clubs and societies or organizing parties and society dos, always taking a share of the revenues. The talk of a 'telly-stocracy' may to some extent be justified.

For the bulk of the population at least, celebrities fulfil some of the functions previously performed by the aristocracy. They influence taste, personal behaviour and standards of conduct, as well as public opinion on national and international social and political issues. In this role celebrities advertise fashion, cosmetics and other goods. In the past companies might have boasted that their products were endorsed by Duke So-and-so. Elevation to the ranks of celebrity to some extent signals a partial step-up in social class.

Celebrities are certainly not universally accepted as upper-class. However, virtually everyone finds it flattering to know them and have them around at a party. The traditional aristocratic and moneyed elites too accept celebrities, often even seeking them out, e.g. by inviting them to birthday parties, weddings and other family occasions, as a way of boosting their own status. Celebrities have the advantage over the traditional upper classes that they are less under fire from the public, because their wealth and status are apparently less envied than that of others of high rank. The inequality of income between a soccer player or TV presenter or pop star and someone on an average wage is criticized much less than the same inequality between a run-of-the-mill businessman and an average earner. Nevertheless, celebrities do not have complete freedom to do as they please. With the territory of being admired goes the risk of ridicule or savage attack should they step out of line.

THE GENTLEMAN

The gentleman is an internationally recognized trademark of England, so much so that many languages – including French and

German – have adopted the word, using it to mean a person of quite specific character and behaviour. On an international level a 'gentleman's agreement' designates a commitment that, although not legally enforceable, is morally binding. The gentleman – who was predominantly male, although the female 'gentlewoman' did exist – was for several centuries the English ideal of humanity. The traditional gentleman in this mould has been described so often by Englishmen and foreigners that his image has become somewhat of a stereotype bordering on the caricature.

Arguably the best portrayal stemmed from a man whose political leanings were quite unlike those of the typical gentleman: someone who instead, as a political scientist and one-time chairman of the Labour Party (1945/46), was always a declared opponent of the established ruling class. The author in question is Harold Laski, and his description contained in the essay *The Danger of Being a Gentleman: Reflections on the Ruling Class in England* (1932) remains unsurpassed. The gentleman, Laski wrote, had reached the height of his ascendancy before the Great War, not only in England, but worldwide: 'The Gentleman had persuaded the world to believe that he was the final term of human evolution.' The Frenchman André Malraux once called the gentleman England's *'grande création de l'homme'*. In the war, he showed courage and character: 'Gentlemen knew how to die' (Harold Laski). Thereafter the traditional gentleman came under attack. He was accused of being an amateur in a professional world and therefore no longer capable or best-equipped to control England's destiny, with no understanding of modern industry, the working classes or democracy, or of how new, up-and-coming states such as the USA would figure. For this reason, the traditional gentleman had become a threat to England, as alluded to in the title of Laski's essay.

After the Second World War the gentleman was targeted even more strongly. He and his virtues were held responsible for England's decline. By the 1960s and 1970s he was reduced to the object of satire, some of it spiteful, in the media and especially on television. For all his flaws and despite being eclipsed by the modern order, there were few who did not feel some sorrow at the gentleman's demise. 'Yet no one, I believe', wrote even Harold Laski himself, 'will see the passing of the gentleman without a brief annotation of regret. In the period of his apogee, he was a better ruler than any of his possible rivals.'

In England the real-life gentleman is as good as extinct, or has at any rate disappeared from view. Which figure in public life would be called a gentleman today – let alone use the term to describe themselves? Therefore, in considering the observations of Evelyn Waugh that 'The basic principle of English social life is that *everyone thinks he is a gentleman*. There is a second principle of almost equal importance: *everyone draws the line of demarcation immediately below his own heels*', we must conclude that, if ever they held true, they do so no longer. Scouring the index of many more recent books about England where one could reasonably expect to find something on the subject given their content, the word gentleman is nowhere to be found. This is true of Jeremy Paxman's *The English – A Portrait of a People* (1998), for instance, although the word gentleman does indeed feature in the chapter headed 'The ideal Englishman'. The term still crops up in phrases referring to the male sex, such as 'the Gents' or the equally lavatorial 'Gentlemen lift the seat', an instruction made famous by British Rail in the 1960s and 1970s. Elsewhere it also occurs in the more or less formulaic 'ladies and gentlemen'. 'For gentlemen' is used as a selling point for guides to gentlemanly behaviour, attire, choice of books, etc. All refer only to external appearances – the inner character is barely mentioned. In the vast majority of cases, the expression is used ironically or even in the contrary sense. The gentlemen of the press, for instance, are nothing of the sort. This ambiguity and lack of seriousness is finally embodied in the latest guide on the 39 steps to being a modern gentleman published in 2015 by *Country Life* magazine:

1. Negotiates airports with ease.
2. Never lets a door slam in someone's face.
3. Can train a dog and a rose.

4. Is aware that facial hair is temporary, but a tattoo is permanent.
5. Knows when not to say anything.
6. Wears his learning lightly.
7. Possesses at least one well-made dark suit, one tweed suit and a dinner jacket.
8. Avoids lilac socks and polishes his shoes.
9. Turns his mobile to silent at dinner.
10. Carries house guests' luggage to their rooms.
11. Tips staff in a private house and a gamekeeper.
12. Says his name when being introduced.
13. Breaks a relationship face-to-face.
14. Is unafraid to speak the truth.
15. Knows when to clap.
16. Arrives at a meeting five minutes before the agreed time.
17. Is good with waiters.
18. Has two tricks to entertain children.
19. Can undo a bra with one hand.
20. Sings lustily in church.
21. Is not vegetarian.
22. Can sail a boat and ride a horse.
23. Knows the difference between Glenfiddich and Glenda Jackson.
24. Never kisses and tells.
25. Cooks an omelette to die for.
26. Can prepare a one-match bonfire.
27. Seeks out his hostess at a party.
28. Knows when to use an emoji.
29. Would never own a chihuahua.
30. Has read *Pride and Prejudice*.
31. Can tie his own bow tie.
32. Would not go to Puerto Rico.
33. Knows the difference between a rook and a crow.
34. Sandals? No. Never.
35. Wears a rose, not a carnation.

36. Swats flies and rescues spiders.
37. Demonstrates that making love is neither a race nor a competition.
38. Never blow-dries his hair.
39. Knows that there is always an exception to a rule.

From the 1970s onwards, few books venture a serious description of the gentleman.[20] Most of those produced are ironic in their portrayal or at least have strongly ironic overtones.[21] Nevertheless, the English gentleman of tradition is not quite dead yet. He lives on as a kind of shadow man, telling the real world how things ought rightly to be done (rather like the shadow cabinet). The gentleman remains a benchmark of moral and behavioural rectitude. This finds expression in modern parlance in such utterances as 'He behaved like a true gentleman' or 'This wasn't gentlemanlike' or 'A gentleman would not have done that.' Indeed, most writers define the gentleman in the negative: 'It is almost a definition of a gentleman to say that he is one who never inflicts pain.'[22] The gentleman is said to be concerned with 'the not doing of the things which are not done'.[23] Among the things that a gentleman does not do, for instance, is to shamelessly accost others in order to gain professional or monetary or other advantage, a practice to which modern networking all too often succumbs. The most pleasing anecdote on this subject concerns F. E. Smith, Lord Birkenhead.[24] A scallywag once asked him where to find the lavatory – not because nature was calling, but because he wished to get Lord Birkenhead's attention. This did not escape Birkenhead, who retorted: 'My dear fellow, go down that corridor and you will see a door on your right on which is written the word "Gentlemen". Don't let that deter you!'

The positive definitions focus more on the ideal member of society than the reality. Like an isolated brushstroke in an Impressionist painting, a single trait does not show the complete picture, but does so perfectly when combined with others. Roger Scruton put it like this:

The gentleman was a sportsman, which meant not someone who always won, but someone who was a 'good loser'. He 'played cricket', after that leisurely, interminable sport of gentlemen which offered opportunities to lose with dignity, while maintaining a seemly distance from both friend and foe and wearing a uniform of unsullied white like an angel. The gentleman was a 'brick', a 'sport', and showed 'pluck' and coolness under fire. He had 'grit' and was able to lead. But he was also willing to serve, and was guided in every emergency by public spirit and selfless concern for the cause. His virtues were precisely those which enabled people to stand together in the face of enemies, and to weather the severest storms.[25]

Probably the most sympathetic description stems from Simon Raven, despite his repeated affirmation, 'I myself am not a gentleman. If I were I would almost certainly not be writing this book.'

And so at last we may see and sum our paragon, the English Gentleman in the last days of his ascendancy. We see that he was an agent of justice and effective action, having the fairness and the thoroughness to examine facts and the integrity to act on his findings. We see that he had much regard for the old loyalties – to country, to kinsmen, to Church – and that as a guardian of such institutions, and no less to assist him in his other duties, he saw fit to adopt a grave and somewhat aloof attitude of mind which was matched by dignified demeanour and a superior, though not an ostentatious, style of maintenance. Deeply conservative, if only as a result of fostering the loyalties with which he was charged, he never forgot his status as a warrior, was always ready, in time of need, to return to the ancient proving ground of his kind; but when there was no call for service, then he preferred to remain on the lands which his ancestors had won by service, for on these lands were at once his proper establishment and his proper occupation. Lacking the passion for intellectual exchange which had made city life tolerable for the Greeks, he held firmly to the Greek rule which pronounced most urban employments to be degrading. He went to the city, therefore, only to carry out the many obligations on which his honour was based. According to this notion of honour, he was bound, not only by such commonplace rules of decency as chivalry to women and charity to the poor, but by a direct and imperative necessity to pay for his privileges by rendering service – service to his Sovereign and his superiors in office, service to his dependants, service to his Church. But even so he set store by his freedom; if he met his obligations it was because honour bade him do so, not because any absolute authority compelled him. Authority he certainly recognized, but only such as his conscience suffered him to obey; he would welcome laws made by man in proper form and would acknowledge a king who ruled with his consent and with regard for his interests; but he would brook nothing from a tyrant who claimed divine right or a priest who dictated through dogma, and in no case whatever would he accept interference from beyond the sea. As his position required, he had pleasing manners intended to reassure his inferiors and to show the proper respect, free of any hint of servility, to those above him; and he was liable to combine such manners with a light scepticism which eschewed enthusiasms and quarrels. But if ever he was tempted to let this scepticism affect his deeper attitudes, then he was apt to receive timely reminders that many of his countrymen took their souls – and his – very seriously, and that if he was to continue in his place then he must look to his morals. For the English Gentleman, over and above all, was the product of English morality.[26]

Being a gentleman was not the same thing as belonging to the upper class. The English gentleman could be made as well as born. Anyone who behaved like a gentleman became one, regardless of which class he was born into, though 'gentle birth' doubtlessly conferred an advantage. Gentlemanly status could also be acquired by initiation. This explains the many volumes and guidebooks containing the criteria for being a gentleman that appeared around the time the term was coined in 1400 and thereafter, such as Richard Brathwaite's *The English Gentleman* (1630) and Henry Peacham's *The Complete*

Gentleman (1622). The difference between upper-class and gentle-man consists in the former's tendency to rely on externals, such as prestige, power, rank, money or privilege, whereas the gentleman – whether or not he also belonged to the upper class – was always more concerned with justice, obligation and duty.

The last item may be the quintessential trait of the gentleman: he adhered to a code of honour which placed duty before self-advance-ment. In *Nobs and Snobs* (1976), Michael Nelson tells an amusing story, re-told by Jilly Cooper in *Class*, on the difference between the gentleman and the aristocrat. Invited to dinner, his grandfather was sitting next to the hostess when he spotted a slug on his lettuce. Rather than embarrass her, he ate it and managed not to be sick until dinner was over. His behaviour bore out the definition of a gentleman as 'a man who never inflicts pain'. An aristocrat would never swallow a slug – or anything else for that matter if he did not like it (although he would also avoid complaining).

HOOLIGAN

Almost equally as famous as the archetypal English gentleman is the English hooligan, a figure not confined to history, however, but very much still alive and kicking. Largely associated with football, this breed of man consumes copious amounts of alcohol and picks endless fights with the fans of the opposing team or anyone else who happens to cross his path. Coincidentally, he also enjoys watching the match, the 'official' reason for being there. Although maybe wearing a little thin, the following joke on the subject can still raise a smile: 'I went to a fight and a football match broke out.' Hooligans, generally aged from late teens to 35, come mainly from working-class and lower-middle-class backgrounds. As a rule they are employed in manual or lower-level office jobs, or to a lesser extent are unemployed or work-ing in the grey economy. For many, they are the bugbear of European football. In Great Britain a whole raft of legislation has been passed expressly to deal with football hooliganism (the Public Disorder Act of 1986, the Football Spectators Act of 1989, the Football Offences Act 1991, the Football Act 1999, the Football Disorder Act 2000), and strict measures have been taken at club level against such excesses. From this perspective hooliganism is simply the rather ugly face of a section of the lower classes.

But there is another way of looking at it: what if the hooligan is regarded as a kind of counter-model to the gentleman, like matter and anti-matter? Supporters of this theory stress that hooligans actually prefer to scare off their opponents and see them run rather than beat them up; that in their parallel universe they apply the same rules of fairness and decency as do gentlemen – but only the other way round, as it were. Likewise, their aggressive and violent clashes are said to be governed by unspoken rules that are no more breakable than the silent rules of the classes above them (although for an outsider this may admittedly be hard to detect).

CLASS IN THIS BOOK

The impossibility of finding a generally applicable definition derives from the fact that class impinges upon just about every aspect of human life. While the official classifications highlight occupation and the resultant material wealth (or lack of it), other factors such as education and language, the words you use and how you pronounce them, what clothes you wear, where your house is located, how you furnish and decorate your home, how you design your garden, which pets you keep, which sports you practise, your behaviour, what car you drive, what you eat and drink, where you shop and how you spend your free time – all play an equally, if not more, important role.

A scientific definition of the word class is not actually required for the purposes of this book. We can make do with the knowledge that social class is a concept readily understood by the average man. The English know classes exist in their country and to which class they belong. From this perspective class, like beauty, lies in the eyes of the beholder. But let us be clear about this: while class may indeed take place in the head, it never exists solely in the mind or eyes of the beholder. Social reality always keeps breaking in. Class is a mishmash of objective facts and the way in which they are perceived and interpreted by individuals. The definition of class that is perhaps best suited for our purposes is that provided by the novelist Jilly Cooper in *Class* (1999):

> A group of people with certain common traits: descent, education, accent, similarity of occupation, riches, moral attitude, friends, hobbies, accommodation; and with generally similar ideas and forms of behaviour, who meet each other on equal terms and regard themselves as belonging to one group. A single failure to conform would certainly not exclude you from membership. Your own class tend to be people you feel comfortable with – 'one of our sort'.

For our purposes here, the most practical solution seems to be to follow the widely held understanding of the English class system, whereby society is divided into three groups – the upper, middle and working classes – with the middle class usually being subdivided into upper-middle and lower-middle strata, or into upper-middle, middle-middle and lower-middle sub-groups as described above. The reader will draw the lines between the classes where he thinks fit.

4

Hard Class Markers

HARD VERSUS SOFT

The traditional perception of class markers and indicators empha-sized traits that can be described as 'hard' factors: in particular family, education, title, occupation, wealth and income. They are 'hard' because they are easy to identify externally, can be measured and weighed, and do not usually change quickly – if at all, for there are some things, such as the school or university attended or family background, that are unalterable. The mainstream view of class among sociologists is based on economic status, and this is essentially the approach still adopted by official statistics today (see Chapter 3) – which explains why terms such as accent, pronunciation, language and terminology are completely absent from the index and text of many books about the English class system and barely discussed.[1]

All the same, occupation, wealth and income have never exclu-sively defined class in England. Just as important were and are characteristics that can be described as soft class markers – for exam-ple, pronunciation, vocabulary, behaviour and who one's friends are. Modern sociology understands these as elements of cultural and social capital, as illustrated most notably by the Great British Class Survey of 2011 (see Chapter 3). There is a shift in the understanding of class from a purely economic notion to one based on cultural prac-tices. However, the hard class markers naturally do not go away, and also often feature prominently when someone is being described. It is no coincidence that in the English media people are nearly always presented as coming 'from background X, educated at school and university Y, and living at address Z', occasionally even with the additional titbit of how much their home is worth ('lives in a £3 million house in Islington').

The **hard class markers** are relatively few in number:

Family	Title	Education	Occupation
Fortune	Income	Address	Appearance

The number of **soft class markers**, by contrast, is practically unlimited. This is because just about every sphere of life can be (although is not necessarily always) permeated by class. The following list aims to give an idea of which aspects of human existence and behaviour can be influenced by class. It is by no means restricted only to 'major' items such as accent and terminology but also, and often more tellingly, includes 'minor' points: whether an Englishman expresses his patriotism by singing the national anthem or flying the Union flag or barely shows it; what he eats and drinks; what he reads and listens to; how he treats waiting staff; whether he goes to church; whether he takes on volunteering roles; how he conducts his love life – these are just a few of many areas that (also) depend on class. The following are some key terms in this connection:

Accent	Garden	Radio programmes
Appearance	Holidays and travel	Religion
Arts	Honorary roles	Servants/personnel
Behaviour	House	Sexuality
Books	Introduction	Shopping
Brand loyalties	Love life	Social commitment
Car	Magazines	Social media
Charity	Marriage	Sports
Clothing	Mobile phones	Table manners
Clubs	Newspapers	Television programmes
Conversation	Patriotism	Terminology and language
Eccentricity	Pets	Voting habits
Follies	Political party	
Gaming	Pronunciation	

There is no razor-sharp division between hard and soft class markers. They overlap with each other and also have a mutual impact. Despite this blurring, hard class markers are tantamount to prima facie evidence. The class to which a member of the Royal Family or hereditary aristocracy or gentry belongs is obvious, even if they decide to work as a taxi driver in London or farmhand in Australia. Classification based on occupation alone is by no means reliable. The Mayor of London can be working-class, as Ken Livingstone was, or upper-class like Boris Johnson. Theoretically, the road-sweeper in the East End can also belong to any class – but only in theory. Members of the professions are assumed to be from a higher class than members of the manual trades. Money alone certainly does not determine class. The working-class lottery winner remains working class, even if he buys a country house in Gloucestershire, a London townhouse on Eaton Square and a luxury car (should the windfall allow). On the other hand, however, it is quite difficult to be seen as a member of the upper classes if one is penniless.

Class is generally underlined by some material goods – though this of course remains unspoken. Mentioning it would be low. Even noblemen who have lost everything but their title suffer from the loss of their houses and estates as well as the 'requisite acquaintance and props' giving evidence of their rank, such as 'the odd watercolour of a grandmother in a crinoline, some two or three decent antiques and preferably a relic of a privileged childhood'. These things are a 'kind of sign language' that indicates where in the class system the owner places himself.[2]

FAMILY

The 'hardest' of all class markers by far is the family one is born into, which no-one can influence. Birth and breeding may perhaps subsequently be denied, concealed or even despised, but they cannot be undone. For the first two decades of human life, the family determines important hard and soft class markers.

It begins already with the family name, a quasi-permanent appendage that *can*, but by no means must, provide an initial pointer as to a person's class. Many surnames exude a particular class, provided one knows one's way around the upper-class world. Smith, for instance, is a very normal and common name that is sure to occur several hundred thousand times in the London telephone directory. But it is also the family name of Viscount Harbledon. The initiated know which Smith is meant. The same applies to the surnames Cecil (Marquess of Salisbury), Grosvenor (Duke of Westminster), Russell (Duke of Bedford) and Cavendish (Duke of Devonshire) – a name the Duke shares with a high-profile English racing cyclist (who is no relation, however). A disproportionately large number of places at Oxford are allegedly taken up by people with Norman Conquest names such as Baskerville, Darcy, Mandeville and Montgomery.[3] Ordinary, simple, honest surnames like Smith, Thomas, Jones and Bond are always good or at least neutral. Double-barrelled names still tend to be regarded as faintly distinguished. Because no-one can do anything about their name, however, jumping to conclusions about a person's class on that basis is highly unreliable.

Although seemingly less popular these days, the search for venerable antecedents for a time created an 'ancestor-manufacturing industry' that operated according to the following principle: the further back in history an ancestor was unearthed, the higher the price. The English media insisted on pointing out that David Cameron is a (distant) descendant of King William IV (1765–1837). The family one is born into also decides one's material wealth (or lack of it), accent and terminology, and shapes one's social circle, taste, education and professional career. Overall, family determines one's class of origin and therefore unquestionably has a 60 to 70 per cent bearing on the class one ultimately belongs to (see Chapter 31).

TITLES AND HONOURS

All millionaires want to be lords.

Observed by a lord during the 1999 debate on the
future of the House of Lords

The visible, official class system is still a strong class marker, being the easiest to identify, at any rate. A member of the hereditary peerage, from duke down to marquess, earl, viscount and baron, need not worry about his place in the class hierarchy, nor does a baronet or member of an old-established landed-gentry family, irrespective of titles or the lack of them. Rather surprisingly, those who have inherited a title and possibly a fortune with it without ever doing anything worthwhile themselves are usually regarded as higher up the class ladder than those who have earned an honour or great wealth by their own efforts, as was normally the case with the first title holder. The English sooner refuse to esteem the first baron or first viscount who has actually done something of merit but revere his descendants, the remoter the better. The 10th duke is more respected than the first. This is understandable if he himself had also achieved something, which was often true; but not if his only distinction was that of the genetic fluke of heredity. From a class point of view it can therefore be more propitious to be the lazy, unintelligent and feckless descendant of a great ancestor than the first in the family to do something great.

After a generation or two, how the first title holder came by his title also ceases to be important for the esteem enjoyed by the incumbent. Successors to titled individuals are still held in high regard although the original title holder has done nothing other than having a mother who slept with the 'right' king, for example the 'royal bastards'.[4] A historic case in point is that of the illegitimate children of Charles II's mistresses, to whom he generously awarded titles: the son of Lucy Walter was created Duke of Monmouth in England and Duke of Buccleuch in Scotland. Catherine Pegge's son was created Earl of Plymouth. The three sons of Barbara Villiers were created Duke of Southampton, Duke of Grafton, and Duke of Northumberland respectively. Nell Gwynn's son was created Duke of St Albans. 'Half the grander entries in Debrett's or Burke's spring from her loins.'[5] All of those mentioned also received further (lower-ranking) titles and usually a source of income as well. Particular good fortune shone on Charles Lennox, the son of Louise de Kérouailles. He was created Duke of Richmond, Baron of Settrington and Earl of March in the English peerage, and Baron Methuen of Tarbolton, Earl of Darnley and Duke of Lennox in Scotland. To this Charles II added an annuity of £2,000 and a royalty of 'twelf pence per chaldron on coal dues at New-Castle', which made Charles Lennox one of Britain's richest men.

Nor does it count against you if your titular line goes back to a person of less reputable worth and occupation. David Lascelles, 8th Earl of Harewood, is a stellar member of the English aristocracy. His father was a cousin of the Queen. He is 54th in line to the British throne, followed by other members of his family in places 55 to 67. The ancestral seat, still inhabited by the family, is the renowned Harewood House in Yorkshire. The progenitor and founder of the Lascelles fortune was Henry Lascelles (1690–1753). He earned his wealth primarily through the unscrupulous exploitation of his positions as a Barbadian customs collector and government-appointed contractor supplying troops stationed in the Caribbean. He established a London commission house which imported sugar for refining, participated in the slave trade and owned a plantation with slaves. When Henry Lascelles died in 1753, having committed suicide by opening the veins in his wrists[6], he was probably the richest man in England. His fortune was inherited by his son Edwin (1713–95), who was created 1st Baron Harewood. He built Harewood House and acquired large plantations and nearly 3,000 slaves in the West Indies. When Edwin Lascelles died heirless, his fortune passed to his cousin Edward Lascelles (1740–1820), who was made Viscount Lascelles and Earl of Harewood. When he died, his fortune and title passed to his son Henry, 2nd Earl of Harewood. Following the abolition of slavery in the British Empire in 1833, Henry received compensation for the release of around 1,300 slaves.

Even if a forebear had simply bought the title, his successors are still very much venerated today. For titles purchased in days of yore, that makes some sense given the passage of time, for example the peerages sold by James I (1566–1625) and his friend, the Duke of Buckingham, such as the earldoms of Warwick, Northampton and Devonshire and the baronies of Teynham and Houghton (bought for £10,000 each). Baronetcies were all about cash from the very beginning. James I instituted the baronetage in 1611 as a means of raising money, issuing the honour only to substantial land owners capable of paying £1,000 a year.

The practice is more difficult to understand in the case of the titles peddled en masse until 1925 by the political parties and prime ministers of the day, notably Lloyd George and his henchman Maundy Gregory, who was symbolically jailed for his part in the affair.[7] The Irish-born British newspaper magnate Lord Northcliffe made no bones about it: 'When I want a peerage, I shall buy one like an honest man.' The purchasers included some still illustrious names. The place occupied by Starbucks, Google, Apple et al today in the public debate about tax evasion was held some 100 years ago by the brothers William and Edmund Vestey, who became known as legal but morally reprehensible tax dodgers after relocating their meat-importing business to Argentina to avoid paying taxes and thereby rendering some 5,000 Britons redundant.[8] When William Vestey bought his peerage in 1922 for £25,000 King George V was provoked to write a letter that a man who refused to pay his taxes should not be ennobled (there was nothing illegal about the practice of selling peerages until the Honours Act was passed in 1925). In the present day, Vestey descendants are close friends of the Royal Family.

To avoid any misunderstanding, most of those who first held the family title earned their honour by honest and decent means. What is striking is the growth over time in the esteem in which their heirs are held regardless of their own life's work.

Everywhere one reads that titles count for less and less. Most people can hardly tell the difference between a sir and a lord, and do not understand the significance of the different handles. The media likewise are no longer correctly versed in the complex rules of the English nobility and honorary titles and make little effort to use them properly. Anyone arriving at a US border control whose passport identifies them as a Member of the House of Lords will arouse considerable suspicion. In the USA Prince, Duke, Earl and Viscount are currently more likely to be understood as first names than as titles. Even in England the incorrect use of titles is these days the rule rather than the exception, at any rate outside a relatively select group of the upper echelons and a few experts. Thus, a viscount who had purchased an air ticket using his name without title was not allowed to fly because the airline mistook the entry Viscount in his passport for his first name and claimed this did not match the name under which he had booked.[9] One might imagine that under these circumstances many title holders could become disenchanted with their moniker, which is actually frequently reported to be the case. The current Duke of Devonshire is said to have 'threatened' to give up his title, preferring to be referred to as Mr Cavendish.[10] This is naturally just affectation and not meant seriously. Who would be 'threatened' if the Duke abandoned his title? The general public would not be losing out; at most the title holder would be depriving himself, which is why no-one actually carries out this 'threat'.

Even Tony Benn (aka Anthony Wedgwood Benn) was disingenuous in this respect. Although he pursued – and famously also won – a legal action lasting for years in order to dispense with his title of viscount, this stance had no impact on his life. He retained his wealth, his house in Holland Park and the Stansgate Abbey family seat. In his will he left nothing to the poor or the Labour Party, but bequeathed everything to his family.[11] Nor had he fully renounced the title, since after his death his son Stephen became 3rd Viscount Stansgate. As everyone knows, to be called sir or lord in England is simply better than the opposite (except if you want to be elected to the House of Commons, that is).

Non-hereditary life peerages entitling the holder to a seat in the House of Lords are also a clear class marker. Although the status associated with a life peerage has been slightly dented by various abuses (such as the indiscriminate appointment of undeserving cronies by Harold Wilson when he resigned as Prime Minister on the infamous 'lavender list', or the 'sale' of peerages under Tony Blair in the infamous 'cash for honours' scandal), a life peerage continues to confer unique social prestige. Titles have obviously retained their old magic. There are plenty of individuals who crave the public prestige and respect such honours still represent and are happy to pay for them. Social equality otherwise so deftly praised seems to be forgotten in favour of old-fashioned snobbery. As one peer observed during the 1999 debate on the future of the House of Lords: 'Lords would like to be millionaires, but all millionaires want to be lords.' Only very few reject these honours. The lesser gongs are very attractive, too. 'I remember the elderly Conservative MP,' remembers the Labour politician Tony Wright,

> desperate to get that self-inflating 'Sir' in front of his name ('Of course I don't want it for myself, but my wife, you know . . .'), explaining how painful it was when honours lists came and went without him. He had done everything asked of him by his party, abased and humiliated himself on command over a lifetime, but still he was made to wait. It's pathetic of course, but it also shows why honours matter. They are instruments of power.[12]

The pain people are prepared to endure in the hope of gaining such honours was recently described by the late David Tang, agony uncle of the *Financial Times*, in the newspaper's House & Home section. He quotes from a letter he says he has received (it may be pure invention, but that's neither here nor there):

> I am chairman of a large British retailer. For six years I sucked up to Dave [Cameron] but got nothing in the way of an honour, not even an MBE. Do I now have to start all over again with Mrs May? What incentive is this for me to use company money to do charitable things, attend breakfasts at Number 10 and write letters to newspapers?[13]

The pleasure from receiving an often coveted ennoblement is not confined to Conservatives and the well-to-do, but has also gripped Labour supporters and politicians down through history. Many have been delighted to accept a peerage, indeed have (surreptitiously) made it their goal, even some who, throughout their political career, vehemently called for the House of Lords to be abolished – e.g. John Prescott and Neil Kinnock. Famous Labour peers past and present have included Philip Snowden (1st Viscount Snowden), Clement Attlee (1st Earl Attlee), Herbert Morrison (Baron Morrison of Lambeth), Michael Young (of meritocracy fame, Baron Young of Dartington), Harold Wilson (Baron Wilson of Rievaulx), James Callaghan (Baron Callaghan of Cardiff), Roy Jenkins (Baron Jenkins of Hillhead), Neil Kinnock (Baron Kinnock), John Prescott (Baron Prescott), Peter Mandelson (Herbert Morrison's grandson, Baron Mandelson), Alistair Darling (Baron Darling of Roulanish). If one wonders what motivates (erstwhile) enemies of the class system to become peers, it is likely to be the recognition after a career in politics that they (and their families) are much better off as lords than as workers. After David Cameron's leaving honours list there were 207 Labour, 257 Conservative and 104 Liberal Democrat life peers in the House of Lords. 'Indeed, the customary reward for a life spent in determined fight against privilege, seems to be an elevation to the peerage,' commented George Mikes.[14]

It is also rather smart to have some of the following letters after one's name:

CH	Companion of Honour
KCMG	Knight Commander, Order of St Michael and St George
KCB	Knight Commander, Order of the Bath
Kt	Knight
DBE	Dame Commander of the British Empire
CB	Companion, Order of the Bath
CBE	Commander of the British Empire
KBE	Knight Commander
CCB	Knight Grand Cross, Order of the Bath
OBE	Officer of the British Empire
MBE	Member of the British Empire

EDUCATION

A person's upbringing is determined by their parents. A child's first years are spent either alone in the family, perhaps with a grandmother lending support, or with a nanny and in a nursery school.

The school and university someone attends identifies them for their entire life as a seal of class not dissimilar to a branding mark on cattle. Once accomplished, it cannot be undone. You may be able to ditch your public school accent or follow the example set by Tony Benn, who attempted to remove details of his education (at Westminster School and later Oxford University) from the salient books and registers, but that does not alter your attendance at these institutions. When it comes to schools, the traditional hierarchy of public schools, grammar schools and state schools still exists, although there are not many grammar schools left now. Among public schools Eton, Harrow, Rugby, Winchester, Westminster, Charterhouse, St Paul's, Marlborough, Stowe and Fettes still top the rankings. When it comes to universities, Oxford and Cambridge (Oxbridge) lead the way, followed by the others in the Russell Group.[15] Not everyone who graduates from these institutions is or will become upper- or middle-class; many of them are proud to be and to remain working class. However, what it says on your CV speaks volumes. Education is an English obsession and closely entwined with class. Many see in education the only way to a fairer or class-free world, which is why education is mentioned in nearly every chapter of this book.

FORTUNE AND INCOME

In England wealth and income do not constitute class markers per se. The Russian revolutionary Alexander Herzen, who lived in England as an exile, wrote the following 150 years ago about the USA: 'The persons who constitute the classes in the society of that country are constantly changing, they rise and fall with the bank balance of each.'[16] His comments are no more applicable to England today than they were at the time. But in conjunction with other signifiers, wealth and income assume great importance. It is considerably easier to be rich and have class than if impoverished. Large sections of today's upper class gained their status by becoming rich and being accepted and assimilated by those already in the top social tier.

One of the hard class markers, maybe the most poignant one, is the ownership of land, in particular rural land. Being the owner of a country estate was for centuries the quintessential token of being upper-class. Though landownership has intensively changed over the last 150 years, it is still an important factor in indicating the class you belong to. In 1873 *The Return of Owners of Land*, a sort of second Domesday Book, was published. Then about 7,000 men owned 80 per cent of England, most of them belonging to the aristocracy and gentry. Through the increase in taxes in the aftermath of the two world wars and in the time thereafter, vast amounts of land changed hands, mainly to companies, charities and government agencies, but also to private individuals. Today's structure of land ownership is as follows: the Forestry Commission with 2.57 million acres, the National Trust with 630,000 acres, the Ministry of Defence with 593,000 acres, company pension funds with 550,000 acres, utility companies with 500,000 acres and the Crown Estate with 358,000 acres. Besides these there are still many private owners. The 36,000 members of the Country Land and Business Association (CLA), 0.6 per cent of the population, own half the rural land in the country. The top ten British landowners own 1 million acres between them in a country of 60 million acres altogether. A third of British land is still owned by aristocrats and rural gentry. 'Country estates remain the beating heart of the English aristocracy.' [17]

As with titles, when it comes to riches, old money is much more revered than new money – although old money was once new money too, and those who inherit or possess old money haven't worked for it. Many of the most famous large country houses in England, whose like is not found anywhere else in the world, have been built or purchased with newly acquired wealth: examples that spring to mind are the previously mentioned Harewood House belonging to the Lascelles family, Renishaw Hall, the home of the Sitwell family, Stowe House, which was owned by the Temple-Grenville family, and Waddesdon Manor, together with other houses in Buckinghamshire ('Rothschildshire') owned by the Rothschild family. Others (more frequently post-1918) were saved from demolition or decay with new money: Cliveden by the Astor family or Sudeley by the Dents, to name but two.[18] Their founders or buyers were in many cases regarded at the time as upstarts or nouveau riche. The Environment Secretary under Margaret Thatcher, Nicholas Ridley (2nd son of the 4th Viscount Ridley and brought up in Blagdon Hall, Northumberland), reminded the members of the Historic Houses Association of this at their annual meeting, to less than unalloyed pleasure: 'Many families who pride themselves on having always lived in a house in fact married into it, bought it or stole it at some point in their murky history, when they were robber barons, property speculators, or simply won the pools.'[19]

Anyone inheriting such a country seat after three or four generations was admired much more highly than its first buyer, even if too incompetent to hold onto it. It is as if today's successful entrepreneurs in the mould of Bill Gates, Steve Jobs, Mark Zuckerberg or Richard Branson were regarded as inferior, but their successors – perhaps degenerate and inept (but with better manners than their founding fathers) – whose vast fortunes had been inherited were held in the highest esteem: a rather absurd idea. The snobbery towards new money may be understandable among the traditional upper echelons with their conservative leanings. Paradoxically, however, it is often the intellectual left-wingers who turn up their noses at it and disapprove of the self-made rich – something which seems at odds with their professed belief in equality of opportunity and meritocracy. Logically, one would expect them to value people who have earned their fortune by their own endeavours more than those who have simply inherited it. However, in this respect a shift has occurred in recent decades (beginning with Margaret Thatcher's premiership): previously, success used to be something vulgar. You didn't need success if you had inherited a fortune. Today success is a good thing – what is vulgar is boasting about it.

The owners of old wealth (land, houses, furniture, art) are not immune from such dual standards either. They dislike the newcomers with their recent prosperity that gives them access to such trappings of success; they consider them upstarts and say as much. On the other hand, they deem it reasonable and legitimate that demand from the newly wealthy should boost the value of their own estates, houses, furniture and works of art, and they are happy to take advantage.

OCCUPATION

Like wealth and income, occupation is not a class marker per se, but it becomes one in combination with other characteristics, and provides strong reasons for assuming a person belongs to a certain class. If someone is introduced as an Oxbridge don, they are more likely to be situated in the upper-middle class than someone encountered as a scrap dealer, say. The starting point of the official (ONS) classifications is always one's occupation (see Chapter 3). One's occupation is also the element of class where the interdependence between class and class marker is particularly pronounced. On the one hand, as stated, occupation is an indicator of class. On the other, someone's pre-existing class is a factor in which professions they are likely to enter. In short, class is determined by occupation, and occupation by class (of origin). For example, being a Queen's Counsel is an indicator of being upper- or upper-middle-class; the child of a Queen's Counsel is more than average likely to pursue a comparable profession.

In England, being a **Member of Parliament** (MP) and therefore a member of the House of Commons unquestionably counts as something quite exceptional: you are one of 650 people who represent and control the 64 million people of the UK. Is being an MP something to do with class? There are two ways of looking at it. One was articulated many years ago by Anthony Trollope, who had himself (unsuccessfully) sought office: 'It is the highest and most legitimate pride of an Englishman to have the letters of MP written after his name.'[20] And many modern politicians think along the same lines. The Labour Party's former Deputy Leader, John Prescott, a man of working-class origins and a former steward in the Merchant Navy, said in 1997 that he had become middle-class, while in 2003 Charles Clarke, a former chairman of the Labour Party, held that all politicians were upper-middle-class. Harry Wallop qualifies elite politicians as the 'modern upper class.'[21] Other parliamentarians emphatically maintain that they have not changed class after being elected an MP. Especially those with working-class roots are keen to reassure their constituents that they are still one of them. At any rate, being an MP appears to be a sought-after occupation, as the Labour MP Diane Abbott put it: 'Being an MP is the sort of job all working-class parents want for their children – clean, indoors and no heavy lifting.'[22]

Employment in the **Civil Service** spans a wide range of classes, from the top-level mandarins with the Cabinet Secretary at their head, who count as upper-class, down to the junior ranks who may even be ranked as lower-middle-class. Being a civil servant in the Foreign Office still has a certain connotation of poshness.

Being an **officer** in the services was generally respectable in the past, when an officer was deemed to be a gentleman. Today, in times of downsizing cuts across the board, the merger of traditional regiments and modest pay rates, it is more difficult. At the apex is the Army, followed by the Navy, then the Air Force. To gain a class advantage in the Army it is advisable to make your career in the Household Cavalry (the Life Guards and the Blues and Royals), Scottish regiments, the Coldstream Guards and the Royal Green Jackets, rather than the (former) Royal Corps of Transport or the Royal Army Ordnance Corps or the Army Catering Corps.[23] In the Navy the helicopter squadrons are more highly rated than the sea-going units. The Royal Air Force is the least interesting socially, and all the more so when you call it the 'Raff'.

The English have a unique relationship with their military officers that extends beyond the 'officer and gentleman' cliché. Serving officers are among the few who are not reproached for being posh or having a public school accent, and certainly not when they go to war for Britain, as they did in Iraq in 2003. Even the *Guardian*, which is not generally noted for its love of the la-di-da classes, marvelled benevolently at the 'admiration that they have occasioned in the media':

They seem so terribly upper, or at any rate upper-middle. While all the rest of us back on civvy street have learned that elitism and class distinction are dirty words, Sandhurst has created a new generation of officer toffs – or 'tofficers'. To judge from the press they have had, you would think our army officers were saints, not military line managers.[24]

Among occupations requiring a certain level of education or skill, the **legal professions** have an edge. Although not always terribly admired and often maligned as shysters and money grubbers, they have generally not seen their position in the class system undermined. This is because, in modern democracies, the law ranks above the people who apply it. No-one need do anything against their will unless this is required by law, and no-one is above the law. This is arguably the greatest achievement that England secured for itself and as a role model for other countries, being one of the first to accomplish this (through the Magna Carta, Bill of Rights, Habeas Corpus Act, etc.).[25] Clearly, a society founded on the rule of law needs people to make the law and be familiar with it; similarly, it will value these people because they are indispensable and accord them higher status in the class system.

The second reason is the traditional proximity of the legal professions to power. In feudal times no king could manage without legal advisers. In the modern era many leading politicians have studied jurisprudence or worked as lawyers, e.g. Tony Blair. Legal experts are still readily chosen for senior positions in the Civil Service. Indispensability and their proximity to power gives the legal professions status, from which class is derived. Within the legal professions, judges rank highest, followed by barristers and solicitors, including Queen's Counsel as a particularly distinguished group – which does not mean that these people's status is cast in stone or beyond censure, however. When in an interview Lord Denning, the most celebrated English judge of the twentieth century, used such expressions as having 'no help' in the house, 'a roast' for lunch on Sunday and referring to his wife as 'Lady Denning', eyebrows were raised among the arbiters of taste.[26] To the working class, members of the legal professions are upper-class or as near as makes no difference.

By the upper classes only those at the apex of the profession are acknowledged as their peers.

Doctors are neutral. The lower echelons think of them as upper-class or thereabouts, possibly influenced by their portrayal as heroes in many television series. By the upper echelons they are regarded more as middle-class providers of services they regrettably cannot do without. Only rarely are they promoted to become genuine friends on an equal footing. Whether the role of doctors in the National Health Service (NHS) is a factor here is an interesting question. The personal physicians of King George V and of Winston Churchill – Lord Dawson and Lord Moran respectively – were of course themselves upper-class due to their closeness to the Royal Family and political power. But these were exceptions. The physicians who attend modern-day prime ministers are eminent and respected specialists without a specific class affinity.

One of the most obdurate and bizarre aspects of class is perhaps the judgement and prejudice affecting its relationship with **trade** and **business**. Large sections of the traditional upper class owe their status to the fact that trade made them rich. Only after making their pile did they espouse a life of leisure, and often rejected their origins. Others had no problem in marrying rich heiresses, whose fathers had made their fortune in trade, to restore their finances, making them duchesses, countesses, etc. in return. Prime examples include the Duke of Marlborough with Consuelo Vanderbilt, and Winston Churchill's father, Lord Randolph Churchill, with Jeanette Jerome.[27] Practically all the present-day rich have their success in trade – be it their own or that of their ancestors or managers in their employ – to thank for their wealth. Furthermore, it is universally accepted that the weal and woe of the entire nation depends on the fate of the economy.

Nevertheless, prejudice exists against those in business – and not only from long-standing, land-owning aristocrats, gentry and other landed society, but also from the respectable professions such as barristers, doctors, civil servants and senior army officers, as well as from the chattering classes, the media, the arts, academia, publishing, charities, think-tanks, quangos, non-governmental organizations (NGOs) and so on. Most of them feel superior to the commercial world and look down on it, as if to say that men in trade are not entirely trustworthy. This is naturally pure hypocrisy. Even those who scorn the world of commerce are more than happy to make money from it, so they usually keep their prejudice to themselves or air it in private.

The reason for this contempt is most often sheer envy on the part of the 'poor' intelligentsia towards the 'rich' doers. 'It is not fair that this ignorant and uncouth person is so much richer than me with my education and polish.' Strangest of all is that the businessmen themselves do not appear all that self-confident either. As soon as their finances permit, they start gathering round them the trappings of the upper classes by buying a country estate, going out hunting, buying boats, leasing a reach of a good salmon river, joining smart clubs and attempting to cancel all evidence of their former undesirable connections – in short, becoming gentlemen in the old sense of the word: that is, living without working or working hard, or at least appearing to live without working, and indulging in high living and leisure.

When it comes to the regard in which the commercial world is held, considerable differentiation is found. Industrialists that manufacture things, ship owners, traditional bankers, oil magnates and art dealers at Christie's or Sotheby's seem to be more respectable than salesmen, estate agents, advertising executives (the exception being Saatchi & Saatchi), hedge fund managers and stockbrokers (although former Prime Minister David Cameron stems from a stockbroking family). Nonetheless, in more recent times the stigma of trade has increasingly been eroded. Many friends of younger members of the Royal Family have been recruited from families which have become wealthy through commerce.

For the majority of other occupations, the classification is relatively clear, roughly along the lines of the National Readership Survey and the National Statistics Socio-Economic Classification (NS-SEC) .

ADDRESS

> *Three addresses always inspire confidence, even in tradesmen.*

> Oscar Wilde, *The Importance of Being Earnest* (1895)

The address at which one lives remains a hard class marker par excellence. Anyone brought up in a house on a council estate will find it hard to shake off this symbol of social class. Aneurin Bevan, a Labour minister in the Attlee cabinet after 1945, who founded modern council housing in the aftermath of the Second World War, aimed to create mixed communities:

> It is entirely undesirable that on modern housing estates only one type of citizen should live. If we are to enable citizens to lead a full life, if they are each to be aware of the problems of their neighbours, then they should all be drawn from different sectors of the community. We should try to introduce what was always the lovely feature of English and Welsh villages, where the doctor, the grocer, the butcher and the farm labourer all lived in the same street.

This wish did not come true. On the contrary, there is a widespread geographical apartheid between the well-to-do and everyone else. The working class live mostly in rented (or bought under right-to-buy) council houses in certain parts of town, while the other classes reside in other districts and mostly in the suburbs. The upper echelons go to some lengths to prevent social undesirables from living too close, as each class generally tries to segregate itself from the class below (see Chapter 29). Taken to extremes this leads to gated communities.

The part of town where someone lives is a symbol of social class. Although in London the claim that north of the Park (i.e. Hyde Park) and south of the river are beyond the pale has ceased to apply, the areas within that boundary are still meccas for the upper echelons. London neighbourhoods popular with the top social tier are Belgravia, Chelsea, Kensington, Knightsbridge, Mayfair, Notting Hill and West Brompton, but also included, in the wake of dizzying hikes in property prices, are Camden, Clapham, Fulham, Marylebone, Putney, Richmond and Westminster. Shoreditch is up and coming.

The residents of many areas that are posh reject this label, preferring 'intellectual'. These include Islington, Hampstead and Highgate. As a place to live, the East End of London is associated more strongly with the working class. Similar distinctions along the line of class are to be found in most English cities as described for Bristol by Will Atkinson in *Class in the New Millennium*. Certain counties too are classier than others, in particular Gloucestershire, Wiltshire, Oxfordshire, Buckinghamshire, Norfolk, Berkshire, Dorset, Herefordshire, East Sussex and Northumberland.

The most exclusive addresses in England are the shortest: no need for house number, street name, town or county; at best, even the country is superfluous. The house name is sufficient, Buckingham Palace being a prime example. It should be added that the number of addresses in London that can be found by the postman on this basis is exceedingly small.

Not so in rural England, where the country house holds sway. While 1,100 such dwellings disappeared over the century between 1875 and 1975, having been demolished, fallen into ruin or burnt down, these monuments to a bygone era still abound. The rather unassuming term of 'country house' can encompass both large properties that could more accurately be described as palaces, such as Castle Howard, Holkham Hall and Blenheim (which actually has the word palace in its name), and medium-sized and rather modest and less well-known residences.[28] If you go on a pleasure flight in a light aircraft or helicopter from Oxford's Kidlington airport, taking off to the north and then circling to the east around Oxford in a clockwise direction over Oxfordshire, Buckinghamshire, Berkshire, Hampshire and Gloucestershire, you can pick out a dozen or more of these jewels of English architecture and living culture, beginning with Blenheim Palace, followed by Stowe House, Waddesdon Manor, Cliveden, Stonor Park, Highclere Castle and Sezincote, to name but the most famous. No less striking are the country houses dotted evenly across the landscape that are neither familiar from pictures nor visible from the road. Every 10 or 20 miles or so stands one of these properties, usually ensconced in parkland and with a lake or watercourse nearby. The sight recalls Shakespeare's description of England as 'this precious stone set in the silver sea' (see Chapter 35), and the author ventures to compare these residences to shining pearls in the verdant ocean of England's rolling landscape. They represent the apogee of a lifestyle and culture that is unique worldwide – something of which past occupants were intensely aware. When Vita Sackville-West wrote: 'There is nothing quite like the English country house anywhere else in the world . . . It may be large, it may be small; it may be manorial; it may be the seat of aristocracy or the home of the gentry',[29] or Lady Frederick Cavendish waxed lyrical about Cliveden, 'When one lives in paradise, how hard it must be to ascend in heart and mind to heaven',[30] they fittingly expressed the spirit of their class.

After a period of decline following the Second World War, the English have taken country houses to their hearts once more, installing them as something of a sacred cow of English national identity. This is reflected in the phenomenal success with which those houses still in private ownership have been marketed by the Treasure Houses of England and the Historic Houses Association, and the various charitable institutions and public bodies ensuring the conservation of these historic places and opening them to the public, such as the National Trust and English Heritage. In the past it was clear that the people who lived in these houses were upper-class or thereabouts – either because they were aristocratic or rich, or both, or simply because this had always been their family home.

Simon Jenkins's *England's Thousand Best Houses* (2001) gives an insight into the history and social class of those who lived in such places: labourers, policemen and haberdashers do not feature.

And what of today? Being the owner of a country house is still an unambiguous sign of being upper-class – which explains why buying a stately pile, if they can afford it, is one of the first priorities for those who aspire to join the smart set. Apart from the agreeable lifestyle thus obtained, it is also a statement of social intent. Within one or two generations, and sometimes even during the first, they will achieve that goal. Just as important, the loss of their house meant for the owners a deep cut into their lives, not only on the outside but also on the inside. It dealt a heavy blow to their self-confidence, which was only rarely taken with a sense of humour: 'The decline of our family began the first time we moved into a house with a number.'

APPEARANCE

Appearance is a complex topic. On the one hand, it is an immutable given, and people cannot change things like their height, stature, shape of head or face. On the other, certain characteristics can be worked on: e.g. hairstyle, weight, and posture.

What has appearance to do with class? Linking appearance and class often leads to entirely false judgements, because people do not all correspond to their stereotypes. Nevertheless, many outstanding analysts of the English class system have sought to define such typical class appearances, including George Orwell:

> The great majority of the people can be 'placed' in an instant by their manners, clothes and general appearance ... Even the physical type differs considerably, the upper classes being on average several inches taller than the working class ... the prevailing physical type does not agree with the caricatures, for the tall, lanky physique which is traditionally English is almost confined to upper classes: the working people, as a rule, are rather small, with short limbs and brisk movements, and with a tendency among the women to grow dumpy in early middle life.[31]

'To this day', noted the architectural historian Nicolaus Pevsner,

> there are two distinct racial types recognizable in England, one tall with long head and long features, little display and little gesticulation, the other round-faced, more agile and more active. The

proverbial Englishman of ruddy complexion and indomitable health, busy in house and garden and garage with his own hands in his spare time and devoted to outdoor sports, is of the second type. In popular mythology this type is John Bull.[32]

These observations made 70 or 80 years ago were barely reliable even at the time. As the grandson of a duke, Winston Churchill was clearly upper-class, but he was neither tall nor had he a narrow head; quite the opposite – he was the John Bull type. Nowadays their accuracy is limited, in the same way as the stereotypes of Uncle Sam for US Americans and John Bull for the English are more caricatures than reality. However, these associations have not disappeared entirely, as the obituaries for Sir George Martin, the Beatles' record producer, show. Virtually every published review of his life following his death in 2016 contained a reference to his appearance and background, viz. 'This posh-looking man [in fact, the son of a carpenter] with tailored clothes and the clipped voice of a kind headmaster' (*Economist*) or, 'His reputation for gentle-manly charm and patrician elegance belied his humble origins. His father was a carpenter' (*Telegraph*). Appearance is important because it is the earliest indicator observable of another person's class (Chapter 10).

Physical beauty is one of the most important traits of a human being. All the world prefers a beautiful face and body to an ugly one, regardless of their sex, whether a promotion is in question or a lift on the motorway or a job interview or a place at a dining table or whatever. Beauty opens doors. Nearly everyone wants to be beautiful, although this is (of course) downplayed or denied by many, includ-ing the beauties themselves. The ever-increasing demand for plastic and cosmetic surgery demonstrates this. However, beauty is not an indicator for class. Sometimes the upper classes like to surround themselves with beautiful actors and actresses – but only for deco-ration, and in full awareness that they do not belong and can be dismissed at any time without repercussions. Their status appears not far from the position of the unofficial court jester. Having said this, a number of actors – as well as other artists – have advanced quite a long way up the social ladder (see Chapter 27).

SOFT CLASS MARKERS

Hard class markers are important. But on their own they are not reliable as identifying criteria. Increasingly they must be combined with other social markers before class assignation can take place. Those 'soft' markers are not spoken about in public, although they may quite happily be discussed in private or out of earshot. There is nothing secret about them, as every Englishman is highly conscious of their presence – they are just never mentioned. The uninitiated cannot read them for this reason. To those in the know, on the other hand, they are an open book. It is fair to say that these days soft class markers play a stronger determining role than those described as hard. 'We know each other and speak the same language.' The outsider alone does not know why he or she is not accepted. Or, to put it another way, when it comes to class markers, soft is the new hard. The soft class markers are the subject of Part Two of this book.

5

Working, Upper, Middle, Under

WORKING CLASS

Britain was the first industrialized nation, and was where the first working class emerged in the eighteenth and nineteenth centuries.[1] On the face of it, 'working-class' could reasonably refer to those who work exceptionally long hours or toil particularly hard – which would make the hedge-fund manager who does a 16-hour day and earns millions working-class. Indeed, if people are asked which class they belong to, they have recently been likely to reply that they work hard and are therefore working-class. The multimillionaire businessman Mohamed Al-Fayed (of Harrods and Princess Diana notoriety) once described himself as working-class. The Earl of Harewood (who was said to work 'at least twice as hard as most men') was called 'a new member of the working class' in an interview.[2] Naturally this should not be taken seriously. The term working-class refers not to the duration or intensity of the work performed, but to its type. Whereas four-fifths of the population lived and worked in the country at the beginning of the nineteenth century, by its end the same proportion was living in towns and cities and working in coal mines, in building and civil engineering, in shipyards, steelworks, textile mills and later also car plants. Together with farm workers, they gave rise at the time to the classic definition of the English working class as people who earn their living by manual labour. This label is no longer applicable today as this group, now known as old working class, has dramatically

86

shrunk. While before the Second World War three-quarters of the working population were in unskilled or semi-skilled manual jobs, this number has nowadays fallen to less than a quarter. The reasons for this are new labour-saving technology, the switch of production to less-developed, lower-cost countries (globalization) and a tendency among Britons to spend higher proportions of their income on services rather than goods. Although the old working class has not completely disappeared, it is now clearly outnumbered by the new working class.

The broadest modern definition of the working class is people who have no means of sustaining a living other than by selling their labour. However, this does not correspond to the general understanding, since it would also include the majority of people working in the public sector, among them university professors, high-ranking civil servants and judges – who are certainly not members of the working class. A universal definition has so far proved elusive. The most constructive approach is probably to list the occupations that are nowadays generally regarded as working class: the remaining members of the old working class together with numerous jobs in the service sector, including office workers, secretaries, sales assistants, those employed in the retail sector (especially supermarkets), call centre staff, personnel in hotels, restaurants and pubs, cleaners, employees in security firms and truck drivers. Not included are teachers, healthcare workers such as nurses, and train drivers. The archetypal working-class figure is the underpaid shelf-stacker in a supermarket. In total, around 12–15 million people are in this category.

On average, the income and assets of the working class are modest. Their annual income rarely surpasses the £20,000 mark. Household savings, if any – which is the exception rather than the rule – are unlikely to exceed £10,000. If they own a house or flat, its value will usually be under £250,000. However, another feature of the modern working class is that some of its members break the mould in extravagant fashion, those most often cited being plumbers or electricians in London in particular, who seemingly effortlessly earn many times the average wage and are able to accumulate substantial assets in terms both of property and household savings. But perhaps these individuals are more middle class.

Given its size, the working class may be assumed to wield significant political influence since each of its members has a vote in the same way as those belonging to other classes. A restriction of suffrage according to wealth such as existed (with varying intensity) in Britain in the nineteenth century (see Chapter 2) is long gone. In the one man, one vote era, the working class actually does have clout. Without votes, including those of the working class, no political party can secure power. By determining which political party is elected, the working class has a decisive influence on society. That said, however, what follows can be described as the first tragedy of the modern working class. Although it is at least partly instrumental in deciding which party governs the country, the politicians chosen by the working class are not (or no longer) working-class themselves. This applies in particular to the party whose very name suggests its working-class allegiance.

The Labour Party was founded in 1900 after workers recognized, towards the end of the nineteenth century, that banding together in trade unions was insufficient to protect their interests in the face of inadequate worker representation by the dominant political parties of the day, the Conservatives and Liberals. The new party quickly gained political ground (heralding the concomitant decline and virtual disappearance of the Liberal Party). The most striking feature of the Labour Party was not only that it advocated the interests of the working class, but also that its leaders themselves had working-class origins. In short, the working class was representing itself. The first leaders of the Labour Party, notably Keir Hardie and Ramsay MacDonald, were themselves working-class. Of the 393 Labour Party MPs elected in 1945, the majority were working-class. In the 20-strong cabinet of Prime Minister Clement Attlee, ten ministers had working-class backgrounds, including such famous names as Aneurin Bevan, Ernest Bevin and Herbert Morrison. Attlee himself, however, was not working-class, having been educated at Haileybury

College and the University of Oxford and trained as a barrister at the Inner Temple.

The 1960s saw the beginning of the trend for Labour MPs and, if elected to government, Labour ministers to be selected less often from the working class and more and more frequently from the middle class, in particular from the public sector and career politicians.[3] The tendency reached its highest level so far with the parliament of May 2015: of the 232 Labour MPs elected, only 16 have past connections with manual labour. Seventy-seven per cent of Labour MPs have a degree. In simple terms, the working class has placed its political fate in the hands of the university-educated middle and upper classes, be they in the Conservative Party (where this has always been so) or with Labour, where this has been the case for a number of decades now.

Politically speaking, the intellectuals of both parties can be perceived as regarding the working class as a lever to accomplishing power. A case in point is Stephen Kinnock, son of the former Labour leader Neil Kinnock. Neil Kinnock was the son of a coalminer turned steel worker. Stephen Kinnock is the son of two members of the House of Lords, his father Neil, Baron Kinnock and his mother Glenys, Baroness Kinnock. He studied at Queen's College, Cambridge and at the College of Europe in Bruges and is married to the former Danish prime minister Helle Thorning-Schmidt. Most of his professional vocational career was spent outside the UK as an employee of the British Council in Russia and Sierra Leone. In 2009 he joined the World Economic Forum in Switzerland, and since 2012 he has worked for a business advisory firm in London. It would be difficult not to characterize him as upper class or upper-middle class, though he describes himself as from 'a Labour and trade union family'. He was selected as the Labour candidate for the safe Labour seat (held by the party since 1922) in the ultra-working-class constituency of Aberavon in Wales and duly elected MP in 2015, without having any personal connection of his own to Aberavon. According to Kinnock's predecessor as Labour MP, Hywel Francis, the working-class candidate in Aberavon, Mark Fisher, 'lacked the academic ability' to represent the area in parliament. Small wonder that many working-class voters do not see eye to eye with middle-class Labour politicians. The journalist Janan Ganesh put it thus: 'It [the Labour Party] is run by the public sector upper-middle class for the working class that it increasingly struggles to understand.'[4]

This explains the hostility encountered by Tony Blair during the second half of his term in government, and even more strongly thereafter from Labour circles that identified themselves as working-class. The working-class voters who elected him suspected he had exploited them as useful idiots and as a springboard for his own political career; he was deemed to have done just enough for working-class people to keep them sweet, while otherwise maintaining Thatcherite capitalism more or less unreformed, and to have made a personal fortune from the political career made possible by the working class when it ended. Even today, ten years after Blair's term in office ended, disapproving articles about him are still being published, by serious journalists like Peter Wilby:

> Blair legitimized Thatcherism and inequality. By refusing even to talk about redistribution, he banished the subject to the political fringes. Inequality was no longer contested . . . Instead of leading the British into more progressive territory and building support for Labour's core values, Blair led them in the opposite direction, conniving with rich newspaper owners, notably Rupert Murdoch, to marginalize the left.[5]

The election by a large majority of the political left-winger Jeremy Corbyn as the new Labour Party leader, following Ed Miliband's resignation after the May 2015 general election defeat, is regarded by many as a counter-reaction to this. After Corbyn became leader, Labour Party membership swelled by 180,000. This does not appear to be a renaissance of the working class, however. Labour's influx of new members is overwhelmingly middle-class, the majority being 'high-status city dwellers as opposed to members in rural areas, among the elderly and from people who are less well-off'.[6] The new Labour leader (as of April 2020) Sir Keir Starmer stems from a humble background but went to Oxford University.

The second tragedy of the working class is that a not-unsubstantial proportion of the politicians it has elected as its leaders and to defend its interests, that is to say the university-educated members of the middle class, secretly despise the working class, because they themselves are better educated and more intelligent, and because the working class is not itself able to appoint politicians from its own ranks. Perhaps the most infamous example of such behaviour was Prime Minister Gordon Brown's darkest hour during the 2010 election campaign. Gillian Duffy, a 65-year-old widow and a lifelong Labour supporter from Rochdale, tackled the Prime Minister on debt, education and Labour's immigration policy. Brown ended the conversation with, 'You're a very good woman. A good family, good to see you.' Back in his car, having forgotten to remove his microphone, he said to his aide: 'That was a disaster . . . Should never have put me in with that woman . . . Whose idea was that?' Asked what Mrs Duffy had said Brown answered, 'Oh, everything. She was just a sort of bigoted woman, said she used to be Labour. It's just ridiculous.'[7] Mrs Duffy was very upset. After the 2010 election defeat the *Guardian*'s economics editor Larry Elliott articulated New Labour's attitude to the working class thus: 'Working-class people are sort of seen as a problem. They drink too much, they smoke too much, they don't look after their kids properly, they're feckless, they're work-shy. Racist. Essentially, that's how they're seen.'

The Conservatives are the traditional party of the upper and middle classes. But they too require working-class votes for electoral victory – which they also receive. One of the longest-standing topics of political analysis concerns the question of why working-class people vote for the Conservative Party. Owen Jones quotes an unnamed former senior Tory figure: 'What you have to realize about the Conservative Party is that it is a coalition of privileged interests. Its main purpose is to defend that privilege. And the way it wins elections is by giving just enough to just enough other people.'[8]

This is not the whole truth, of course. Under both Conservative and Labour governments the living standard of the working class has improved dramatically since the Second World War. Likewise, both parties have not only called for greater opportunities for professional and cultural advancement while in opposition (which goes without saying), but have also substantially extended these once in power. This is also a consequence of the working class's electoral potential, which every party must (also) target. It is therefore logical for both main parties to give and promise the working class enough for them to obtain sufficient votes from that quarter to retain or gain power.

The third tragedy of the working class is how it is perceived and depicted by the other classes, and also by members of the working class itself, as well as by the media and many politicians. Its image is not very flattering. The dark side of the working class – the violence, drunkenness and squalor, as feared and portrayed primarily by intellectuals – has of course always existed.[9] But these are distortions. As a rule, the working class was respected, including and in particular by political leaders. Prime Minister Benjamin Disraeli had dubbed the working classes 'angels in marble', and they were considered the 'salt of the earth'. Miners were 'labour aristocracy', and Prime Minister Harold Macmillan went as far as to call them 'the best men in the world'. Up to the Second World War and for some time afterwards, terms such as respectable, decent, honest, hard-working, solid, self-help and cleanliness dominated the way the working class was represented, setting an overridingly if not exclusively positive tone, as reflected in George Orwell's *Road to Wigan Pier* (1937), for instance, and Richard Hoggart's *The Uses of Literacy* (1957). 'In a working-class home', wrote George Orwell almost romantically,

> you breathe a warm, decent, deeply human atmosphere which it is not so easy to find elsewhere. I should say that a manual worker, if he is in steady work and drawing good wages . . . has a better chance of being happy than an 'educated' man. His home life seems to fall more naturally into a sane and comely shape. I have often

been struck by the peculiar easy completeness, the perfect symme-
try as it were, of a working-class interior at its best.

That has changed. For around 40 years, the working class has been
seen predominantly in a negative light. In 2007, looking back, the
philosopher Julian Baggini described how he had experienced the
working class as a young man:

> In the homes of the working-class families I saw, the fathers were
> usually shadowy presences to be feared, while the overworked
> mothers were always shouting. Meals were based around baked
> beans and chips, and the kids were sent out onto the street, to keep
> them from under the feet of the parents. The *Sun* or the *Mirror*
> would lie folded on the arm of father's worn, nicotine-infused
> armchair, with the television permanently on and tuned to ITV.[10]

Soap operas probably carry the most weight in this connection,
because they claim to show people's everyday lives, and are also
understood as such by most viewers. Thanks to their regularity and
the continuity of their rolling plots, they to some extent co-inhabit
our world. Ferdinand Mount summarized the portrayal of the working class on television as follows:

> We see moral and physical degradation shown with a lurid relish that
> Dickens might have envied. The women are slags, either scrawny
> with straggly blonde hair, or grotesquely fat and bulging out of their
> tracksuit bottoms. The children are surly, whining, spoilt, wolfing
> down their junk food with no concept of manners and not much
> grasp of their native language. The men in the regulation get-up –
> T-shirt, earring, shaven head – are equally surly and incoherent,
> callous and faithless to their women, sentimental about their chil-
> dren but liable to forget to pick them up at school and prepared to
> leave home and abandon them if they meet a bit of skirt in the pub.
> There is never any suggestion that the Downer men might be inter-
> ested in anything except sex, drink, cars and football.[11]

The cause of this shift in perception is generally deemed to be the aspirational ideologies promoted by Margaret Thatcher and Tony Blair.[12] Both prime ministers promoted social mobility as going hand in hand with meritocracy: anyone could make it if they tried hard enough. If people are poor this is because they are lazy or lack aspiration. Thatcher and Blair encouraged the working class to strive hard so they could climb the ladder to the middle class. In Theresa May's first speech as prime minister she said: 'We will do everything we can to help anybody, whatever your background, to go as far as your talents will take you.'

Under these circumstances it is understandable, if not very endearing, that people with working-class roots who have achieved wealth and success congratulate themselves on escaping from the working class. "'I'm middle class. I got out of the working class as quickly as I could. The working class is violent and abusive, they beat their wives and I hate their culture."'[13] The old socialist motto 'Rise with your class, not above it' has been replaced by a new call to 'Rise above your class.' Of the 'massive transfer of wealth and power to ordinary working people' advocated by Tony Benn and other reformers of the left, nothing remains.

The question is whether these descriptions of the working class are accurate or mere caricatures. The majority do not bear objective scrutiny, but can be blamed on the media's unhealthy obsession with misery and perversity as a means of attracting viewers and readers. Lynsey Hanley has impressively documented the existence of the 'old,' respectable working class, even on a large council estate.[14] The truth here does not simply lie somewhere in between, but in the co-existence of extremes: from anti-social behaviour, gang culture, drugs, guns and what Lynsey Hanley calls 'estatism' to people's pride in their community and their way of life, a sense of belonging, strong family bonds, love for their children, respect for each other, cleanliness, honesty and hard work. In her book about St Ann's council estate in Nottingham, Lisa McKenzie has found a metaphor for these contradictions and complexities that borders on the lyrical:

I remember walking under one of the underpasses that links the estate together under a main road, walking though the litter-strewn concrete subway, covered in graffiti (and not the type of artistic or clever graffiti you might see in Bristol, Brighton or in Shoreditch). As you walk you have to watch your feet and look at the floor, because you don't want to step into dog shit, at the same time keeping an eye on what is happening around you – it is, after all, a dark subterranean alley reminiscent of a scene from Stanley Kubrick's interpretation of *A Clockwork Orange* . . .

I remember emerging one day from this underpass to the smell of washing powder, the overwhelming smell of clean washing. At the backs of the houses on this windy day, and in the small square back yards, were rows of large, white, clean and fresh smelling sheets. The contrast was overwhelming, and it is this contrast that symbolizes the story I wanted to tell: the difference between stale piss and clean washing, side by side.[15]

As individuals, members of the working class have little or no influence on society. On their own, workers do not count for much. Although isolated members of the working class can achieve great or outstanding popularity, such as the celebrity Jade Goody on television, for example, or someone who has saved another's life, or an exceptional sportsman, such one-offs do not shape society. Furthermore, popularity is generally associated with increased income which, for the majority of these individuals, means leaving the working class behind and becoming middle class. On the other hand, the collective clout of the working class over society is substantial and derives from the potential for million-fold multiplication. If a particular fashion has become popular in the working class or is on the verge of a breakthrough, it will be copied by a large number of companies manufacturing similar products. Many businesses tailor their product range to working-class customers. This applies not only to fashion, but also to other products that depend on customer taste, such as music, furniture, cars, newspapers and magazines, television and radio programmes, holiday destinations and types of sport.

Nevertheless, the working class does not determine its own fate. Rather, it is shaped by higher social classes, in just about every key aspect. The representatives of the media who fly the flag for the working class are primarily university graduates, the most prominent contemporary example being the left-wing journalist and political commentator Owen Jones (author of *Chavs* and *The Establishment*), who studied at Oxford. Most of the makers of entertainment for the working class are not themselves workers, but university graduates. Virtually everyone involved in providing culture for the working class – be it in museums, concerts, education, travel, literature or the theatre – has completed tertiary education. The vast majority of products manufactured by industry for the working class to buy are developed and produced by companies whose senior managers hold degrees. The advertising for products targeted specifically at the working class is devised almost exclusively by graduates. The fashions worn by the working class are rarely designed by their peers. The films enjoyed by the working class in the cinema or on television are made by directors who are generally well educated and professionally qualified. The working class receive tips about diet and food from Jamie Oliver, himself not working-class, and other celebrity chefs. The suburbs, estates and houses built for the working class are designed and planned by university-educated architects and town planners. That the entire literary canon about classes and class society in England was written not by workers, but by members of the middle class, hardly bears mentioning: the working class lacks the requisite education. A member of the working class who acquires such learning ceases to be working-class and becomes middle-class instead. In short, the lives of working-class people are framed not by workers but by the middle and upper classes – or as Ferdinand Mount would have it: the lower orders do not run their own affairs (any more), but are managed by the upper classes.[16]

There are of course exceptions, but a worker will hardly ever reach the dizzy heights of power and still remain working-class; rather, in the vast majority of cases, the working-class child leaves that class after finishing school and university. Even those whose intentions

96

vis-à-vis the working class are well-meant (and that is far from every-one who speaks or writes to that effect) do not actually believe in the working class's ability automatically to do what is best for it. Of course, most of these supporters of the working class act not in the working class's interest, but very much in pursuit of their own agenda.

There are only a few areas in which the working class excels through active participants. In football, for example, the bulk of players at English clubs (still) have a working-class background. But here too caveats apply. Many club managers are retired players coming from the aforementioned working-class background. However, a growing number of managers have an intellectual grounding in addition to their experience of the game, and successfully give football a scientific dimension that is no different from any other form of intellectual activity. So in the higher echelons of both football clubs and the English Football Association, an increasing number of well-educated people, many of them graduates, are ensconced. In pop music in 1990 the working class still held sway, accounting for around 80 per cent of musicians (although some were only pretending to be working-class, such as Jim Morrison, who claimed his parents were dead rather than admit that his father was, in fact, an admiral). Here, too, we find an increasing trend towards the middle class among successful popstars, e.g. James Blunt and Dido.[17] Acting is becoming more and more of a middle-class profession as well, with many of the best, highest-earning and award-winning actors having been privately educated, e.g. Kate Winslet, Eddy Redmayne, Damian Lewis, Tom Hiddleston. Even sports appear to be going that way. Just a third of today's top athletes went to state schools.[18]

The one sphere in which the working class has the edge is elector-ally. Here the balance of power is reversed, on polling day at least. By electing an MP, voters place their authority in that individual's hands and forego their individual power – until the next election day, that is.

There is no such thing as a homogeneous working class; rather this term subsumes a finely differentiated hierarchy. This was particularly striking in the past. In Robert Roberts' book *The Classic Slum* (1971), he describes how the Salford proletariat was arranged in an elaborate status hierarchy covering all men, women and children in a closed urban village of crowded streets, rooted in the different market and work situations of workers with different levels of skill, the arbiters of status mostly being women. It was common for them to try to prove to others that an adversary and their kindred were low class or no class at all, by for instance brandishing their own 'clean' rent book (that great status symbol of the times), in the knowledge that their rival had fallen in arrears.

The jobs people did were also classed in a clear hierarchy. Once, the miners had the highest status because they could bring the country to their knees – and indeed did so in the 1970s. A parallel caste system existed among those working in service. A servant employed in the large house belonging to a duke such as Chatsworth was higher up the ladder than someone engaged by a baron or commoner. In large households a strict pecking order was observed among domestic servants: from butler at the top, to valet, footman, parlourmaid, chambermaid, etc.

The most general divide was between respectable and rough, the latter typically drinking too much, making too much noise, fighting in public, swearing all the time and occasionally neglecting their wife and children. Traditionally, at the bottom of the working class were those members of society who shunned virtually all social order and obligation. They were often referred to as the undeserving poor (as opposed to the deserving or respectable poor), or what Karl Marx called the 'Lumpenproletariat'. The modern view discerns a social order outside the recognized class structure: the underclass (see below).

It is no longer possible to encapsulate the working class in a single axiom or phrase. While 'I'm working class and I'm proud of it' neatly fits the attitude of the old working class, the new working class is more likely to maintain, 'I hate this job. I can and will do better'.

UPPER CLASS

The upper class is a peculiar beast. It seems not even to exist. There is hardly an Englishman alive who would admit to being upper class, or indeed who would publicly acknowledge belonging to the

Establishment or elite. The available figures indicate that less than one per cent of the population belongs to the upper class. The highest value was stated by the Great British Class Survey of 2011, which put the elite at 6 per cent of society. Many people declare that the upper class, if it exists all, is no longer relevant. Scientific studies of the upper class, its size and influence, are few and far between. Even the media do not pay these much attention. All this creates a completely false impression.

Who belongs to the upper class? Many people, especially sociologists, define the upper class purely in terms of money, in other words their assets and income. This approach requires amounts or at least a ballpark figure to be stated, yet the majority of authors fail to comply. They speak of the 'super rich' or the 'seriously rich' or 'the one per cent' (or even less). Not so the authors of the GBCS 2011: they regard 6 per cent of the population as belonging to the class they have designated the 'new ordinary elite', having an average household income of at least £89,000 p.a., household savings of £142,000 and a house value of £325,000.

This very broad interpretation of the elite does not coincide with the traditional understanding of upper-class. People who match these figures are neither very wealthy nor seriously rich, a category which would surely only start at a multiple of these amounts. The moneyed upper class (admittedly not the same thing) is drawn from owners of businesses and large estates, captains of industry, bankers and investment managers; top-earning members of the so-called free professions such as lawyers, engineers, doctors and tax experts; highly-paid figures from the entertainment industry such as sportsmen and -women, media stars and journalists; high-status executives of international organizations such as the World Bank, International Monetary Fund, World Trade Organization, European Union, etc.; senior civil servants, including judges, as well as eminent professors and vice chancellors of the great universities; high-ranking soldiers, leading politicians and, last but not least, sundry celebrities. With his education at a private school and Oxford University, decades of high political office, his election as Prime Minister of the United

Kingdom on three occasions, prodigious national and international connections and assets of several million pounds, Tony Blair epitomizes England's modern upper class. His example illustrates the partial – but not complete – overlap between the upper class and the Establishment or elite. The boundaries with the middle class are likewise blurred, especially with the upper-middle order, where the crossover with the upper class is in any case ongoing.

As already mentioned, the financial aspect is not sufficient to define someone as upper class in the traditional sense. A certain minimum level of culture and behaviour must additionally be present. Consequently, the National Lottery winner who buys himself a country house in Buckinghamshire, a flat in London's Eaton Square and a Rolls-Royce in no way qualifies as upper class. Maybe he can join its ranks, but it's a big maybe. Becoming upper class is very, very difficult, and only few people succeed (see Chapter 32). Normally, it takes one to two generations for the newly rich to be assimilated by the existing upper class – although being extremely rich naturally speeds things up.

On the other hand, as we've already seen, it is fairly difficult to be upper class without any money at all – difficult, but not impossible. A high level of education, culture and behaviour, coupled ideally with intellectual achievement, opens the doors to the upper class. Writers, artists, scientists, university lecturers and distinguished actors are included in this category. Examples that spring to mind are Oscar Wilde, who was hard up all his life but not only belonged to the upper class himself, but was also accepted by it as such (until he was disowned when his homosexuality, which was illegal in England at the time, became known); and Patrick Leigh Fermor, a war hero, famous writer and lifelong friend of the late Deborah, Duchess of Devonshire who, she wrote, 'nearly belongs to the family'. The same applies to the actor Laurence Olivier and the painter Lucian Freud, who became rich themselves.

Like the working class, the upper class is far from homogeneous, but rather stratified. From the outside, for those who do not belong it, members of the upper class may appear identical and indistinguishable. The view from the inside is entirely different. As with nearly all privileged groups that arouse envy in others, how they are perceived depends on whether they are viewed internally or externally. To outsiders, the differences in wealth, income and status within the group are imperceptible or barely recognizable. Football fans who watch the professional game see players who are all similarly skilful and all very well paid. Within the team, however, there is a pronounced hierarchy. Each player knows that their footballing skills are far from equal and differ enormously. And the money they earn varies just as greatly. The stars of the team can easily take home ten times more than the run-of-the-mill players. For a worker watching the match at the weekend, the outward impression is more or less exactly the same, whether the player is earning £1 million or £10 million a year.

It is a similar story with university professors. From the outside they generally appear to be a relatively homogeneous group of well-paid academics whose level is much the same. Yet there are huge differences between professors, especially when it comes to peer recognition. Apart from the usual petty jealousies among academics, they are very clearly aware of who is 'top notch' and who is more or less coasting, with no motivation. An academic honour is therefore 100 times more significant for those inside the group than for outsiders who have no clear idea of its meaning. It is a similar tale with the upper classes. To an outsider, fortunes of £100 million or £1 billion are much of a muchness. To the rich, the gulf between them could hardly be greater. Within the aristocracy the order of precedence, from duke down through the ranks, is relatively clear and straightforward. However, this does not preclude serious rivalries over status among the nobility. At a particularly splendid gathering, teeming with grandees, the Duchess of Buccleuch and the Duchess of Northumberland made their entrance together, as neither wished to concede rank to the other.[19]

The upper class wields disproportionate influence. It has economic power and consequently obtains (at least indirect) political authority at all levels of state. Through the media it can influence public opinion. In many respects it is the arbiter of taste. The vast influence of the upper class derives from multiple factors. They own or, through their companies, control the productive resources. They therefore decide which businesses are created, wound up or moved elsewhere, with all the associated consequences for the workforce and dependent entities such as suppliers, as well as the public coffers of the community where the company is based.

The upper class is fully networked, both within and outside the aristocracy. Although not everyone knows everyone else, they recognize each other when they meet and develop a certain mutual solidarity. They tend to inter-marry. Many of them come from a common background, as regards their families, schooling, university education and early professional experience. Their investments crisscross into various companies, as do directorships. Multiple directorships are the norm.

They are flexible about both their place of residence and their capital, placing them at the forefront of modern globalization. If they no longer feel at ease in one country, they can relocate to another, both in person and with their capital. Most of them are patriotic, but only up to a point.

Should they work in the media or even own media outlets, e.g. major newspapers, they have a huge influence on public opinion which, although hard to quantify, is clearly there.

Under these circumstances, it comes as no surprise that governments of every stripe pay heed to these people. Because they can sponsor, finance or bribe political parties and politicians, they can create dependency among the latter. They can use jobs for employees as a lever to influence votes, which are the politicians' bread-and-butter. The creator of a thousand jobs can expect the red carpet treatment from every politician in the world. Some quid pro quo is invariably expected in return.

Most people, especially the members of other classes, are unaware of the upper class's dominance, and it is relatively rare for the upper class to be criticized or come under real pressure, provided it does not overstep certain limits. This is no coincidence. In a democratic age, the supremacy of a minority is regarded as improper and contrary to the will of the people. This situation must therefore be kept from the majority – something achieved by silence, downplaying, contradiction, concealment, etc., culminating in the phenomenon of class denial (see Chapter 7).

In one respect alone does the upper class not have an edge on the other classes. Each of its members has only one vote, and so it is automatically in a minority in democratic elections and unable to achieve political power through the ballot box. As history shows, however, this has far from caused its decline. Through the media or think tanks, for instance, it can have a certain impact on voters. It has access to those wielding political power and can mould them. And it can bring influence to bear at many levels of society below the ruling elite, by providing financial backing for specific points of view and attitudes, for example.

Opinions on the upper class have fluctuated throughout history. Decades of respect were followed by a growing chorus of criticism following the First World War. Someone whose voice stood out among the detractors was George Orwell, whose comments have since become famous:

> England is a land of snobbery and privilege, ruled largely by the old and silly . . . At any normal time the ruling class will rob, misman-age, sabotage, lead us into the muck . . . England is a family with the wrong members in control . . . For long past there had been in England an entirely functionless class, living on money that was invested they hardly knew where, the 'idle rich' . . . The existence of these people was by any standard unjustifiable. They were simply parasites, less useful to society than his fleas are to a dog.[20]

The usually so perspicacious Orwell was not quite fair in this assessment: members of this class (and other classes too) were among those who most valiantly risked their lives in the First World War, sustaining heavy losses. Their conduct in the Second World War was no less distinguished, as Toby Young rightly wrote in a piece headlined, 'The Battle of Britain was won by members of our clapped-out ruling class.'[21] For them, duty was more than something to be paid lip service to.

'The upper classes in every country' declared Denis Healey at the 1945 Labour Party Conference, 'are selfish, depraved, dissolute and decadent'. (It almost goes without saying that, in later life, having served as a minister several times, he became upper-class himself and entered the House of Lords as Baron Healey.) More damning still was the indictment of the dramatist John Osborne who in the 1950s, together with Kingsley Amis, was the most famous of the 'angry young men' (*The Entertainer, Look Back in Anger*):

> I can't go on laughing at the idiocies of the people who rule our lives. We have been laughing at their gay little madnesses, my dear, at their point-to-points, at the postural slump of the well-off and the mentally under-privileged, at the stooping shoulders and strained accents, at their waffling cant, for too long. They are no longer funny, because they are not merely dangerous, they are murderous. I don't think I want to make people laugh at them anymore because they are stupid, insensitive, unimaginative beyond hope, uncreative and murderous.

Descriptions and appraisals of the modern upper class of the past 50 years are relatively hard to come by. This may be because of its heterogeneity, which is not conducive to general characterization. Another reason may lie in the deliberate efforts of today's top tier not to be seen as such. If judgement is passed, entrepreneurs, company directors and CEOs, together with bankers and particularly politicians, seem to be less trusted and respected than senior civil servants and soldiers, scientists, artists and media stars.

A special role in the upper class is played by the hereditary aristocracy. According to the German sociologist Max Weber, a person's place in society is defined by their power, wealth and status. Until around 200 years ago the British aristocracy combined all three criteria, over which it had virtually a sole monopoly. It occupied the positions of political power and governed the country. It was wealthy, primarily as a result of land ownership, and enjoyed the highest social esteem.[22] This exclusive grip on power, wealth and status faltered at the end of the eighteenth and during the nineteenth centuries. By that time industrialists, merchants and bankers were becoming just as rich as the aristocrats, if not richer, as their activities replaced agriculture as the backbone of the economy. Many patricians lost their fortunes because the economic world had changed or through sheer ineptitude or high death duties, particularly after both world wars, forcing them to sell their estates and land, their homes and heirlooms. From the mid-nineteenth century onwards they saw their political power eroded with the birth and growth of democracy. Today they have disappeared completely as a governing force. In the House of Lords, where just 92 hereditary peers remain following the 1999 reform under Tony Blair, they constitute a minority of around 12 per cent. Hereditary peerages are no longer awarded: Margaret Thatcher was the last prime minister to create a small number of hereditary lords. David Cannadine impressively chronicles these events in his book *The Decline and Fall of the British Aristocracy*. In more recent publications on who is running Britain, peers no longer even feature or are confined to historical footnotes.[23]

As might be expected, the English aristocracy has deeply divided opinion over the past 200 years. Until roughly the time of the First World War, the aristocracy's belief in its unique role and unequalled influence, wealth and prestige was also shared by the general populace. The aristocracy's pre-eminence was regarded by virtually all Englishmen and Britons as the natural order of things, having ever been thus. Above all, it was also perceived as fair and deserved. When Lord Curzon quoted the French historian Ernest Renan's conclusion that 'all civilizations have been the work of aristocracies' with reference to England, this was hardly surprising, given his own impeccable aristocratic credentials (Marquess Curzon of Kedleston, Viceroy of India, foreign secretary, renovator and owner of several stately homes, renowned traveller and writer). The plaudits, along with the admiration and deference frequently shown to the aristocracy, stem primarily from the responsibilities encapsulated in the motto *noblesse oblige*: to rule the country well, be a model of courage in times of crisis or war, protect those they govern and provide for them, and generally to be an upstanding citizen. Peregrine Worsthorne, in his book *In Defence of Aristocracy* (2004), summed this up as follows: 'I've always thought the English aristocracy so marvellous compared to other ruling classes. It seemed to me that we had got a ruling class of such extraordinary historical excellence, which is rooted in England almost since the Norman Conquest.'[24]

It should also be borne in mind that, during the era when the political leadership of England and Great Britain was recruited almost entirely from the aristocracy, the British Empire was being established and maintained, over a period spanning more than 300 years. This was achieved against fierce rivalry from the other European powers and not infrequent resistance from the subjugated peoples. The men (and only men were involved – Queen Victoria was more of an onlooker) who shaped these destinies were no simpletons or cowards. Although our moral judgement of overseas European colonialism (and not just the British Empire) has changed, the creation and upkeep of such an empire, encompassing a quarter of the world's surface area and population, remain an astonishing feat. It called for intelligence, energy, character, hard work, physical effort and personal sacrifice. Even today, and with all the benefit of hindsight, we can still explain and understand the English gratitude towards their aristocratic rulers.

With the rise in wealth away from the land, in industry, trade and banks, and the growing consciousness of a working class around the middle of the nineteenth century, the first cracks appeared in the feelings of esteem and appreciation. The extraordinary proliferation of aristocratic titles outside the traditional landowning class exacerbated the trend. The two world wars saw a restoration of standing thanks to the exemplary bravery of soldiers from noble families. After the Second World War the aristocracy again lost face, amid the notion that this class could not (or could no longer) best determine the future of the British people. The mood was symbolized by the election defeat

of Prime Minister Winston Churchill in 1945 and the victory of the
Labour Party under Clement Attlee. A barrage of press reports about
individual immorality among the aristocracy added fuel to the fire.
Someone with an intimate knowledge of the English aristocracy and
who counted many of them as close friends was James Lees-Milne,
who devoted his long life to rescuing country houses through his work
for the National Trust. In 1996, a year before his death, he evoked the
full spectrum of emotions, from contempt to awe:

> I have come to the conclusion that the aristocracy have always
> been shits, and that in my youth I was too beguiled by them.
> Nevertheless, I still maintain that the decent and educated ones
> attain a standard of well-being and good-doing which has never
> been transcended by any other class in the world.[25]

Today, the hereditary aristocracy remains, if not alone, then pretty
much unchallenged at the top of the class pyramid, despite strong
criticism from some quarters.[26] Many of its members are still rich.
Around one-third of the 300 wealthiest Britons are nobles, bearing
testament to a remarkable continuity across the generations – something incidentally that is also found among moneyed commoners.[27]
As a result of the gigantic leap in land prices in Great Britain, estates
that have been severely pared down are often worth more today than
before, when their acreage was much larger. This applies not only to
building land, which notably made the Duke of Westminster rich, but
also to farmland, prices for which have reached unheralded heights.
But even without a substantial fortune, members of the hereditary
aristocracy – and not only the title holders, but the rest of their family
too – are seen as upper-class by a clear majority of English people. A
hard-up earl would have to work in a very down-at-heel job indeed to
cease to be regarded as a member of the upper echelons. Several lords
have famously become police officers in real life, and were perhaps
the inspiration for the television series *The Inspector Lynley Mysteries*,
in which Detective Inspector Thomas Lynley, 8th Earl of Asherton, is
seconded to Scotland Yard. The series feeds off the contrast between

Lynley and his female sidekick Detective Sergeant Barbara Havers, whose background is working class. Lynley's own social pedigree is never in doubt.

Of the three criteria power, wealth and status, the aristocracy has effectively completely lost the first and partially lost the second. However, its status has remained fundamentally intact. Admittedly, many see the aristocracy as a marginalized relic of a past age with no particular role in contemporary British social and cultural life. It is variously regarded as eccentric and quaint, un-modern and largely irrelevant, outmoded and ill-equipped for the modern world, yet people still contrive to find its foibles quite endearing – a view readily adopted by the media, including television, and not a few scientists.[28] This attitude is, I feel, akin to the repression encountered with social class. Its existence is denied – not so much as a statement of fact, but more as a wish that it might go away. Some sections of society may exist for which the aristocracy is so far removed as to be practically non-existent.

But for the bulk of the population and certainly for the middle classes, the situation is very different. Why do members of the aristocracy come first on any guest list or seating plan? Why are they so often invoked as the arbiters of taste? Why are they the subject of endless films and television series? Why is a commoner 'marrying up' if they wed an aristocrat, but the latter then 'marrying down'? Why do clubs, corporations and foundations strive to secure a grandee on the board, or better still as chairman? Why are aristocrats patrons of so many events? Why are so many sporting trophies awarded by dukes and duchesses and other nobility who otherwise have little to do with the sport? Why do most people behave 'differently' if a lord or lady is present? Why are people generally fascinated if they come face-to-face with the blue-blooded owner of a country house and even prepared to pay to have dinner in his company? An invitation from a member of the nobility is studied more closely than any other, none more so than an invitation to a garden party at Buckingham Palace. In the light of the foregoing, can we really be expected to believe that aristocrats are just mortals like the rest of humanity?

In England the aristocracy's social status is also officially preserved in an institution whose like is seldom found in a democracy. The Order of Precedence, details of which can be looked up on the internet, contains elements that, to an outsider, appear incomprehensible and preposterously undemocratic. That the sovereign (male or female) should rank highest is understandable and logical because the monarchy is supported by the people; it is upheld by Parliament, although the latter could abolish it. Beyond that, however, many questions arise. Why do MPs – who have earned their position by personal effort, represent the people and make the laws that every British citizen must obey, regardless of status – rank below a hereditary peer who has personally done nothing to obtain his position, having merely inherited it? Ordinary MPs are not even mentioned in the Order of Precedence (only the speaker of the House of Commons is included on the list). Even the monarch's grandson is placed higher than the prime minister and the speaker of the House of Commons.

The present-day attitude of most Englishmen towards hereditary peers is one of the surprises of English society. On the one hand the English roundly reject unwarranted individual privilege. They could therefore logically be expected to have greater respect for life peerages than for the hereditary kind, since the former are awarded to people who have themselves achieved something notable (apart from those which have been bought or given for tactical political reasons). In fact, the opposite is the case. Hereditary peers are valued more highly. The majority of English citizens look up not only to the hereditary monarchy – by definition a bastion of unmerited privilege – but also to hereditary peers. Besides, it would be remarkable if, in a state headed by a queen with an extended family – the acme of class privilege – the remaining aristocracy were not to play a role too. The aristocracy and the monarchy form an indivisible whole. If the monarchy is the tree, the aristocracy are the branches or the roots – depending on your perspective; the one cannot live without the other.

Again and again we read that the age of deference is over. For the greater part of the population this is mistaken. It is true that an Englishman, on discovering that he is speaking to an earl, will on no account grovel. On the contrary, he is quite likely to attempt to behave 'super-normally', as with any other compatriot, and as a consequence appear rather stiff and unnatural. Nevertheless, his perception and his behaviour will change. Quite unconsciously, he expects the earl's conduct, pronunciation, occupation, conversation and table manners to be out of the ordinary. If the earl fails to live up to this image, a comment is passed: 'Who would have thought it!' If a school class or university cohort includes a viscount, and a pecking order is created among pupils or students, the viscount is certain to be at the top – not because of any deliberate effort on his part (which would be unthinkable), but because this is imposed upon him by the others. If he is absent from an event, people will ask why he is missing. If someone makes a mistake or messes up at cricket or rowing, say, everyone's first thought is: will he help the unhappy one? When he (naturally) obliges, what stands out is the attention this attracts. The situation is certainly no longer as described by Harold Laski in 1932:

> As a people, said Bagehot, the English have a genius for deference; by which, I take it, he meant that they know their betters when they see them . . . That is why *The Times* will print a letter, however absurd, from a duke in large type, and one, however important, from the secretary of the Trades Union Congress, in small. That is why, also, the births, marriages and deaths of even the remotest members of the Royal Family cast light and shadow upon every home in England, why the coming of age of a great gentleman like the Duke of Norfolk, of whose character and intelligence nothing is known, is almost a national event, and the fit subject of leading articles in the press.[29]

But these lines are still likely to resonate somewhat, even with a twenty-first-century Englishman. Shrouded in mystery, titles have retained their popular fascination. What would otherwise explain the reports of sons of lords who were known simply as 'Mister' (e.g. Mr Churchill) until their fathers died and they succeeded to the title? Their testimony reveals that people's behaviour towards them changed quite remarkably on their succession. In their dealings with officials or officers of different ranks, people automatically assume that the lord is superior to the plain 'mister', even if the opposite is true. Now as before, lords are approached to become chairman, president or patron of institutions or charities without any investigation of their qualification or suitability. If the lord in question suggests that someone else might be a better choice, having greater interest or knowledge, the inquirer inevitably dismisses the idea on the grounds that they do not have a title.

This 'fine distinction' also gives peers an edge over those who have become upper class or upper-middle class on personal merit, something of which the English are acutely aware. A highly cultivated and educated man who works as a lawyer in Gloucestershire and lives in an idyllic English village explained this to me as we were walking past the manor house, owned by his friend John C, that dominated the village.

You would be hard pushed to find any differences between John and me. We went to the same school and both went to university, we hold the same honorary positions in our town, both actively support the museum, have very similar political views, speak the same English, behave in the same way, go hunting together and so on. Any outsider would describe us as social equals. Yet that is not correct. We are only 98 per cent equal. He ranks 2 per cent higher than me. Sometimes those 2 per cent matter more than the remaining 98 per cent.

It is because his family can be traced back in this village to 1066. Of course, I have just as many ancestors as him, and everyone else for that matter. But his are recorded in ancient tomes and have been members of the upper echelons for more than 30 generations. Mine are unmentioned in the history books, and my father was the first to make it to the top. That makes all the difference. Even if I were extremely rich and John poor, and he wished to sell me his house, nothing would change for a very long time, maybe not until three generations had passed.

When one examines the reasons for this deference, a law of modern market economics comes to mind: things that are rare rise in value and are put on a pedestal. With new hereditary peerages no longer being created, the hereditary aristocracy is destined for extinction. But until then it stands to gain from its rarity value. Aristocrats are valued because they are so few in number. A similar principle applies in the case of the elephant or rhinoceros: the rarer they become, the higher the price for their tusks and horns. When there is only one duke left in England, he will probably be idolized and weighed in gold. This is the undoubtedly accidental consequence of political intervention. Perhaps the English custom and tradition of honouring the past is a factor here, or maybe too an age-old faith in the 'purity of blood'; perhaps it is also the widely held longing for a wise leader who can guide people's fates better than they think they are capable of themselves; a belief fundamental to democracy itself. This deference is – with some exceptions – to be found in all classes. 'As an Englishman', admitted the artist Grayson Perry, 'even a jumped-up prole like me feels genetically drawn to crumbling faded glory.'

The relationship of the aristocracy to the rich is straightforward: they are linked by a huge mutual interest. Members of the nobility, especially if hard-up, are interested in the money they hope to gain from the wealthy. And the rich are interested in class, which they hope to gain from the nobility. It is, to use a modern cliché, a win-win situation. 'There is no stronger craving in the world', wrote Hesketh Pearson, 'than that of the rich for titles, except perhaps that of the title for riches.'[30] The knock-on effect of these interests can be seen in the widespread practice of having at least one hereditary lord on company boards.

This is not a new-fangled notion. As early as the nineteenth century many rich individuals kept aristocrats as if they were pets or elegant dogs, to give themselves the appearance of genuine class, as typified by the scheming magnate Augustus Melmotte's treatment of Lords Nidderdale and Grendall in Anthony Trollope's *The Way we Live Now* (1874). And to this day, impoverished nobles marry wealthy

commoners strikingly often. 'She gave me money,' as one particular
lord put it: 'I gave her class.' The entire 'philosophy' of the relationship
of the self-made Englishman to the aristocracy is reflected in a letter
recently published in the 'Dear Mary: Your problems solved' section
of the *Spectator*. All the clichés are to be found: pride in one's own
accomplishments; the desire to show success tempered by the fear
of boasting about it, resulting in a display of humility; pride in the
upward mobility that comes with marrying an aristocrat; admiration
for the aristocrats' superior taste; the aristocrats' definition of vulgarity as naturally demonstrated by the self-made man; and reluctance
to reveal one's wealth and upper-class connections by withholding
one's own name. The letter was about the vulgarity or otherwise of
security gates. Abridged, it reads:

> Don't forget that humble farmers like us have to have our modest
> electronic gates, as cattle grids are not trustworthy. (As a common
> little self-made man I long to have massive gates with coats of
> arms, but my aristocratic wife says that would be vulgar and likes
> our battered wooden gates.)
>
> Name and address withheld[31]

It is difficult to find a pithy saying to characterize the English upper
classes, because they result from a 'circulation of elites' that is well
under way. Those who have inherited their status stand alongside
people who have created their wealth through their own endeavours, aristocracy alongside the arts, politicians alongside rich people,
intellectual plodders alongside highbrows, recluses alongside public
figures. The perspicacious author and journalist Harry Mount knows
who belongs and who does not. While for centuries aristocrats ruled
the roost, 'Now cash, good looks and celebrity are king. The poor,
the plain and the unknown will never make it to the king's court,
however deserving they may be.'[32]

Young royalty and aristocracy are now just another arm of the
international, rich celeb glamocracy (Harry Mount again). The phrase
that perhaps best captures the traditional upper class is 'born to rule';

the expression which sums up the modern upper class, 'I believe in meritocracy'.

THE MIDDLE CLASS(ES)

> *I come from the middle classes, and I am proud of the ability, the shrewdness, the industry and providence, the thrift by which they are distinguished.*

Neville Chamberlain

> *I am glad that she has gone . . . she has a decidedly middle-class mind.*

Oscar Wilde, *The Remarkable Rocket* (1888)

In theory, defining the middle class is easy. In reality, it is the section of society hardest to pinpoint. One reason for this is that – unlike the upper and working classes – it is bounded by not one social caste, but two, and therefore any definition must delineate its scope with reference to these two other categories.

A more serious problem is that, while the presence of the upper and working classes has never been doubted, there have always been voices that have denied the middle class's very existence. In 1980 Arthur Scargill claimed that 'There is no such thing as a middle class.' And many of those who accepted the presence of a middle class believed that its days were numbered, most prominently George Orwell in *The Road to Wigan Pier* – 'and we of the sinking middle class . . . may sink without further struggles into the working class where we belong' – while 40 years later George Mikes maintained that 'Britain has . . . a middle class which is not in the middle but is sliding fast to the bottom.'[33] Both are wrong, both about the past and most definitely about the present: there has been and continues to be a middle class, and it is larger and more influential than ever; it is certainly not sliding to the bottom, let alone vanishing.

The difficulty with a positive definition results from the broad spectrum of different professions, educations, accents, vocabularies, lifestyles, etc. that count as middle class, and from changes in the upper and working classes. In the upper class, the traditional aristocracy and landed gentry have been joined by the plutocratic elite of entrepreneurs, financiers, executives and celebrities – in other words the wealthy. The working class, when understood to mean manual labourers, has shrunk substantially, and a separate underclass (see below) has split off from it. Consequently, the middle class comprises a vast, heterogeneous mass of all backgrounds, incomes and occupations, rather fittingly referred to in a 2006 study by the Liverpool Victoria friendly society as the 'muddle class'.[34] Many prefer to define the middle class negatively, by what it is not: divided from those above by the scale of the latter's wealth, and from those below by not doing and believing what they do and believe.

The wide span of the middle class has led to it commonly being subdivided into lower-middle, middle-middle and upper-middle strata. Probably the best yardstick when describing the middle class is to use the professions it traditionally includes. The lower-middle class comprises mainly office workers in low-level civil service jobs in local and regional government, sales assistants, travel agents, and administrative staff in factories and large properties. Lower-middle class people generally do not have a university education (at least, this was the case before the expansion of higher education in recent decades). The middle-middle class consists of teachers, managers, engineers, doctors, accountants, architects, solicitors, social workers, civil servants and soldiers – people in jobs that generally call for a university degree. The upper-middle class to a large extent practises the same professions as the middle-middle class, but occupies the highest echelons, working as barristers, Queen's Counsel, senior judges, high-ranking civil servants, top executives in companies, university professors, headmasters of bigger schools, successful artists and writers.

The assets and income of members of the middle classes are as diverse as their occupations. They can earn anything from around £20,000 p.a. at the bottom end of the scale to seven-figure sums.

As anyone can see, the middle class has a dominant influence at practically every level of English society (occasionally together with the upper class). The middle class has assumed roles that in many areas used to be the preserve of the working class. In politics, this is symbolized by the fact that more than 90 per cent of all Labour politicians are middle-class rather than working-class, as was once the case. Through its size, the middle class also makes up the majority of all voters. In England policies against the middle class are a non-starter.

Unlike for the upper and working classes, no uniform similarities can be found for the middle class by way of class markers, although some clusters are evident. Virtually all hard and soft class markers are present among the middle classes. This may explain why many members of the middle class are uncertain about their own class status, and therefore seek greater guidance about class than members of the upper or working classes. Some observers regard it as an actual characteristic of middle-class people that they live in a constant state of insecurity – feeling nervous, unsure of their tastes, preoccupations, behaviours and sensibilities. To be middle-class is to hesitate and dither at every turn, consumed by the fear of potential embarrassment and social catastrophe. Awkwardness takes over.[35] Books with titles such as *Your Place in Society* or *What is Your Class?* and the relevant self-help books for learning the 'right way to behave' are bought almost exclusively by the middle class. The English penchant for apologizing too much (saying 'I'm so sorry' to someone who has just stood on their foot) is much more pronounced among the middle classes.

The members of the middle class are also the ones who most want to know which class they belong to. Of the 161,000 people who took part in the self-assessment part of the Great British Class Survey in 2011, well over 80 per cent belonged to the traditional middle classes, and only just under 20 per cent were working class (although the GBCS itself used other categories).

Another touchstone of the middle classes, at least since the Second World War, is their desire to own the property they live in. This wish has also come true for the vast majority of middle-class people. The more people own their own homes, the better for democracy (and the Conservative Party), according to Prime Ministers Harold Macmillan and later Margaret Thatcher, who scored her biggest ever domestic coup with the right-to-buy programme, by which the tenants of council houses were entitled to buy them at a discount. 'An Englishman's home is his castle' is not simply an aristocratic motto, but also reflects a middle-class preoccupation. This trend has been fuelled by the near-continuous rise in property prices since the 1950s. Joining the property ladder was almost without risk. However, with house prices soaring out of reach of many middle-class citizens, in recent years, the tide is turning. After a longstanding association, home ownership and the middle classes are no longer inseparable.

If a house purchase is for most middle-class families the largest single investment of their lives, this is closely followed by expenditure on the education of their children. Just about every member of the middle class places inordinate emphasis on their children being well educated, because they believe this will improve their life chances and allow them to go further than they themselves have.[36] Consequently, they send them to the best schools they can find and afford, be they public schools, grammars or highly-rated comprehensives. For a place in a good school they are prepared to drive miles. Some even move house to be in the catchment area of a reputable school, and to this end are willing to pay a premium on their house price. England is probably one of the few countries in the world where house prices are influenced (among other things) by whether a property is situated in the designated area of a sought-after school. The better the school, the higher the house price. After school, the goal for nearly all middle-class families is for their children to go to university. Here too they are ready to make considerable financial sacrifices to enable their offspring to study at a prestigious institution.

Reflecting the breadth of the middle class is how it is described, which veers from less than flattering to full of praise. On the one hand, we have Julian Baggini:

> Even worse [than the working class] were the aspiring 'middle classes' in whose homes I felt suffocated under the oppressive veneer of respectability. In many ways, these homes were rather like the ones on the council estate, which is not surprising, for

117

they had the same cultural roots. Father was also a little feared, only they called it respect and his superiority was not expressed through profane shouting. Mother also did all the household work, but with fewer kids and more money, she was not so much harassed as bored and frustrated. Dad also had his somewhat plusher chair, and here too the television was almost always on – only this time tuned to the BBC. But as on the estates, the new Channel 4 was only for left-wing homosexuals.[37]

The opinion of the lower middle class expressed by Peter Jay, the son-in-law of the Labour Prime Minister James Callaghan and former ambassador in Washington, was even more derogatory:

> We felt nothing but hostility for them. We thought they were silly and selfish, with narrow, primitive, semi-educated attitudes. We grew up viewing them with contempt, and saw them as preoccupied with money so they could 'better themselves'. They made themselves ridiculous. They were contemptible, and therefore it was easy for governments to squeeze them.[38]

On the other hand, there is Neville Chamberlain (quoted above), or the owner of a small business who declared: 'I'm proud of being middle-class. If there wasn't a middle class, we'd be Britain, full stop. There'd be very little of the "Great" left, wouldn't there?'[39]

Despite all the aspersions cast on the middle class as parochial, avaricious, hypocritical, fawning, obsequious, narrow-minded and bigoted, everyone can ultimately see that the middle class is indispensable. The dominant position it has held for some time as a result of its intelligence, industriousness and resultant competence is being further consolidated in the England of today. Pick up any book about the state of the nation, and you will find sentences such as:

> The middle classes represent the enterprise and genius of the nation; they are the people who recognize what needs to be done and set about achieving it.[40]

They provide specialized knowledge, operate the machinery of the state and direct every form of commercial enterprise.[41]

Nearly all our political and personal liberties have been secured through middle-class education.[42]

This book deals with the present conditions and the prospects of the middle classes, from whom the nation's brains, leadership and organising ability are derived.[43]

Without being unfair to the other classes, the middle classes provide the country with the bulk of its talent and its genius – and have done so for more than 200 years. They have produced long lists of successful scientists, engineers, civil servants, judges, soldiers, pioneers, explorers, entrepreneurs, inventors, teachers in schools and universities, writers, painters, composers, playwrights, novelists and poets. Let there be no doubt, without the middle class there would have been no Industrial Revolution, no rise as a world power, no parliamentary system that has won such admiration; England would not have attained the level of culture and civilization the country currently enjoys.

Only in politics was the hour of the middle class slow to come. Until the end of the nineteenth century, the upper classes and the aristocracy in particular largely called the political shots – albeit to a diminishing extent[44] – but since then the middle class has gradually grown in influence. Nowadays, the hereditary aristocracy has ceased to play a role in politics. Despite a significant number of voters, the working class has secured very few positions of political power. The vast majority of these are clearly held by the middle class (see Chapter 8).

The word that probably best sums up the middle class (apart from its most upper-crust elements) is 'aspiring'. Virtually all members of the middle class strive to exceed their current status quo, which is why they enjoy talking so much about their future plans: 'We found this house quite by chance when we urgently needed somewhere to stay. But we are looking for something a bit more suitable.' 'We've hung onto this car because we grew so fond of it, but we're getting a new one.' 'Our daughter is a medical assistant at the moment, but she is taking a course so she can study medicine.'

THE UNDERCLASS

The phenomenon of the English underclass has been publicly debated for around 40 years.[45] It refers to those people who are outside the classic division into upper, middle and working classes. As far as we can tell, it has existed in every human society. Karl Marx described the *'Lumpenproletariat'* as follows:

> thieves and criminals of all kinds, living on the crumbs of society, people without a definite trade, vagabonds, *gens sans feu et sans aveu* . . . discharged soldiers, discharged jailbirds, escaped galley slaves, swindlers, mountebanks, *lazzaroni*, pickpockets, tricksters, gamblers, *maquereaux*, brothel keepers, porters, literati, organ grinders, ragpickers, knife grinders, tinkers, beggars . . . this scum, offal, refuse of all classes.

The left-liberal thinker Gunnar Myrdal defined it in 1963 as an under-privileged class of unemployed, unemployables and underemployed who were essentially and helplessly set apart from the nation at large. More recent definitions and descriptions, particularly after the riots of August 2011 in London and various other cities across England, are less indulgent. Biressi and Nunn gathered references to the underclass including 'fecklessness and criminality', and phrases such as 'poverty of ambition, poverty of discipline, poverty of soul'. Many are abandoned or divorced. Some are of low intelligence, most of low educational attainment. They produce 'problem children, the future unmarried mothers, delinquents, denizens of borstals, sub-normal education establishments, prisons, hostels for drifters'. They are the dangerous classes, idle thieving bastards, benefit scroungers, neo-rabble. They lead inactive lives on benefits and without any sense of society and shared purpose. They are unsocialized and often violent, drop-outs from the world of work; street thugs, failures, losers with character flaws and behavioural deficiencies. Some are economically inactive NEETs – young people not in employment, education or training.'[46] Their prime characteristic is that they do not, or only occasionally, work and are dependent on social benefits for survival. After the August 2011 riots the phrase 'feral underclass' was frequently used.

However, the word underclass tends to be avoided by politicians. Since members of this underprivileged group have a vote, and votes are what count for politicians, the latter have sought more palatable expressions and come up with terms such as 'social exclusion', 'disconnected' and 'precariat'. In science and in sociology in particular, opinions are divided on the existence and position of the underclass. While some simply cannot see it as such, others assign it to the (lower) order of the working class. No-one denies the phenomenon exists.

6

Class Matters

*To say that class doesn't matter in Britain is like saying
wine doesn't matter in France; or whether you're a man
or a woman doesn't matter in Saudi Arabia.*

Nick Cohen, quoted in Owen Jones, *Chavs* (2011)

*Without class differences England would cease to be the
living theatre it is.*

Anthony Burgess, *Remark* (1985)

CLASS EXISTS

That a class system exists, and acceptance of this as fact, is in the
DNA of all Englishmen. George Orwell's description of England as
'the most class-ridden country under the sun' may have been overdone even at the time of writing (1941); nevertheless, the results of
every study and survey clearly demonstrate the population's certainty
that class still matters, that it is still the most common source of social
identity, that the class structure remains an obvious feature of life in
the twenty-first century, that modern Britain is a society shaped if
not predominantly then palpably by class, and that the class system is
still alive and well. Around 90 per cent of all English people take this
view. A denial that class exists should be taken with a pinch of salt.
It is merely a sign that the denier is either happy with their status or
unwilling to say what they think.

There is much evidence for the persistent recognition of classes in England. Take the twice-yearly honours list, whereby the Queen distributes titles, baronetcies and peerages to recipients nominated by government. There are a great many people, plenty of them already rich and powerful, who are desperately keen to win peerages, knighthoods and even the lesser gongs. Why? This is not just some harmless eccentricity. Rather people know that, with a handle to their name, they will be accorded a new degree of respect and deference. Being addressed as Lord Wilson or Sir George instead of just plain Mr Wilson makes all the difference. Some will stop at nothing, and even use money or bribery to secure such elevation, as exemplified by the 'cash for peerages' affair. This was no different under Tony Blair than it had been under Lloyd George and the elder Stuarts.

The very titles of the most popular English television series are exercises in class-consciousness: *Upstairs, Downstairs, The Good Life, Keeping Up Appearances, Coronation Street, The Royle Family, Dinnerladies, EastEnders, Downton Abbey* and *The Edwardian Country House*, to name but a few. A never-ending series of books, newspaper articles and internet posts on the subject serves to acknowledge the existence of classes, even if the published content seeks to negate them. Why bother otherwise?

The most striking empirical and numerical evidence for the extreme interest in questions relating to class is shown by the public reaction to the BBC's Great British Class Survey (see Chapter 3). If it was already astonishing that more than 161,000 people took the trouble to spend 20 minutes of their time answering questions about their economic situation, cultural tastes, leisure interests and social networks, the biggest surprise was yet to follow. After publication of the BBC's results in 2013, an interactive Class Calculator was installed on the internet, whereby people could tap in replies to questions about their income, savings and house value, their cultural interests and their social networks. They were then told into which of the Class Survey's newly developed classes they fitted.

The outcome was staggering: within a week seven million people – roughly one in five of the British adult population – clicked on the

Class Calculator to find out their class. Social media buzzed with debate, and a wave of popular and academic comment poured forth. Train passengers chatted about which class they were in now and schoolchildren talked in the playground about class. Sales of theatre tickets in London increased by an average of nearly 200 per cent in the week after the GBCS launch, the reason apparently being that the Class Calculator had identified theatre going as an indicator of belonging to a higher class. Social class is a very powerful force in the imagination. People in Britain are interested in and also upset about class.[1]

Just as upward mobility is possible by virtue of a good education, valued profession and ample income, social demotion can occur if assets and income are lost and people turn away from culture and civilization (see Chapter 32). This is also common knowledge, and explains the striving of many to better themselves – proof in itself of widespread class awareness.

Some call class 'Britain's dirty little secret'. That misses the point. Class is not a secret, since everyone knows about its existence. It is not little either, since its social significance is substantial. Whether it is dirty is divisive – some think so, others disagree. To paraphrase Oscar Wilde somewhat, class is the Englishman's love that dare not speak its name. There is much to be said for Stein Ringen's oft-quoted hypothesis: 'What is peculiar to Britain is not the reality of the class system and its continuing existence but class psychology: the preoccupation with class, the belief in class and the symbols of class in manners, dress and language.'[2] It is actually impossible not to notice class in England, unless behaving like the child playing peekaboo who covers her eyes and thinks no-one can see her. If certain individuals nonetheless maintain that there is no such thing as class in England, this is due not so much to poor insight as to their own vested interest in negating the existence of class. Politicians, business leaders and media figures like to do this to suit their own objectives (see Chapter 7).

If evidence were needed of the present-day existence of classes and their permanent place in the English consciousness, it was provided by Prime Minister Theresa May in her first speech in the job. In a short statement of some 650 words delivered outside 10 Downing Street, she dealt only briefly with the reason for her premiership – the Brexit vote – but spoke at length about the English class system. Although she did not dwell on the term, her every word resonated with the language of the English class system:

> One nation . . . whoever we are and wherever we are from . . . burning injustice . . . if you are black . . . the working-class boy . . . university . . . state school . . . top professions . . . educated privately . . . own your own home . . . country that works for everyone . . . ordinary working-class family . . . getting your kids into a good school . . . interests of a privileged few . . . the powerful . . . the mighty . . . the wealthy . . . advantages of the fortunate few . . . whatever your background.

'We will make Britain a country that works not for a privileged few,' she concluded, 'but for every one of us'. Theresa May could not have been clearer in articulating her view of modern England as a class society. The current buzzwords of the class debate were referenced exactly.

PLACING
If the English had no credence in such a thing as a class system, they would be unable to determine their own position in it. Yet not only is this within their powers, but it is exactly what they do. In the same way as modern cars, ships and aircraft are equipped with a Global Positioning System that tells them their location on the Earth at any time, the English have a Class Positioning System that helps them identify their place in the class system. This identification does not always have to be objectively correct from the viewpoint of an anthropologist or sociologist, for instance, but this self-positioning in the class system proves that people believe in classes.

Should the individual have certain ideas about their class and feel ambivalent about it, or about belonging to any class at all, this does not prevent those around them from forming an opinion. They automatically extrapolate which class an individual belongs to from the class markers they observe, regardless of whether this is objectively correct or incorrect or, in particular, whether it is right or wrong in the eyes of the individual concerned. A judgement is made. In other words, the individual Englishman need not indulge in the national pastime of placing and assigning people to a social class, either for himself or for others, so his active participation is not required – but he cannot stop the continual, automatic process of placing himself in a social class, and is therefore always party to it, passively at least.

Getting another person's social status wrong should be avoided at all costs, too. That is why the English have turned their ability to identify each other's class into a national obsession. The English are generally good at this too, relying for their success on a number of open and hidden class markers.

BELONGING

Belonging to a class or group is important for the English. There is a subconscious urge on their part to create

> the illusion that England, or rather the England of the upper-middle and upper classes, is criss-crossed with a million invisible silken threads that weave them together into a brilliant community of rank and grace and exclude everybody else. There is little dishonesty in it, for as a rule they understand each other.[3]

This feeling and this desire to belong to a large club also lead to a general reluctance to admit not knowing another member of the club, even someone never seen in reality and completely unknown. Instead of answering 'I have not met him', an Englishman of a certain background would therefore say, 'Well, I have met him. But he wouldn't remember me.'[4] Hence there is a curious need on the part of the upper classes to demonstrate that they all know each other and do the same things with the same people. One of the joys of belonging to a class is to feel included, to belong to a club and be able to open doors that are closed to others. Ian Buruma tells a good story on the subject.

> One afternoon in May Dominic and I decided to watch the cricket at Lord's. Dominic was a member of the MCC, for which the waiting list is so long that most aspiring members can only hope to be accepted in their dotage. His magic pass allowed him to bring one guest. We went up to the pavilion – members only, of course. At the entrance was a stout man with a bulbous red nose. His manner was officious. His Cerberus role was to keep non-members out. He took his time, enjoying his brief moment of authority, turning Dominic's pass this way and that, asking him questions about precisely who I was. Something about the man, his nose, his puffed-up airs, sent me into a silent rage. After we had finally been let in, my rage became more vocal. Silvery heads in the Long Room swivelled in our direction. And Dominic said to me, with a patience my outburst hardly merited, 'But don't you understand? This is the whole point of being a member. This is what English life is all about.'[5]

The English have a general affinity for exclusivity. Leave three Englishmen in a room and they will invent a rule that prevents a fourth joining them. A hallmark of the upper classes is their absolute discretion about privileged admissions or memberships, or being a guest where others have to buy a ticket. To admit that would be rather low. The very idea denotes a lack of breeding. All this adds up to a desperate desire among many Englishmen to belong to a class or circle from which they have (so far) been excluded: there is something that you have and I do not – therefore I want it too. The efforts to gain membership of prestigious London clubs and the success of private member clubs of the type of Soho House and its rivals (see Chapter 28) illustrate this. The same function is fulfilled by the use of nicknames in a group (see Chapter 13).

As with so many English rules, the rules of belonging to a particular group are well concealed to outsiders. Who belongs? Who is allowed to join? Why do people leave? How are group roles assigned? The members already know the answers – and they keep them to themselves. This secret knowledge is summed up in a member's remark about a club: 'Nobody goes there any more – it's too crowded.'

THE FINE ART OF CONDESCENSION

> We must be thoroughly democratic and patronize every-
> one without distinction of class.

Bernard Shaw, *John Bull's Other Island* (1904)

> Dame Barbara Cartland being asked on the *Today* programme whether she thought the class barriers had broken down: *Of course they have, or I wouldn't be sitting here talking to someone like you.*

Quoted by Jilly Cooper in *Class* (1999)

Nowhere is it more obvious that class matters than in the fine English art of condescension. Evelyn Waugh defined the basic principles of English social life in 1956:

> that everyone thinks he is a gentleman and that everyone draws the line of demarcation immediately below his own heels. The professions rule out the trades; the Services, the professions; the Household Brigade, the line regiments; squires, squireens; landed families who had London houses ruled out those who spent all the year at home; and so on, in an infinite number of degrees and in secret, the line is or was, drawn.[6]

George Mikes distilled it further:

> An English acquaintance of mine – let us call him Gregory Baker. He, an English solicitor, feels particularly deep contempt for the following classes of people: foreigners, Americans, Frenchmen, Irishmen, Scotsmen and Welshmen, Jews, workers, clerks, poor people, non-professional men, business men, actors, journalists and literary men, women, solicitors who do not practise in his immedi-ate neighbourhood, solicitors who are hard-up and solicitors who

are too rich, Socialists, Liberals, Tory-reformers (Communists are not worthy even of his contempt); he looks down upon his mother, because she has a business mind, his wife, because she comes from a non-professional county family, his brother, because although he is a professional officer he does not serve with the Guards, Hussars, or at least with a county regiment.[7]

The fine art of condescension is by no means confined to the upper and middle classes. Snobbery, defined as the joy of looking down upon others, is similarly widespread in the working class.

Skilled workers look down upon unskilled workers, unskilled workers upon labourers, foremen upon ordinary workers, store keepers upon a lorry driver and a lorry driver upon his co-driver, all of them upon a coalman, who in turn looks down upon a dust-man, and all those who are looked down upon look down in turn upon those snobbish fools who look down upon them.[8]

Naturally, no Englishman would admit to this kind of snobbery. It is now a badge of honour to refrain from being an overt snob, and not only for the well-educated. The higher the social class, the greater the desire among people to distance themselves from any snobbery, patronization or condescension. In interviews held as part of the Great British Class Survey, people tended to preface their remarks with disclaimers such as, 'I don't mean this in a snobby way . . .' or, 'I know this might sound snobby, but . . .' They asserted an openness towards other people's preferences – 'I would never ever condemn other people's taste' – and were at pains not to appear snooty: 'He is from a real working-class background, but very intelligent, brightest working-class person you will ever see.' Such statements, however, are usually followed by exactly the kind of snobbery that the speaker claims to eschew. Having defended the right to individual tastes, these are then judged pejoratively. 'I love jazz, and I feel really sorry for the people who don't, because of what they are missing.' Or, 'Given her background, it's hard for her to really get pleasure from opera.' Sometimes the judgements are very direct: 'These heavily branded

129

and labelled clothes are so naff and gaudy', 'It's not that I'm a snob, but he's so common.' In this way, overt snobbery is avoided, but the speaker nevertheless sets himself apart. It is still class snobbery. More refined, but perhaps even more devastating, is the talent of the English upper and some of the middle classes to express their contempt for someone else by being scrupulously polite. It has been said that in Britain good manners often are an act of passive aggression.

CROSS-CLASS MARRIAGES

As anyone can observe just by looking around them, and as is borne out by the statistics,[9] most people marry within their own class (according to the principle of assortative mating). There are various reasons for this. One is undoubtedly having the opportunity to meet. Gone are the days of the so-called 'season', when young, upper-class debutantes 'came out' under royal patronage, which ended in 1958 but was continued by Peter Townend until the 1980s. Nevertheless, similar activities and interests are still a crucial part of getting to know one's future spouse. Today's mating places are universities, the workplace, leisure and events venues. Academics marry academics, doctors nurses, tennis players other tennis players, actors actresses. The motive behind a marriage between equals of keeping other classes out and especially away from one's personal fortune has lessened in importance, but has not disappeared completely. Weddings between poor and rich are not uncommonly viewed with suspicion by the moneyed side and often derided as gold-digging or fortune-hunting.

Just how close class is to people's hearts in England and what role it plays becomes clear when marriages take place across the class divide. Anyone thinking that class in relationships was just an issue in Jane Austen's time or had died out with the Edwardian era should think again. It is still very much a talking point today, although the terms have shifted somewhat. As has been the case for centuries, it is still a favourite topic of English literature, as it is of the counselling industry, which offers guidance to would-be couples from different social backgrounds. More recently it has cropped up in science as well.[10] The astute commentator Ferdinand Mount summed it up beautifully in the title of his book *Mind the Gap* (2004). He recalls a whispered aside at a wedding: the 'Mind the gap!' warning drew attention 'to the social distance between the bride's family (unmistakably upper-class) and the groom's family (embarrassingly middle-class).'[11]

While such cross-class marriages may be on the increase these days – and one need look no further than the present royal family – their perception as unusual has not altered. If there were no classes or if classes were irrelevant, no-one would take a blind bit of notice. The phrases 'marrying up' and 'marrying down' say it all. Should a socially mixed marriage fail, the standard reaction among family and friends and, in the case of a famous couple, in the media too is: 'It was never going to work out: the class difference was too great.' Many accounts by people in this situation have their funny side, but if suffering was involved they are also touching.[12] In this instance class obtrudes on the most intimate sphere of people's lives.

CLASS LABELS

The English know very well that their position in the class system has an impact on nearly every aspect of their lives: occupation, income, marriage, children, children's education, divorce, health, life expectancy, circle of friends, electoral behaviour, food and drink, activities such as television, reading, pubs, sports, games, holidays. This is also the reason why the presentation of someone in the media nearly always mentions their background, frequently in more general terms such as, from a 'humble' or 'privileged' background. Even after death, scarcely a single obituary neglects to refer to the subject's social background. Take just one of many published in January 2017: 'Clare Hollingworth was born into an upper-middle-class family in rural Leicestershire.'[13] The practice is equally prevalent among measured intellectuals and writers. Alan Rusbridger, long-time editor of the *Guardian* newspaper, writes quite unselfconsciously of Philip Feeny, 'one of my closest friends at Cambridge', that he was 'a working-class boy who had won a musical scholarship to Winchester.'[14] This kind of thing is rare outside England. All the more astonishing, then, that the English, in public at least, dismiss all knowledge of class and even deny it outright.

7

Class Denial

We are forever being told we have a rigid class structure.
That's a load of codswallop.

Prince Edward Mountbatten-Windsor,
Daily Mail (1996)

Interviewer: *Would it be right to say you come from a*
comfortable middle-class family?

Lady Longford: *Upper middle class . . .* [startled, then
continuing hastily] *That was what we were told. I never*
knew what it meant.

P. N. Furbank, *Unholy Pleasure or*
The Idea of Social Class (1985)

Lady Hodmarsh and the Duchess immediately assumed
the clinging affability that persons of rank assume with
their inferiors in order to show them that they are
not in the least conscious of any difference in station
between them.

Somerset Maugham, *Cakes and Ale* (1930)

Perhaps the most interesting aspect of the English class system is
class denial. Until a few decades ago, the English were untroubled by
belonging to a specific class and said as much. In particular, they had
no qualms about describing themselves as working-class. Since it was

perceived as a matter of fact, acknowledging it was no more conten-
tious than saying it was or wasn't raining. Members of the upper
classes likewise made no effort to conceal their status, although they
tended to keep a lower profile except on official occasions. However,
in recent decades, the English have become increasingly reticent
about divulging their class, or try to give the impression of belonging
to a different category.

THE GREAT SILENCE

> *The word class is fraught with unpleasant associations,*
> *so that to linger upon it is apt to be interpreted as the*
> *symptom of a perverted mind and a jaundiced spirit.*

R. H. Tawney, Equality (1931)

Ideally, the English prefer not to talk publicly about class at all. This
was already the case back in Nancy Mitford's day, and she came
in for serious criticism, including from her friends, for her book
Noblesse Oblige, not so much for the content, but because she had
brought class to light at all. Right across the social spectrum, the
English tend to suppress the topic of class, which they seem to find
embarrassing, preferring to talk about someone's 'background' or
'upbringing'. Although calling someone working-class is not taboo,
most people speak diplomatically of 'the ordinary people', the 'less
privileged', the 'rank and file', 'the man in the street', 'those on low
incomes' or the 'less educated'. The journalist Owen Jones sees 'a
conspiracy of silence over class'.[1] Take books dealing with etiquette
and manners, for instance.[2] 'Manners maketh man', runs a familiar
motto, but they also make his class. In spite of this, in Debrett's *New
Guide to Etiquette and Modern Manners* (1996) by John Morgan,
class is mentioned only in the preface: 'courtesy and civility are not
a matter of snobbery or class (we all know of duchesses who behave
disgracefully!). Good manners are purely and simply a way of showing consideration and sensitivity towards others. As such, they
are classless.' So far, so uncontroversial. But what follows are 360

(eminently readable) pages about the class behaviour of the upper and upper-middle classes, or at least how they should behave, with lots of qualifiers such as proper, correct, suitable, unacceptable, inappropriate, bad manners, and, on the other hand, 'out of the question'. The working class have little use for such a guide, the occasions on which they are invited to meet royalty, partake of a hunting weekend or attend a diplomatic reception being rather rare.

More important still is the new tolerance that has grown up in matters of class and class rules. The old class markers are still there. But it has become a no-no to remark on other people's ignorance or flouting of these rules, let alone to ostracize or punish them for it (except perhaps in very private family circumstances). The manners of class cannot be criticized, and people cannot be seen to receive preferential or discriminatory treatment because of social differences. There is a ban on all (overt) differentiation on class grounds. The infamous remark about Michael Heseltine attributed to Alan Clark in the House of Commons as the kind of person who 'had to buy his own furniture' could never be said today without exposing the speaker to universal contempt. The comment is widely recognized as not only old-fashioned but also morally repugnant or, to use a word of the moment, unacceptable. Even those who may hold a different view in private are compelled outwardly to show disdain unless wishing to attract similar opprobrium. In particular, the upper classes no longer dare to insist on the enforcement of their own code, be that in addressing someone personally or on the envelope of a letter or even in matters of language and accent.

Where the great silence does not prevail, everything relating to class is denied: its existence, belonging to a class oneself, its impact on people's lives. And they are all at it: politicians, the media, businesses, often even scientists and artists, as well as those, of course, whose particular status is in question. What varies is the way in which denial is expressed from class to class.

If denial does not work, because class quite clearly does exist, it is resoundingly rejected. Deborah, Duchess of Devonshire, the last of the famous Mitford sisters, who died in 2014, put it rather sweetly:

'I think class is the biggest pest that has ever been invented.' It may be easier to say this if you are a member of the upper-upper class yourself.

UPPER-CLASS DENIAL

> *Being perceived as upper-class in contemporary Britain*
> *is the kiss of death.*

Toby Young, *Spectator*, 25 January 2014

Upper-class denial is by no means a new phenomenon. Virtually every feudal lord down through history has preferred to describe himself not as what he is (a ruler), but as someone who serves. 'I am my country's first servant' was the motto of the Prussian absolutist monarch Frederick II, otherwise known as Frederick the Great. This was of course subterfuge, as was clearly revealed when the 'servant's role was threatened. Then the self-proclaimed 'servant' did everything in his power – including the use of violence and murder – to defend his 'service'.

The emphasis on serving rather than ruling was important to make being ruled palatable for the ruler's subjects. In England this principle of class denial is embodied in the Queen's use of language – 'I feel an obligation to serve you' –and the Prince of Wales's motto 'Ich dien' (I serve). Even Prince Charles's son Prince Harry, widely regarded as the most modern member of the Royal Family, said in an interview in June 2017 that they were 'involved in modernizing the British monarchy. We are not doing this for ourselves but for the greater good of the people.' None of the royals wanted to be king or queen, he added, 'but we will carry out our duties at the right time.' Just about every freshly appointed prime minister in the last 100 years has expressed a desire to serve Great Britain and its people: ruling or wielding power are never mentioned. No member of the upper class asks, 'Do you know who I am?', and no aristocrat introduces himself with his title.

In the upper echelons of English society members of the younger generation have always been inclined to deny their class, some seemingly uncomfortable about their privileged status. They copy the behaviour of those below them in the pecking order, by speaking with a working-class accent, or using the kind of phraseology they believe is used by the man in the street; they avoid class symbols such as dress, and generally adopt working-class manners. Far from being a recent phenomenon, this has been the case since time immemorial. Alan Coren provides a vivid description of this with reference to students at Oxford University in the years 1957–60:

> I seem, here and there in this chronicle of gilded youth, to have hinted that class still ran its fading blue thread through the social woof of Oxford.
>
> And so it did, albeit oddly.
>
> For in these, the immediate post-Angry years, new heroes and new hierarchies had burgeoned, overgrowing the old. New prides were everywhere, which in turn meant new pretensions and deceptions. One was constantly bumping into people who referred to themselves as one, blushed, and corrected the offending emblem to you. Tall willowy lads with inbred conks and hyphens might be found, in the dead of any night, burning their cavalry twills and chukka boots in lay-bys along the A40, thereafter changing into blue jeans and Marks woollies. They stood before mirrors, abbreviating their drawls and lopping their aitches; they defended, with a heartbreaking desperation, their entitlement to membership of the new order.
>
> Thus: 'I'm not saying the family aren't merchant bankers now, I'm only trying to point out that in the early fourteenth century they were solidly behind Wat Tyler. I mean, bugger me, squire, there's nowt tha can teach me about t'working-class struggle, tha knows!'
>
> And: 'Oh, god, roll on my twenty-first, I'll be able to renounce my title and just be plain Auberon Fitzwilliam de Brissac Giles Corkseeping-ffearfful . . .'[3]

Twenty years later Philip Howard described the same thing:

> We are all equal these days, or, at any rate, we are all nervously
> wearing masks . . . To stand out as a snob or merely different is the
> deadly social solecism. Twenty-five years ago public-school boys
> hastened to hoist their old school ties as soon as they left school,
> as a badge that they were U or at any rate adult, depending on the
> school. Today they would not be seen dead in them.[4]

The modern manifestation of this is the wearing of the kind of baggy
trousers worn by inmates of American prisons by upper-class schoolboys who call each other 'bro' and 'homie'.[5]

Adults too can be seen to distance themselves. Rachel Johnson's
father was a conservative member of the European Parliament. Her
brothers are Boris Johnson, the Eton and Oxford-educated Tory
politician and MP, long-time mayor of London and currently Prime
Minister; the Conservative peer Jo (now Lord) Johnson; and Leo
Johnson, who is a partner at PricewaterhouseCoopers. She is married
to Ivo Dawnay, who is communications director of the National
Trust. As former editor of the *Lady*, a magazine read mainly by posh
women, she is a success story in her own right. Nobody would deem
her less than upper-class, as she speaks in the same cut-glass accent
as her brother Boris. Nevertheless she claims, 'I'm definitely middle-
class, but I am married to a man who is upper-class . . . I've never felt
remotely within the bloodstream of the class system'.[6] If this is not
hypocrisy, then it is the epitome of British understatement.

The Royal Family likewise downplays its class in the interests of
popularity. Since the eponymous BBC documentary (1969) was
commissioned by the Queen, if not before, the Windsors have been at
pains to come across as a normal, modern family.[7] The trend reached
a certain high-water mark with the marriage of Prince William to
the commoner Kate Middleton, the couple now being known as
the Duke and Duchess of Cambridge. Some members of the Royal
Family have declared their wish not to be styled Royal Highness
(HRH), but to have effectively a plain surname, and for their children

to be treated likewise. Sophie, Countess of Wessex, wife of Prince Edward, Earl of Wessex, chooses to be addressed as Sophie Wessex and, by prior agreement with the Queen, their two children do not use the title prince or princess or the style HRH either. The endeavours of the Royal Family not to be seen as detached, arrogant and altogether upper-class in the pejorative sense have been successful, as confirmed by the spectacular and overwhelmingly positive media coverage and marketing of the wedding between William and Catherine, as well as the recent approval ratings for the monarchy in Great Britain. Whereas support for its retention has run at 65–75 per cent for decades, the level is currently close to 80 per cent.

Funnily enough, the rules of class denial extend even to those who go to the greatest lengths to ameliorate their class by winning a peerage or a knighthood. Many of them feel the need to apologize for accepting the honour, and do this indirectly by explaining that it will now be easier to make the world a better place or (more tongue-in-cheek) to book a table at a restaurant.

RICH? ME?

The phenomenon of upper-class denial resembles and often runs parallel to the paradox of champagne socialists/communists. Such individuals espouse the views of the far left not only in their youth but also throughout their lives, calling for the dispossession of the rich and higher taxes for plutocrats and fat cats, and demanding the wholesale expansion of the welfare state. Their activism includes becoming members of communist or socialist parties and committing themselves to the relevant causes. Yet the lives they live in practice are capitalistic in the extreme. They shun paying taxes and give little or nothing to the poor from the wealth they have thus amassed. Not unusually, these people relish the limelight and are happy to receive acclaim for their socially minded and humanitarian views.

Take the left-wing intellectual, who calls for higher taxes but employs every trick in the book to reduce his own tax bill ('I did pay my fair share of tax and more'), or the right-winger who does the same while preaching the traditional values of putting the public good before one's own self-interest. Then there's the artist who despises and decries capitalism and the rich, yet at the same time complains that artists are underpaid and his own works in particular are worth much more money. If he gets the higher prices he claims are justified, he gives not a penny to needy, up-and-coming artists or other people in poverty. The key test for champagne socialists is to ask how much of their assets and income they give away to vulnerable members of society. The answer is usually nothing.

Another part of this dissimulation strategy is to keep quiet if you have inherited an easy fortune. Those who cannot conceal it play up the responsibility undertaken, the burden of preserving jobs, or of being only a custodian for the next generation, etc. In 2010 Earl Spencer (Princess Diana's brother), for instance, formulated the custodianship argument as follows: 'We belong to our possessions, rather than our possessions belong to us. To us, they are not wealth, but heirlooms, over which we have a sacred trust.'[8] The recently deceased Gerald Grosvenor, Duke of Westminster, commented in the same vein: 'Given the choice, I would rather not have been born wealthy, but I never think of giving it up. I can't sell. It doesn't belong to me.'[9] This reinterpretation of private ownership as public trustee-ship been resoundingly successful in England, as demonstrated by institutions such as the National Trust, English Heritage and the Historic Houses Association, with their many millions of members and visitors. This is probably the most elegant way to date of distract-ing attention from one's own class.

Similarly, no-one can admit to enjoying their wealth and lead-ing a life of indolence and luxury. Rather, they must emphasize how hard they work – first in and last out of the office each day, toiling away even at weekends – all from a deep sense of responsibility for the family, the workforce and society, never for personal gain and certainly not for the money's sake.

The reluctance of the rich and affluent to show their wealth often spills over into their everyday behaviour. Displays of wealth are unseemly. Suppliers of luxury items are asked to remove the price tags, to use neutral packaging, and to deliver the goods in a nondescript vehicle. The rich family may live in a penthouse, but they give their address as a simple house number. Yes, their children go to a public school, but only because it's the closest one. Luxury foodstuffs? Yes, but purely for health reasons. A luxury SUV? Yes, but with a modest mid-range car parked alongside. One would, of course, never dream of flying first class or by private jet unless it was a matter of life and death (or economy class was fully booked). That designer dress and those designer clothes for the children? On sale – what a stroke of luck! The wealthy are 'completely normal people' whose children 'grow up just the same as anyone else's', with no special privileges. But one is never 'truly rich' no matter how much money one has; that status is reserved for those who have even more.

THE MASTER CLASS

The most prominent and complex case by far of upper-class denial is Princess Diana, who died in a car accident in a Paris tunnel in August 1997. Born as the daughter of the 8th Earl Spencer, she was clearly upper-class, a status heightened still further – if that were possible – when she married the heir to the British throne, Prince Charles, in 1981 and joined the ranks of the Royal Family. Thus by birth she was a member of the traditional aristocratic upper class.

Princess Diana was without doubt one of the most striking personalities of her time: vastly popular and admired, even loved, by many. It cannot be denied that she put her immense popularity to good use for commendable humanitarian efforts such as banning land mines. And it is indeed true, at least to some extent, that the English showed less stiff upper lip and more emotion, empathy and public displays of sorrow after her death. This became abundantly clear in the expressions of sympathy at her funeral and the candid remarks of her sons, Prince William and Prince Harry, in a TV documentary to mark the twentieth anniversary of Diana's death.

But that is not the whole story. She clearly enjoyed all the privileges afforded to someone of her rank: wealth, respect, servants, flattery, luxury. Not one iota of these did she ever give up. At the same time, she presented herself as a victim of this class, intimating that she had been badly treated by it, in particular by her parents-in-law. One might say that she despised her class of origin, or at least pretended to despise it. The people, politicians, the media, virtually everyone believed in Diana the martyr and loved her for it. In her class denial achieved its most consummate perfection. Not only did the lower classes not envy her privileged status, but they even went as far as to see her as a casualty of her advantage, a victim made vulnerable and in need of help. No class denier could ask for more: not only to be spared the envy or scorn of the underprivileged for their unearned favour, but also to be loved.

Such analyses of Princess Diana's behaviour were for some time regarded as politically incorrect and rejected. Indeed, Prime Minister Tony Blair prevented the publication of an article criticizing Diana by a philosophy professor.[10] Today a more realistic assessment is emerging.[11] Princess Diana's lawyers published her will on the internet. She left her fortune of around £20 million to her sons (apart from a small sum for members of her staff). The poor, the needy and charities got nothing.

THE HEART HAS ITS REASONS

Why do so many members of the upper classes deny their station? Some have feelings of guilt or a bad conscience. They believe that their wealth and their status 'under wiser and humaner laws would belong to the community,' as the Labour MP Sir Charles Trevelyan put it in 1929.[12] Others fear an uprising by the lower classes – afraid the latter might break into their homes, kidnap their children and take away their assets, their income and their privileges. Although no such threat actually exists, the facts matter less than feelings. In the extreme, they react by living in gated communities and holidaying in places where they cannot be followed by the hard-up lower classes. Class denial becomes an instrument of defence against the danger embodied by their social inferiors. If the lower orders do not even know how those at the top live, then they cannot become envious and demand, 'We want what you have.' This sentiment, pivotal to the plot of John Lanchester's novel *Capital* (2011), is the message the residents of houses on a well-to-do street in London keep finding in their letterboxes. People who cannot conceal their wealth attempt to rebuff the feelings of envy by arguing that their affluence has been achieved by their own hard work. Heirs to a fortune that cannot be disguised try to present themselves not as the rich owners, but as guardians of national heritage and English culture and identity (see above).

Class denial is also used to pre-empt professional prejudice. A victim of reverse discrimination who has been turned down as a children's television presenter because 'his accent was too posh'[13] will next time try everything to disguise his pronunciation and hide his class. Class denial is also a means of warding off attacks from the media. Up until the Second World War or perhaps even later, belonging to the top tier of society gave people a certain protection from exposure and censure should they make a mistake or stray from the straight and narrow. Occasionally the faults of the great and good were even regarded as more excusable than the small man's failings. Those days have gone. The protective varnish of deference has been removed. The media apply great effort to expose and apportion blame ('in the public interest' of course), and the public have become hostile towards transgressing members of the upper echelons who are rich, famous or powerful (with some exceptions being made for celebrities, sportsmen and actors, but even then not always). Better therefore to hide your class from the beginning. And of course one should not forget those who deny their class simply for personal gain, seeking either to earn more money, like pop stars, or to attract votes, like politicians. Finally, there are those who deny being upper-class because they find it lacking in certain things they hope to find in the proletariat: strong roots, down-to-earthness, human warmth, authenticity, community, solidarity. Whether these aspirations are borne out is a different matter.

UPPER-CLASS DENIAL DENIED

Like so many things in England, upper-class denial should not be taken entirely at face value. It is extremely doubtful whether those who deny their class are being perfectly candid. When asked about the reasons, the standard answer appears to be because they are fighting for a better, more just world. When it matters – in other words, when choosing a career, a place to live, a partner, a school or university for the children, or when choosing friends and acquaintances and pursuing hobbies – the same class deniers tend to be very class-conscious and do whatever serves their class interests. Anyone who believes that the members of the upper class who deny their background really wish to join the lower orders with all the consequences this entails is mistaken. The duchess who extols the virtues of her housemaid does not of course wish to have anything to do with her personally, any more than Marie Antoinette in her rural retreat at Versailles truly desired to be a shepherdess, let alone wish to be treated as an equal by peasant women. Though adept at the manners of self-deprecation, the upper-class person never forgets his superior rank and all the prestige owed to him, nor does he allow others to. He asks to be treated as an 'ordinary man', but gets shirty if it happens. Beyond the respect he believes he deserves, he even expects some sort of emotional recognition for denying the class he belongs to and being so modest.

Most class denial is a facade or a way of securing personal advantage under the cloak of the common touch. It is an absolute hallmark of upper-class denial that those who practise it give up not one jot of their own privileges. Those 'children of the purple who reject their upbringing in their way of living, their philosophy, their chosen partner and their choice of address, mostly take their snobbery with them absolutely intact in their new life, being as or even more dismissive than before'.[14] Who isn't familiar with the twenty-five-year-old children of rich parents who bleat about capitalism, consider their privileges highly unfair and, faced with the prospect of a large inheritance, would prefer to 'run for the door, slam it and keep on running', as the late Gerald Grosvenor, Duke of Westminster once told the BBC?[15] Yet you almost never hear that someone has passed up their inheritance. Rather, the heirs are overjoyed that their ancestor has undertaken careful tax planning to protect them from inheritance tax.

Also to be taken with a pinch of salt are invitations from members of the Royal Family or the aristocracy to drop official forms of address such as Your Royal Highness, or to call them by their first name, as offered by the aforementioned Duchess of Devonshire during a television interview, when she allowed her pet name Debo to be used. And does Prince Harry, sympathetic as he is, really understand his role exclusively as his duty 'for the greater good of the people'? Anyone really wishing to dispense with their title can do so. In reality the aim is to have the best of both worlds: to retain the privileges and fend off possible resentment and envy from Joe Normal. One is reminded of the millionaire who at every opportunity complains about the affliction of his wealth and praises the merits of poverty. The burden of wealth is easily eliminated: give it all away! By doing so you may even win fame and honour. The world's once richest man Andrew Carnegie famously did it ('The man who dies rich, dies disgraced') and won fame and honour.

And whether the gurus for whom class has supposedly ceased to be relevant really believe what they say and write is questionable, as Edith Lever, the heroine of Julian Fellowes' novel *Snobs*, who has married Charles, the future Earl of Broughton, reflects when she dreams of the feudal world of the past before the Great War:

> It seemed at first to her troubled brain that the media had been right all along, that these dreams and ambitions were outmoded, that no one nowadays wants titles and rank and inherited power, that these are the days of the self-made man, of talent, of creativity. But then, looking about at the office workers and sweepers and job interviewees who loitered near her in the park, she was struck by the dishonesty of the media pundits of our time. Was there one here who would not change places with Charles if they could? Was it not possible that the small screen gurus praised meritocracy because it was the only class system that would accord them the highest rank? Even if unearned riches and position had no moral merit, even if they embodied the Dream That Dare Not Speak Its Name, it was still a dream that figured in plenty of people's fantasies.[16]

ESTABLISHMENT AND ELITE DENIAL

Like upper-class denial, Establishment denial exists too. One way in which the Establishment is denied is by disputing it as fact. What rubbish! For of course power is exercised in every country, by a bigger or smaller number of people. It really cannot be disputed that a member of the Cabinet has greater power than a production line operative or supermarket checkout girl. Each country has its establishment, only with different members. In capitalist countries these include rich people, in communist states they are the party leaders. In the vast majority of cases, the denial comes from members of the Establishment who, while acknowledging its existence, claim and perhaps feel they are not a part of it. The Establishment, they say, 'in reality means those with the power. I am not one of them, I am against them.' An almost absurd example was provided by John Prescott, in a column written for the *Daily Mirror* in 2013: 'Britain is still ruled by the elite. Those who are born into wealth and can afford to buy into privileged networks will continue to dominate the Establishment.' Though coming from a humble background, having once been a waiter in the merchant navy and a member of the radical left, Prescott became one of the pillars of the English Establishment by becoming the nation's Deputy Prime Minister under Tony Blair and, after stepping down as an MP in 2010, a member of the House of Lords he had long campaigned to abolish. Prescott seems to be implying that, despite his career, he was not a member of the Establishment. Was he deluded or was this just spin?

Margaret Thatcher boasted that she had never belonged to the Tory establishment. Tony Blair promised the Labour conference in 1999 to fight 'the forces of conservatism, the cynics, the elites, the Establishment'. The most radical anti-Establishment stance is adopted by the media, including the right-leaning *Daily Mail*. For journalists and writers likewise, fighting the Establishment is a way of life, a prime example being Owen Jones in *The Establishment – And How They Get Away With It*. Jones was educated in Oxford, is on good speaking terms with many members of the Establishment whom he otherwise couldn't describe. He earns a lot of money and wields power by writing influential books and columns in the *Guardian* and appearing on television. It may be that he would prefer not to be a member of the Establishment, but he is.

It is quite astonishing to find that the fiercest attacks on the Establishment (on private schools, for instance, or Oxbridge or the rich) come from journalists who have themselves (partly) made careers in the Establishment and in particular are graduates of Oxford or Cambridge or other Russell Group universities. Take the *Guardian*, for example, whose contributors seem almost neurotically obsessed with the Establishment and the elite. The current editor-in-chief of the *Guardian*, Katharine Viner, was educated at a grammar school and Pembroke College, Oxford, and her predecessor for two decades, Alan Rusbridger, was educated at a private school and studied at Magdalene College. The current political editor, Anushka Asthana, is Cambridge-educated, and the paper's political editor, Heather Stewart, studied at Oxford. The *Guardian*'s editorial team have also enjoyed an elitist education.

It is also no coincidence that the satirical magazine *Private Eye*, whose mission is to pillory the 'vice, folly and humbug' of the powerful, famous and rich – a very English sport – should be a product of the public school system. *Private Eye* was founded by a group of friends at Shrewsbury School at the end of the 1950s. As one would expect, the present-day editors, writers and columnists all (or nearly all) are university-educated. The editor of *Private Eye*, Ian Hislop, arguably Britain's most famous satirist, who has no qualms about ridiculing the ruling class and pulls no punches, has clearly become part of the Establishment himself. The writers who are most outraged by private schools, Oxbridge, etc. but have themselves benefited from them are legion, and include, alongside Owen Jones, Stuart Jeffries, Polly Toynbee and Carole Cadwalladr. A shining example is Seumas Milne, who joined the *Guardian* in 1984. He has never concealed his far-left political views, having at one time held sympathies with the Communist Party, and was appointed by Jeremy Corbyn as the Labour Party's executive director of strategy and communications (aka spin doctor) in October 2015. What makes Seumas Milne interesting is his background. He is the son of the former BBC director general Alasdair Milne, who went to school at Winchester College before studying at New College, Oxford. Seumas followed in his father's footsteps, also attending Winchester and studying at Balliol College in Oxford. Both his children were sent not to the local comprehensive but to top grammar schools some distance away. One subsequently went to Oxford, the other to Cambridge. Milne received an inheritance from his father and lives in a £2 million house in Richmond in south-west London.

These new elites are not arrogant, aloof or contemptuous of ordinary humanity. Quite the opposite. They apologize for being elitist and are ashamed of their elitist hobby. They are afraid of appearing a snob. But this is nothing to do with snobbery. In reality these are elites in disguise. They are 'an oligarchy of professional egalitarians. Their aim is not the public interest or to make the world a better place but to exploit mass taste, mass gullibility, or mass spending power for their own advantage.'[17] There is only ever one reason for Establishment and elite denial and that is to remain a member of that very Establishment and elite. The effect, like its upper-class equivalent, is two-fold: the deniers thereby avoid the accusation of wielding power, which is regarded as something indecent, and they leave the ruled in the dark about their rulers. Ignorance of who your rulers are leaves you impotent to regulate them or call them to account. In his book *Twilight of the Elites* (*Le crépuscule de la France d'en haut*) (2016), the French writer Christoph Guilluy studied the new elites, which he branded 'bohemian-bourgeois', and concluded:

> These new bourgeois have 'seized power' by enunciating 'morally superior' principles: they back globalization in the name of tolerance, openness and multiculturalism, describing critics as 'backward-looking' or 'racists'. In effect, they have allowed a system to thrive that only works for them.

WORKING-CLASS DENIAL
In 1991, 46 per cent of the population identified themselves as working-class, 8 per cent as upper-working-class, 27 per cent as

middle-class, 2 per cent as upper-middle-class and 2 per cent didn't know.[18] Nowadays, approximately half those who previously described themselves as working-class now state that they are middle-class. Others classify themselves as working-class by one criterion but middle-class by another. 'By way of income I'm working-class. By way of education I'm middle-class' would be a common answer today. What we see is a flight from the working class.

Being working-class has now become a more pejorative term, associated with people who do not work, benefits scroungers, chavs, pikeys, etc. Small wonder many Englishmen do not wish to be categorized in this way.

MIDDLE-CLASS DENIAL

No one ever describes himself as belonging to the lower-middle class.

George Mikes, *How to be Inimitable* (1960)

The class denial of the middle order is equally complex. For those seeking to distance themselves from being upper- or working-class, there is only one alternative in each case. The middle-class denier has a choice of direction: either up or down. For centuries, the middle-class person who pretended to be upper-class was the object of ridicule and caricature.

A more recent phenomenon has been the middle-class person who pretends to be working-class, or at least goes to great lengths to point out that he comes from a working-class background and is proud of it. Particularly for those who have achieved success in the creative industries, such as filmmakers, photographers, magazine editors, advertising executives, artists, fashion and interior designers and architects, it is a must to de-gentrify their backgrounds. In these sectors to become rich and famous you must first pretend to have been poor. The effect is doubly absurd if these individuals sing the praises of the meritocracy, claiming that what counts is where you are going rather than where you come from. This is all very well unless you belong to the upper echelons, when the consequences are negative and your background is clearly an affliction necessitating apology. A working class-background, by contrast, is a blessing, to the extent that if need be it is invented.

In the end, the picture is a strange one: there are classes and there are class rules. The English know that and, in their closest circles, they also talk about it. But in public they change their tune: there are no (longer) any classes; class rules have been abolished. And if not (yet) abolished, breaches are not punished. The most prominent exponents of class denial are politicians.

8

Class and Politics

I don't know. Middle class, I suppose. I've never really thought about it. Does it matter?

> The politically correct answer to the question of which class a politician belongs to.

I come from an ordinary middle-class family in an ordinary town.

> Prime Minister Gordon Brown during the 2010 general election campaign.

Far from being limited to the purely private sphere, class in England is a highly political construct that dates back virtually to when records began. Few English politicians have not commented on class and, as far as can be established, the subject has been addressed by every prime minister in the past 200 years. While it is true that the word class itself tends to be inferred rather than spelt out in the current political discussion, it is inherent in everyday expressions such as elitist, privileged, background, etc. Even political decisions on which the major parties agree are determined by class. In the lead-up to the Brexit vote on 23 June 2016, both the Conservatives and Labour campaigned for Remain. Commentators unanimously attributed the majority for Leave to the voters' class. Sentences such as the following, from just one newspaper, abounded:

It is all about social class, age, education and mobility. This has been Britain's most class-based vote of recent decades.[1]

At its heart, leave was fuelled by a sense of betrayal among working-class voters.[2]

The vote for Brexit was an English working-class insurrection.[3]

THE MAGIC QUARTET

Politics and social class form a particularly complicated couple. In a democracy there are four facts that politicians must face.

First, the goal of all politics and all politicians is power, either to win it or hold onto it. Of course no politician says that, but instead expresses a desire to change the world for the better, bring about justice and so on. But to make the world a better place, you need power.

Second, the way to power is through the ballot box. The right to vote is impervious to class. Be they poor or rich, idle or hard-working, stupid or intelligent, righteous or unrighteous, feckless or responsible, everyone is equally entitled: one man, one vote. And this vote is what politicians need to win power. The British first-past-the-post electoral system provides the best illustration of this, when sometimes scarcely more than a handful of votes decide on which candidate wins the seat and thus attains power, thereby excluding from power all the other contenders, even if, together, they accumulated many more votes than the person elected.

The third aspect is that the voters belong to social classes that lean towards certain parties. Members of the working class tend more strongly towards the Labour Party, middle-class voters more towards the Conservatives. This dichotomy no longer sums up the modern British party landscape entirely, when one considers how many votes are received by other parties such as the Liberal Democrats, UKIP and, in Scotland, the SNP. However, since these votes have not been translated into seats at Westminster (apart from in the case of the SNP), the two-way split remains a useful description of how power is distributed between the parties. Although not always members, many electors (core voters) maintain a close, lifetime allegiance with their party and never waver in their loyalty. For politicians these are the 'useful idiots' whose support can be more or less taken for granted.

The fourth element is that the class-based core vote is not sufficient in many constituencies to secure a party's electoral success. To win an election therefore, the Labour Party needs votes over and above those of the working class, and the Conservatives have to attract votes beyond the bounds of the middle class. Tony Blair's election victories in 1997, 2001 and 2005 were made possible by opening up the Labour Party to voters outside the working class. He knew he could count on the core vote from working-class people 'who had nowhere else to go'. But because the working-class vote alone would not have yielded election success, the party had to reach out to other sections of society: 'My job is to appeal to the great mass of people on issues that the Labour Party generally speaking is just not interested in.'[4] At the other end of the spectrum, Theresa May also demonstrated her understanding of the situation when she succeeded David Cameron. In her first major speech on domestic policy in September 2016, the then prime minister chose to address education. Coupled with her desire to make Britain a 'great meritocracy', the whole thing was a homage to the working class. May promised to put the interests of ordinary working-class people first and singled out those on modest incomes of between £19,000 and £21,000 a year. A quick count reveals that the words 'ordinary working-class people' occur ten times in the speech, whereas the middle class gets not a mention. From the viewpoint of a Conservative politician who believes she must appeal more to working- than to middle-class voters, this makes perfect sense.

These four facts define the relationship between politics and social class.

POLITICIANS, PARTIES AND CLASS

By virtue of their job, politicians are very well informed about the existence of classes and class voting patterns. The study of the population and in particular the electorate for certain attitudes, similarities, differences, etc. plays a central role in politics, and this is reflected in the plethora of people and institutions engaged in this field and the many reports and analyses they produce. Among the things specifically targeted by modern election strategy and tactics is the class identity of voters. How politicians react to the magic quartet of power, one man, one vote, core voters and the need for a majority depends on the class not only of the voters but also of the politicians themselves.

Politicians' comments on class are often hard to interpret because, as with all political pronouncements, while politicians may say what they truly think, they can also lie and say things they do not. Whether they are truthful or dishonest depends on which is politically more advantageous. The classic observation on this subject comes from George Orwell (who else?), in his famous essay *Politics and the English Language* (1946): 'Political language . . . is designed to make lies sound truthful and murder respectable, and to give an appearance of solidity to pure wind.' A more modern take is the question every journalist must ask himself when interviewing a politician: 'Why is this bastard lying to me?' The line is attributed to many journalists, including Harry Evans, the long-time editor of the *Sunday Times*,[5] the BBC interviewer Jeremy Paxman, the *Times* journalist Louis Heren or an unnamed American newspaperman.[6] No less a politician than Jean-Claude Juncker, the head of the Eurogroup at the time and former President of the European Commission, said in 2011 with reference to the euro crisis, 'When it becomes serious, you have to lie.' For politicians, well-employed lies are no less valuable than the truth, although the risk of discovery must be borne in mind. Consequently, while everything a politician says may – and usually will – be the truth, it is equally possible that he is lying. History is littered with as many political lies as political truths. When it comes to comments on class, such statements can have a direct effect on politicians' chances of being elected.

Down through history the traditional position of the Conservative Party has been to deny that classes exist or to assert that the classes interact in harmony, as summed up in the catchphrase 'one nation'. Prime Minister Benjamin Disraeli (1804–81) is often credited with inventing the one-nation concept. This is not so. He neither used the phrase nor advocated what it stood for. In fact, he had clearly recognized that society was divided, in the most famous passage from his novel *Sybil* (1845):

> Two nations between whom there is no intercourse and no sympathy; who are as ignorant of each other's habits, thoughts, and feelings, as if they were dwellers in different zones, or inhabitants of different planets; who are formed by a different breeding, are fed by a different food, are ordered by different manners, and are not governed by the same laws. 'You speak of' – said Egremont hesitatingly, 'THE RICH AND THE POOR'.

His acceptance of class differences probably outweighed his desire to dismantle them.[7] What he did promote was a principle of duty of the upper classes towards the lower classes. Nevertheless, Disraeli is regarded as the father of one-nation Conservatism, a concept propagated by virtually all Conservative politicians. Prime Minister Stanley Baldwin's unerring message in the interwar years was 'union among our own people'. He found there was a 'brotherly and neighbourly feeling which we see to remarkable extent through all classes', and in 1937 concluded, 'I think that in recent years in spite of all the troubles we had there has been a much better understanding among all classes in the country of each other's lives and methods of thought.'[8] During the 1959 general election Prime Minister Harold Macmillan announced: 'The class war is over,' and he did not forget to add, 'and we have won it.' Margaret Thatcher didn't believe in class: 'Class is a communist concept. It groups people as bundles and sets them against one another.' A year after Margaret Thatcher had come to power the Conservative leader of the House of Commons, Norman St John Stevas, said in 1980: 'I think that class is largely an irrelevancy in contemporary British society.'[9] The Conservative ex-Chancellor of the Exchequer George Osborne's 'We are all in this together' and ex-Prime Minister David Cameron's 'big society' were in the same vein. In the latter's speech, delivered in August 2015 to mark the first 100 days of Conservative government following the May 2015 election, he said:

'One hundred days ago I stood on the steps of Downing Street and told the British people that the first Conservative majority government for 18 years would govern on behalf of everyone. One nation, one United Kingdom.' The same outlook was expressed by Theresa May in her first statement as prime minister in July 2016. She spoke of her desire to continue the one-nation policy of her predecessor and a mission to make Britain 'a country that works for everyone, not just the privileged few', something she repeated several times and in a variety of ways in her speech to the party faithful at the Conservative party conference in 2016.

For decades, there was no question of the Labour Party denying class and class differences. On the contrary, the party was founded specifically to represent the interests of the working class (see Chapter 5). For the best part of the twentieth century Labour supporters more often than not regarded the Tory Party as the class enemy, and they made no bones about it. 'No amount of cajolery', declared the great Labour politician Aneurin Bevan, 'and no attempts at ethical or social seduction, can eradicate from my heart a deep burning hatred for the Tory Party ... So far as I am concerned they are lower than vermin.'

The Labour MP Tony Wright describes how, as an 11-year-old boy during the 1959 general election, he had driven the Conservative candidate out of town by planting fireworks in the back of his Land Rover that exploded as he furiously drove away: 'We had expelled the class enemy from our territory.'[10]

It was not until after the election defeat against John Major in 1992 that the Labour Party began practically to eradicate the words class, class consciousness and above all class war from public debate, most determinedly under Tony Blair. New Labour was so afraid of using the word class that at the end of the 1990s the Labour government renamed a committee appointed to revisit the official social classifications used for national statistics: 'Social Class Based on Occupation' became 'National Statistics Socio-Economic Classification'.[11] In 1999 Tony Blair proclaimed that 'The class war is over.' At the 2007 Labour conference Gordon Brown claimed that 'a class-free society is not a slogan but in Britain can become reality.'

Labour leader Ed Miliband, who was often accused of wishing to reignite the class war, made the one-nation concept the centrepiece of the Labour conference in 2012:

> I do believe in one nation . . . We won a war because we were one nation. We rebuilt Britain because we were one nation . . . Every time Britain has faced the greatest challenge, we have only come through the storm because we were one nation . . . Here is the genius of one nation . . . We must be a one-nation party to become a one-nation government to build a one-nation country.

In private, of course, politicians knew very well that the class system was still alive and well, notwithstanding ten years of Labour government under Tony Blair and Gordon Brown. A number of Labour ministers, including Alan Milburn, Stephen Byers, Peter Mandelson and Estelle Morris, have indeed admitted that class division in Britain during Labour's governing years not only persisted but in some important ways appeared to have deepened.[12] Under Labour leader Jeremy Corbyn, the pendulum swung back towards the notion of class conflict again.

Politicians who do not suppress or deny the existence of classes generally call for them to be abolished. Shortly before becoming prime minister in November 1990, John Major said, 'I think we need a classless society and I think we need to have what I refer to as social mobility.'[13] Major was being honest: he accepted that classes existed, and therefore he called for their elimination. It is easy to explain why politicians in democratic countries in particular deny that classes exist or call for a classless society: they do it to win or to retain power. For, notwithstanding all their very real social differences in terms of wealth, income, occupation, education and culture, all people have one asset in common: their vote – and politicians will leave no stone unturned to secure it.

Politicians must treat every voter well. They do this by making or promising gifts, and steering clear of anything that might rub electors up the wrong way. Politicians need and will accept every vote, be it from intelligent, hard-working and responsible voters, or from stupid, idle and feckless types: losers have votes too. Modern politics has recognized that more points can be scored by creating a feel-good atmosphere in which disparities are played down than by fomenting divisions. In such a strategy class and class differences have no part, and this is reflected in rhetoric like 'co-operation, not confrontation', 'big society', 'mums and dads', 'all in this together', 'one nation', etc. One of the mantras of modern democracy is that all men are equal and there's no such thing as class, or at least that there shouldn't be. This is what most voters want to hear, and the politicians are only too happy to oblige. It has nothing to do with political party or inclination.

This explains why politicians deny not only class differences, but even those that are biologically innate, like being of above or below average intelligence. On polling day they don't wish to alienate a single potential supporter. To call voters stupid would be the kiss of death for any politician, but this doesn't stop them thinking it (and even saying so in private), especially if they then lose the election. In public their reaction is likely to be tempered by correctness: 'We didn't make our message sufficiently clear.'

Class disappeared from the radar of political observers too. The first edition of Anthony Sampson's classic book *Anatomy of Britain*, published in 1962, even contains an interview with the Labour leader at the time, Hugh Gaitskell, on the influence of class on voting behaviour. In the 2004 version, entitled Who *Runs This Place – the Anatomy of Britain in the 21st Century*, the term class only comes up in connection with access to university education. In science and sociology in particular, following the collapse of communism in 1989, the thesis gained considerable traction that classes no longer existed, in books like *The Death of Class* (1996), by the Australian sociologists Pakulski and Waters. In the index of Anthony King's book *Who Governs Britain?* (2015), the words 'class' and 'social class' are nowhere to be found, although he does deal with the subject, as he inevitably has to, in Chapter 4. The wilful suppression of class by politicians and the media is regarded by modern political authors of all colours as dishonest. They accompany their criticism with a call for class to be put back on the political agenda.[14] It may well be that the fierce current debate on inequality (Chapter 2) is the class debate in a new look.

POLITICIANS AND THEIR CLASS

So which class do top politicians belong to? If one considers the two parties that have dominated political life in Great Britain for the past 90 years – Conservative and Labour – the class origins of the politicians in these parties are essentially as follows: Conservative politicians have traditionally been recruited largely from the upper half of the population, their Labour counterparts mainly from the lower. Of course there have always been exceptions. In the Labour Party these have included figures such as Clement Attlee, Sir Stafford Cripps (who was said, in his day, to be the highest-earning barrister in Great Britain), Tony Benn, Viscount Chandos and Lord Sainsbury. Prominent exceptions on the Conservative side are John Major, Norman Tebbit, Kenneth Clarke and Edward Heath. A glance at the parliaments elected in 2010 and 2015 reveals that, while this generalized picture still applies to the Conservatives, massive changes have occurred in the Labour Party (see Chapter 5). True working men in the mould of Aneurin Bevan or John Prescott have become virtually extinct, having been replaced by career politicians with university degrees. Of the MPs elected in 2015, approximately 75 per cent are university-educated, the party-by-party breakdown being as follows: Conservatives 81 per cent, Labour 77 per cent, Lib Dems 100 per cent, SNP 75 per cent. Only 13 per cent were former manual workers, 7 per cent of these belonging to the Labour Party. A prime example of this new political breed is the Labour MP Jo Cox, who was tragically murdered in June 2016. Her mother was a school secretary, her father worked in a toothpaste and hairspray factory. Cox went to the local grammar school and after that to Pembroke College, Cambridge, where she graduated in social and political studies. Thereafter she worked as an adviser to the Labour MP Joan Walley, later for two years with Labour MEP Baroness Kinnock, after that for Oxfam, Gordon Brown's wife Sarah Brown, Save the Children, the NSPCC and the Bill and Melinda Gates Foundation, until in May 2014 she was chosen as the Labour candidate for the constituency of Batley & Spen, a seat she won in the 2015 election. Her husband was an adviser to Gordon Brown during the latter's premiership and a campaigner for International Justice, an organization also affiliated to the Gates Foundation.

A common criticism of MPs is that, in terms of class, they are not representative of the British people, and that the working class in particular is not adequately represented in Parliament numerically and therefore lacks influence. This is true – but could it be any different? No parliament in the world is the 'snapshot of the people' once wished for by the German politician Otto von Bismarck. In Britain voters cannot vote for whoever they like, but only for one of the candidates the parties in their constituency choose to nominate. Hence in practice the local party decides who the local MP is going to be, especially in safe seats,[15] and apparently those making the selection prefer university-educated, middle-class people over manual workers.

POLITICAL CLASS DENIAL

All politicians worthy of the name automatically check their own class credentials to establish whether or not the voters will approve. As a result, they choose to highlight their class of origin or try and obscure it, depending on what they consider to be more attractive to voters. For the Labour Party this was for many decades quite simple: appear as working-class as possible. Jeremy Paxman described the ideal biography of a mid-twentieth-century Labour politician:

> He has their father killed in a mining accident caused by the callous indifference of the aristocrats whose fortune is built on the sweat of the poor. Their widowed mother struggles to bring up seven children single-handedly in a back-to-back terrace until, exhausted, she dies of a curable disease when our hero is aged about 13. There may then be a kindly schoolteacher who takes an interest in the orphaned child, introducing them to books, paintings and, most importantly, The Struggle. A light has been lit but,

because our hero has no money, there is no possibility of further education. By the middle teenage years, school has been abandoned, for money must be earned to support younger brothers and sisters. By the age of 20, the fight for social justice is embedded irremovably in the soul.[16]

This is of course no longer possible, since such life stories are no more. Many Conservatives have a different problem. They consider themselves too high up on the social ladder and need to downgrade. To be upper-class and blatantly make no bones about it is political suicide. A similar difficulty faces more and more Labour politicians too, now that the party is no longer led by members of the working class. For centuries the English were happily ruled by the upper classes, indeed even approved of the situation, assuming that the latter were best qualified to govern. This has changed completely, both legally and socially. A peer cannot become prime minister, which is why in 1963 Lord Home famously renounced his title. For electoral success, social acceptance is key. In modern democracies with the ideal of equality, this calls for a difficult balancing act. On the one hand the politician has to be a man of the people, an everyman type not unlike the people he rules; on the other he has to be recognizably different in order to be accepted as their ruler. In the politician's mindset the voting public should say and believe not only that 'he is one of us' but also that 'he can do it'. They should be certain of his competence and of course feel allegiance to him as well. To project the image of an everyman – something which by definition they cannot be – politicians put on a mask, presenting themselves not as the people's elected representatives, but as their best pals. To close the gap between them and those they govern still further, they choose not to be addressed by their official title (Prime Minister, Minister, etc.), or their surname (Mr Blair, Mr Cameron, Mr Miliband, Mr Clegg), but on first-name terms instead, at any rate when the TV cameras are rolling: 'Call me Tony/Dave/Ed/Nick.' They are seen cycling to the Commons rather than riding in an official limo (although occasionally the car follows a few hundred yards behind, carrying the red boxes or ministerial briefcase). If they need to pull rank in order to push something through, they never say 'I want' (in public at least), but cite the common good or de facto constraints or 'our shared values'.

Since the votes of only one class are not enough to win power, all politicians also depend on obtaining the votes of other classes apart from their own. This results in the phenomenon of denying their own class, a trend most pronounced among upper-class politicians. When George Osborne spoke to workers at a Morrisons' supermarket distribution centre, he seemed to have lost his cut-glass RP accent and replaced it with Estuary English. 'Briddish people badly wannit fixed', he said of the benefits system, complete with glottal stops and other affectations of what people call 'mockney'. Tony Blair had done the same (see Chapters 7 and 14).[17] While they prefer a cup and saucer in the comfort of their own home, if the TV cameras are watching they drink tea from a mug. They walk into a branch of a low-class food chain and order some pasties – but only if being filmed, of course.[18] For a politician from working-class origins, having an accent can be problematic. He must fear rejection from middle-class voters. He is therefore best advised not to hide his working-class background, but not to overplay it either, and to pay particular attention to making clear how he has worked his way up through his intelligence and industriousness and is consequently electable across class boundaries. The majority of politicians seek to avoid this dilemma by describing themselves indiscriminately as middle class, to some extent the lowest common denominator and liable to cause the least offence.

A further variant of political denial is power denial, which is similar to Establishment and elite denial. Many politicians, from the prime minister down to the simple backbencher, maintain that actually they have next to no power at all. 'Power?' said Harold Macmillan. 'It's like the Dead Sea Fruit. When you achieve it, there's nothing there.' According to the former Tory MP Rory Stewart, 'Anybody running a small pizza business has more power than me . . . in our situation we are all powerless . . . we pretend we're run by people. We're not run by anybody. The secret of modern Britain is there is no power anywhere.'[19]

This is nonsense. Of course a prime minister does not have the power of a dictator (thank God!), and naturally a single MP who is one of 300 in his party has only a three-hundredth of the power. But both have a lot more power than the normal citizen. The prime minister of the day is undoubtedly the most powerful individual in the political system and arguably the country. Ministers (still) decide. MPs make the laws and to a certain degree control the government and hold it to account – and can make life difficult for the government by rebelling against their party line in the Commons, something that seems to have become more and more of an option for backbench MPs.[20] The assertion of powerlessness, however genuinely it may be felt, serves their political image: a desire to appear more human, more a friend and a servant than a ruler. As de Gaulle once put it: 'In order to become the master, the politician poses as the servant.' It is the same impulse that prompts the CEO of a 50,000-strong company to say he answers to his wife. Furthermore, powerlessness is a good excuse for failure.

CLASS AS A WEAPON

A recurring manifestation of the political struggle in England for some decades now has been the use of class as a weapon against a political opponent, although it is only ever used one-sidedly. People are attacked as upper-class or toffs, or for having excess wealth or being educated at public school and Oxbridge.

Such assaults, usually by Labour against the Tories, are nothing new. The most legendary were the relentless attacks by the Labour leader Harold Wilson on the Conservative Prime Minister Sir Alec Douglas-Home, the former 14th Earl of Home, because of the latter's aristocratic background. Wilson asserted that Douglas-Home's roots prevented him from knowing the problems of ordinary families: 'After half a century of democratic advance, of social revolution, the whole process has ground to a halt with a fourteenth earl' – to which Douglas-Home famously retorted: 'I suppose Mr Wilson, when you come to think of it, is the fourteenth Mr Wilson.' In the 1997 election campaign, Tony Blair did not play this card against John Major – for the simple reason that John Major's background was much humbler than Blair's own. The grocer's daughter Margaret Thatcher was also immune to any attack of this kind.

A more recent example is David Cameron. After he had become the leader of the Conservative Party in 2005, and most noticeably after the general elections in 2010 and 2015 which made him prime minister, he was criticized for being too rich and too posh, and derided as a descendant of King William IV. The son of a well-heeled stockbroker, Cameron was educated at Eton and Oxford and is a millionaire. The same holds true in principle for the ex-Chancellor of the Exchequer George Osborne. Even a Tory MP described Cameron and Osborne in 2012 as 'two posh boys who don't know the price of milk'. And Nadine Dorries did not stop there:

> Unfortunately, I think that not only are Cameron and Osborne two posh boys who don't know the price of milk, but they are two arrogant posh boys who know no remorse, no contrition, and no passion to want to understand the lives of others – and that is their real crime.

The reproach of attending the 'wrong' school and university is most striking, given the English obsession with their children's education. Parents who are politicians have no less desire to secure more for their children than 'bog-standard' state schools. However, political correctness and voter sensitivity require politicians' children to go to the same schools as the bulk of the population. This leads to unimaginable contortions and disagreements, especially in the case of politicians who publicly extoll equality of education. Attending the 'wrong' school or university, or sending one's children to the 'wrong' school or university, can have substantial consequences: when the barrister Charles Falconer (later Lord Falconer of Thoroton), one of Tony Blair's closest friends, was due to be nominated as the Labour Party candidate in a safe seat in 1997, the selection panel demanded that he remove his children from their private schools and send them to state schools, if he didn't want his candidacy to be ruled out.

163

Falconer refused and was not selected (though he went on to have one of the most impressive political and civic careers possible in the UK). Jeremy Corbyn reputedly divorced his wife because she had sent one of their three children to a selective grammar school, something incompatible with his political beliefs.[21]

THE GENIUS OF TONY BLAIR

It was Tony Blair's political genius that in the 1997, 2001 and 2005 election campaigns allowed these contradictions to be overcome, assisted of course by the decline of the Conservative Party. His own background was far from working-class: on the contrary, it was middle-class at least. Likewise his academic career – from fee-paying Fettes, the Scottish Eton, to Oxford and employment at the Bar – was indisputably upper-middle class. However, the members of the working class (unlike some Old Labour diehards in the party) did not hold this against him too much. What's more, he was now the leader of the Labour Party, and they would naturally never vote Conservative just because the Labour leader was himself upper-crust. His charm and attractiveness to women voters swept aside the last remnants of resistance. Old Labour supporters voted for him because, after 18 years in opposition, he represented the only means of regaining power, something for which, out of sheer desperation, they were prepared to pay any price.[22]

Blair's class-transcending image also played a key role. The middle class could see in him a secret ally because of his background: although (inevitably) he was talking the language of the left in deference to working-class voters, they believed he fully appreciated middle-class values, would not seriously damage their position and would uphold the central tenets of Thatcherism – as famously turned out. This made Tony Blair eminently electable for the middle class as well, which resulted in his first two resounding election victories and remained sufficient for the third. He had recognized that appealing to a classless society and one nationhood would bring electoral success where encouraging the class struggle would not.

There was more to Tony Blair's genius, however: a talent for making money and building his personal fortune. Wikipedia puts the wealth he is said to have earned since stepping down at between £20 million (a figure Blair has indirectly acknowledged) and £75 million.[23] Other sources refer to tax-efficient structuring. No other Labour politician has ever become so rich because of his office. Tony Blair has taken literally Peter Mandelson's infamous remark that 'New Labour is intensely relaxed about people getting filthy rich, as long as they pay their taxes.' The former minister under Tony Blair and Gordon Brown and member of the House of Lords since 2008, where he sits as Baron Mandelson, has become rich himself through extensive consulting activities. According to press reports, in 1997 he lived in a one-bedroom flat worth £250,000; in 2011 he moved with his partner into an £8 million home in North London. Mandelson subsequently disowned his 'filthy rich' comment as 'spontaneous and unthoughtful'. But by then he had made his pile. Tony Blair's children have been brought up as the offspring of rich parents with first-class connections and high cultural status. When they come into their inheritance, they will be rich too.

Blair and Mandelson share their attitude to money with a not insubstantial number of other politicians,[24] and not only in Britain. Between 2010 and 2014 the presidential couple Bill and Hillary Clinton together grossed US$102.5 million.[25] Yet their behaviour must not be regarded as reprehensible. Their attitude is very human: being rich is better than being poor. Otherwise, why do millions do the lottery? Why does no-one forego a lucrative inheritance? In both cases, people wish to get rich quick without having to work for it. What is astonishing, however, is that no-one has asked these politicians whether they have given any of the wealth they have accumulated thanks to working-class votes, to the working class.

Part II

Soft Class Markers (Then and Now)

9

Rules, Soft and Silent

Our culture contains many silent symbols more powerful than money. It contains keys that can't be bought, which gain access to rooms whose existence you can barely imagine.

Lynsey Hanley, *Respectable* (2016)

'WHAT IS YOUR CLASS?'

When two Englishmen meet for the first time, an interesting game begins. Both ask: What do you do for a living? Only they don't say it out loud – at any rate, not unless they are already at the top of their tree and therefore not bound by the rules. When, during a party, Randolph Churchill in obviously truculent mood barked at a guest: 'Who are you? What do you do?' this was the privilege of the prime minister's son.[1] It couldn't have happened the other way round. Etiquette prohibits asking someone directly what they do. You have to guess. And to find out you have to spot the clues and interpret them correctly. How this guessing game works is amusingly described by Kate Fox.[2] As the Conservative politician Julian Critchley remarked, 'Class is every Englishman's parlour game.' Of course, the other person's class becomes clear long before the game is concluded, and far from all Englishmen even play. The small circle of the upper classes need not join in.

It is one of the features of the upper classes that most of them know each other, in particular the aristocrats. Many are related to one another, as is the case with all 26 dukes. The same holds true for most of the rich. They have common interests, common sorrows. How do I protect my money from the lower classes? How do I prepare my children for the responsibility of handling a fortune? Such concerns unite. That's why the rich make their homes in the same places – London, or the Hamptons on Long Island – and spend their leisure time in the same destinations – skiing in St Moritz, playing polo in Sotogrande, yachting at Cowes. For those not personally acquainted, some other method of class identification must be found. With enquiries as to the hard class markers of profession, income, address and education ruled out, this is where the soft class markers come in.

It is a particular feature of soft class markers that they are chiefly noticed by the people who observe them, rather than those from whom they emanate. Who would think that, by combing their hair in public, someone is demonstrating their membership of one class and inviting ostracism from another? Who considers the class implications when choosing a dog? Of course, the opposite may be true, and the individual may be trying very hard, by displaying certain class markers, to signal membership of a specific stratum by doing something they believe gives that impression – buying a certain model of car, joining a particular club, taking up certain sports or using pronunciation and terminology that differs from that learned in the parental home. In the case of some social climbers, this can assume near-ludicrous proportions, as described by John, Duke of Bedford in his *Book of Snobs* (1965). However, on the whole, class signals are sent out entirely subconsciously.

CHANGING AND UNCHANGING

It is not surprising that the soft class markers have changed in recent decades. Some seven years ago, in *The Fall of the Sloane Rangers*, Peter York wrote that the Sloane style which he and Ann Barr had documented in 1982 in the *Official Sloane Ranger Handbook* had gone completely out of fashion as early as the 1990s.

By the 90s the Sloane style couldn't have been more unfashionable. The accent, the language, the dress code, the 'miniature stately

168

home' interior styles were all wrong, wrong, wrong in the world of mild mockney, the 'information super-highway' and mid-century modern. Sloane seemed archaic and unprofessional – only for the magic world of Richard Curtis romcoms – in the new high-maintenance world of Big Money London.[3]

In part he was correct. Many words in the Sloane Dictionary contained in the *Official Sloane Ranger Handbook* are not used at all today, regardless of the speaker's class. On the other hand, some soft class markers, amazingly, have survived for decades. Many behaviours and uses of language and pronunciation Nancy Mitford clearly categorized as 'U' and 'non-U' ('U' being upper-class) back in 1956, and similarly assigned to specific classes in Debrett's *U and Non-U Revisited* in 1978 and Jilly Cooper's *Class* of 1999, still had the same connotation when Kate Fox published her second edition of *Watching the English* in 2014. These include 'pardon' (instead of 'what' or 'sorry'), 'toilet' (instead of 'loo' or 'lavatory'), 'serviette' (instead of 'napkin') and 'lounge' (instead of 'sitting room' or 'drawing room' or 'hall'): terms whose utterance Kate Fox describes as 'deadly sins'.

There is therefore every reason to doubt the long-term reliability of Peter York's diagnosis. Instead, it seems more likely that many of the old rules still exist, but that many people are too embarrassed to espouse them in public. In particular, they are no longer upheld by, say, social ostracization; rather it is tacitly noted who masters the rules and who does not. Those in the know then privately draw their own conclusions. These proprieties may be buried underground now, less visible, and unspoken at least in public – but they're there. They may have become even more important than when manifestly evident. Camouflage has become the instrument of the arbiters of taste. What really matters is usually left unsaid. It comes across in small signs, a gesture, tiny give-aways, the odd phrase. When you join a group of people or you are addressed personally or on the telephone, you recognize the markers at once: the clothes, the style, the voice, the mannerisms. Nobody who knows the codes believes otherwise. The rules, although hazy, most definitely exist. Everyone is measured by them, and either passes or fails. Except that they are never told. No-one knows who makes these rules, hence the nebulous references to the 'arbiters of taste' or 'the smart set'. Style rule-makers in the manner of Beau Brummel or Beau Nash are a thing of the past. The rules are probably the result of mutual observation and imitation, should the other person's actions and words be deemed to be 'the right way'.

Alongside accent and terminology, leisure activities have emerged as an increasingly important soft class marker, reflecting the general tendency for class to be determined not only by how one earns one's money, but primarily also by how one spends it: in a word, lifestyle. Among the reasons is that people now have much more time on their hands, and so a much greater amount of money is spent on recreation. Whereas after the war around a tenth of people's expenditure went on relaxation, today that has risen to a quarter.[4] The broadest definition of leisure activities is everything that is not work and which people do in their spare time. A detailed breakdown includes such things as holidays, sport, television, gardening, games, going to the pub, clubbing, reading, socializing, eating out, travelling, visiting people, radio, shopping, going to the theatre, opera and concerts. Historically, only the upper classes had an opportunity for leisure pursuits because they did not have to work for a living.

CLASS AND TASTE

Taste is woven into our class system.

Grayson Perry, *Daily Telegraph* (2013)

Taste and class feed off each other.

Stephen Bayley, *Taste: The Secret Meaning
of Things* (2017)

The notion of taste so often goes hand in hand with class. Taste is the most universal of the soft class markers because it is reflected in so much of human behaviour. To say of someone they have taste may well be a compliment, but on its own it is meaningless. We need to know what their good taste applies to: is it clothes or furniture, make-up or music, or garden planting schemes, maybe?

Can good or bad taste be characteristic of a whole section of society? People thought so once. The preferences of the upper echelons, in particular the aristocracy, set the benchmark. Anyone wishing to move up in the world observed how the nobility dressed, furnished their houses and behaved, and tried to copy them. Any other style was common or just plain bad. However, this discrimination was not really an issue until the late-eighteenth century. It was an invention of the middle class, recently emerged and now flourishing. The gentry gave no thought to taste, and how its members spoke or acted would never have been judged aesthetically as either pleasing or otherwise: it was just what it was. The middle orders were the first to identify the differences between themselves and the upper and lower classes and begin to describe the relevant proclivities as good or bad taste.

What constitutes superior or inferior taste has constantly morphed over time. Though hard to believe today, even the works of Shakespeare were found to be weak, crude, 'dunghills', repulsive and tedious by wordsmiths of near-equal renown including Dr Johnson, Voltaire, Bernard Shaw and Tolstoy. A similar fate was suffered by many artists – the Impressionists, for example, were initially regarded as downright tasteless, only to become the ultimate in good taste. In a nineteenth-century experiment, museums were established for items whose design was deemed 'utterly indefensible'. One was the Chamber of Horrors, which displayed items from the Great Exhibition of 1851 decreed to be in bad taste. These days most of them are nigh-on priceless.

The differences between good and bad taste have since become blurred, but have not disappeared. Nowadays we measure good taste by our own choices and those of style mavens whose more sophisticated judgements we therefore admire. The time-worn 'them and us' divide takes on new meaning in relation to taste: 'them' is bad, 'us' is good. Arrogance and snobbery have become ominously close.

ENGLAND: A CLASS OF ITS OWN

Characterizing other people's taste as inferior creates a class boundary and keeps other tribes at bay.

That said, bad taste seems to be transient anyway these days. Something decried as tasteless one minute will be seized upon the next moment by an avant-garde artist or lifestyle guru as the acme of renewal or intelligence or non-conformism or disruptive thinking. The art market and the consumer sector latch on and millions of copies are produced, to the extent that what had been condemned as tasteless ends up setting a new trend. Many members of the upper classes take pride in wearing clothes or buying furniture considered tasteless to embrace a reputation as a free spirit. In a world in which new is automatically good, and old – with a few exceptions – automatically bad, it follows that tastes quickly change. Recently, two paradigm shifts appear to be afoot. Works once regarded as high art are starting to be seen as a con (part of the output of Damien Hirst and Jeff Koons), while paintings by forgers (Han van Meegeren, for example, or John Myatt, Shaun Greenhalgh and Wolfgang Beltracchi) are being hailed as works on a par with the masters they've copied.

Although the relationship between class and taste is still considered symbiotic, as borne out by Grayson Perry's Channel 4 documentary series *All in The Best Possible Taste* in 2012[5] on how the different English social classes understand taste, class and taste do not correlate. The woman who buys a tasteful dress can come from any class. Her husband may wear beautiful clothes but live with ugly furniture. If someone speaks with a certain accent, this may reveal their class, but not their taste. And while wealth and occupation may signify social standing, taste is clearly a different kettle of fish.

HARD IMPACT OF SOFT MARKERS

Soft class markers may also have material consequences, in that they may ease or obstruct one's access to various professions. For some professions this is obvious, since certain soft class markers are a prerequisite of the job. Anyone hoping to earn a living as an art dealer or owner of an exclusive London club should be familiar with the accent and terminology of their clientele and dress and behave accordingly. Someone selling fish at the market is more likely to find favour with their customers if they speak the same language.

However, soft class markers also have a bearing in cases where one might assume that objective criteria such as academic credentials or A-levels would be the sole determinant. In a study entitled *A Qualitative Evaluation of Non-educational Barriers to the Elite Professions* (2015), the Social Mobility and Child Poverty Commission concluded, with reference to five elite law and accountancy firms, that although intelligence and hard work – evidenced by psychometric tests and academic credentials, including A-levels – are indeed a basic prerequisite when hiring new recruits, a range of non-educational skills and attributes is also required in accordance with the firms' definition of talent, such as drive, resilience, strong communication and debating skills, and above all confidence and 'polish' as shown at interview. These blue-chip firms find people with these attributes mainly among candidates educated at fee-paying or selective state schools and applicants with degrees from a Russell Group university. In top law firms, close to 42 per cent of graduate trainees were privately educated, and in leading accountancy firms up to 70 per cent of job offers were made to former students of private or non-comprehensive state schools. Typically, 40 to 50 per cent of applicants were educated at a Russell Group university, and these applicants received between 60 and 70 per cent of all job offers. In simple terms, where candidates' intelligence and skills are equal, it is soft class markers that determine who is admitted to the elite professions.

However, not every career flourishes to the same extent as a result of soft class markers. An upper-class appearance, accent and terminology may give an edge in certain professions. But in others they can be an impediment. Being judged as 'too posh' rules out many who aspire to be television reporters, journalists on provincial newspapers, actors or pop stars. They are not 'authentic' enough. Allegedly the prospect of an Old Etonian being hired once triggered a mass protest by employees on the grounds that he was 'not one of us'. Naturally, such reasons are not stated in any rejection letter, or aired in any interview.

SOURCES

The following chapters contain a collection of soft class markers. The sources go back as far as the 1950s. Nancy Mitford's classic *Noblesse Oblige*, with its quotes from Alan S. C. Ross on 'U and non-U' – meaning upper-class and not upper-class – was published in 1956. The book created a social bombshell at the time, and to this day remains a kind of bible of class markers. When Prime Minister Harold Macmillan selected his cabinet in January 1957, he noted in his diary:

> The forming of the whole administration . . . has meant seeing nearly a hundred people and trying to say the right thing to each. In the circumstances many considerations had to be borne in mind – the right, centre and left of the party; . . . – and last but not least, U and non-U (to use the jargon that Nancy Mitford has popularized): that is, Eton, Winchester etc. on the one hand; Board School and grammar school on the other.

As the son-in-law of a duke, Macmillan knew what he was talking about. Further sources include George Mikes' *How to be a Brit* (1984), Debrett's *U and Non-U Revisited* (1978), Ann Barr and Peter York's *The Official Sloane Ranger Handbook* (1982), Jilly Cooper's *Class* (1999), Ferdinand Mount's *Mind the Gap* (2004), Julian Fellowes's *Snobs* (2004), Not Actual Size's *The Art of Being Middle Class* (2012), as well as Kate Fox's *Watching the English* (2014), Will Atkinson's *Class in the New Millennium* (2017) and others mentioned in the notes or the appendix. Other examples are drawn from English newspaper articles, television programmes, films and also my own personal experience, as well as occasionally from social media.

It should come as no surprise that Facebook, WhatsApp, Instagram, Twitter and the like have their own part to play in the English class game. As one observer puts it, 'The internet has become snobbery's greatest forum.'[6] I believe we are still just finding our way, although class differentiation is already apparent. How people use social media in their professional lives says little about their class; we can learn far more from social media's use for pleasure.

In this respect the upper classes seem more reserved. They certainly refrain from broadcasting compromising details about their private lives, which of course is a matter of prudence as well as class. But using social media automatically sends out class signals. A selfie from Ascot sends a different signal to a post from the dog track. Status updates about a recent weekend trip (to a country house or Blackpool Pleasure Beach?) or the journey there (in a rich friend's private jet or by coach?) reveal a great deal – as they are meant to.

Social media are the perfect playground for exercising snobbery.[7] The class difference lies in whether one chooses to take part. The notion that Facebook and co. could level out social stratification or even make it disappear is just as wrong – and naïve – as similar claims made in the past about fast food, cheap furniture or affordable clothing. But perhaps social media will become an influencer of taste and a judge of class-related behaviour. By 'liking' certain content, users can decide what is – and is not – tasteful and generally accepted within their own circles. It will be interesting to see whether the independent thinkers of the upper classes will succumb to the pressure of the 'like' button or endure a 'shitstorm' of abuse.

HOW MANY NATIONS ARE THERE?

The following chapters are generally organized into two contrasting columns to represent social difference. Of course, this two-fold presentation does not adequately reflect reality. A three-way breakdown into upper-class, middle-class and working-class would be more appropriate. More accurate still would be to have subdivisions within the classes since, as we have seen in Chapter 5, these are far from homogeneous. This would involve differentiating between the aristocracy, the wealthy and the powerful in the upper class; between upper-, middle- and lower-middle class within the middle class; and between the respectable and the undeserving poor within the working class, where even more complex distinctions are conceivable. Some observers have performed these dissections to humorous effect and characterized the phenotypes of the relevant class quite literally by name, like Jilly Cooper in *Class*, where we meet Harry Stow-Crat (aristocracy), Gideon Upward (upper-middle class), Howard Weybridge (middle-middle class), Bryan and Jen Teale (lower-middle class), Mr Definitely-Disgusting (working class) and Mr Nouveau-Richards (a millionaire). Harry Wallop in *Consumed* introduces us to the Portland Privateers (high earners and high spenders whose children are delivered in the private Portland Hospital in London), the Rockabillies (wealthy individuals with a rural attitude to life whose ideal holiday is spent at the resort of Rock in Cornwall), the Hyphen-Leighs (whose status aspirations are asserted through spending on brands and labels and choosing double-barrelled names for their children), the Sun Skittlers (a low-income group who nonetheless usually own their own homes and spend their money on leisure, not fashion), the Middleton classes (Sun Skittler escapees from a red-top-reading, blue-collar, hire-purchase background and proud members of the middle class), the Asda Mums (who put their children's well-being and status first despite limited incomes), the Wood-Burning Stovers (devotees of garlic presses, wood-burning stoves, farmers' markets and Birkenstock sandals).

However, three or more columns would have hampered readability too much. On the other hand, this simple, two-way split is not quite without basis in fact. Indeed, a great many English people fully relate to this dichotomy between 'them' and 'us' or 'upper' and 'lower'. The English use these words – seriously or ironically – to describe the uppers and the lowers. They have some similarities with the historic descriptions in Chapter 3, albeit with a more modern twist. In contrast to Chapter 3, the order in the following table is purely alphabetical, so that the word pairs are not linked. In all the subsequent tables word pairs are linked. Incidentally, for the most part employing the terminology is not dependent on class. Members of both the upper class and the working class call the head of a bank a fat cat.

aristocratic	ASBO youth/kids
(the) better sorts	benefits scroungers
chinless wonder	blue collar
classy	chav/chavette/chavvy
county	coarse
elite	common
establishment	council estate
exclusive	disadvantaged
fat cats	dispossessed
flash Harry	down-market
green welly brigade	dross
high-class	Essex man/girl
higher echelons	flashy
high-ranking	hoi-polloi
hoity-toity	hoody
hooray Henry	hooligan
idle rich	ill-bred
la-di-da	infra dig (from Latin infra dignitatem = below one's dignity)
(the) man	kappa slapper
(Tim) nice–but–dim	lad/ladette/laddish
nob/nobby noble	less educated
old boy network	less privileged
old money	lout
old school tie	lower echelons
posh	low-income groups
posh git	mob
privileged	mock-Tudor
public school	Mondeo man
rah/wrah	naff
rentier	ned (non-educated delinquent)
respectable	new money
(the) rich	non-U (not upper class)

ritzy	nouveau riche
scion	oik
select	ordinary people
Sloane Ranger	parvenu
smart	peasant
smug	pikey
snob/snobby	plebs/plebby
snooty	precariat
stuck-up/posh tart	proletarian/prole/proll
swell	riff-raff
swish	scally
toff	socially excluded
top-drawer	state school
top-notch	suburban semi
U (upper class)	tabloid reader
upmarket	TOWIE (TV show The Only Way is Essex)
upper class	townie
upper-class git	trash/trashy
upper-class twit	uncouth
upper crust	underclass
upscale	vulgar
well-born	white man van
well-bred	working class
yah-yah/yar yar	yob/yobbo/yobby
young fogey	yuppie

HOW TO READ THE SOFT CLASS MARKERS

This collection is not a guide to good or bad behaviour or a recipe for how to get on in society. It is all about differences. It is therefore less about manners when coughing, or the correct way to dispose of chewing gum, or how to eat prawns, or when to switch off one's mobile phone, and more about how people use different words for the same thing or choose different pets.

Many of the differences recorded here are outdated. But isn't it interesting to know how people spoke, dressed, thought and felt in the past? Let us take as an example the idea of the weekend (or country weekend), a term nowadays accepted as normal parlance by every class. Between the wars and for a decade or two after, the expression of choice among the upper echelons was 'a Friday-to-Monday', or later 'a Saturday-to-Monday', a coinage that clearly drew attention to the fact that one did not have to work again until Monday morning. These phrases are no more. Today the idea of a visit lasting three days would fill host and guest alike with dismay: for the host, because they want to have their home to themselves again, and for the guest, because they have to work in the week and do not wish to spend their two days off with the same people. These days such visits seldom begin before Saturday lunch and are over shortly after lunch on Sunday. Consequently, this book is also a historical record.

The order chosen for these soft class markers is determined by solid English pragmatism and follows the process of becoming acquainted. To start with, what counts is the overall visual impression conveyed by appearance. Besides figure, looks and gait, there is dress. Next, the two people meet and introduce themselves and exchange names. (The saying 'What's in a name?' may now be relevant.) This is the moment of truth for accent and pronunciation, as well as terminology: a chance to discover the other party's style of conversation, and their behaviour, comportment and attitude. Perhaps the two then get into the same car and share a meal, whether at a restaurant or at home (table manners and food and drink). As they become better acquainted, they may be invited to each other's homes, where they discover each other's house, garden and pets, and meet their spouse and possibly children. They find out where the latter go to school or which university they attend, and learn about each other's education. From there, the discussion leads on naturally to leisure activities (sports and holidays) and other aspects of their lives and surroundings: their reading preferences, membership of clubs or the local church, political leanings, voluntary work, and which charities they support.

Alongside pronunciation the most important class marker is terminology. It too permeates every sphere of existence. Class-related terminology exists for people's appearance and their clothing (gum boots or wellies), as well as for their car (he drives a Merc) and their house (loo or toilet); it defines the food they eat (back bacon or streaky), and even the sport they do (riding or horse-riding).

In weighing up whether to assign the different words and their usages to the relevant areas of life – appearance, clothing, cars, etc. – or devote a separate chapter to the subject of terminology in general, I have opted for a bit of both. Terms used specifically in the aforementioned categories are noted in the relevant section under terminology, while all other differences are discussed in 'Vocabulary and Language'. Thus, shirt or blouse can be found in the chapter on clothing, loo or toilet in the chapter on houses, riding or horse-riding in the chapter on sports. Choice of word, on the other hand – party or do, pupil or scholar, father and mother or mum and dad – is examined under 'Vocabulary and Language'.

The motley assortment of differences juxtaposed in the columns set out in Chapters 10 to 28 are intended not to be read at one sitting, but rather to be browsed and dipped into. Consequently, most are not arranged by topic or importance or occupation. Which brings us back to the conclusion that (see Chapter 1) there is, contrary to its designation, nothing systematic about the English class system.

Last, but by no means least: if you find the whole thing nonsensical, politically incorrect, or just plain crazy, please don't fret. No, indeed: to get the most from this book, be guided, as Kate Fox urges (with apologies to Oscar Wilde), by a basic tenet of English life: *The importance of not being earnest.*

10

Appearance

It is only shallow people who do not judge by appearance.

Oscar Wilde, *The Picture of Dorian Gray* (1891)

There is this saying that you should never judge on appearance; actually, I think you should always judge on appearance. Because people haven't arrived there by accident, it's not like the colour of your skin. Everything else they have completely chosen.

IT consultant Benedict, interviewee for the Great British Class Survey, in Mike Savage, *Social Class in the 21st Century* (2015)

In his (still highly readable) 1980 book *Class: Image and Reality in Britain, France and the USA since 1930*, Arthur Marwick begins with an anecdote about his own appearance. After featuring on a BBC television show, he received the following letter from a viewer:

I wonder whether, before you come into my sitting room again, you could make some effort to improve your unkempt appearance. It was clear from your accent and dress last night that you have risen, by dint of hard study, from the working classes. Your accent is completely acceptable, but your appearance is NOT.

On first encounter, a momentary glance is exchanged that takes in gender, race, ethnicity, age, height, posture, gait, the way someone stands or gesticulates, their face, eyes, nose, mouth, smile, hair. These characteristics are observed initially from a certain distance, then in greater proximity, finally at arm's length. Each attribute is also an early indicator of the other person's class which, whether consciously or otherwise, they are transmitting. Class has its own body language. The principle that one should never judge by appearances has always been unrealistic. Who can avoid that first impression when someone enters a room? There is some truth in the quip that you never get a second chance to make a first impression. Appearance is a mixture of hard and soft class markers. Many are also changeable, and therefore soft: hard is one's height, soft one's hairstyle. What counts is how they come together. And naturally the traits of appearance are not unique to any one class but found across the social strata, to varying degrees. Winston Churchill – the grandson of a duke – looked very much like John Bull, whereas in appearance George Martin of Beatles fame was invariably singled out, despite his working-class origins, as upper-class (see Chapter 4). For this reason the following lists relating to appearance, which also include the hard class markers, should not be taken too seriously.

FIGURE

Uncle Sam type	John Bull type
tall and thin, lean	stocky, sturdy, obese
stooping shoulders	
long neck	short neck
long arms and fingers	short arms and fingers
thin hands	strong hands
thin legs and feet	stout legs and strong feet

HEAD

narrow stoat's head	bulkier in the face
relatively small eyes	
often hanging eyelids	
relatively small mouth	
thin lips	
good teeth	bad teeth
look younger than they are	look older than they are

HAIR

hairstyle under forty: as you like it over forty: brushed backwards	
medium long to long	very long or very short, crew cut, shaved head, spiky hair
floppy haircut	
parting north of the outer corner of the eye	
hair only slightly over the ear	
cut just above the collar	
often crispy curls at the nape of the neck	
sideboards to entrance of the eardrum	long side-whiskers
not too careful	overcareful (parting)
but never too sloppy	too sloppy
seldom bald; if so, don't hide it	wig or hairpiece
do not dye their hair (men)	dyed hair
discreet dyeing (women)	conspicuous dye
washed hair	hair greasy
no spray or gel	hair gelled sometimes in spikes
simple moustache OK, less so full beard	
haircut once a month at barber's	haircut by wife
never comb their hair in public	

Lord Whitelaw, Lord President of the Council in Margaret Thatcher's cabinet, is said to have mistrusted his colleague, the Defence Secretary Michael Heseltine, as 'the sort of man who combs his hair in public'.[1]

SKIN

delicate pink and white skin	
or reddish	
skin flushes up at parties and in hot places	
hidden wrinkles which break when laughing or getting angry	
tan slight if any	too deep a tan
discreet make-up	too much make-up

EMBELLISHMENTS

piercings in ear if any	piercings in ears, eyebrows, nose, tongue, nipples, belly button, tattoos

PACE AND GESTURES

Appearance is determined not only by the physical realities of height, build, shape of head, hairstyle, etc., but perhaps even more revealingly by how someone uses them – which is why even the best waxworks in Madame Tussaud's collection tell only half the story. A fleeting movement of the arm or head, the way one crosses one's legs, stands up or sits down can considerably alter first impressions. Such is the actor's bread and butter.

slow pace	rapid scuttle, bouncy walk
slow, lethargic, languid, unexcited	excited, harassed, attentive, tensed
poker face, deadpan look	pull faces, roll their eyes, raise their eyes to heaven
don't gesticulate	lively gesticulations, jerk their head, wave their hands, shrug their shoulders

See also Chapter 17, Stances and Behaviour

11

Clothing and Dress

He had a horror of showing white hairy shin between sock-top and trouser cuff when sitting down, legs crossed – it was in some ways the besetting and prototypical English sartorial sin.

William Boyd, *Ordinary Thunderstorms* (2010)

We know them when we see them – hoods up, trousers halfway down to their knees, swaggering along the pavement in small groups, playing loud music on their phones, swearing, spitting . . . these are the educational underclass.

Charlie Taylor, *Telegraph*, 7 March 2002

Apart from the alliterative link, clothing and class have a great deal in common in England. They have gone hand in hand throughout history, although their relationship today is not quite the same as in the past. On 27 September 1826, an elegantly dressed German nobleman boarded a ship in Rotterdam bound for London. He planned to stay for some time and indeed did, as well as sojourning in Wales and Ireland, before leaving England's shores on 1 January 1829. He had access to the highest echelons of English society, but also mingled happily and anonymously with the general populace. He was a perceptive and empathetic observer of England, and he recorded his impressions and experiences in weekly, sometimes daily, letters to his divorced wife in Germany. He was fascinated by the obsession, as he saw it, of the upper classes of English society with clothes. Changing attire several times a day – for breakfast, lunch, tea, dinner and ball – was not unusual. With some astonishment he concluded that, in English society, by 'tacit understanding indeed an absolute mistress had been crowned: not the aristocracy but fashion, a goddess which only in England could reign as personally and despotically'.

The German in question was Prince Hermann von Pückler-Muskau, whom we will encounter again in Chapter 34.[1] What he was describing was the aftermath of dandyism – a social, class-specific and sartorial phenomenon that flourished in England at the beginning of the nineteenth century. Behind its birth was the greatest dandy of them all, George Bryan 'Beau' Brummell, who for many years was the arbiter of gentlemen's fashion in England and in London society in particular.

Brummell is regarded as the inventor of a new style of male attire, with perfectly fitted and tailored dark coats and full-length trousers, immaculate shirts and an elaborately knotted cravat, as well as – most famously – high, starched collars. The entire look was characterized by what we would today term simple elegance and understatement: a far cry from the extravagant embellishments and knee breeches with stockings that had previously been the rage. For a number of years Brummell was befriended by the Prince of Wales (later the Prince Regent and King George IV); he moved in all the best circles, and his mode of dress was considered the undisputed epitome of 'exquisite propriety', of what was 'good and great'. To fail to dress accordingly was to risk social ostracism or at the very least contempt. Things went so far that a duke reportedly died of a broken heart when, having sought Brummell's opinion about his coat, he received the rather disparaging reply: 'Bedford, do you call this thing a coat?' Even after he had quarrelled with the Prince of Wales and fled to France to escape his creditors, Brummell was for a long time still considered the doyen of English aristocratic fashion.[2] Of course, these affectations were probably not quite so caricaturish at the time, but undoubtedly in England the way someone dressed played a significant role in how they were regarded. Even a hundred years after Brummell and Pückler, in the period between the two world wars, people maintained that they knew a gentleman (or his opposite) when they saw one. George Mikes put it like this:

> Before the War you could place a man by his clothes. The rich – particularly at weekends – went around in rags; the working class wore cloth caps; prostitutes wore foxes around their necks and smoked cigarettes in the street; wives of rich brewers wore mink coats and wives of dustmen were dressed as today only Eliza Doolittle is in revivals of *My Fair Lady*.[3]

All this is history, for many nowadays little more than occasion for incredulity. But that is not to say that dress has lost its relevance to class, for what one wears plays no small part in the first impression one makes. Clothes don't just add to one's appearance: often they *are* one's appearance. Once Englishmen and -women have taken in the overall picture, the figure and face of another person, they switch their attention to what they have on. Of course, one of clothing's functions is to protect the human body from the cold or the heat – and from nudity: there are few things more embarrassing than someone who is naked when everyone else is fully clothed. And people tend to buy clothes as a kind of self-expression of their personality and style. But at the same time they are transmitting a signal about their class. Whether they like it or not, sartorially they are making a social statement. The class-related judgement is made in the eyes of the beholder, not the wearer. So what do your clothes say about your class?

It is often said that dress rules have become much more relaxed. While this is true, it has by no means diminished the class aspect of clothes, and if anything may have amplified it. These days the whole thing is fraught with far more uncertainty. There is nowhere to find out how to dress correctly for a particular occasion. Worse still, if you get it wrong, barely anyone will tell you or explain why. The lapse is simply noted and if necessary condemned, without a word being spoken. Knowing what is 'right' to wear on which occasion is simply expected. The Labour politician and former chair of the Equality and Human Rights Commission, Trevor Phillips, contributes an illuminating story.

> I was recently invited to what was described as a small informal supper at a stately home. The invitation said 'no dress code' and the guidance from people who'd been before uniformly vague. The lesson was that what 'no dress code' really means is that, if you don't already know what the code is, are you sure you really belong here?[4]

Certain sectors with strict dress codes still exist. For instance, if you're going to the races at Ascot during Royal Week, you can look up the *Official Royal Ascot Style Guide* on the internet. But such codes have no bearing on our current discussion because they are prescriptive, and so the potential for making a mistake is pretty much ruled out. Much more interesting are the unwritten rules maintained even without any apparent prescription, merely by acting 'in concert', a case in point being the colour of men's shoes (see below). Nor is it only what one wears that matters: it's also how one wears it.

Take fashion brands. When the lower classes buy them, they flounce around in them as a way of showing what they can afford. The upper echelons like to wear designer labels too, but they don't flaunt them. Neither are they too perfectly or immaculately dressed. A spanking new outfit is suspect, as are too many accessories. A real gent is hardly ever seen in very new attire. Sartorial perfection and overgrooming are the trappings of a spiv. Dress has far from lost its purpose as a class marker, but it has become much harder nowadays to categorize people according to their clothes, and well-nigh impossible among the young, although slightly easier as they get older. For this reason, we will limit our comments here primarily to adult males.[5]

GENERAL

more clothes	fewer clothes
little flesh	a lot of flesh
underdress	overdress
observe dress code	seek attention
out of fashion	in fashion
start fashion	follow fashion
look stylish	look like a fashion victim
old clothes	new clothes
made to measure	off the peg
expensive clothes looking old	cheap clothes, air of austerity
excellent material, obviously good	overdone and fussy
natural fibres: wool, cashmere, leather, silk, cotton	man-made, synthetic fibres: nylon, plastic, polyester, Lurex, Crimplene, etc.
muted colours: grey, blue, brown, dark green, rust	bold colours: yellow, orange, purple, gold, pink, royal blue, brilliant white, jet black
discreet, unobtrusive, inconspicuous	screaming, conspicuous, ostentatious, flashy, coquettish
no clothing with initials	initials on shirts, etc.
no or small token of 'source'	logo-studded designer clothes
thin stripes	wide stripes
clothes and accessories don't match	matching clothes and accessories (e.g. all in red)
have reservations about casual Friday	like casual Friday
small boys (up to eight years) wear short trousers	long trousers for small boys
	visible braces

HEADGEAR

normally hatless	baseball caps, especially backwards or at an angle, cloth caps
outdoor hats and caps	
bowlers on occasion	
straw hats on occasion	
	fascinators (decorative headpieces consisting of feathers, flowers, beads, etc. attached to a comb or hair clip) instead of hats, for women

Headgear is a good example not only of the vagaries of fashion (which are to be expected), but also of changes in the class indicators associated with it. Until roughly the First World War it was a must for gentlemen (and incidentally ladies too) to wear a hat outside the house. Those failing to do so were neither upper-class nor gentlemen.

This class rule was so firmly entrenched that, in 1911, it was even employed to force members of the House of Lords to vote in a specific way. In July of that year the vote was due to be taken on the famous People's Budget proposed by the Chancellor of the Exchequer David Lloyd George, which was intended to remove the Lords' right of veto over the budget and tax legislation and open the way for the landowning upper classes to be deprived of power and, through high taxes, ultimately dispossessed. This was clearly understood by the Lords. A minority, with Lord Willoughby de Broke as their spokesman, went to extreme lengths to persuade the other peers to oppose the bill and above all just to take part in the vote. To keep a certain duke inside the House, Willoughby hid his top hat and coat, believing he would never dare leave the House of Lords without them. In the event he fled anyway.

After the First World War the requirement that a gentleman wear a hat was relaxed, but by no means ceased. The bowler hat rose to fame in England as a hallmark of the 'City gent' who worked in London's financial district, its most prominent wearer probably being the British Prime Minister Winston Churchill. Since the 1970s the upper classes have largely gone about their business bareheaded, reserving the wearing of hats for special occasions. Sometimes the headgear itself changes class. In keeping with Burberry clothing in general, the Burberry baseball cap with its iconic check pattern began life in the luxury segment. However, more and more pictures gradually appeared in the media of the caps being worn by football hooligans and other unsavoury types, not infrequently as they were being arrested by the police. In autumn 2004 Burberry withdrew its baseball cap from the market because it had become the trademark of the 'wrong wearers'.

SUITS

in London	
two-piece or three-piece suit	light-weight suits in light colours, tracksuits
dark grey, navy blue; when in doubt opt for navy	crude, garish, clashing colours or black
no brown suit in town	country clothes in London
white tie for an official occasion	
black tie for a dinner party	
morning coat for a wedding	
never wear waistcoat without jacket	go out wearing waistcoat
bottom button of waistcoat undone	
in the country	
tweed jacket	city clothes in the country, blazer with badge
flannel trousers or corduroy trousers	
green, dung-coloured or brown	
frumpy and out of date	
leather patches on the elbows of coats	
'normal' jeans	loose-fitting jeans
shorts for sports, gardening, running, walking only	shorts as normal wear
ancient khakis	new shorts
long shorts	short shorts

SHIRTS

white or blue, plain, pale	glowing blue, pink, yellow, bright and/or shiny
no dark or black shirts	black or dark blue shirts
single solid colour	multi-coloured
discreetly checked or striped	
long-sleeved shirt	short-sleeved shirt
	frilly evening shirts
	button-down shirt
no T-shirts and sweatshirts	T-shirts, especially sleeveless, sweatshirts
	round-neck T-shirts under shirt
	T-shirt under leather jacket
polo shirts	
shirt sleeves rolled up below elbow	shirts sleeves rolled up above elbow
shirts buttoned up or with top button undone	shirts with two or more buttons undone, bare chest

TIES

dark, subdued colours	fresh, garish, brash colours
small, discreet patterns dark blue with red dots	loud patterns, cartoony or jokey ones
striped (but not with dark suit)	
no old school tie, college tie, regimental tie, club tie. Exceptions: Old Etonians and Guards	
tie and handkerchief don't match	matching tie and handkerchief
	scarf rings

SOCKS

silk or cotton	synthetics
colour of suit or trousers	contrasting with trouser colour
never white with non-white suit	white socks with dark trousers
no skin visible	too short, skin visible
	shoes without socks

SHOES

He's a gentleman: look at his boots.

George Bernard Shaw, *Pygmalion* (1916)

A head waiter once told me: I can always tell people by their shoes. People who are only trying to show off and impress you, wear fabulous clothes but are not prepared to spend a lot on their shoes. A real gentleman always wears first-class shoes.

John Duke of Bedford, *Book of Snobs* (1965)

A pair of brilliantly shined shoes ... is the signature of a true gent, before any word is spoken.

David Tang, *Financial Times* (May 2017)

first-class shoes	shabby shoes
shoes made to measure	
leather shoes	trainers, sneakers, shell shoes
brogues or half-brogues	sandals, flip-flops
lace-ups	
penny loafers	tassel loafers
normal heels	heels too high
polished	unpolished
'no brown after six'	
'no brown east of Windsor'	
gumboots, green or black	yellow or blue

One of the delights of the English class system and English society in general is the fascination with the colour of men's shoes. At the risk of irreverence, the urge to paraphrase Shakespeare's Hamlet in this context is irresistible: 'Brown or black, that is the question.' Although the colour of someone's shoes is unlikely ever to have decided a 'to-be-or-not-to-be' issue, it has undoubtedly influenced social mobility (up or down), success or the lack of it, and even marriage itself.

When young men were scarce after the First World War, Jemima Lewis's great aunt considered herself lucky to have found a smart and handsome fiancé. But disaster struck because of the colour of his shoes. When the young suitor visited her in London, he wore a navy-blue suit with brown shoes. The engagement was broken off forthwith, and the great aunt remained a spinster for the rest of her life.[6] It is difficult to know whether to laugh or cry, especially given the great aunt's fate, or simply shake one's head at such folly.

When the City veteran Brian Winterflood started his first job at the London Stock Exchange in 1951, he wore brown shoes to work, only to be greeted with cries of 'Brown boots, brown boots!' He got the message and hastily bought a pair of black shoes, having understood that a career in banking would be ruled out if he wore brown.[7] Can we at least laugh at this today? After recounting the anecdote about Brian Winterflood, an observer no less astute than Harry Wallop comments that 'Hardly anyone remembers these rules now. Brown shoes are a common sight in the city.'

Really? In the introduction to the 2017 edition of *Spear's 500,* a publication listing manufacturers and service providers who stand ready to satisfy high-net-worth individuals' every whim, the (aptly named) editor-in-chief William Cash writes: 'Turning up for an interview in brown shoes would be like saying you have never heard of the *Financial Times.* No would-be banker to a Global Citizen wears brown.' In an August 2016 study entitled *Socio-Economic Diversity in Life Sciences and Investment Banking* (amazing the things taxpayers' money is spent on!), the Social Mobility Commission was shocked to find that 'Some investment bank managers still judge candidates on whether they wear brown shoes with a suit rather than on their skills and potential.' The study caused a furore in the English press, including quality newspapers such as the *Financial Times* and *Telegraph.*

The attention to shoe colour on its own might be considered trivial. Why shouldn't an employer expect his staff to dress in a particular way? Doesn't the fashion business do this too? But what is significant is that the English regard the colour of one's shoes as a class indicator. The journalist Jemima Lewis headlined her earlier quoted article thus: 'The prejudice against brown shoes is a classic case of class snobbery.' In his amusing book *Rules for Modern Life* (2016), the *Financial Times*'s former agony uncle, the late David Tang, fondly dedicates several pages to the right shoe colour under the heading 'Shoes – brown or black?' Tang writes that he has received a great deal of mail about brown shoes and had many more discussions with friends. It is clearly a very important matter.

The following guidelines have been compiled for those wishing to be in the know. In London shoes are always black: 'No brown east of Windsor'. With a dark blue or grey suit (and others are a no-no), black shoes are again de rigueur. Brown shoes are only acceptable in the country, best kept for tramping the hills, fields and meadows, for soil and mud, for gardening, fishing, shooting, farming. Even the time of day must be considered: 'No brown after six'.

BELTS

shoes and belt match suit	
brown shoes and belt with beige trousers	
belt same colour as shoes	shoes black, belt brown
modest belt buckle	conspicuous belt buckle

COATS

blue or grey	brown, green, light-coloured
no brown except camel	
sheepskin coat in the country	duffel coat

JUMPERS AND SWEATERS

blue or grey sweaters	glowing colours
fitting	baggy, tight fitting
jumper with college logo	jumper with university logo

Anyone sporting a University of Oxford sweater has almost certainly not studied there. Someone who has will, if any, choose one bearing the logo of their college.

HANDKERCHIEFS

kept in pocket	kept in sleeve of jacket
breast pocket handkerchief	
no flowers or patterns	

GLOVES AND SCARVES

gloves to protect from cold or in sports	
leather, no knitted gloves	knitted gloves, often home-made
scarves to protect from cold	
	Paisley pattern

JEWELLERY AND WATCHES

discreet watches	ostentatious metal watches, especially gold ones
simple leather strap	metal strap
prefer thin watches	prefer thick watches
cufflinks: small, simple, unobtrusive	cufflinks: big, flashy, showy
no chain or medallion around neck	chain or medallion around neck
signet ring on little finger of left hand	signet ring with initials
plain wedding ring	rings with stones
no tie pin or tie clip	

In common with the place where one usually shops (see Chapter 21), shopping for clothes has its own class connotations. Where one makes one's purchases naturally depends on the quality required and the price one is willing and able to pay.

For men it is undoubtedly still considered smart to buy suits –
whether ready to wear or made to measure – in London's Savile Row,
Jermyn Street or Bond Street. Mail-order purchases are acceptable,
provided the source is right-on, e.g. Boden.

Women have a bit more freedom. If they absolutely have to have a
dress by Escada, then they must visit an Escada store. But it is equally
chic to make a find in non-label stores or discover a vintage piece in a
second-hand or charity shop. Showing off a bit with such purchases is
more socially acceptable than flaunting an expensive designer dress.
That would be stuck-up.

TERMINOLOGY

clothing, wardrobe, garments	outfit
Macintosh	raincoat
change coat	
evening dress (worn at home)	hostess gown
white tie, black tie	evening dress
morning dress	morning suit, morning coat, cutaway (American)
dinner jacket, black tie	dinner suit
tuxedo	tux
tweed jacket	sports jacket
boating jacket	blazer
(polo-neck) jersey	sweater, pullover, jumper, woolly
	ball gown, evening gown
dressing gown	bathrobe
underpants	pants
knickers	panties
gym shoes	plimsolls
gum boots	wellington boots, wellingtons, wellies
swimming costume	swimsuit
bag	handbag
cardigan	cardi

12

Greeting, Introduction, Addressing People

The aim of introduction is to conceal a person's identity.

George Mikes, *How to be an Alien* (1946)

My name is Sherlock Holmes. It is my business to know what other people do not know.

Arthur Conan Doyle, 'The Adventure of the
Blue Carbuncle' (1892)

Class distinctions associated with greeting, introducing and address-ing have, in common with many other features of class, become blurred but not vanished entirely. Like many social conventions, these practices have become less formal in recent decades. Naturally, someone who fails to use the correct form of introduction or address is no longer snubbed or turned away. But that is to miss the point. By getting these formalities wrong, they may be unable to unlock the invisible door to the social class they aspire to join. Forms of greet-ing, introduction and address are still among the codes by which members of the upper echelons identify one another, albeit with less weight. People who greet others with the words 'Hey mate' signal that they belong to a different class from those who proffer a 'How do you do?' Addressing someone with a 'sir' or 'love' is similarly revealing. More than just the phrases themselves, gestures too play a part: a high five is not the same as a handshake.

GREETING

On greeting someone, distinctions apply, depending whether you're meeting for the first time or have already met before, and of course on the level of trust implicit in the relationship.

First meeting: 'How do you do?' Answer: 'How do you do?' Both spoken as a statement, not a question.	'Hello/Hi' 'Nice/pleased to meet you'
Further meetings: 'How are you?' 'Very well, thank you!', 'I'm well'	'Fine, thanks' 'I'm good'
Look the person in the eye	Look away or down
Handshake at arm's length	Long handshake
	Clasping, forearm-patting, hug, back-pat, high five
Kiss on one or each cheek (woman to woman, man to woman) Touch cheek against cheek	air kiss

INTRODUCTION

George Mikes' observation applies only to introductions in a social context: invitations, parties, exhibitions, etc. The days when members of one and the same club would cross paths for decades without knowing each other's names have long gone. But slurring one's name to be sure it gets lost still seems to be very popular. And any additional information, such as what people do for a living, their title or where they live, is definitely not divulged in polite society. 'Peter, this is George Hamilton. George, this is Peter Johnson,' is the way to do it – even if George is a highly exotic and gifted painter and Peter the largely unknown commanding general of the British troops in the Falklands. At business meetings, on the other hand, stating one's name clearly makes sense and is essential. Usually one adds which institution one comes from, be it a company, university, public authority or law firm, and if this is not familiar, where the latter is based. Visiting cards are acceptable in a business context, but frowned upon at social gatherings.

In the upper classes self-introductions are very low-key. First name and surname suffice: 'I am George Hamilton.' Anything more is excessive. 'Hello, I'm John Smith' or 'Hi, I'm Bill. How are you?' are over the top. Academic ranks and qualification as a doctor or professor are overtly suppressed, as are aristocratic titles. Someone who introduces themselves in upper-class circles as Professor Famous or Doctor Clever has blown it (unless the latter is a physician on a house call). If you meet Sir Michael Caine, for example, he will announce himself simply as Michael Caine. A member of the nobility such as Lord Queensberry is just 'Queensberry'. It is perfectly acceptable for military officers, on the other hand, to introduce themselves as Captain Brown or General Battle.

If people who do not know each other are being introduced by a mutual acquaintance, the procedure is similarly to the point: 'Peter/ Mr Jones, may I introduce George Hamilton,' or 'Peter/Mr Jones, this is George Hamilton,' or an economical 'Peter Jones – George Hamilton'. Then again, eyebrows would be raised if the person being introduced were presented as 'CEO George Hamilton'.

The way peers are introduced by others differs from how they introduce themselves. The title of Sir or Lord is stated, and the appellation 'lord' is also used generically for marquesses, earls and viscounts, as well as barons. 'May I introduce Lord Queensberry and Lady Williams,' say those in the know. 'May I introduce the Marquess of Queensberry and the Baroness Williams,' flounder the unknowing. Here too military titles are accepted.

ADDRESSING PEOPLE

A whole host of books and websites offer advice on how to address people. Many variations are found. The level of formality varies by class, at least among adults who do not know each other. The older the person and the higher their class, the more formally they will address people, and vice versa. Young people make fewer distinctions.

Women workers circa 1940 taking their lunch break.

All dressed up in evening wear.

Couples at dinner, with the maid pouring the soup.

Supping wine in the living room.

Businessman reading a newspaper.

Eton College pupils cycling to their 'posts' during rifle-shooting practice. A parashooter's detachment to patrol Eton was formed and it includes 50 Eton College boys, all members of the Officer Training Corps and all aged 17.

Worker in the 1950s holding a wrench and looking delightedly at his paycheck.

Bank Holiday Cheese Rolling Festival. This annual tradition which is thought to date back to Roman times, draws competitors from far afield to race the cheese 200 yards down a near-vertical slope in pursuit of a seven-pound Double Gloucester cheese. Injuries are commonplace, and have forced the cancellation of the event in the past.

Spectators pose for a portrait at the Henley Royal Regatta in July 2019. An important part of the English social season, it is held annually over five days on the River Thames.

England captain Joe Root reacts during day five of the second Test Match between England and India at Lord's Cricket Ground in August 2021.

Participants in the Eton Wall Game ruck for the ball during the traditional St Andrew's Day match, November 1936.

Awaiting the arrival of Queen Elizabeth II at the Royal Enclosure at Royal Ascot in June 2002. The traditional annual horseracing event, attended by the Queen and other members of the Royal Family, is one of the highlights of the social season for Britain's upper classes.

Row of brick 1950s detached houses.

Filming of *Quadrophenia* in Brighton, based on the Mods and Rockers battles of the mid-1960s, starring Phil Daniels and with British rock group The Who providing the music.

'I look down on him because I am upper class…' (L-R) John Cleese, Ronnie Barker and Ronnie Corbett in the class sketch from the television series *The Frost Report*, in 1966.

The audience waves flags and sings along during the climax of the Last Night of The Proms at The Royal Albert Hall in London, on 8 September 2012.

The Prince of Wales refuses to give an autograph to local builder, Hedley Venning, during his visit to north Cornwall on 2 February 2005.

'Sir/Madam'	'love, my love, darling, dear(ie), sweetie, duck(ie), treacle, mate, hen, pet'
'old boy, old fellow, old chap'	'Mister, Man, Hey Man'
'Mr Hamilton'	'Mr George Hamilton'
Just 'Hamilton' is dying out	

Across all classes, calling someone by their first name is more common than it used to be. The working class and the aristocracy have always used first names widely, the latter helped by their small numbers and family ties. The middle classes, especially at the upper end, have tended more towards last names when addressing people of any class and any professional rank. Today the first-name basis is widespread in many areas of life, including the business world and academic circles. Some companies even use first names as a matter of policy, and a growing number of schools and universities recommend that teachers and students call each other by their first names.

This is not to everyone's liking. When Princess Anne addressed the former Prime Minister Tony Blair's wife as Mrs Blair, the response was, 'Oh, please call me Cherie.' The princess replied, 'I'd rather not. It's not the way I've been brought up' (also reported as, 'Actually, let's not go that way. Let's stick to Mrs Blair, shall we?'). If there is a class-based rule about being on first-name terms, it is perhaps that the upper classes are more hesitant than the lower classes to use first names with one another, and are more likely to prefer a last-name basis with members of other classes.

The correct way to address a peer, a baronet or a knight does not of course depend on the speaker's class. The relevant rules can be found in many publications. But in reality some substantial differences are apparent. Dukes and duchesses are addressed by some as 'Duke/Duchess' and by others as 'Your Grace'. Some people address all other peers under the single title of Lord or Lady, i.e. Lord/ Lady Queensbury. Others distinguish between titles: Marquess/ Marchioness of Queensbury, Earl/Countess of Shaftesbury, Viscount/ Viscountess Maugham, Baron/Baroness Gladwin. People who are less familiar with the peerage are more likely to use titles such as My Lord, or Lord Peter. Sir Michael Caine is 'Sir Michael' to some and 'Sir Caine' or 'Baronet Caine' to others.

When referring to peers (as opposed to addressing them), a baron is not called 'Baron X' but 'Lord X', as opposed to marquesses, earls and viscounts, who may be referred to as such or as lords. Hence 'The event was attended by Earl X/Lord X'. But 'The event was attended by Lord Y' (not 'Baron Y').

Addressing army officers by their military rank, on the other hand, is very common and welcomed by many, even after retirement. However, care should be taken to get it right. 'Captain Brown' and 'General Battle' are correct, but lieutenant-colonels should always be referred to as 'Colonel'. The rank of lieutenant is not used as a form of address. A lieutenant called Jones is always addressed as 'Mr Jones'.

13

What's in a Name?

Nomen est omen.

> Latin saying: literally, 'Name is fate.'

I then went to the Viceroy's Lodge and asked to see Lord Irwin (as he then was) without delay. I shook Lord Halifax (as he then was not yet) by the hand in the friendliest manner but spoke to him sternly: 'Mr Wood', I began (as he no longer was), 'I've just had a message from Mr Churchill' (as he then was) 'about Second Lieutenant Birch' (as he still is) etc., etc.

> George Mikes, *How to be Inimitable* (1960)

Don't worry. I have a niece called Smith.

> Queen Mary's answer when the Duchess of
> Devonshire apologized for her son Charles
> Cavendish marrying the dancer Adele Astaire in 1932

No-one can help their name, and so jumping to conclusions from someone's name about their class is extremely unreliable. But names can still provide an initial clue about class. Surnames are more of a hard class marker, because they are relatively unchangeable. These have already been discussed in Chapter 4.

First names are more revealing than surnames since they can convey the class of the parents who have chosen them. Beyond revealing something about the parents, the name a child is given can also foreshadow social status and therefore influence the infant's life path. In fact, many first names, such as Kevin and Tracy, have become the object of satire in recent years. Simple, old names are generally best. They give at least a connotation of neutrality, if not of being upper class.

MEN

Charles	Arnold
Edward	Callum
Frederick	Darren
Gerald	Gary
Henry	Gavin
Louis	Jayden
Michael	Kevin
Philip	Norman
Richard	Roy
Robert	Sidney
Rupert	Stanley
William	Terry

WOMEN

Anne	Chantelle
Camilla	Jessie
Caroline	Joyce
Catherine	Kayleigh
Deborah	Lesley
Diana	Michelle
Elizabeth	Molly
Fiona	Sharon
Victoria	Tracey

The first names of the lower classes tend to follow fashion much more than those favoured by the upper echelons. In the same way as the rings on a tree indicate when it was planted, some names can reveal the exact year in which someone was born. A more recent trend among those lower down the social scale is the giving of highly exotic or hyphenated Christian names. A stand-out example is Kayleigh and its many iterations that emerged in the years from 2010 onwards, including Demi-Leigh, Chelsea-Leigh, Tia-Leigh, Honey-Leigh, Kaydie-Leigh, Everleigh and Lilleigh: no fewer than 128 in total.[1]

The philosophy of names is not just imagined. According to an article in the *Daily Mail* in 2005, children with middle-class names were eight times more likely to pass their GCSEs than those with names like 'Wayne and Dwayne'. The travel firm Activities Abroad – which offers exotic adventure holidays in the high-priced bracket such as huskie safaris in the Canadian wilderness, Finnish log cabin holidays and that sort of thing – sent a promotional e-mail to the 24,000 people on its database quoting said article and wondering what sort of names were likely to be found on an Activities Abroad trip. The answer came in the form of two lists: one of names you were 'likely to encounter on Activities Abroad trips' and one of those you were not. Alice, Joseph and Charles featured on the first list, Britney, Chantelle and Dazza on the second. The firm concluded that they could legitimately promise 'chav-free activity holidays'. Not everyone was amused.[2] But the firm's increase in sales in the aftermath of the furore was a substantial 44 per cent, and the company management was unrepentant, pointing out that the middle classes did not need to apologize for being middle class or wishing to escape from chavs when on holiday.[3]

Not surprisingly, the class implications are again something no-one wants to talk about, and merely mentioning any link between names and social class is politically incorrect in the extreme. This was demonstrated by the appearance of the *Apprentice* star Katie Hopkins on 4 July 2013 on ITV's *This Morning*. 'I think you can tell a great deal from a name,' said Hopkins during a discussion about baby names.

For me, a name is a shortcut to finding out what class that child comes from and makes me ask: 'Do I want my children to play with them?' It's the Tylers, the Charmaines, the Chantelles, the

Chardonnays. There's a whole set of things that go with children like that, quite a disruptive influence in school.

The normally unflappable presenter Holly Willoughby was visibly shocked: 'That's terrible! Listen to what you are saying!' Hopkins continued, 'I tend to think that children who have intelligent names tend to have fairly intelligent parents, and they make much better playmates for my children.' The author Anna May Mangan, also a guest on the programme, took Hopkins on: 'I can't believe that you're such an insufferable snob. Working-class children are doing incredibly well at school. For you to categorize them by their names – which they didn't even choose – is cruel, snooty, unkind and so old-fashioned.' Before a smiling Hopkins could respond, an increasingly irate Willoughby cut her short saying, 'Oh, stop. Stop right there.' 'You know', Hopkins also confided to the presenters, 'parents often come up to me in the playground and say, "I read your article about class and children's names and . . . [whispers] I wouldn't say it, but that's what I do too."' Willoughby, her fellow presenter Phillip Schofield and Mangan all shook their heads vigorously, obviously dismissing Hopkins's suggestion that parents were so class-ridden.[4]

Within two days of being broadcast, the programme had attracted three million hits on YouTube and caused a storm of outrage on social media, a sure sign that Hopkins had touched a nerve. Any opinion expressed in the media may be the truth, but it can also be a lie, because in public many people say not what they think, but what they believe people want to hear. How otherwise can the lack of outcry over the many books written about which names are upper- and lower-class and the impact of their moniker on those concerned be explained? Harry Wallop takes a large number of first names (many more than those listed above) and assigns them to the different social classes, quoting from the Acorn database:

Statistically if you are a Crispian, Greville, Lysbeth or Penelope you are about 200 times more likely to be in the 'wealthy executive' top class than in the 'inner-city adversity' bottom one. Seaneen,

Terriann, Sammy-Jo, Jamielee, Kayleigh and Codie are the six names most disproportionately skewed towards the 'struggling families' category, a group of people Acorn works out as most likely to live in a social rented accommodation, work in a routine occupation, read the *Sun* newspaper and play bingo.[5]

And William Hanson writes:

> If you want your child to be accepted into the higher social circles, then think carefully about what to name him or her ... It's always a good idea to check the Office for National Statistics for the current year's rankings of most popular baby names before branding the benighted child for life. Avoid anything in the top ten, and arguably in the top 100. Name him Harry or George or her Amelia or Grace in the next couple of years, and the chances are that he/she will be among six or seven similarly named in the same classroom, office, dinner party, whatever for the rest of their lives. For the same reason avoid calling him Hugo, Sonny, Seth, Elliott, Theodore, Rory or Ellis; or her Mollie, Ivy, Darcey, Tilly, Florence or Violet.[6]

There is no evidence of any backlash similar to that triggered by Katie Hopkins. This is probably because reading is done in private, and no Englishman is likely to be taken aback, far less outraged by passages like these, because they are simply confirming what is common knowledge. English politicians know it too. Darren Jones, a new Labour MP, said after the 2017 election that he was proud to be the first politician called Darren ever elected to Parliament. The *Spectator* seized the opportunity to list other MPs whose first names 'have been subject to snobbish derision from some quarters', such as Gary, Gavin, Keith, Kevin, Lee, Michelle, Sharon and Tracey.[7]

Names are also the subject of class denial, especially by the upper classes. A famous case in point was Anthony Wedgwood Benn who, after the death of his father, became Viscount Stansgate. Not only did he renounce the title (after a long legal battle), but he shortened his name to Tony Benn and further to just Tony when talking to voters. Less often mentioned but in the same vein is Tony Blair who, when standing for the first time as an MP in a 1982 by-election, was still known as Anthony Blair. From 1983 on he stuck to Tony. Politicians do this to enhance their popularity and look less aloof.

It is difficult to 'upgrade' one's name, except perhaps through marriage or by hyphenation with another surname to make it double-barrelled. Pronouncing one's name in a foreign or exotic manner, as did Hyacinth Bucket in the 1990s TV series *Keeping Up Appearances* by insisting her surname was pronounced 'Bouquet', risks being lampooned. A title or gong on the other hand (see Chapter 4) gives a name additional refinement.

NICKNAMES

> *Nobody ever makes up nicknames. A nickname is your*
> *real identity, jumping out from behind you like an afreet.*

> Robert Robinson

Nicknames are very common in England, particularly in the upper echelons of society, and they have an important class function. We are not speaking about widely-known nicknames that mainly comprise short forms or names derived from someone's proper name, which can be found on the internet under 'common nicknames'. The class function of nicknames lies in their ability to exclude outsiders, as Julian Fellowes makes clear:

> I have always been uncomfortable with the *jejune* pseudo-informality implicit in the upper-class passion for nicknames. Everyone is 'Toffee' or 'Bobo' or 'Snook'. They themselves think the names imply a kind of playfulness, an eternal childhood, fragrant with memories of Nanny and pyjamas warming by the nursery fire, but they are really a simple reaffirmation of insularity, a reminder of shared history that excludes more recent arrivals, yet another way of publicly displaying their intimacy with each other. Certainly

the nicknames form an effective fence. A newcomer is often in the position of knowing someone too well to continue to call them Lady So-and-So but not nearly well enough to call them 'Sausage', while to use their actual Christian name is a sure sign within their circle that one doesn't really know them at all. And so the new arrival is forced back from the normal development of friendly intimacy that is customary among acquaintances in other classes.[8]

When it comes to nicknames, just about anything goes, including among the highest social orders. The Duke of Edinburgh's pet name for the Queen was said to be 'Cabbage'. Peregrine, 12th Duke of Devonshire even signs himself 'Stoker Devonshire', using his life-long sobriquet. Louis, Earl Mountbatten of Burma was always known simply as 'Dickie', an appellation unhinted at by his other given names (Francis Albert Victor Nicholas). Many families don't stop at one, but give members several nicknames and as a result become positively famous. Take Deborah, Duchess of Devonshire, née Mitford (a sister of Nancy, the author of *Noblesse Oblige*). She was variously referred to by her sisters and parents as Debo or Hen or Swiny or Nine (supposing she would never mature beyond that age) or Miss or Stubby (after her short, fat legs, which could not keep up).[9] However, here too there are limits: Sharkie, Fastfingers, Snakeyes, Dollface, Jailbird and others of that ilk are not recommended.

14

Accent and Pronunciation

Accent is the snake and the ladder in the upstairs down-stairs of social ambition.

> Melvyn Bragg, *The Adventure of English* (2003)

As soon as a man opens his mouth, we can tell in what sort of school he missed his education.

> George Mikes, *How to be Decadent* (1977)

You called me an attack dog because I've got a Glasgow accent.

> Labour politician John Reid to Jeremy
> Paxman on *Newsnight* (2005)

Ability must be the test, and ability is not to be measured by upper-class accents.

> Harold Wilson, *The New Britain:*
> *Labour's Plan* (1964)

I have a languid upper-class voice.

> Ferdinand Mount, *Mind the Gap* (2004)

The English working class, as Mr Wyndham Lewis has put it, are 'branded on the tongue'.

> George Orwell, *The English People* (1947)

These quotations highlight the central importance of accent and pronunciation. Little is revealed about this key social marker when people are introduced. The moment of truth comes thereafter, but by then the die is cast. Particular accents no longer engender hatred and contempt. However, they immediately brand the speaker. They pinpoint the region of England they come from: 'Good morning' is enough to distinguish a native of Sunderland from a Geordie living 12 miles away. Secondly, they define the speaker's class. It is why no English person has any difficulty associating a particular accent with the upper class or the working class. As a class marker, pronunciation ranks above language usage. Whereas learning the terminology of a different class is achievable (although difficult), shaking off the accent acquired as a child and assimilating that of another societal group as an adult is very hard indeed. This makes pronunciation more reliable than terminology as an indicator of class.

However, as a touchstone of class, pronunciation is slippery. As with taste, different isn't necessarily wrong, as the famous Latin maxim *De gustibus non est disputandum* reminds us. Pronunciation changes faster than vocabulary and idioms, be it from one generation or one person to the next, or within the same individual. We are inclined to assume that the pronunciation we learn in childhood will stay with us and serve us well for our entire lives. Far from it: the Queen speaks quite differently and much more 'normally' today than when she acceded to the throne. And the accent of younger members of the royal family, including Prince William and Prince Harry, is different again. Hardly anyone would understand Queen Elizabeth I today. What was considered impeccable English in 1800 would have likely been the exact opposite one-and-a-half centuries later and vice versa.[1] Queen Victoria did not consider her own English to be particularly refined, but always thought herself dowdy in comparison with haughty Whigs. One precept that has not altered, however, is that pronunciation maketh class.

GENERAL

'General' is perhaps not the best heading for this section, since all manners of speaking are evident across all classes. The Queen's cut-glass accent, for example, is very different from the mutter-and-mumble style for which her pre-predecessor Edward VIII was well known. He is even said to have had slight traces of cockney in his accent and to have spoken 'mid-Atlantic'.

Upper-class speakers do not use regional accents, except (possibly) to poke fun at them. They naturally use a form of received pronunciation (RP), formerly sometimes also called BBC English, which, however, is not homogeneous. The Queen's accent, clear though it is, is no longer typical of most types of RP. Her tendency to use a long vowel in words like *lost* and *gone*, which sound like 'lawst', 'gawn', marks her out as no longer a mainstream RP speaker. Colloquial non-U terms to describe upper-class speakers are: *cut-glass accent* (also applicable to middle-class speakers), *mumble and mutter*, reflecting the tendency of some speakers to enunciate less clearly in an attempt to sound modest and self-effacing, and *speaking quietly, in measured tones*, the more positive side of the phenomenon. Colloquial U terms to describe non-U accents are: *a thick accent*, or simply *has an accent*.

VOWELS AND CONSONANTS

A typical feature of upper-class usage is to pronounce unstressed vowels even less clearly than is otherwise the norm, and in some cases to omit them entirely. With words like *history* or *secretary*, upper-class speakers would normally drop the second and third syllables respectively, pronouncing them as *hist'ry, secret'ry*. *Corduroy* becomes *cord'roy* and *happenstance* becomes *happ'nst'nce*. During a philosophy course in Oxford it took me several repetitions to realize *ph'los'phy* meant *philosophy*. Where the unstressed syllable is retained, such users prefer the schwa, i.e. the mumbled vowel [ə], as in the second syllable of *father*, to a pronunciation with a full vowel or diphthong. Thus the word *magistrate* upper-class speakers would pronounce to rhyme with *candidate*, not with *allocate*. The latter pronunciation is more characteristic of working-class but also of some middle-class speakers.

Dropping your aitches, i.e. not pronouncing the letter h where it would be spoken in RP, is a typical shibboleth which marks off a non-standard speaker, and is thus common among working-class speakers in most parts of England from London to Manchester and Leeds. Because it is such a prominent feature, dropping your aitches is eschewed by the middle class, which caused George Orwell in *The Road to Wigan Pier* to quip,

> And then perhaps this misery of class-prejudice will fade away, and we of the sinking middle class . . . may sink without further troubles into the working class where we belong, and probably when we get there it will not be so dreadful as we feared, for, after all, we have nothing to lose but our aitches.

So in most cases a pronunciation like *'undred* for *hundred,* or *'orse* for *horse,* marks the speaker at once as working-class.

A second shibboleth is the use of the glottal stop in words like *bit, better, butter,* where the 't' is replaced by a glottal stop, i.e. a very short pause in articulation, as in *a bi' of be'er bu'er.* However, unbeknown to most RP speakers, they too use the glottal stop in lieu of 't' before a consonant, e.g. in *that man,* and there is evidence that the use of the glottal stop is spreading among RP users even before a vowel, as in *that evening.*

London working-class speech (cockney) has had a big impact on the English of the South-East. Examples of this are pronunciations like *Dive* for *Dave, trine* for *train,* but also *town* for *tone, loud* for *load.* Similarly, the final l is vocalized, i.e. turned into a vowel similar to 'oo' in *till, well.* In traditional cockney 'th' is often replaced by 'v' or 'f', e.g. *Fings ain't what they used to be.* Likewise *bruvver* for *brother* and *bovver* for *bother.* Cockney has also influenced the rise of Estuary English, a compromise between cockney and RP which shares some features of cockney like the vocalization of 'l', but avoids the replacement of 'th' by 'f' or 'v'. As a compromise variety Estuary English has the advantage of being more acceptable than cockney but avoids the extremes of upper-class usage – not many people want to sound like Jacob Rees-Mogg.

Away from the South-East, working-class speech in the North and Midlands is also a marker of regional identity, a typical feature being the pronunciation of 'u' (and 'o' in some words), e.g. *mud* rhymes with *could* or *good*, similarly the 'o' in *other* or *money*.

MISCELLANEOUS WORDS

In words where the traditional pronunciation diverges markedly from the spelling, speakers from higher social classes tend to prefer the traditional pronunciation, while working-class or middle-class speakers normally use 'spelling pronunciation', i.e. a pronunciation remodelled to fit the spelling, e.g. *forehead* (traditional *forrid*, spelling pronunciation *fore-head*, where *fore* rhymes with *more*) and *waistcoat* (traditional *weskit*, spelling pronunciation *waist-coat*). Similarly *scone* (traditional *scon*, spelling pronunciation *scoan*). The name of the letter 'h', *aitch*, is pronounced *haitch* by some working-class speakers, no doubt aware of the perils of 'dropping your aitches'. In Northern Ireland this is also a shibboleth between Protestants and Catholics, with the former using *aitch*, the latter *haitch*.

In words which traditionally had 's', 'd', or 't' followed by a 'yoo' sound, higher social classes aspire to the original more careful pronunciation, whereas lower social classes are less inhibited, e.g. *issue* (traditional: *iss-yoo*, non-traditional *ish-oo*), similarly *tissue*, and *media* (traditional: *meed-iya*, non-traditional: *mee-jer*), *tuition* (traditional: *tew-ish-on*, non-traditional: *chew-ish-on*). A rather different case is *schedule*, where the question is whether it should be pronounced as in German, i.e. as 'sh', or in Italian, i.e. as 'sk'. The traditional British pronunciation is 'sh', preferred by higher social classes and older people, while lower social classes and younger people opt for the 'sk' pronunciation, which is also the norm in American English.

In French words ending in -et or -é there is a tendency in higher social classes to pronounce the ending more carefully as '-ay', whereas in lower social classes the diphthong is weakened to a short 'i'.

Examples of this are: *ballet* (more careful: *ballay*, weakened to: *bally*). Similarly *buffet, croquet, fiancé(e), café* (in very informal working-class speech reduced even further to *caff*). In *garage*, originally a loanword from French, some people in higher social classes affect a more French-like pronunciation, viz. *gur-rahzh* (with stress on the final syllable), with working-class speakers opting for a more English pronunciation, i.e. *garridge* (cf. *carriage, marriage*), which can also be heard in upper-class usage.

STRESS

There seems to be a tendency among higher-class speakers to stress the first syllable of polysyllabic words where other speakers stress the second syllable, e.g. *cóntroversy* as opposed to *contróversy*. Other examples are *amicable, coronary, exquisite, formidable, hospitable, lamentable, preferable, primarily*. Similarly *ínteresting* (normally *ínt'resting*, but some working-class speakers stress the third syllable, i.e. *interésting*) and *témporarily* (stressed on the third syllable by some speakers: *temporárily*).

PLACE NAMES

Many British place names are irregular in their pronunciation, because their pronunciation has changed, while the spelling still reflects an earlier pronunciation, e.g. Derby is pronounced *Darby*. Although some regional speakers may pronounce this *Dur-by*, thanks to the well-known horse race the majority of all social classes will say *Darby*. Knowledge of the standard pronunciation is the norm among higher social classes, but not necessarily in lower social classes, especially if the place is small and less well-known. Some examples:

Beauchamps *Beecham*, Beaulieu *Bewly*, Belvoir *Beaver*, Greenwich *Grénnidge* or *Grénnitch*, Harwich *Harridge*, Hertfordshire *Hart-ferd-sher* (the older pronunciation without 't' is dying out), Holborn *Hoe-burn*, Norwich *Norridge* or *Norritch*.

Magdalen College (Oxford), Magdalene College (Cambridge), both *Maudlin*, although some sources claim that the Cambridge college is pronounced *Mag-da-leen*.

ENGLAND: A CLASS OF ITS OWN

PEOPLE'S NAMES

There are virtually no rights or wrongs. All you can go on is what people say themselves. An example well-known is that of the brothers Charles and Jonathan Powell. The former was Margaret Thatcher's foreign policy adviser, the latter Tony Blair's chief of staff. Charles rhymes his surname with *toll*, Jonathan with *towel*.

The pronunciation of people's names is essentially without class connotations. Either you know it or you don't. However, that knowledge may have class-specific overtones in certain cases, insofar as getting it right reveals a familiarity with the people concerned and their social set. Speaking the name Cholmondely correctly with ease suggests an at least hypothetical connection with the aristocratic world. Someone who reels off a cockney name that an uninitiated compatriot would struggle with based on how it is written demonstrates a close association with working-class Londoners. A few examples: Buccleuch *Bucklóo*, Cholmondely *Chumly*, Colquhoun *Cahóon*, Fiennes *Fines*, Home *Hume* (former prime minister Alex Douglas Home), St Clair *Sínclair*, St John *Sinjen*, Wemyss *Weems*.

WHICH ACCENT IS BEST?

Where does all of the foregoing fit alongside BBC English, Oxford English and educated English? Well, first of all, although very closely related, these are not the same. For the majority of the population BBC English is just as posh as U-English. The upper classes have sometimes had their doubts about BBC English and Oxford English. The Oxford accent smacked of intellectuality, and intellectual achievements were seen as slightly suspicious. With the need to earn a living this has of course changed, and a good Oxford accent is more of an asset than a liability. It would however be a mistake to imitate an Oxford accent. That would be a deadly sin, in particular if a trace of cockney or some other non-U pronunciation were to seep through. Dishonest U is much worse than honest non-U.

The importance of having the 'right' accent has declined. Young people with a working-class accent who in the past would have been likely to acquire a BBC accent in order to pass themselves off as middle-class no longer feel the need to do so. Having a regional twang, be it Yorkshire, Geordie (Tyneside), Scouse (Liverpool), Brummie (Birmingham), West Country or cockney (London), is no longer a source of shame and certainly not a terminal affliction. On the contrary, it is frequently perceived as genial, original, distinctive and gritty, and regional dialects are experiencing a revival in the national media and in television in particular.[2] RP coexists alongside a rich variety of regional accents. However, without a command of BBC English as well, the exclusive dialect specialist is not particularly prized. The kudos in class terms goes to those who master both. A. H. Halsey, who was born in Kentish Town, north London, 'learned two languages in order to survive the day in a grammar school and the evening in the village street'.[3]

In and around London, Estuary English and multicultural London English have sprung up. Estuary English is Standard English with features of cockney and working-class London speech with its trademark glottal stop. It is spoken in the south-east of England, especially along the River Thames and its estuary, particularly among the young. By and large, it is neutral in class terms. Multicultural London English is a hybrid dialect spoken by many young working-class people, comprising elements of Caribbean, South Asian, African and American speech patterns and vocabulary.

Unsurprisingly, class denial and attempts to disguise one's class are again in evidence here. Given the general tendency to play down one's class (see Chapter 7), those bred with an upper-class accent tend to deny their mode of speech and copy how the other classes talk. In their search for street credibility and to appear cool, they affect an Estuary or working-class accent and use associated words. The result is often derisively called mockney. The following dialogue from Peter York and Olivia Stewart-Liberty provides an illustration:

Said	Meaning
A: Yo Blud! Exeat this kend?	Hello, my friend. Are you going home for the weekend?
B: Londres innit.	Yes. to London.
A: Same!	I'm also in London for the weekend.
A: Safe! Let's hook up tomoz. Anyone for the KR?	Excellent, let's meet tomorrow. Does the Kings Road suit?
B: Wicks!	Great idea.
A: Later's bruv!	Goodbye, my friend.
B: Later's!	Goodbye.[4]

This is by no means a new phenomenon. Alan Ross reports that U-speakers (particularly young ones) were rather addicted to slang, at least up to 1914.[5] Alan Coren describes the upper-crust scions thus: 'They stood before mirrors abbreviating their drawls and lopping their aitches.'[6] Jilly Cooper describes how, in the 1960s, working-class became beautiful and everyone from Princess Anne downwards spat the plums out of their mouths, embraced the flat 'a' and talked with a working-class accent.[7] One girl had elocution lessons to try and get her accent made less patrician so she would be accepted at demonstrations.[8] This stance was also spotted 40 years ago by Richard Buckle, who coined the term double-U.[9] The trend seems to have been growing in the last two decades in the quest to put equality first. Ferdinand Mount wrote in 2005 that young people of the middle classes had never been keener to imitate the accent of their lower-class peers.[10] Tony Blair was said to have adopted some features of Estuary English to sound more ordinary and more appealing to Joe Public. Language courses are available on 'How to de-posh your accent'. Even *The Times*, under the heading 'Voice coaches in demand to rub polish off posh accents,' reported that business was booming for companies coaching upper-middles from sheltered backgrounds to sound more 'with the people' and to lose the blah in their voices.[11]

More difficult to explain is the so-called Oxford stutter or stammer. Although not encountered quite so often these days, it still exists. Popular exemplars include the actor Hugh Grant in the film *Four Weddings and a Funeral* (1994) and the Prime Minister, Boris Johnson. This has nothing to do with the natural stutter, a medical disorder which can fortunately be successfully treated nowadays and is consequently encountered less and less. The Oxford stutter is peculiar to people who have studied in the city of that name (or at Cambridge); they do not have any speech impediment and are able to speak stammer-free. Their stutter is intentional: instead of saying 'I wonder,' they say 'I – I – I – wonder' or 'p – p – please'. They continue to cultivate this verbal stumbling until it becomes their natural diction. Why? I most like the theory that the graduates of Oxford and Cambridge, all too aware of their intellectual superiority, wish to appear more human. By seeming to lack confidence by the way they speak, they make the person they are talking to feel reassured that they are not quite perfect after all, and therefore feel more at ease themselves. The Oxford stammer is meant to endear a snob to the average person.

We are not talking here of those who, in the words of John, Duke of Bedford, practise anti-sour-grape snobbery. These are people who speak with a naturally acquired Oxford accent but complain of their 'awful' voice and express their desire to get rid of it. What they are trying to say is: 'Half of humanity is dying to speak the way I am actually speaking, but look at me – I do not even attach any importance to such ornaments.'[12]

Others try to 'improve' their pronunciation. This is extremely difficult, since it involves losing the accent one has had and replacing it with a new one. Some people are particularly good at acquiring a different, especially an upper-class, accent. The Welsh seem to have a talent for it – think of Richard Burton or Roy Jenkins. It is dangerous for your class affinity if you don't entirely succeed. Prime ministers Ted Heath and Margaret Thatcher had elocution lessons. When they appeared on television the whole country waited for their first slip. Celebrities such as David Beckham and his wife Victoria have changed their way of speaking to tone down their cockney and Essex roots. That so many people are sent to elocution lessons by their partners and bosses or do it on their own initiative is a clear indication that pronunciation counts when it comes to class.

Admittedly, these modifications to speech can be short-lived. The upper-class speaker who adopts non-U English at university reverts to U-English in the family setting (unless still an aspiring revolutionary, of course), and someone who has previously spoken with a working-class accent, but has learned U-English, slips into their original accent again when back home. Linguists have coined the term code-switching for it. But most know only too well that they are only pretending. As Nicholas Monson wrote:

> As I was mixing with 'real' people I . . . affected an accent that owed its origins to Cilla Black, California and the East End of London. I was uncomfortable with this voice, so I said little but nodded vigorously and tried to look tough. We also sneered at a certain lecturer who . . . talked posh. It was at such an airing of bigotry that I realized to my acute embarrassment that I was guilty of the same crime as before. I was a snob.[13]

This is often called 'inverted snobbery'. It is highly questionable whether those who cast off their original mode of speech are always completely happy with their new idiom. Some feel they are betraying their roots and paying what is possibly too high a price for their 'promotion' in job and society.

15

Vocabulary and Language

All choice of words is slang. It marks a class.

George Eliot, *Middlemarch* (1871)

The next class determinant after pronunciation is vocabulary – which words do people use? It can even lead to radical rejection of a person if they use what the upper class see as one of the 'seven deadly sins':

pardon instead of *what* or *sorry*,
toilet instead of *loo* or *lavatory*,
lounge instead of *drawing room* or *sitting room*,
settee instead of *sofa*,
dinner meaning the midday meal, which in their view should be
    called *lunch*,
serviette instead of *napkin*,
sweet, *afters* or *dessert* instead of *pudding*

as vividly described by Kate Fox.[1] Using these words in the presence of the higher classes will at once unmask an Englishman as 'not like one'.

Countless lists exist of words that are 'right' and 'wrong'. Many have always been deemed unsuitable or have become so, while others have remained above reproach. Every day new trends emerge as words enter and exit fashion. They differ between young and old, whether influenced by Americanisms or not, and of course according to the region of England concerned. The English language has always been subject to a relatively high level of flux, and the pace of change has quickened in recent years with the rise of English as a world language that is spoken by more people as a second language than as their mother tongue. This applies not only to pronunciation but also, and perhaps to an even greater degree, to terminology. This development is documented by the entries in the *Oxford English Dictionary* (*OED*) and many literary works about the English language.[2] As the language in general has evolved, so the elements of English signifying class have changed. With each passing generation, traditional, upper-class language has absorbed more words found in common usage or terms that had previously been regarded as non-U, and these have become so established that any disapproval at their utterance would meet with blank looks. Examples include such expressions as cinema, weekend, mirror, glasses, radio, ice cream and photo. The assimilated words are incorporated with their intrinsic meaning and without being understood as 'foreign', rather than as an exercise in appearing in touch with ordinary people by adopting working-class vocabulary that peers might shun or use only ironically or as an in-joke. Nevertheless, do not be fooled into thinking that 'anything goes'. Many words still signal the social status of the person who says them.

What we are talking about here are sociolects or social class dialects, an area of study in sociolinguistics.[3] Unlike dialects, which are defined as the language habits of the population in a certain geographical region (e.g. a county), sociolects are understood to be variants of language used by socially defined speech communities, e.g. members of an occupation, ethnic group or age group, students in general or those attending a particular university or school. They can be specific to individual families or even, at their most extreme, to siblings: one thinks of the private language of the Mitford sisters. These speech groups also include the social classes.

To avoid any misapprehensions, it should be stressed that the left and right columns in the following list are definitely not intended as a simple juxtaposition of U versus non-U or upper-class versus working-class, far less of right versus wrong. Many in the right-hand column would hardly ever be used by members of the working class, while many of those on the left belong to their everyday speech. It would therefore be wrong to interpret the list as meaning that 'sweat' is an upper-class word and 'perspire' a lower-class one. Indeed, both say 'sweat', while the alternative 'perspire' is more widely favoured by some sections of the middle class. Exclusivity is not a feature of language usage in the social classes since they all employ one another's words. However, there are clearly certain expressions that are used with greater frequency or infrequency by each class, which applies its 'own' words rather than those preferred by others in line with typical recurrence patterns. The left-hand column thus contains language familiar to every Englishman, and that he may well also himself use, but encountered statistically more frequently among the upper and upper-middle strata, while the terms on the right occur markedly less often in upper-echelon parlance. The list is not restricted to modern phraseology but also records developments in usage since the 1950s. It is in no particular order but simply random. It stems from the above-mentioned sources (Chapter 9) and my own observations.

GENERAL VOCABULARY

What? Sorry? What did you say?	Pardon? I beg your pardon? Come again?
smart, upmarket, posh (ironically)	posh, classy
county (adjective)	
naff	
thank you	thanks, ta
goodbye	bye-bye, ta-ta
photographs	photos
anyhow	anyway
antique/old	vintage
repartee	banter
frightfully	terribly

she is a nice woman, she is a nice girl	she is a nice lady
he is a nice man	he is a proper gentleman
one (ironic)	I
my husband and I	my husband and me
university	uni
to read law	to study law
knave (at cards)	jack
mad	mental
Navy	Royal Navy
rude	smutty
cheeky	risqué
hurrah	hooray
pleasant	enjoyable (meaning pleasant)
gym (gymnastics)	P.E. (physical exercise)
notecase	wallet
takeaway	carry-out, Deliveroo
schoolmaster, mistress	teacher
frightened	frit
Friday/Saturday to Monday	weekend
I'm English, Scottish, Welsh	I'm British
beaker	mug
Mothering Sunday	Mother's Day
Shrove Tuesday	Pancake Day
of good family	well connected
U accent	Oxford accent
quite well now	are you quite better now?
wash up	do the dishes
I'm just going to give them to you	(cigarettes) coming up
John is attracted to the au pair girl	John fancies the au pair
very stupid	dead stupid
cold	a bit parky

bad	chronic
well done	very crafty
conceited	big-headed
half past two	half two
yes	that's right, that's the idea
I didn't hear you	I didn't (quite) catch that
leave it to me	leave it with me
help yourself	be my guest
I don't know	I wouldn't know
I was ashamed	was my face red?
exactly right	bang on
sunglasses	sunnies
I understand	I follow you
pleased with oneself	chuffed
I'll hit you	I'll thump you
I'll beat you up	I'll do you
bad smell	pong
to sell	to flog
uninterested	disinterested
to imply	to infer
bum bag	fanny bag (originally AmE)
he is good at arithmetic	he is good at figures
strata (plural)	strata (used as a singular)
girl	young woman
lover	partner
off sick	on the sick
I hope	hopefully (meaning I hope)
scurf	dandruff
ring me, call me	give me a tinkle, give me a bell
good	perfect
I don't know	I couldn't say
woman	lady

writing paper	notepaper
snobbish	toffee-nosed, cliquey
peerage	titled people
Royalties	Royals
Scotch	Scottish
to telephone, call	to phone, ring up
he said 'Let's go!'	he was like, 'Let's go!'
film	movie (originally AmE)
party	affair, do, function, shindig
public school, independent school	private school
great	awesome
sweet	charming
attractive	cute
the police	the law
maître d'hôtel	maître D (pronounced Dee)
really or very	real (a real good time)
to have a bath	to take a bath
wine merchant's	off licence, liquor store
paper handkerchief	tissue, Kleenex
do you understand me?	do you get me?
to go down to the country	to go to the country
to go up to London	to go to London, down to London, into town
male (animal)	fella (meaning male animal)
isn't it?	innit?
could I have?	can I get?
red (hair)	auburn (hair), copper (hair), red top
scent, fragrance	perfume, pong
the general	the general public
invitation	invite
(wedding) ring	rocks
hit (in war)	wounded (in war)

influenza	flu
constipating	very binding
sick (after drink)	ill (after drink)
I was sick on the boat (vomit)	I was ill on the boat
I was ill (in bed)	I was sick (in bed)
ill	has he been taken bad?
hurt (to)	pain (to)
rich, well off	wealthy, high net worth, people in the money, moneyed class
expensive, dear	costly
broke	skint
rich, upper-class	exclusive, select
rise (of pay)	raise (of pay) (originally AmE)
money	folding stuff, lolly, brass
unique	very unique

Saying 'like' or 'sort of' or 'you know' several times per sentence is not cultivated English.

POSH OR ARCHAIC?

There are words and phrases that lead a twilight existence. Some have virtually died out, dinosaurs of the *OED*. Others cling desperately to life, perhaps in tiny niches, but with the resilience of hermits in the desert. Many are relics of the basic vocabulary of the aristocracy, the gentry, the cultivated rich, public schools, Oxbridge, the old boy network and intellectual circles such as the Bloomsbury Group. For them, the endangered vocabulary has always been simply an every-day tool, like using a knife and fork to eat, and nothing to do with class. Examples include the language used by Bertie Wooster and his servant Jeeves ('a gentleman's gentleman') in the P. G. Wodehouse novels, or by characters in the Malory Towers series by Enid Blyton. Many, perhaps most, of these words and phrases are today seen as old-fashioned, outdated, posh or arrogant. Politicians and populists avoid them, and people who do use them – in many cases non-native speakers of English, it seems – are likely to be accused of being ironic or simply trying to sound posh. There may be some truth to this, but these linguistic 'relics' are in fact still very much alive and kicking. Some people do still call each other old bean, old chap, old boy, old chum or old fruit, with no irony at all.

said	meaning
to dash off	to leave quickly
spiffing	fantastic, excellent
splendid	excellent, brilliant
capital	fantastic
bish-bash-bosh	something completed quickly and well
ghastly	frightful, unpleasant
divine	splendid
that is most unsporting	not fair
simply (marvellous, dashing, livid)	used for emphasis (cf. absolutely)
pip pip, cheerio	goodbye
to fag	to work hard, chore, toil
jolly hockey sticks	describing humorously a hearty, sporty, gung-ho public schoolgirl
dash it!	damn!
good egg	agreeable, trustworthy person
rather!	I strongly agree, yes indeed
poppycock!	nonsense, rubbish
loathe	to hate
faux pas	mistake
blub	to cry
what ho?	hello (greeting)
I say	listen! or I'm surprised
good/bad show	good/bad thing
bottoms up!	finish your drink, down the hatch
marvellous	awesome, outstanding
jolly good/bad	very good/bad

bate (mood)	angry, in a bad mood
tight	drunk
blotto	very drunk
gigs	glasses, spectacles
bind	problem, fix, jam
ass	fool
brick	reliable, trustworthy person
to shriek	to scream
bore (a crashing bore)	boring person
ravishing	extremely beautiful, gorgeous
yonks (it's been yonks since . . .)	ages
a good sport	fair loser, co-operative person
beastly	nasty, unpleasant, horrible
righto, right-ho	OK, I agree
bally good (bally good coffee)	very, bloody
just the ticket	exactly what I need, the right thing
to put some welly into	to put effort, power into
bad form	questionable or offbeat behaviour
skive	be lazy, bunk off
(feel) seedy	(feel) unwell, ill, suspicious
thrilling	extremely exciting
pish tosh!	bullshit
terribly (terribly good)	extremely
absurd	silly, ridiculous
utterly	completely, totally
sups	dinner, supper with friends

Given the popularity of cricket, it comes as no surprise that many cricketing terms have entered the general vocabulary with a literal or figurative meaning. As cricket has traditionally been played most widely among the upper classes, this is where most cricket-based expressions are still found today. Some are now seen as slightly old-fashioned.

ENGLAND: A CLASS OF ITS OWN

said	meaning
to play (with) a straight bat	to behave honestly and decently *or* avoid giving a direct answer to a question
it's (just) not cricket	that's not fair, not done, not acceptable
to have a good innings	to live a long and good life
on a sticky wicket	in a tricky situation
I'm bowled over	I'm overwhelmed or surprised
I was hit for six	I was overwhelmingly surprised, shocked
rolled the pitch	cleared the way

A striking number of words considered to be outdated or posh are found in expressions of surprise, amazement, delight or shock.

said	meaning
hey do	disappointed or surprised
by Jove!	exclamation of surprise
golly, gosh, golly gosh!	signal of surprise
blimey!	wow!
good grief/gravy!	expression of surprise or shock

Oxford colleges dispense with the college tag.

New	New College
Merton	Merton College
Magdalen	Magdalen College
The House, or Christ	Christ Church College

BAD LANGUAGE

Swearing and the use of obscenities are heavily class-laden.[4] Historically we have seen similarities between the upper and working classes in terms of other soft class markers too that distinguish them from the middle class. The English working class has always been famous for its rich repertoire of obscenities and swear words that will forever remain unfathomable for foreigners and which, even for Englishmen, sometimes rely more on delivery than on concrete meaning. Likewise, the upper classes, and the aristocracy in particular, are far from averse to a vulgar turn of phrase,[5] although they may be coy about using such language within earshot, reserving it more for private conversations among friends. 'Swearing was simultaneously the vice of princes and of prostitutes, kings and kitchen maids.'[6] It was the middle classes, in their endeavour to set themselves apart from the working class, that labelled various words offensive, such as bloody, ass, bugger, bitch, damned, shit, fucking, piss. Use them, and a gentleman could lose his status and cease to be recognized in society. Although plenty of such expletives are found in the works of Chaucer and Shakespeare, they became off limits in literature, plays and films from the eighteenth to the mid-twentieth centuries.

After the Second World War, the class aspect appears to some extent to have receded. Tolerance of swear words and obscenities has increased greatly. In the media, pop music, the theatre and cinema their use is commonplace. Fans who binge-watch crime dramas will most likely be assailed by a fusillade of profanities. Even in the romantic comedy *Four Weddings And a Funeral* (1994), Hugh Grant says the word 'fuck' seven times and 'bugger' once in the opening scene, all in the space of a few minutes[7] – something that did the film no harm at all, of course. The most striking thing is the way many words previously taboo in the upper echelons of society now seem to form part of that class's everyday parlance. Reading Alwyn Turner's *A Classless Society* about Britain in the 1990s or James Graham's play *Labour of Love* (2017) and, more excessive still, Tom Bower's *Broken Vows: Tony Blair, the Tragedy of Power* (2016), one gets the impression that the political leadership of the UK hardly held a single private conversation without resorting to the word 'fuck' in all its permutations, including 'fucking', 'fuck you' and 'fuck off'. Some celebrities too take pleasure in swearing ad infinitum. In an interview she gave in November 2015 lasting for around an hour and a half, the singer Adele used the word 'fuck' 15 times and 'cunt' twice. Here's a taste:

> How the fuck did that happen? – I used to fucking love the drama of all of it – I've got to clear a lot of stuff the fuck out – Right, fuck, OK, what shall I play first? – Everyone fucking does it – It's fucking hard – That's over and done with, thank fuck – That's been over and done with for fucking years – Everyone thinks I live in fucking America – I love it, it's fucking sick – I'd been shitting myself about standing on that fucking B-stage on my fucking own – George fucking-Clooney's – It's not me trying to be like fucking anti-famous cunt-y – on the West Norwood fucking Overground platform – If I can do that I'll be really fucking happy.[8]

Adele has a fantastic voice and is rich and famous and has been honoured with an MBE. But which class does she belong to?

As for the most abusive terms, a shift has occurred towards sexist and racist words. 'Paki' and the N-word are now at least as offensive as 'cunt' and 'queer', although these days a lot depends on who is saying them (see Chapter 33).

FAMILY RELATIONSHIPS

my wife or first name	Mrs X, Lady X, the wife, my missis, the missus, my better half, trouble and strife (cockney rhyming slang)
my husband or first name	Mr X, my hubby, other half
to spouse: darling	to spouse: dear, pet
have you a wife and/or children?	have you any family?
having a baby, pregnant, with child	expecting, starting a family
baby	tiny tot
the baby	baby, my baby, my little girl
baby is making a noise	baby isn't half creating
child, children, kids	kiddy, kid, kiddies, kids

the girls/boys	my girls/boys
how's your boy?	how's your son?
can I bring George and Fiona?	can I bring my kids?
to look after, to care for children	to mind children
nanny	the au pair
father, mother, parents, relations	folks
single parent	lone parent
my father, my mother	my dad, my mum, my old man, my old lady/woman
mummy and daddy, mama and papa	mum and dad, mam(my)
grandmother, grandma, granny	nanny, nana, nan
grandfather, grandpa, grandpapa	grampy, grandy, grandad, poppie
youngster	lad, lass
to fall in love with	I fell for X
betrothed, engaged	fiancé(e)
Aunt Mary	Auntie Marie, Aunty Marie
	children call any older person 'Uncle or Auntie'

BIRTH ANNOUNCEMENTS

In newspapers	
name, date, gender, parents	child's name, mother's maiden name, name of the hospital
On 1 April, to George and Jane a son	little brother for . . . much awaited sister for . . . long-awaited grandchild for . . .
Announcement cards	
Mr and Mrs . . . are happy to announce the birth of a girl/boy George Charles,1 April 2017	Picture of a stork on the front My name is . . . I weigh 10 lbs My happy Mum and Dad are . . . From love came life

GRAMMAR

It is not only accent and vocabulary that vary by class, but also grammar. The grammar of the upper classes tends to be Standard English. In other classes, wide deviations from standard grammar can be found. Here are a few examples:

Can I have a lend of your pencil?
I better come (instead of I'd)
I would of come
He was stood there on the court
I've been sat there
The film what was on
We done lots of work
John will take baby
I ain't done nothing
Look at them houses
I came like I said

Linguists nowadays no longer tend to prescribe language (what is right and wrong) but rather simply describe it (what people really say). Language should be democratized, they say, far removed from acting as the elite guardians of language. Some populists applaud this development. Others lament it and insist that there is indeed such a thing as 'correct' and 'incorrect' English. Be that as it may: people who speak in a certain way cannot avoid being assigned to a certain class by their listeners, whether they want to or not. This does not hold true, of course, for Prince William's utterance when speaking to the crowd waiting outside the hospital shortly after the birth of his first child: 'I know how long you've all been sat out here.' (See Chapter 33, Breaking the Rules.)

CLASS DENIAL

Denying one's one class can be a matter of changing one's accent (as we saw in Chapter 14), code-switching or simply using different words. This can begin at a very young age, as a letter to Dear Mary, an agony aunt at an English magazine illustrates: 'The heir to a colossal inheritance attends both state (in London) and private (in the country) nurseries. The problem is that the state school reprimands him for saying "What?" and tells him to say "Pardon?", but the reverse then happens in the private school.' Mary's succinct replay: 'There is no problem here. It is good for the boy to learn to be bilingual and, when in Rome, to do what the Romans do. The camouflage may well be essential in the coming years.'[9] It would be interesting to know what career in the coming years Mary might suggest for the young boy.

16

Conversation

The great English art of conversation is something of which English people are rightly proud. Conversation's class relevance derives primarily from the topics that are discussed. Naturally some subjects exist that people of every class can, and do, speak about, such as the weather, which is an inexhaustible source of English conversation, or the national team's prospects or performance in various sports. There are also issues that the English, whatever their class, prefer to avoid. The upper echelons are still bound by the golden rules of conversation that religion, politics, money, illness and sex are all a no-no. For novices and those of a more cautious disposition, this may well be right. The confident conversationalist may talk about these issues, as long as they don't go too far. Raising the subject of physical disability in the company of someone with a bad limp is not exactly a stroke of conversational genius. Some areas that are happily debated at length by one class are excluded altogether or broached only with great reticence by another. In many respects the topics also differ in the way they are approached, which in no small measure is down to class.

avoid speaking about: money, servants, politics, secrets, religion, illness, sex	
don't ask: 'What do you do?'	ask: 'What do you do?'
never ask what someone earns	
don't speak about prices of things	discuss prices of everything

never boast about extravagant expenditure	
may boast about having made a bargain or saving	
don't comment on their house	house talk is central: price, costs, defects, renovation
don't comment on children's likeness to their parent(s)	'a chip off the old block'
rarely allude to famous names	excessive name dropping
never claim kinship with those in a more elevated station	brag about friendship and acquaintance with high-ranking people
refer to Baron, Viscount, Earl, Marquess as 'Lord'	refer to peers as 'Earl' etc.
don't utter radical views	adopt a radical stance
don't talk about class	discuss class distinctions
do not gossip much	enjoy a good gossip
try not to sound too well-informed and knowledgeable – 'I'm not good at this'	try to impress
comment reluctantly on other people's appearance: 'Are you all right?'	'You look tired. Have you been crying?'
rarely speak about themselves	speak mainly about themselves
don't mention their plans	talk about great plans
rarely make jokes	tell jokes compulsively
rarely interrupt	often interrupt
dialogue	monologue

One of the trickiest markers, perhaps the most tricky class marker of all, in relation to conversation is the topic of class itself. No member of the upper echelons would (publicly) describe themselves as such. Nor would they (publicly) categorize another human as belonging to a certain social class. They would not get involved in a discussion of the English class system ('we are all descended from Adam'). They would most certainly not play the class card by complaining that they had been belittled because of their class. All of these would be low-class indicators.

17

Stances and Behaviour

In theory, stances and behaviour are easy to tell apart. Stances are internal: what someone thinks and feels. Behaviour is external: how someone speaks and acts. Stances can give rise to behaviour: if I value someone, I pay them a compliment; those I can't stand I ignore. Or, to give another example, if someone has done something amazing, e.g. sailed across the Atlantic, I ask them how they did it. The question of class arises on both levels: 'What am I allowed to think and feel?' and 'What am I allowed to say or do about it?' Traditionally it was acceptable for the upper classes to feel the pain of a child's suffering (obviously), but not to express this feeling too overtly. The terminology of stances and behaviour overlaps. Many phrases designate both an internal attitude and the associated behaviour, e.g. stiff upper lip, grace under pressure, being pushy with one's children. In case of doubt, we have assigned them to stances.

STANCES

do not care what someone else thinks of them	care very much about what other people think
indifferent to public opinion	What will the neighbours think?
don't care what the media say	fear of the press
politically incorrect	political correctness
do not think about their place in society	feel unsure of their status

seem unaware of their privileges	proud of their position in society
take their life and circumstances for granted	fear of losing what they have achieved
take their class for granted	think about class distinctions
are never awed by wealth or luxury or higher ranks (irreverence)	deference, in awe of wealth, luxury and high rank
a certain insouciance	pore over problems
'I will solve the problem when confronted with it'	rack their brain over the future
don't rely on the welfare state	rely on the welfare state
not envious	envious
think they have a chance in life	survive
not very ambitious, no swots	often over-ambitious
give their children their head	push their children
reluctant to meet new people because they already know everybody worth knowing	keen on connecting and networking
when receiving hospitality, think they are doing the host a favour	when receiving hospitality, feel they are being done a favour
amiable lack of interest towards newcomers and guests	make a fuss of guests and newcomers
lack of interest in other people's hobbies and circumstances	nosey about other people's hobbies and house, furnishings
just take note of an insult	snap back with aggressive response
no shame	shame
hidden arrogance	
colossal self-confidence: 'I can do what I like'	
obsession with rank	reject ranks but do not object openly to them
work moderately and play moderately	work hard and play hard
leisure activities: just mindless pleasure-seeking	meaningful leisure activities under guidance

self-deprecating	blow their own trumpet
understatement, measured	ostentation, over-reaction
stiff upper lip	effusive
grace under pressure	feel badly done by
don't lack feelings, but don't express them	crave for attention when grieving
sportsmanship	gamesmanship
eccentricity, folly	less eccentricity
fairly tolerant of someone breaking the rules	tend to stick to the rules
sentiment towards own house and inheritance	aspire for more

That members of the aristocracy tend to take their own status for granted and automatically regard their personal trappings of class as superior is reflected in an anecdote told in England in various versions and with a variety of protagonists, but generally about elderly dukes or earls. The punchline is always the same: 'Fellow praised my chairs, damn cheek!' In his biography of *Lord Derby* (1959), Randolph Churchill recalls the visit to the former in the 1920s by the art expert, the Earl of Crawford and Balcarres:

> Noting the general ugliness of the furniture, Lord Crawford felt moved to say to Derby, 'That's a very fine set of Charles II dining-room chairs.' Derby made no comment, but after his guest had left he snorted and said, 'Damn cheek, that fellow noticing my chairs!' Neither he nor any of his ancestors had noticed them before. Evidently he thought it an impertinence, and even rather common, that a guest should draw attention to something which all his life he had taken for granted.

Similar outrage is said to have been expressed by the dukes of Argyll and Fife, as well as other aristocrats.

The only other place where we may encounter this phenomenon of 'misplaced' praise in everyday life is in hierarchies. Put simply, those higher up the ladder are allowed to applaud those lower down, but not vice versa. If a colonel tells a captain that he has fulfilled his duties in an exemplary manner, then both can feel pleased. On the other hand, a captain would be sticking his neck out if he said something similar to his colonel. Paying compliments is often regarded as 'naff'.

Something peculiar to the upper classes is their habit of making light of serious events and responding to trivialities with great passion. Whether this is simply a mode of expression or also signals an underlying attitude is hard to judge. Most likely it is a combination of the two, resulting from their instinctive understatement, modesty and non-ostentation. When an event is called a 'complete and utter disaster' this means a mild mistake. 'A bit of a show' or 'quite a party' or a 'spot of bother' are apt to refer to a heavy battle or fierce and bloody fight. A minor social upset such as a getting an introduction wrong is called a 'horror'. A traffic accident where someone narrowly escaped death would probably become 'a slight spill'. Behaviour that is slightly unconventional is described as 'completely mad'. A host whose priceless Ming vase has been destroyed by a guest will probably be a 'bit peeved', whereas he will be 'simply livid' if someone has accidentally broken off a flower-head. Financial ruin or serious illness may be dismissed by the sufferer as 'rather a bore'.

The oft-vaunted immunity of the upper classes to what the neighbours think is not without exception. It very much depends on who the neighbours are. For the upper classes too the opinion of the people next door can serve as a yardstick or benchmark if they are of comparable social rank. Keeping up with the Joneses is not confined to the lower and middle classes. When John Russell, the future 13th Duke of Bedford, reached the age of maturity at 21, he was still living on the allowance of an impoverished student, although he was destined to inherit one of the oldest titles and largest fortunes in England. He ran into debt and tried to borrow money in anticipation of his inheritance. This was his 'only recourse to keep up with the titled Joneses'.[1] Not every aristocrat was as self-assured as the Duke of Norfolk, who always wore appalling clothes. These garments were old and comfortable, and he liked them. When members of his family kept telling

241

him that he couldn't go about dressed like that, the Duke retorted: 'Why not? No one knows me in London. And everybody knows me here – so what does it matter?'[2]

BEHAVIOUR

Manners maketh man.

Motto of Winchester School and
New College, Oxford

It is by politeness, etiquette and charity that society is saved from falling into a heap of savagery.

William of Wykeham, founder of Winchester
School and New College (*c.* 1382)

Many people say that the motto 'Manners maketh man' is outdated, arguing that there are more significant and weightier matters in life, such as education and career, income, relationships, a home. These things are important – no-one would deny it – and they also determine how an individual is valued by society, but not absolutely, and only on a superficial level. A person is defined by more than their bank account. Admittedly, behaviour is only external. But it is the way we express our attitude to other people. Someone of modest means and humble origins who treats others with courtesy is respected and well regarded. The rich man from a privileged background who feels entitled to bark at waiters and belittle shop assistants because he is splashing his money around in their restaurant or shop is despised. The richer and more powerful he is, the greater the revulsion because he should know better.

don't offer sightseeing tour of their house	present their house and furnishings
as hosts may put friends and guests through discomfort (bad food, primitive accommodation)	excessive generosity with gifts, invitations, treats
open doors without knocking	knock timidly and several times

with guests stay at home for evening meal	take guests out for a meal in the country
go outside in bad weather	stay inside in bad weather
refuse (an invitation) with a short excuse	elaborate excuses
leave someone's home quickly, without more ado	make leaving a protracted operation
'Goodbye'	'It was so nice seeing you!'
thank-you letter or call on day after invitation or receiving a present	
handwritten letter with envelope addressed to the wife	email
don't say 'sorry, excuse me' all the time	
polite, 'please' is enough	overpolite, 'terribly grateful'
occasional off-handed rudeness	
like to sound informal	formal, stilted speech
don't complain	sob and weep in public
hide their grief	show their grief
stick to 'never explain, never complain'	
veil a command as a request	
polite to subalterns	rude to servants and waiters
polite to shop assistants and waiters	bully shop assistants and waiters
men leap to their feet when a woman enters the room	remain seated
don't look over the person opposite's shoulder to spot someone more important	
remove sunglasses when speaking to someone else	keep sunglasses on during chat
make eye contact with the waiter or raise a hand	bellow across the room or snap their fingers
	make the 'thumbs up' sign

	remove their shoes in their own home and ask their guests to do the same
	wear slippers at home
	wear curlers and pinny outside their home
	excessive physical intimacies or overly affectionate in public
	talk with cigarette hanging from mouth
	smoke, chew gum on the street
	men sit with their legs wide apart
	tap feet when sitting
	fans of street parties and fêtes

One characteristic of the higher echelons is their inclination and ability to maintain appearances, especially the facade of a happy family life and successful career. To admit personal and family problems is still regarded as socially 'not done' and also ill-bred, an attitude fully consistent with the wish not to trouble other people with one's own misfortunes. So people comment on how harmonious and happy their family life is, how well the children are doing at school or in their careers, and how pleased they are with their children's partners. Many couples appear entirely contented with their lot, and so the news one day that they have split up or one of their children has filed for bankruptcy comes as a complete surprise to those around them. Professionally we are all familiar with those losers or unfortunates who survive only because they are married to a teacher but are always raving about their next fantastic career opportunity, be it the chance to join a friend's business, open a wine shop, launch a hotel in Madeira, become a big shot in the software industry or write a book. 'Things are going really well for us and we have so much to be thankful for', they say – until the day their home is repossessed.

Some aspects of social class are reflected in the way parents behave towards their children. One of the most striking things here is the phenomenon already observed elsewhere of similarities between the upper and working classes. In this case it refers to the care and effort made to 'train' their children – or rather the absence thereof. Both groups give their children relatively free rein without constantly lecturing them on what is and isn't done. For this reason, upper-class children who play with all the other youngsters in the neighbourhood regardless of their class frequently acquire a terrible accent. This does not bother their parents in the least, because they know it 'will turn out all right' in the end. The working-class parents pay no heed to their children's accent either since it is that of their surroundings. It is the middle classes, in their insecurity about their place in society and their endeavours not to put a foot wrong, while always having an eye on moving up in the world, who plague their children from morning to night with dos and don'ts. Don't mumble; speak slowly and clearly. It is important to be well spoken. Avoid whispering and shouting. Put your hand to your mouth if you cough or yawn. Hold doors open and let adults go first. Hold your knife and fork properly. Don't slurp. Comb your hair. Say please and thank you (Mind your Ps and Qs!). Why are your shoes not clean? And so on without end. The outcome is not unusually two types of child: the self-confident upper- and lower-class sorts in their respective milieu, and the self-doubters in the middle.

See also Chapters 10, Appearance, 11, Clothing and Dress, 16, Conversation and 19, Table Manners.

18

Cars

*To argue that a car is simply a means of conveyance is
like arguing that Blenheim Palace is simply a house.*

Jeremy Clarkson, *Sunday Times* (1999)

After first setting eyes on an Englishman, being introduced and
getting to know his name, his accent and speech, the next thing
you might find out is what car he drives. Like clothes, at first glance
cars have a function – to convey the driver from A to B – and so are
no different from taxis or buses. Modern automobiles are superbly
engineered for the task. But as everyone knows, cars are not just a
means of transport, but are probably the single everyday item (apart
from clothing) with the greatest symbolic meaning and the strongest
emotional connotations. They are also the most prodigious pretext for
lies. People claim that they have bought a particular car for objective
reasons (its reliability, engineering, design, handling, speed, performance, comfort, fuel consumption, test results, eco-friendliness or
because it represents good value for money) – never for its social
image or status or out of vanity or in order to impress colleagues
or neighbours or the world at large. Maybe the buyer really believes
what he is saying and therefore is not lying. But that is just how he
sees it. Like it or not, others will associate his choice of car with a
great deal more than these rational qualities, namely status and class.

MAKES AND VEHICLE CATEGORIES

expensive or ultra-small cars	mid-range cars
Land Rover, Range Rover, Jaguar, Bentley, Daimler, BMW, Mercedes, Audi, Mini	Ford ('Mondeo Man'), Volkswagen, Japanese marques, Vauxhall/Opel, US cars, big SUVs, especially Mercedes and Bentley
vintage cars	souped-up cars with extras
sports cars	pickups

Exterior	
black, navy, dark grey or green	white, mauve, red, two-tone
dirty, neglected, battered look	spotless, shiny
washed only when you can't see through the windscreen and colour becomes indistinguishable	washed and polished by the owner's own hand
impeccably clean only when done by chauffeur/driver	
	weekend is washing and polishing time
number plate with initials is just about acceptable	
Interior	
normal equipment, few extras	drinks cabinet, games console, high-tech luxuries, e.g. video screen
racks for country activities, e.g. guns	decorative objects, trees, nodding dogs and cats, scented dangly things
untidy, general disorder, rubbish, apple cores, biscuit crumbs, bits of paper, horse- and dog-related dirt	very tidy
old smell	new smell
jacket slung on the back seat	jacket hung on a coat-hanger or hook
	stickers, what you like and where you have been

	mock tiger-skin seat cover or rugs
	go-faster stripes on the side of the car
	furry steering wheel
	name of driver and his girlfriend
	across the top of the windscreen
	tinted windows
	racing wheels

The following description of the car in which an earl took his family and their guest on a picnic on his estate may smack of caricature but is not completely far-fetched:

> An ancient Land Rover that was now a skeletal husk of its former self, it threatened to fall apart as we climbed aboard and folded ourselves into what was left of the seats. Doors were missing. Hooks swung from the ceiling, festooned with scraps of animal carcasses and deceased-bird by-products matted with dried blood. Wellington boots jostled for floor space with decrepit gardening implements, insect carapaces, muddy, torn country-pursuits magazines, and broken-off sections of farm machines. It smelled really bad, a noxious mixture of dead things, stale things and oil.[1]

WHERE TO SIT AND OTHER RULES

Almost on a par with the class implications of the seating plan at a dinner party, where and how couples arrange themselves in a car is considered a tell-tale sign of class. Leaving the front seats to the men and letting the women sit in the back is regarded as working-class. Middle-class husbands place their wife next to them in the front and the other couple in the rear. The upper classes seat the guest's wife in the front next to the host at the wheel, and the others get into the back, with the man sitting behind the driver.[2] Of course the fairest way is to ask the ladies where they would like to sit.

Inevitably the rules do not stop there. Having a chauffeur is naturally all right, at which point a spotless car is also permitted. Not owning a car has become smart and environmentally sound, since the idea that gentlemen do not travel by bus has become outdated. However, the upper classes regard motorcycles and bicycles as solely for leisure or pleasure and not as serious methods of transport. For politicians, riding a bike in London can also be a ploy to appear in touch with the people (see Chapter 8).

TERMINOLOGY

Mercedes	Merc
roadster, sportscar	convertible
limousine	limo
BMW	beemer
Rolls-Royce	roller

19

Table Manners

On the continent people have good food; in England they have good table manners.

George Mikes, *How to Be an Alien* (1946)

To some extent a distinction must be made between superficial and deeper facets. Of surface importance are the things everyone takes for granted: the no-slurping-no-burping rules; no talking with your mouth full; bring the fork or spoon to your mouth, rather than lowering your head towards the plate; no elbows on the table; say please and thank you when food is being passed or served. Anything else is beyond the pale. More interesting is the underlying distinction between those who know what to do in theory and those who get it absolutely right – or, to put it another way, the difference between satisfactory and superior, the small nuances that outsiders won't even spot and are therefore so hard to detect. As ever, a kind of conspiracy of silence prevails here too. No-one mentions, far less criticizes, someone else's table manners (at least not until later behind closed doors). The imperative not to cause offence is occasionally taken to such extreme lengths that someone with impeccable table manners will modify their behaviour to match that of the rule-breaker so that attention is not drawn to the latter's faux pas. The anecdote is often told of the guest who drank from the finger bowl only to be copied by their host. At table, while noiseless and invisible, the class radar is very much switched on.

eat in the kitchen if it's large enough and suitably designed	always eat in the kitchen
	eat in front of the telly
relish and sauces served in sauce boats or dishes	relish and sauces served in the bottle
all-purpose knives	special fish knives/steak knives
tablecloth	coasters, place mats
cloth napkin	paper napkin
napkins folded simply	napkins folded into over-elaborate shapes
	folded napkins standing upright in glasses
	napkins placed in napkin rings
napkin loose on lap	napkin tucked into waistband or collar
gentle dabbing with napkin	scrub or wipe vigorously at one's mouth
napkin left carelessly crumpled on the table	napkin folded up carefully
don't touch fork and knife before everyone is served	start eating without waiting
start eating, say nothing	say 'Enjoy your meal' (originally AmE)
fork in left hand	fork in right hand
knife handle rests in palm	knife held like a pen
eat slowly with composure	eat in a hurry and greedily
food is cut up and eaten piece by piece with knife and fork	all food is cut up small and then eaten with a fork
peas on the back of the fork	peas on the concave side of the fork
salt not on food but on plate	
take bread with left hand	
break off bread piece by piece	cut bread with knife

tip soup plates away from oneself to retrieve the last spoonful	
spread butter or marmalade onto the broken-off piece of bread	spread butter or marmalade on the whole slice and bite off
say nothing or Good health!	say cheers, *skol*, *prost*, *santé*, etc., clink glasses
no second drink before dinner	
port after dinner must go clockwise	
loose tea leaves in pot	tea served bag in cup
drink tea from teacup with saucer, ditto coffee	drink from mug
drink espresso from a demitasse	
pour milk after tea or coffee	milk first in tea or coffee
no or silent stirring	noisy stirring
	cake or biscuit dunked in tea or coffee
don't comment on host's food except when host himself cooks	
high tolerance towards food	extreme sensitivity about food
conversation beats food	food beats conversation

Not everyone has the same idea of what constitutes correct table manners, not even the arbiters of taste themselves. The late 13th Duke of Bedford, John Russell, expressed his revulsion at making a toast before drinking with alarming vehemence: 'I would rather bite my tongue off than raise my glass and utter the word Cheers. Or words to that effect. But my whole point is that you should not say anything. Just have your drink and keep quiet about it.'[1]

Fish knives and the class implications thereof have been debated for as long as they have existed. Some find them quite intolerable, others think them classy. While the Royal Family (it is said) does not use them, other venerable families (reportedly) very much do. At one time fish was 'correctly' eaten with two forks.

Putting the milk in first, i.e. pouring the milk into the teacup before adding the tea rather than the other way round, was a tell-tale sign of being 'non-U'. Individuals were pigeonholed as 'MIF people'. But even the authors of Debrett's are no longer sure. Debrett's *New Guide to Etiquette and Modern Manners* (1996) stated that milk, cream, lemon or sugar should be added *after* the main beverage, be it tea or coffee. Twelve years later Debrett's *A-Z of Modern Manners* (2008) draws a fine distinction: 'Pour the milk and add the sugar before dispensing the tea. Lemons should be added afterwards.'

When dining out, being rude to waiters, calling out across the room or, worst of all, snapping one's fingers to attract attention are regarded as low class. Raising a hand slightly, endeavouring to make eye contact or a gesture of the head are deemed proper. The bill is not discussed at the table and certainly not divided to the last penny. Payment is made as discreetly as possible.

TERMINOLOGY

lunch, luncheon (formal)	dinner
tea (4-5 p.m.)	afternoon tea (4 p.m.)
supper, maybe dinner (grander)	tea, high tea, evening meal
first course	starter
pudding	sweet, afters, dessert, pud
napkin	serviette
to offer bread	to offer crumb or crust
salt cellar, pepper pot, mustard pot	cruet
vegetables	greens
to snack	to nibble
to eat, to scoff	to stuff oneself (vulgar)
a cup of tea	cuppa
Have some more tea? Yes, please. No, thank you	How is your cup? I don't mind if I do. I'm doing nicely, thank you
a cup of coffee	a coffee

to have a drink (meaning alcohol)	to have a drink (meaning tea)
pint	jar
	euphemisms: partaking of liquid refreshment, imbibing potations, just a wee dram
	bar terminology: snorter, one for the road, a few jars, a few sherbets
I'm finished	I'm done, I'm full, I'm stuffed (vulgar)

Like the saga surrounding the colour of men's shoes (see Chapter 11), the names given to meals and the different courses are another delight served up by the English class system, as expressed at least partially by the list above. Breakfast is always called breakfast, but the traditional formula of bacon, eggs, sausage, baked beans and toast is variously known as a full English or cooked breakfast to avoid confusion with the so-called continental version. The distinctions are much clearer when it comes to the midday meal. The upper echelons have lunch or luncheon, the lower classes dinner. According to Kate Fox (Chapter 15), using these words incorrectly is no less than one of the seven deadly sins. The grave consequences are revealed in the popular anecdote about a frustrated employee who can't understand why his boss doesn't give him the recognition and promotion he feels he deserves. The penny finally drops when, after a busy morning, his boss tells him, 'Well, I must break for lunch and you should go and have your dinner. We'll continue afterwards.' For the upper classes tea is something to be enjoyed in the long gap between midday and the evening meal, typically between 4 and 5 o'clock. Tea comprises cakes, scones with jam and cream, biscuits and dainty, crustless sandwiches (cucumber being a favourite) with tea to drink. For the working class by contrast tea is the evening meal consumed at around 6.30 p.m., and is also known as high tea or meat tea. To distinguish between the two forms of tea, the working class refers to 5 o'clock tea as afternoon tea. The upper classes either have supper around 7.30 p.m. or, a little later, dinner, which is a more elaborate affair. The working classes use the general term meal, whereas those further up the social scale specify whether they mean breakfast, lunch, tea, supper or dinner. Arguably even trickier are the designations of the courses. The meal begins with the first course, which some people call the starter or, if appropriate, the soup. The term main course is used along with meat course or cold cuts by those at the top, while those lower down the ladder refer to the roast or the joint or the entrée. If you are upper-class, what follows the main course is always termed pudding, whatever it consists of. A sorbet is just as much a pudding as an apple tart. Lower-class people talk of sweet or dessert or afters. Pudding may be followed by cheese, with fresh fruit to finish, which is called dessert by the upper echelons.

See also Chapter 20, Food and Drink.

20

Food and Drink

If you take a labourer in Marseille and a CEO in Marseille, they will eat approximately the same food. In this country there is no link between what a guy who is working on a building site in Southampton eats and the guy who runs that site – they eat completely different things.

Jonathan Meades quoted
by Stuart Jeffries, *Guardian*, 12 March 2004

There is a correlation between class and food in Britain, but it is non-linear. Middle-earners eat better than the poor, urban professionals eat better than middle-earners, but people at the top do not eat better than urban professionals.

Janan Ganesh, *Financial Times*, 24/25 February 2017

Despite the fact that everyone needs to eat and drink, food, like table manners, is a strong class indicator. What do you eat? What do you drink? Where do you buy it? When do you eat and drink? What do you call your food? What do you call your meal? Where do you eat out? The invasion of fast food from America and the first Wimpy bars in the 1950s prompted many to believe that eating would become classless or class-neutral. Far from it! Fast food's classlessness simply became a euphemism for low-class: 'Junk food for the junk classes.'[1] Neither the dizzying choice of myriad foodstuffs in British supermarkets nor the abundance of restaurants dispensing foreign-cum-exotic fare have eliminated class divisions. The answers to the basic questions listed above still define the consumer's class and status. The efforts of celebrity chefs and cookery writers like Nigella Lawson and Jamie Oliver to get everyone eating well and the staggering profusion of television programmes designed to appeal across the class spectrum have not changed anything. Food and drink and everything that goes with them are still strong pointers to class.[2]

What do you eat and drink?	
fresh, organic, local food	cheap, processed, packaged food
lardons, prosciutto, speck, serrano ham	bacon bits, pork scratchings, bacon-flavoured crisps
	cutlets in lacy paper/with paper frills
	prawn cocktail with pink cocktail sauce
	egg and chips
	pasta salad with mayonnaise
	toast with HP sauce
	rice salad
	fish and chips
	baked beans
	savouries
	pasties, sausage rolls
	tinned fruit
	sliced hard-boiled eggs
	sliced tomato in a green salad
	tinned fish
	chip butties, chips sandwich
	shredless marmalade
	jelly

	individual fruit pies
	blancmange
bread unsliced, toast sliced	sliced bread
potted meat	Spam
mustard from earthenware jar	mustard from squeezy bottle
white, black pepper, whole peppercorns	powdered pepper, ground pepper
	chewing gum
offer any chocolate	offer luxury chocolate
Cadbury's chocolate	Fry's chocolate
Earl Grey or China	Indian tea
tea unsweetened and weak	strong and sweet, 'builders' tea'
fresh ground coffee	instant coffee
beer, spirits, wine (dry not sweet), and soft drinks	sweet or creamy beverages like Baileys (women)
gin and tonic, whisky and soda, dry sherry, Armagnac, champagne	brandy, dry ginger, whisky, pink gin, sweet sherry, cocktails (men)
whisky, water no ice	whisky with ice

WHERE DO YOU SHOP?

Sainsbury's makes me feel good about myself. I am rich and I am living well. Shopping here is part of all that.

Customer of Sainsbury's quoted by Stuart Jeffries,
Guardian, 12 March 2004

Whereas shopping in general is dealt with in Chapter 21, shopping for groceries is somewhat special. Apart from some gourmet and exotic foods, organic produce and baking specialities, virtually every type of food is nowadays sold by supermarkets. All of them offer a previously inconceivable array of products to suit all tastes. Those so inclined can choose from more than a hundred types of coffee alone. Some supermarkets offer pricier products, others cheaper lines, many the whole gamut. A single supermarket chain can sell the same foods at very different prices depending on the location and presumed purchasing power and price tolerance of customers. Like supermarkets in general (see Chapter 21), their food halls also count as class markers. 'Tell me where you buy your groceries, and I will tell you what class you belong to,' may be an exaggeration, but there is some truth in it. In a lively article Stuart Jeffries describes which caste buys its food in which supermarkets and also compares the stores' prices for a number of items.[3] Accordingly, the top-down ranking in 2004 was: Waitrose, Sainsbury's, Tesco, Safeway, Marks & Spencer, Asda, Morrisons, Lidl, KwikSave, Netto and Aldi. Whether this hierarchy still applies today is not clear. Lidl and Aldi in particular have made substantial inroads. However, it is likely to be more or less accurate, which was reaffirmed by Harry Wallop in 2013.[4]

And when it comes to getting the groceries in, the snobbery of the English knows no bounds. How did a woman shopping in Waitrose describe her feelings when receiving a delivery from Ocado, the Waitrose home-delivery service? 'Oh, I use Ocado all the time. When the van pulls up, I can see the net curtains twitching. I feel almost intolerably smug. The only way one could trump it is if Harvey Nicks had home-delivery vans. That would drive the neighbours wild.'[5]

See also Chapter 19, Table Manners, which discusses the different names of meals and courses.

21

Shopping

An entire class philosophy has evolved around shopping. Where do I shop? What do I buy? How much do I pay? Do I talk about it? What bag do I use to carry my purchases in? In Chapter 20 we have already looked specifically at shopping for food and drink. In his book *Consumed*, Harry Wallop investigates the relationship between supermarkets and consumers' class and argues not only that the name on their carrier bag indicates a shopper's social status, but also that supermarkets prop up the class system and are crucibles of snobbery.[1] Indeed, the class implications of a single company and its products are discussed.

Some shopping rules cut across class boundaries. Flaunting expensive purchases is taboo whatever your status, and asking how much something has cost is just not done. Telling others you have got a bargain, however, is permitted. Class differences are revealed by who shops where. The distinction is more subtle than simply that the upper classes shop in expensive boutiques and the lower ranks in cheapjack stores, although there is some truth to that. In the upmarket, flagship stores of international fashion retailers on Oxford Street or at Harrods in London you will naturally encounter more patricians (and of course tourists) than plebeians. The prices alone see to that! But many upper-crust women (and this refers primarily to women as in the vast majority of cases they are the 'shoppers' of the family) derive satisfaction from buying things that catch their eye or are especially good value from budget outlets, including charity and second-hand shops, which are rather despised by the working class. Books about the lifestyle of the well-heeled (and those with ambitions to join them) such as Ann Barr and Peter York's *Official Sloane Ranger Handbook* and Peter York and Olivia Stewart-Liberty's *Cooler Faster More Expensive,* give the addresses of establishments frequented by the 'beautiful people'. This dichotomy is carried over to catalogue shopping as well. Here Boden, the White Company and OKA stand out as examples of suppliers to the upper echelons.

If one attempts to generalize about who shops where, then the lower half of the population favours retailers like Asda and Morrisons, Poundland, Costcutter and Iceland, while the upper half prefers Sainsbury's, Waitrose and Marks & Spencer. More likely to be chosen by the lower orders are the two German chains Aldi and Lidl, but their place in the class system is still undefined, perhaps because they are seen as foreign. This breakdown is not reliable, however, since the items stocked by the same supermarket differ in well-to-do areas from those offered in deprived ones. And that's not all. In the same supermarket chain the prices for an identical product vary depending on the store's location. The same bottle of champagne that costs £10 in poor neighbourhoods comes at a much higher price in more affluent postcodes. These days caviar can be obtained from discount stores, while Harry Wallop claims to know a duchess who is a card-carrying member of the warehouse whole-saler Costco.[2]

Marks & Spencer (M&S) appears to occupy a particular place in the English class system. What makes M&S so special is the diver-sity of its product range – from furniture to clothes and toiletries to bed linen, as well as food and drink to go or eat in, all sold under its own brand. If you want to know an Englishwoman's class, don't enquire about her background, occupation, income or education, ask her what she does and does not buy at M&S. Kate Fox calls it the 'M&S test'.[3] The upper middles purchase things that are not instantly identifiable as from M&S: underwear, basic items, towels, bed linen and food. They do not buy sofas, curtains or cushions, party dresses or shoes or anything bearing a trademark M&S pattern. The middle middles buy M&S food (but get their cornflakes and loo paper at Sainsbury's or Tesco), as well as sofas, cushions and certain 'unseen' garments. They sometimes purchase patterned clothing, although they do so with caution. Lower-middle and upper-working-class customers like M&S clothes, feeling they represent value for money, but have a problem with many other goods, especially M&S food, cushions, duvets and towels, because of the price.

Marketing experts employed by the supermarkets painstakingly analyse the retailer's demographic so that everyone receives offers that are right for them (i.e. appealing and likely to encourage them to buy). With this aim in mind, they classify consumers according to diverse criteria such as income (an obvious factor), postcode area, car ownership, leisure activities, communication channels, etc. The underlying purpose is to find out what can be sold to whom where at the highest price. The conventional class schema described in Chapter 3 is not suitable for this task, and so the analysts have drawn up their own categories which focus much more closely on the characteristics of potential customers. But overlaps and parallels do of course exist, which makes looking at them worthwhile. Part of the interest lies in the fact that these categories do not have to adhere to, or are less restricted by, political correctness (in the past, at least). The Mosaic 2004 Classification Groups and Types produced by analysts at Experian divide the UK into 11 main groups and 61 distinct types, and use tongue-in-cheek labels such as Golden Empty Nesters, Dinky Developments, White Van Culture, Town Gown Transition, etc. In addition, they cross-refer to the classic designations upper, middle, skilled, working and poor and include first names regarded as representative of the class concerned (see Chapter 13). A brief description of the group and the channels through which it obtains information are also mentioned.

Group	Distinct types	Percentage of UK households	Typical names	Social groups	Description	Media
Symbols of Success (A)	Global Connections Cultural Leadership Corporate Chieftains Golden Empty Nesters Provincial Privilege High Technologists Semi-rural Seclusion	9.62	*Rupert and Felicity*	Upper middle and middle middle class	This group represents the wealthiest 10 per cent of people in the UK, set in their careers and with substantial equity and net worth. These people tend to be white British but with some Jewish, Indian and Chinese minorities. Tend to contain older people advanced in their careers.	Internet, some TV
Happy Families	Just Moving In Fledgling Nurseries Upscale New Owners Families Making Good Middle Rung Families	10.76	*Darren and Joanne*	Lower middle class and middle middle class	Families from Middle England, focused on children, home and career. Tend to be in new suburbs in more prosperous areas of the UK, mostly white with few minorities	Sky TV and internet
Suburban Comfort	Asian Enterprise	15.10	*Geoffrey and Valerie*	Lower middle class	People in comfortable homes in mature suburbs built between 1918 and 1970, moderate incomes, includes middle class Asian Enterprise	Internet, *Daily Mail*
Ties of Community	Town Centre Refuge	16.04	*Lee and Noreen*	Lower middle class and skilled working class	People focused on local communities, families concentrated near industrial areas, includes lower-income Asians	*Mirror, Sun*
Urban Intelligence		7.19	*Ben and Chloe*	Mixture of middle classes	Young educated people in urban areas starting out in life, includes significant minority presence and students	*Guardian, The Times,* and internet

Welfare Borderline		6.43	*Joseph and Agnes*	Working class and poor	Poorest people in the UK, urban with significant ethnic minority presence	*Sun*, and high TV viewing
Municipal Dependency		6.71	*Wayne and Leanne*	Working class and poor	Poor people in council houses and dependent on benefits, mostly white British with few immigrants	*Sun*, and high TV viewing
Blue Collar Enterprise		11.01	*Dean and Mandy*	Skilled working class	Enterprising rather than well educated, includes White Van Man, few ethnic minorities	*Sun*, and high TV viewing
Twilight Subsistence		3.88	*Percy and Ada*	Working-class pensioners	Poorer pensioners in council houses, few ethnic minorities	*Sun*, and high TV viewing
Grey Perspectives		7.88	*Edgar and Constance*	Middle-class pensioners	Pensioners in comfortable retirement and traditional values	*Daily Telegraph, Daily Mail*
Rural Isolation	Upland hill farmers	5.39	*Huw and Gwenda*	Mixed	Rural people with relatively low incomes but high non-liquid assets, traditional values, very few ethnic minorities	

Needless to say, its publication was followed by the customary moral outrage. Subsequently Experian introduced Mosaic Public Sector with more politically-correct segment names.

Where there is class, there is also class denial. A peculiar type of class snobbery has emerged with the advent of so-called bags for life. Where once supermarkets provided customers with neutral, single-use plastic carriers, these reusable bags clearly sport the logo of the supermarket that supplied them – and with it distinguish between 'cheap' and 'luxury' brands. Some people shop in a high-end store and use a correspondingly upmarket bag for their purchases, or conversely buy from a less prestigious outlet and use a cheap bag. However, others buy in a cheaper shop but place their items in a luxury bag, while others still patronize upmarket stores but put their goods in a less-expensive-looking bag. In response to the question about what bags his customers use to pack their purchases, a commercial director from Waitrose replied: 'We have found some customers putting their Waitrose goods in Tesco bags, because they are nervous that their neighbours will think they are decadent for shopping at Waitrose.'[4]

22

House

*The Englishman's home is more than his castle. It is his
face, his taste, his refuge and his family hearth.*

Simon Jenkins, *England's Thousand Best
Houses* (2003)

The Stately Homes of England,
How beautiful they stand,
To prove the upper classes
Have still the upper hand.

Noël Coward, 'The Stately Homes of England' (1938)

While a house's location and address are hard class markers which
cannot be changed, a dwelling's construction, alterations, use and
above all how it is furnished, provide pointers as to the occupants'
class. Scrutinizing other people's homes and furniture borders on
an English national obsession. The house, its good and bad points,
planned improvements and value are at the heart of many English
conversations – although not among the upper echelons, who think
such talk vulgar. So these discussions are of themselves indicative of
class. If the house itself is status-laden, the furnishings are even more
revelatory. It was a widely held belief that, with the arrival of almost
universally affordable, mass-produced furniture, class differences
would disappear. Habitat, in its heyday an iconic English brand, and

its Swedish counterpart, IKEA, encapsulated this idea. For some, it was a step towards democratization: democratic furnishings for a democratic age. The theory was that, if visiting someone's house, their taste would be apparent, but not their social class. Nothing could be further from the truth. A mere glance inside someone's home is enough to reveal the owner's class. Like it or not, your home, like life, is a stage, which is why the salient literature on English houses also volubly describes the class-related aspects.[1]

GENERAL

inherit house	buy or build a house
redecorate old house	buy a modern house
leave house as they acquired it	paint and decorate house all the time
houses tend to be shabby, frayed and unkempt	tidy, clean and over-careful, neat, pristine, effortful, designed
	satellite dish
simple doorbell	chiming doorbell
	dimmer switches
chimney piece	electric logs, log-effect fire
cold house	warm house
inherit their furniture	buy their own furniture
bare floorboards	fitted carpet, patterned carpet, deep pile, shag pile, acrylic pile
old Persian carpets or threadbare rugs	tiger skin imitation
curtains	net curtains
threadbare and mismatched furniture	brand-new suites of matching settees and armchairs, dining tables and chairs, extremely expensive items
Muddled-up style and origins of paintings, tables, wallpapers, velvets, tapestries, embroideries, sideboards	everything matching and new, streamlined
	repro antique furniture

	furniture called up-market names like Eton or Cavendish
	flying ducks
either no television or visible, not hidden	TV focal point of the room, large flatscreen
stereos hidden	High-tech music centre with big speakers
	music in all rooms all the time
genuine paintings	copies and fakes
shelf of the chimney piece stuffed with notes, invitations, letters, etc.	collections from package holidays or mail-order catalogues (dolls, glass and plastic animals, figurines, spoons, etc.)
awards and photos in the downstairs loo	awards and photos in the sitting room or entrance hall or other prominent place
heritage colours: rose, red, gold, ice blue, green (in London)	modern colours
colours faded into softness by antiquity	
	tassels (on chairs, curtains, cushions, carpets, tablecloths, skirts, umbrellas)

Inheriting one's furniture and therefore not buying it was long considered a hallmark of the upper class. It cost nothing (bar inheritance tax, perhaps) and said more about the taste of the person making the bequest or their ancestors than the preferences of the current heir. This does not imply that all inherited furniture is necessarily good stuff, as anyone who is left a houseful of gimcrack furniture will testify. Many young people are not keen on ancestral hand-me-downs and would rather make their own choices. When you furnish your home yourself you are making a statement about your class.

Sitting room	
bookshelves	DVD shelves
red damask sofa, fabric sofa, old leather sofa	brand new leather sofa
painted portrait of the owner	
photos in silver frames	
	bar behind books
	'candle' wall lights with fake drips

Bedroom	
normal furnishing without gimmicks	huge oval bed humming with dials
	matching bedspreads, cushions and curtains

Bathroom and loo	
high quality with single bath and shower	onyx and marble double bath with gold-plated mixer taps
	fancy Jacuzzi bath
cracked wooden toilet seat	plastic toilet seat
reed diffuser by the White Company	reed diffuser by Next Home or Airwick
bar of soap	liquid soap, individual guest soaps
normal water in the lavatory	bright blue water in the lavatory
loo paper white and un-textured	loo paper coloured or quilted

The class significance of the downstairs loo, which is also likely to be inspected by guests, depends not only on the name it is called – be it loo, lavatory, toilet, WC or some other designation (see terminology) – but also on how it is furnished (beyond the essential fixtures and fittings). People's lavatories also eloquently evoke the social status of those who live there. As long ago as 1982, Ann Barr and Peter York's *Official Sloane Ranger Handbook* lovingly devoted two pages to loo accoutrements: amusing cartoons, postcards from peripatetic friends, the Kipling poem 'If', photos of the master and mistress of the house as children (ideally clutching a hockey stick, rugby ball or cricket bat), easy reads and a few back issues of magazines like *Punch* and *Private Eye*. A good 35 years later and not much has changed. 'Bogside reading' is still a useful class indicator.[2] 'Condensed into this cubicle', writes Harry Wallop,

> must be the following items, all framed: a school or university sports team photo; a university matriculation or graduation photo (double points if it is of one of those we-are-all-wearing-loo-seats-as-necklaces-larking-about group shots of the Junior Common Room); any newspaper clipping in which you have appeared (triple points if it is an appearance in *Private Eye*); a photograph of you posing outside Buckingham Palace clutching your MBE; any awards (though a jokey 'Most catches dropped in a season' certificate is clearly preferable to a 'legal 500 rising divorce lawyer' accolade); a photograph of the loo's owner posing with a celebrity, sports star or world leader (double points if it is signed with a personal message).[3]

Suitable books are those with convenient sections that can be dipped into while going about one's lavatorial business, such as *Xenophobe's Guide to the English* by Antony Miall and David Milsted or *The Situation is Hopeless, But Not Serious: The Pursuit of Unhappiness* (1993) by Paul Watzlawick. A National Trust handbook or crossword collection with a few still left to do are perfect – as of course is this book, ideally with a bookmark inserted at this page. The whole idea is to remove the whiff of unpleasantness from a rather unglamorous function and make a joke of it – which is why loos with pricey original pictures or chandeliers are in bad taste.

Kitchen	
Aga (cooker) – oil or gas	
cafetière	coffee machine
cookery books by Constance Spry, Mrs Beeton, Mary Berry	cookery books by Jamie Oliver, Gordon Ramsay, James Martin
	a hostess trolley
	decanter tags
round plates	square plates
soup plate	bowl (for soup)
dessert cutlery	grape scissors
one sort of knife and fork	fish cutlery, steak knives
cloth napkins	paper napkins or kitchen roll

TERMINOLOGY

An Englishman's home is a central aspect of his personality. His class is reflected not only in the actual house and its furnishings, but also in the terminology that he uses for them. It is no coincidence that, of the seven deadly sins relating to terminology (see Chapter 15), no fewer than three refer to the interior of the house, namely toilet vs loo or lavatory, lounge vs drawing or sitting room and settee vs sofa.

they have a nice house	they have a lovely home
at home (invitation)	
place, villa, cottage	'house' fits all
historic house	stately home
painting one's house	home improvements
do up the house	decorating and DIY (do it yourself)
basement	lower ground
terrace	patio
sitting room, drawing room	lounge, front room, living room
looking glass	mirror
chimneypiece	mantelpiece
nursery	playroom

guestroom	guest bedroom
loo, lavatory, bog, thunder box, 'I'll show you the geography'	toilet, gents, ladies, bathroom, restroom, the smallest room, facilities, convenience, cloakroom, WC, dub(by), little girl's room, This is it (sign on the door), the littlest room
the television	the box, telly, the TV
wireless	radio
photograph	photo
lavatory paper	toilet paper, loo paper
basin	bathroom suite
bath cap	shower cap
deep freeze	freezer
silver	cutlery
spin dryer	tumble dryer
tea cloth	tea towel
daily	cleaner

Terminology can be deceptive. The billiard room in a great house is generally not reserved for playing a game that involves knocking coloured balls into pockets with cues, but is used for after-dinner recreation. Similarly, the drawing room is not where people get creative with a pencil (as many foreigners think), but a room to which one 'withdraws' and where guests are entertained.

See also the section on addresses contained in Chapter 4, Hard Class Markers.

23

Gardens

'Gravel path!' Lord Emsworth stiffened through the whole length of his stringy body. Nature, he had always maintained, intended a yew alley to be carpeted with a mossy growth. 'Most decidedly not. Try to remember, McAllister, as you work in the gardens of Blandings Castle, that you are not back in Glasgow, laying out recreation gardens.'

P. G. Wodehouse, *Blandings Castle and Elsewhere* (1935)

Gardening is probably one of the most delightful obsessions and passions of the English and spurs them on to true greatness. The English are a nation of gardeners and English gardens are world-class. They cover more land per person than in any other country. Gardening is therefore seen as one of the quintessential traits of the English character, and no book about England or the English would be complete without a chapter on the subject. This also explains why many more garden books are published in England than in other countries. Likewise, the landscapers and keepers of English gardens, together with gardening writers, enjoy cult status in England and sometimes beyond. Examples include Lancelot (Capability) Brown, Humphry Repton and Joseph Paxton (who designed the Crystal Palace, of which more later) from bygone eras as well as, more recently, Vita Sackville-West (of Sissinghurst fame),

Gertrude Jekyll, Christopher Lloyd, Rosemary Verey and Robin Lane Fox. It therefore comes as no surprise that class plays a role in this key aspect of Englishness[1] – not so much in terms of wishing to have one, however, since most Englishmen do. To have one's own home and a bit of garden, even if only in suburbia, has for decades been the thing most people have dreamed of, and this is still true today. Nor does it concern the garden's size, as that comes down to money. Rather, it is a question of the garden's design and content: the boundaries, the paths, the trees, the shrubs, the flowers, the plant stands and urns. Any weeds in evidence? Garden gnomes? Is there a pond?

As a rule of thumb the class aspect can be described as the antithesis of ordered and wild.[2] On the one hand there is orderly perfection: a regimented appearance, strict geometrical lines, rectangular or oblong shapes, an untainted newness, overzealously manicured lawns, consummate neat-and-tidiness; on the other, there are gardens that look casual, less effortful, giving the impression of a charming confusion or fine carelessness, a certain shabbiness, wildness and disorder. Of course these gardens are not actually neglected, but are artfully created to appear so. The intended natural look is often the result of jolly hard work. This principle is borne out by the details.[3]

paths: stone chippings, gravel, York stone	tarmac or concrete, crazy paving, stepping stones in the lawn
little or no earth visible between the plants	
muted or subtle colours	more garish, cheerful, gaudy colours
weeds and wild flowers welcome	weeds and wild flowers removed
trees preferably indigenous: oak, beech, lime, yew, chestnut, white double cherry, willow in natural habitat, hawthorn, box. Also cedar and very exotic foreign trees (in parks)	almond, lilac, conifers, silver birch, willow outside their natural habitat

white daisies, white and green tobacco plants, dark red wallflowers, blue roses, brown iris, pink forget-me-not, daffodils, tulips, rhododendrons, clematis, fig, vines, wisteria, azalea, ivy, Albertine, laburnum, harebell	marigold, salvia, zinnia, petunia, busy lizzies, chrysanthemum, gladioli, begonia, asters, fuchsia, Californian poppy, yellow daisies, Oxford blue lobelia, scarlet geraniums, white alyssum, laurel, privet, pink and yellow roses, red and mauve tobacco plants, calceolarias
rosemary, lavender, honeysuckle, sweet peas, lupins, hollyhocks, delphiniums, pinks, mignonettes, pansies, sweet William, white stocks, phlox, Canterbury bells, lilies, moss	heather, pampas grass, bamboo, plastic grass, plastic flowers
wooden garden chairs and table	tubular steel chairs and table
square wooden pots with balls for plants	ornate rockeries, hanging baskets
Tudor-revival patterns	
Arts-and-Crafts patterns	plastic Venus de Milo
pottery flowerpots	plastic flowerpots
	crocus in a wheelbarrow
	garden gnomes
	pink plastic pelican on the front lawn
stone artefacts	plaster cherub
stone vases	plastic vases
	plastic dolphin vase
	dolphin regurgitating water
	garden Oasis (foam blocks to ram flowers in)
	basket held by a naked Cupid
	toadstool lamps
	coolie-hat lamps
	flowerbeds floodlit
	the patio: a mosaic of Italian tiles with plastic urns filled with striped petunias, deckchairs with foot-rests, canopies, seed-packet upholstery, sun umbrellas

Fewer differences exist in herb and vegetable gardens. Here, the fine carelessness to some extent ceases because it would be rather counter-productive. Class is reflected only by what people choose to plant. This also applies to the greenhouse and its complement of vegetables.

The world's biggest gardening achievement to come out of England is probably the conservatory, a habitat in its own right. It ranges from the small, glazed extension attached to private houses to the largest glass-and-steel structure of its kind ever built, the Crystal Palace, created for the Great Exhibition in 1851 by Joseph Paxton. With their conservatories the English kill several birds with one stone: they bring a part of their precious garden into the house, shorten the winter, gain more daylight hours and outsmart the English weather, and many also turn the beneficial heating effect to their advantage. In the conservatory class influences seem strangely less acute. Gladioli, begonias, chrysanthemums and fuchsias, all frowned upon when grown outdoors, are universally acceptable in the conservatory. Perhaps this is because of the joy shared by all classes at overcoming the ravages of nature. Success in a common struggle brings people together.

TERMINOLOGY

the grounds, the gardens	the garden
car shelter	carport
chrysanthemums	chrysanths
daffodils	daffs
gladioli	glads
rhododendrons	rhodies
cauliflower	cauli
tomatoes	toms
flowers	fresh flowers
pull up a lettuce	pick a salad

24

Animals

Animals are a bit like clothes and cars. The owners are often self-deluded, denying their pet has anything to do with status, having allegedly been chosen out of a love for animals or pity or to please the children. Any notion it might be a class statement is roundly rejected. In many cases this may indeed be true. But as with other soft class markers, the beholder forms their opinion irrespective of the thoughts and intentions of the object of their gaze. Which type of pet is kept by whom and in which house is (among other things) a signal to the outside world of social class, even if the individual concerned is neither aware nor complicit. You need only buy a horse, a Labrador, a cat, a hamster or a snake to realize what we are talking about.

Among pets, dogs take pride of place. A canine companion is within the means of many Englishmen and women, and England is 'fluent in dog' (Mark Easton). Dogs are universally loved, in many cases more than human beings. If bitten by a dog, as a rule it is the victim who is blamed. People who are disliked by dogs are treated with suspicion, which is why every Englishman tries to make friends with their host's pooch: hit it off with the dog and soon you will have the master on your side. Tell the canine off, or worse still object to its behaviour, at your peril – even if the animal has unconcernedly mistaken your leg for a tree. Dog racing (with greyhounds) was invented in England, where it enjoys its greatest popularity. The English national symbol is the bulldog, which is also used for political purposes. In the election campaign that culminated in his landslide victory in May 1997, Tony Blair deployed a bulldog named Fitz in a Labour Party election broadcast entitled 'British spirit', to emphasize New Labour's patriotism. The bulldog had the dual advantage of symbolizing the ordinary Englishman John Bull, as well as Britain's great twentieth-century politician Winston Churchill.

The symbolism of dogs is not limited to national stereotypes: get a Staffordshire bull terrier if you want to appear hard, while a French poodle might suggest you are gay. It comes as no surprise to discover that, in England, dogs are also bound up with class. This historic entanglement runs deep. For centuries there was a division between the ruling class's thoroughbred hunters and the peasants' working dogs. In the Middle Ages hunting with hounds was the privilege of the ruling elite. The Game Act 1671 even made it a criminal offence to keep hunting dogs for all but those who owned estates or were heir *apparent* to the nobility. This canine class divide only ended in 1831. Unspoken clashes between the classes relating to dogs nevertheless persisted for many decades thereafter, setting town against country and working animal against pet. The Dangerous Dogs Act of 1991, by which the ownership of certain dogs was banned in response to serious attacks on people, was understood by some as a throwback to former times, since some breeds preferred by the lower classes were found more likely to bite than those favoured by the upper echelons.[1] While the dogs themselves are not aware of class (or at least not to our knowledge), their masters most certainly are.

The other animal with special status is the horse. Horses are fewer in number than dogs and also much dearer to buy and keep. Horse ownership per se does not say much as people from all social backgrounds may have a horse. But buying racehorses or owning a stable or stud is of course a marker of belonging to the upper classes. Horses are still very high up the social ladder, and most things horsey have the cachet of class. The English horse is the most symbolically charged animal in the world after the cats of pharaonic Egypt and bulls of Mithras and Spain.[2] Some artists, such as George Stubbs, made their name and their fortune by painting almost exclusively horses. Cleaning out your stables yourself is not something to be ashamed of but a mark of your love of horses and country life. One step better is to be an accomplished horseman or woman. Best of all is probably to play polo - but then you must remember to call the horse a pony.

horses and ponies	guinea pig, hamster, mice and rats, goldfish, exotic fish, birds, rabbits
cats in country house only	cats in flats
dogs: Labrador, Corgi, Golden Retriever, King Charles Spaniel, Springer Spaniel, Jack Russell, Norfolk Terrier, Hunt Terrier, Dalmatian, English Setter, Whippet	Rottweiler, Alsatian, Poodle, Afghan, (Cocker) Spaniel, Collie, Airedale, Boxer, Doberman, Bull Terrier
	Aggressive-looking guard dogs
dog names: Badger, Ranger, Bertie, Snipe For the Queen's dogs' names see Wikipedia, 'Queen Elizabeth corgis'	Emma, Jessica, Funny, Cassandra, Sophie, Jason, Wellington, Melchester, Sport, Blacky, Patch, Snowy, Lady, Duchess, Rex, Prince, Duke, Earl, Baron, Tyson
have as many as possible	
idolize their dogs	adore their dogs
dogs occupy best places in house	
bury dog in corner of garden	
plain brown leather collar with address on tag	dog's name in inverted commas
	dress up dogs in garish collars, bows, etc.
horse and pony shows	dog shows, cat shows, obedience tests
huge tolerance of mess caused by animals	slightly less tolerant
	sticker in car back windows pointing out animals, e.g. 'Show dog in transit', or on the front door 'Beware of the dog'

Terminology	
dog, canine, hound	doggie, pup, puppy, pooch
bitch	lady dog
cat	pussy, pussycat
to put down (a dog)	to put to sleep (a dog)

25

Sport

Sports and games are an essential part of English culture and heritage. Many sports (rugby, football, baseball, tennis, cricket, hockey) were invented in England (golf in Scotland); for others (boxing, hockey, racing, polo, rowing, swimming, bridge, even skiing), the English were the first to create the rules by which they continue to be played today all over the world. There is probably no other race that takes part in so many different sports and games. Any book about England or Englishness worthy of the name must therefore consider this aspect of national life. Sport can be a class-free zone (see Chapter 30). The selection of the Oxford or Cambridge eight is based not on social class, but on rowing prowess. Engaging jointly in a sporting activity brings different classes together. But in sport too, class affinities persist. Some differences depend on whether participation in the sport is active or passive (as a spectator). Football in particular is keenly followed across the social spectrum, at least at international level (with England vs Germany being the jewel in the crown), but the players are more likely to come from the lower classes, for whom the game is potentially a springboard to prosperity and social mobility à la David Beckham. Some sports are favoured more by the upper sections of society, others by those nearer the bottom. In the first instance, this generally has something to do with the costs, which put such activities beyond the reach of the ordinary citizen.

The sports whose participants come from virtually all strata are surprisingly many. They are not seen as class-specific, but as socially neutral, which is why it has been necessary to introduce a middle column in this case. Nevertheless, class differences may even exist within the same sport. The game of rugby, for instance, is played according to two different codes: as commentators never tire of pointing out, rugby union's origins in the UK are posh and so are its fans ('rugby is a hooligan's game played by gentlemen'), whereas rugby league, with its history of professionalism, has its roots in the working classes.

That sport is not immune to class considerations is clearly demonstrated by media comments on sportsmen and women's social backgrounds should they achieve major success in their field. Polo is reputedly the sport of kings. Prince Philip played, as did Prince Charles. So do Prince William and Prince Harry. Richard John de la Poer Beresford has been one England's most outstanding polo players since his youth. Now 34, he has a handicap of 6 goals, making him one of Europe's finest professionals.[1] Because of his athletic ability he has always attracted attention in polo circles. When his grandfather died in 2015, his father Henry inherited the title of 9th Marquess of Waterford, since when Richard, as the latter's son, has held the courtesy title of Earl of Tyrone. In the intervening years coverage of him in the media has proliferated. With the ubiquitous references to his aristocratic background and his good looks, it would be easy to forget that he is a top-notch polo player. And when a full-page advert from the exclusive polo outfitter La Martina appears in the magazine *Polo Times*, it is no coincidence that the handsome young man pictured on a polo pony wearing a jacket and trousers (red of course) is name-dropped as George Spencer-Churchill, Marquess of Blandford and the future Duke of Marlborough.

At the opposite end of the scale the focus on class remains tangible, although the emphasis is less pronounced. If a working-class sprog attains a high polo handicap, their success will assuredly be noted as particularly impressive given their origins. It was a similar story in tennis in the decades following the war if a former ballboy, say, won Wimbledon – which actually happened in the case of the Spaniard Manuel Santana. The converse is also true, should a child from an aristocratic background reach the top level in a sport dominated by the lower classes. If an earl's son were to play for a Premier League football club, it is inconceivable that the press would not allude to his 'unconventional' background.

TERMINOLOGY

Sport has evolved its own language, with each discipline having its own specific jargon. Any non-native speaker who can understand an English radio football commentary is to be congratulated on their supreme linguistic skills. Sporting vocabulary generally cuts across the classes: there is only one way of saying the defender scored an own goal. Also irrelevant in terms of social class is the terminology specific to a single sport – shooting, for instance. Here a bag is not a piece of luggage, but the amount of game shot on that day, and a gun is not only a weapon, but also a member of a shooting party. By analogy, the word shot describes not only the firing of a gun but also the person doing the shooting. The stand is a butt when shooting grouse and a hide when hunting duck. In all other cases the appropriate word is stand or peg. A pair of grouse, partridge or pheasant is called a brace, whereas two wild ducks are a couple. A point-to-point is not a straight line encountered in geometry, but a race over fences across the English countryside usually involving the horses used in hunting. Being familiar with the lingo is handy if at a hunt, but not knowing it because such sports leave you cold will not count against you as a social black mark. Class is revealed when different words are used for the same thing, as is generally so often the case. Consequently, depending on your class, you will say hunting rather than foxhunting, riding instead of horse riding and use the term hounds in preference to dogs.

riding	horse riding
racing	horse racing
pony (polo)	horse
red coat	pink coat
my horse – was too fresh and bucked me off – gave me a fall	I was thrown from the horse which was very frisky
horse goes up with me	horse keeps rearing
hunting	fox hunting
hounds (hunting)	dogs
hounds give tongue or speak	bark
pack (of hounds)	
to ride to hounds	to ride with hounds
to shoot over a dog	to shoot with a dog
charlie	fox
grouse	the bird
oarsmen (the Boat Race)	rowers

EVENTS

Matches involving the national soccer team are of interest to nearly every Englishman, regardless of social status. This does not mean, however, that everyone will want to be there in the flesh. Normally, people's participation is limited to watching on television. But at a few sporting events, being there is what matters. While the sport itself is important, so is the opportunity to meet and greet certain individuals, have a drink, talk to people, dine together. For attendees, what counts above all is to be seen and therefore recognized as belonging. Probably the most famous occasion of this sort is Royal Ascot, a week-long race meeting traditionally attended by the Queen and other members of the Royal Family. The racecourse is laid out along exclusive, hierarchical lines, with the Royal, Queen Anne and Windsor enclosures, as well as car parks 1 and 7 for the highest-ranking guests. The rest follow on behind.

Flat racing
Derby at Epsom, June
Oaks at Epsom, June
St Leger Stakes at Doncaster, September
Royal Ascot at Ascot, June
Goodwood at Goodwood, July
King George VI and Queen Elizabeth Stakes at Ascot, July
National Hunt racing
Cheltenham National Hunt Festival (Gold Cup) at Cheltenham, March
Grand National at Aintree, April
Rowing and sailing
The Oxford and Cambridge Boat Race in London, March/April
Henley Royal Regatta at Henley, July
Cowes Week on the Solent, August
Tennis
Wimbledon in London, June/July
Cricket
Eton versus Harrow in London at Lord's, June/July
The Lord's Test, usually June onwards
Horse trials
Badminton at Badminton House, May
Burghley Stamford at Burghley House, September
Polo
Queen's Cup Windsor at Guards, May/June
Gold Cup at Cowdray, June/July

SPORT AND POLITICS

Naturally, politics cannot ignore sport and its class ties. The guiding principle for politicians is to demonstrate an allegiance with the game or activity that can win them the most votes. Accordingly, every politician must be a football fan. Upper-class and elitist sports are to be avoided. The repercussions of choosing the wrong sport were experienced first-hand, and to his great chagrin, by the then

Deputy Prime Minister John Prescott in summer 2006. Despite his impeccable working-class credentials (see Chapter 7), he fell foul of his own ilk when, while deputizing for his boss Tony Blair, who was away visiting George W. Bush in the USA, he was photographed playing croquet with aides on the 'manicured lawns' (as they were unfailingly described) at his grace-and-favour country residence, Dorneywood in Buckinghamshire. A media storm followed ('He's supposed to be running the country, not playing croquet'), and Prescott subsequently even gave Dorneywood up. Just about every commentator pointed out that croquet was a game of the upper and upper-middle classes. It seems reasonable to assume that no-one would have batted an eyelid at Prescott's behaviour if he had joined in a kick-about or played darts with his staff or friends or taken two hours out to walk, jog or slog it out in the gym. Evidently a politician's credibility depends on whether, when he picks up a mallet, he intends to knock a stake into the ground, hammer a nail into wood or hit a ball through a small hoop. His accusers and critics were not his political opponents, but members of his own party, among them Labour backbenchers in particular.

Sport found itself at the centre of what might be termed a sporting class war that pitted left against right, upper against lower, country against town. The dispute concerned foxhunting with hounds, a centuries-old leisure pursuit in the countryside that was once widely perceived as quintessentially English and inimitably and immortally characterized by Oscar Wilde as 'the unspeakable in pursuit of the uneatable'. In July 1997 the Labour peer Ann Mallalieu described it as 'our music, our poetry, our art, our pleasure, our community, our whole way of life'. The 2004 Hunting Act imposed a ban on foxhunting. The official justification for the law was to prevent cruelty to animals, but politicians and the wider population understood there was more at stake: those on the political left saw foxhunting as an upper-class pastime of the privileged elite, sufficient reason in their eyes for its prohibition. The counter movement, embodied by the Countryside Alliance, saw an attack on freedom and tolerance towards minorities. In 2002 it successfully mobilized around half a million people in London in protest against the ban, of whom all the indications suggest only a very small number were actual toffs. The others were 'everyday' country folk. Commenting on the 1999 bill to ban foxhunting in Scotland, the Duke of Buccleuch said: 'This is ninety-five per cent about class warfare and five per cent animal welfare.'[2]

26

Holidays and Travel

Travelling was for a long time the prerogative of the prosperous classes. No-one else had either the time or the money, and certainly not for trips abroad. In the seventeenth century the well-to-do began to travel in their own country, from the provinces to London or, for the season, to take the waters in spa towns such as Bath, Cheltenham, Malvern, Scarborough and Tunbridge Wells. The trend reached its apotheosis with the 'grand tour', an extended trip across Continental Europe undertaken by wealthy young Englishmen in search of the art, culture and roots of Western civilization.[1] Their itinerary led them from Dover to Belgium or France and onward to Paris, then to Switzerland (often to Geneva or Lausanne), and from there to Italy – first to Turin, then Florence, and finally Rome, sometimes with a side trip to Naples to visit Herculaneum and Pompeii. On the way back they took in Venice, often stopping in Innsbruck, Vienna, Dresden, Berlin or Munich, Heidelberg and Cologne en route for Holland and Flanders, before returning across the Channel to England. A grand tour could take anything from several months to several years. One of its most famous exponents was Lord Byron. In the nineteenth century and during the first third of the twentieth the journey across Europe became a tour of the colonies and often also the world.[2] Although linked to social status, class differences did not arise since only the affluent echelons had access to travel of this kind.

These days virtually every Englishman has the means and the opportunity to take a holiday in Britain or abroad because his employment also entitles him to a number of weeks of paid leave.[3] Modern class differences are revealed not by whether people have a vacation or not, but by where they go and how they get there. As might be expected, the answers to these questions indicate considerable similarities between the classes. Many destinations are visited by people of all backgrounds, in particular the most celebrated sights. An Englishman who wishes to see Athens, Paris, Rome or Berlin or the Pyramids or Angkor Wat can expect to find compatriots of every social hue there. The same applies to spots without any particular sightseeing merit that are thought of simply as places to relax and which appeal to everyone, such as the Algarve in Portugal. Nevertheless, destinations with specific class associations very much exist, where members of various sections of society are wont to congregate. Go to Brighton and you will meet a different sort of visitor from those who frequent the beaches of Brancaster in Norfolk. The means of transport are also largely neutral in class terms: everyone drives, everyone flies. Therefore, as with sport, a middle column is introduced here. Alongside the choice of destination, class differences are expressed most tellingly by the activities undertaken as a tourist and on vacation. For anyone doubting the social implications of travel and holidays, the example of the English travel company that enjoyed great success by promising 'chav-free' holidays (see Chapter 13) should make them think again. As many places, like types of sport, are not associated with a particular class, a third (middle) list of 'neutral' places is included here.

Winter destinations		
Scotland: Aviemore France: Verbier, Meribel, Courchevel, Val d'Isère Austria: St Anton, Lech Switzerland: Klosters, Zermatt, St Moritz, Gstaad	Spain: Lanzarote, Tenerife	Switzerland: Interlaken USA: Disney World Florida Thailand: Ko Samui

Summer destinations		
UK: Brancaster, Burnham Market, Norfolk; Suffolk; Padstow, Cornwall; St Ives, Cornwall; Croyde, North Devon; Polzeath, Cornwall; Scotland, Hebrides; Channel Islands France: Côte d'Azur (partly), St Tropez	UK: Rock, Cornwall Spain: Ibiza, Majorca, Marbella, Canary Islands, Malaga Portugal: Algarve Greece: Corfu Germany: Berlin	UK: Brighton, Blackpool, Skegness, Margate Italy: Amalfi Coast Spain: Benidorm, Torremolinos
Italy: Tuscany, Umbria, Sardinia Spain: Andalusia, Sotogrande Greece: Kefalonia Portugal: Madeira		Greece: Mykonos, Faliraki, Rhodos Greece/Turkey: Cyprus Turkey: Bodrum USA: Miami, India: Goa Indonesia: Phuket

Means of transport		
(own or friend's) yacht	car	package tour on coach or aeroplane
private aeroplane	easyJet, Ryanair, Wizz	cruising

What to do		
activity holiday		beach holiday
riding		get sunburned
yachting		
		binge drinking
tuition, education		stag and hen parties
		have fun, let off steam, go a bit mad
		change of role (clerk to adventurer)
eat local food		eat English food

27

The Arts

The close and complex interplay between art and class cannot be explained by 'them-and-us' or 'upstairs-downstairs' clichés. The arts occupy a huge space in both the private and public spheres. First take the people themselves: creative artists such as painters, photographers, sculptors, composers, choreographers, installation artists, authors, (some) architects and designers of gardens and furnishings, fashion designers, furniture designers; stage, film and television actors, singers, dancers, musicians, conductors. Some combine several disciplines, such as singer-songwriters or film makers. They and their works are collectively rooted in the great institutions of the art world: theatres, opera houses, concert halls, museums and art galleries, exhibitions, the media including television, performances and events, art periodicals, universities, art schools and music conservatoires, as well as competitions and awards such as the Turner Prize for the visual arts or the Booker for English-language fiction.

Then come the financial backers. In the English public sector the main funding body is Arts Council England. Private sponsors include numerous foundations together with individual and corporate bene-factors. A major financial role is played by the commercial art scene with its galleries, art dealers, auction houses such as Sotheby's and Christie's, art fairs and internet trading. Questions abound as to the part of class in all this. What class do artists come from? Does being an artist make someone change class? Which class buys what art? Do art collectors belong to a specific class? What kind of people work in the institutions that support the arts?

In the past the position was very clear. The upper classes (the nobility, the rich, the Church) commissioned a large part of the art produced, notably paintings, sculptures, architecture and music. This relationship was manifested in the portraits done of the patron and his family, with or without pets, often in his house or palace or on his estate. For centuries the country houses of the English aristocracy were home to many of the largest and most valuable art collections in Europe. Alongside the museums, this remains the case today, as amply illustrated by Harewood House, Waddesdon Manor, Petworth House and Sudley House, to name but a few. With the exception of a few writers, the artists were only rarely upper-class themselves, being mostly from the middle orders. They were not recognized as social equals by those who commissioned their work. When the artist Sir Alfred Munnings went to paint Viola, Duchess of Westminster at Eaton Hall he was not invited to dine with the duke and duchess.[1] The vast majority of art's consumers – those who read the books, attended performances, looked at the paintings and listened to the music – came from the upper and middle strata and were hardly ever working-class. In this respect many things have changed.

Working artists have scaled the social ladder in recent decades, particularly if they are famous and successful. Then they count as upper-middle, or indeed upper-class in some cases if their art has made them rich. The painters Lucian Freud and David Hockney, the writer Patrick Leigh Fermor and pop musicians Elton John and Paul McCartney. The loftier ranks of society befriend them in all sincerity. At the same time they bask in the artists' glow, assuming an aura of cultural and intellectual superiority while simultaneously documenting their compassion and open-mindedness towards other sections of the community. If artists behave badly and contrary to upper-class norms they are generally forgiven. Indeed, the media even condones their behaviour as an expression of a natural and irrepressible vitality.

As artists' social standing has increased so, unlike in previous centuries, members of the aristocracy have felt free to engage in artistic endeavour, some even professionally. Ideally, they do it for fun, but for some it is a way of earning money. They are particularly given to penning their memoirs or writing historical works or books about art or nature or travel accounts. A career in journalism is all right, and photography is clearly favoured, with several lords (Anthony Snowden, Patrick Lichfield and Christopher Thynne) making their name in this field. Even acting is accepted. Actually, today's aristocrats can take up any occupation in the arts they please without eyebrows being raised by their peers, except perhaps to a lesser extent ballet-dancing.

From all of the above it follows that artists can achieve upward social mobility. A contemporary role model is Tracey Emin, the daughter of a Turkish-Cypriot father and an English mother of Romanian extraction and in the 1980s the *enfant terrible* of the Young British Artists movement. Today she is rich, holds a CBE and is a member of the Royal Academy of Arts, where she is professor of drawing. She has lectured at leading art institutions such as the Victoria and Albert Museum, the Art Gallery of New South Wales in Sydney and Tate Britain. She votes Conservative and has become, in a word, Establishment.

Through their work gifted artists receive a ticket to society's uppermost realms. Not all artists wish to use it, and some who would like to are refused entry. But it is undeniably a chance for fame and fortune and access to the high life. A certain contradiction is evident in the attitude of bohemians to the English class system which, virtually without exception, is criticized and roundly rejected. The upper classes fare particularly badly. A leitmotif of the English novel is to depict those positioned on the upper rungs of the 'official' class ladder as narrow, hard-hearted, arrogant, weak and sometimes even inhuman, while 'true' humanity is found nearer the bottom, among poor relations, servants, miners or waiters. From Jane Austen's *Mansfield Park* to George Eliot's *Middlemarch* and Zadie Smith's *White Teeth*, great works have been written on this theme.[2] The ire of nearly all modern artists is directed against the elites and the Establishment, whose mask they insist must be stripped away. A revolution in the

way of thinking and how art is expressed is called for, as well as political revolt in some cases. Art must be redefined as something for the
many, not the few. Boundaries must be removed, barriers torn down.
Art must provoke. The state must be exposed and emasculated. Peace
to the slums! War on the palaces! Middle-class morals must be eradicated. The same artists have no qualms, however, about taking money
from the elites, the Establishment or the state – or even about asking
for it. Admittedly, some artists do exist who willingly reject the upper-
class lifestyle afforded by their success, but the list is not very long.

Within the English class system a special role is played by the
institutions that run the arts and support artists as funding providers, event organizers, museums and art galleries, professional artists'
associations, etc., such as Arts Council England, the Royal Academy,
the Royal Opera House, the Royal Shakespeare Company, the
National Theatre, the British Museum, the National Gallery, the Tate
Gallery, and so on. Until a few decades ago, these institutions were
bastions of the upper echelons. Their chairmen, board members,
directors, general secretaries and other functionaries were primarily university-educated members of the upper classes, the Great and
Good, as Jeremy Paxman so aptly put it under the heading of 'The
Arts Tsars'.[3] Today an interesting dynamic occurs in such bodies: if
you already belong to the upper echelons, you have a good chance of
being appointed to one of these institutions; if not, such an appointment will secure you a place at the highest level of society.

Roy Shaw was born in 1918 as the son of a steelworker whose
father had been a miner. With a mother who had worked in a factory
during World War I, his background was pure working class. When
he died as Sir Roy Shaw in 2012 at the age of 93, he was celebrated
by glowing obituaries in *The Times* and other leading British newspapers. In the intervening years his life had been dominated by, and
had dominated, the arts, with a lifelong commitment to expanding
access to the arts for all, including as head of adult education at Leeds
and Keele Universities and as a member of the Board of Governors of
the BBC and of the British Film Institute. He was also a co-founder
of the Open University. He reached the pinnacle of his career as the

Secretary-General of the Arts Council of Great Britain (as it was known at the time), a position he held from 1975 to 1983, thereafter becoming a theatre critic and author. From working-class beginnings he ended right at the top. Like artists, prominent arts administrators are attractive to the upper classes.

Having been appointed Chairman of the Royal Opera House, Covent Garden in 1974, an office he held until 1985, the celebrated statistician Claus Moser later recalled in an interview:

> Until I became Chairman of the Royal Opera House, by which time I was fifty-two, I had never, but never, met anybody royal: now I was entertaining them month after month. Suddenly this new world had opened itself to me. When I was a frequent visitor to Covent Garden, or even on the board, some people would scarcely speak to me. Yet literally the day after my appointment as Chairman was announced, a very distinguished woman whom I would prefer not to name, who had previously cut me dead, rang up, to invite my wife and me to spend the weekend with them in Scotland. It continued like that for all the years I was chairman. From that moment onwards I saw a totally new layer of British life.[4]

In 2001 Moser was made a life peer as Baron Moser. Art opens the doors to high society. Consequently, membership of these organizations is also favoured as a promising stepping stone to state recognition, an honour from the Queen or even a life peerage – especially if the role is combined with financial sponsorship of the arts through donations to museums or similar. Occasionally even ugly deeds can be concealed by artistic renown. It is widely held that Anthony Blunt, who was revealed as a Soviet spy by Margaret Thatcher in 1979, was saved from earlier exposure by the positions he held (alongside many other honorary fellowships) as professor of the history of art at the University of London, director of the Courtauld Institute of Art and Surveyor of the Queen's Pictures.[5]

The commercial face of art, the art business or art industry as it is sometimes referred to, is also heavily class-ridden. High-end art collectors and buyers are by definition moneyed. A glance round the saleroom at a major art auction or at the names of famous art collectors is sufficient to make out the movers and shakers: members of the working class are nowhere to be seen. Art collectors' motives vary: a pleasure in beauty is one, as well as the hope that their investment will pay off financially – a wish fulfilled remarkably frequently in recent decades. Some desire to create a legacy for posterity, and quite a few to raise their social status by association with art and artists. Buying and owning art demonstrates high status.

Many children of wealthy parents also seek a career in the art business, often more as a hobby than as a means of subsistence. They enjoy the upmarket environment, the great works of humanity, the rubbing shoulders with the well-heeled – work that pays well and is agreeable all round. With the right knack and good luck, art dealers and auctioneers may even become rich. It is a scene that also attracts the scions of the aristocracy and one in which they are in demand. They are presumed to have immaculate manners, be well-connected and have some idea of paintings, furniture and sculptures because of the artefacts surrounding them at home. While they readily satisfy the first of these expectations, the last is more rarely encountered. This is not a problem, however, for the millionaire whose key aim in buying art is to acquire a certain class, esteem and respect.

And so we come to the people who consume art, those who seek enjoyment of the works of others by reading, looking and listening. Which class appreciates what art? This is where minorities and the majority inevitably meet. Art has always included an elitist aspect. Not all art appeals to everyone; not everyone 'gets' all art. Not all art wishes to appeal to everyone. On the contrary, art is more strongly associated with the few than with the many. Some of the greatest works of all time were not only created by minorities (to which artists inherently belong), but were only appreciated by minorities too. A work that pleases the majority from the outset is more liable to be a dud than a masterpiece. That the minority opinion may be shared by the majority in the course of time is a different story. Some attempts at categorization have been made, roughly along the following lines:

theatre	Hollywood blockbusters
opera, ballet, classical music, concerts	country music, golden oldies, easy listening
go to museums and art galleries	games machines and gizmos
like world music	dislike world music
like jazz	dislike jazz
art history	'kitschy' art, 'kitsch'
archaeological exhibits	
English or foreign literature	English 'chick lit'
	Beryl Cook or Jack Vettriano

Under the heading of cultural capital, the Great British Class Survey (GBCS) also examined the affinities between class and the arts, but without reaching any clear-cut conclusions. Although, as a general trend, the above kinds of divisions could be stated to exist as a definite (albeit declining) paradigm among the older generation, overall and in the younger generation in particular a wide-ranging eclecticism appears to be emerging. The members of the upper echelons pride themselves on being interested not only in classical, highbrow culture but equally, and sometimes even more enthusiastically, in all art forms and cultural activities. When it comes to music especially, they are just as keen on pop as the lower classes. On the other hand, the lower classes are engaging to an ever-growing extent in forms and works of art they would have once eschewed. The fantastic crowds attending even 'challenging' exhibitions in English art galleries and museums demonstrate the active interest at all levels of the population in art, which was previously viewed as appealing more to the intelligentsia. While not all Englishmen care for every type of culture, more and more of them are increasingly widening their preferences. Jilly Cooper's observation that 'Mozart, Haydn, Vivaldi and Purcell are upper-class composers, Brahms, Mahler, Schubert and Beethoven are upper-middle, Tchaikovsky, Grieg and Mendelssohn are lower-middle,'[6] could no longer be made today, any more than the suggestion that the Beatles made working-class music.

28

Etcetera

Class pervades all aspects of English life and culture.

Kate Fox, *Watching the English* (2014)

Nearly every book about class contains this or similar sentences. It is virtually impossible in England to find a sphere of activity that is not affected by class to some degree – if never entirely, then always at least slightly. The domains in which class plays a role are countless (see Chapter 4). However, it is worth taking a look at some less obvious aspects – small tokens that signify class. Often they tip the balance in determining where someone is placed.

Some spheres, however, are often described as class-free zones – i.e. settings where class does not matter, popular examples being pubs, sport, the church, hobbies and universities. On closer inspection, however, the term is deceptive. Class differences are set aside temporarily, but even then not completely. If the office goes to the pub for a drink after work, the respect shown to the boss in the workplace is replaced by an ironic mock-deference. But there is no question of equality of the kind that peers enjoy. The (so-called) class-free zones merit a chapter to themselves (Chapter 30).

BOOKS

England is the land of books. More than 150,000 are published there each year, a greater number per head than in any other country in the world. Traditionally class was indicated not so much by reading books, as by not reading them. In the upper echelons the excessive study of books was regarded with suspicion, thought likely to damage or weaken character, which was far more highly prized. The famed public-school ideal corresponded to the muscular Christian of Dr Arnold's Rugby rather than the sensitive intellectual. However, none of this prevented the higher ranks from acquiring beautiful libraries with leather-bound, gilt-edged, luxury editions of antiquarian and contemporary books, for which bespoke wooden bookshelves with glass doors were built. These can still be admired today in many a country house. But only very rarely were these volumes actually perused. Jokes abound that the only works ever picked up by an aristocrat during his lifetime were likely to be *Burke's Landed Gentry, Debrett's Peerage and Baronetage* and, at a push, the *Bloodstock Yearbook*. No books were read either by the working class. That left the middle classes, who believed that reading books was a means of social advancement.

Of course in reality this was never quite the case. Without a modicum of reading there was a risk of remaining uneducated, a fact not wasted on the ruling classes of the past, who consequently generally did make the effort to obtain at least a rudimentary education. These endeavours were furthered from the mid-nineteenth century onwards, when their sons were sent to university, usually Oxford or Cambridge. What is striking is how many members of the upper classes have written fantastic books, not to earn money in most cases, but for the sheer joy of writing or to impart something to mankind. Given their status, they need not have taken the trouble. Shining examples that achieved fame in the English-speaking world and in some cases beyond are the works of Lord Byron, Lord Chesterfield (of letters to his son fame), Vita Sackville-West (also renowned for her garden at Sissinghurst), Nancy Mitford, Bertrand Russell and Winston Churchill. The latter even won the Nobel Prize for Literature (although in Churchill's case the money from his writing was an important reason to do it).

For the females born into the nobility the distrust of books and reading continued on until the 1970s. Although women's colleges already existed at universities, Oxford and Cambridge included, these were frequented more by the daughters of the middle-class intelligentsia than the posh girls or 'girls in pearls' as they were known at the time. With their compulsory schooling complete, upper-class young women attended a finishing school, where they would obtain social polish, brush up their foreign languages, improve their general knowledge and also enhance their sporting prowess, with skiing in Switzerland being particularly popular. Thereafter they would come out as debutantes and, before its demise, take part in the London Season. As their next step they might seek a not-too-challenging job, preferably employed by friends or relatives. Reading clever books was never a priority. Their aim was rather to find Mr Right, ideally a member of the wealthy aristocracy but, failing that, a less affluent blue blood or someone from the moneyed bourgeoisie.

With the daughters as with the sons, this attitude has now died out. While there is no need to become a bluestocking, for someone wishing to be a member of the upper classes a university education is really very helpful. Of course, beauty remains a fantastic competitive asset (as is well known, men think with their eyes), but girls who are completely devoid of intellect are nonetheless rather out of place in the social stratosphere. The last conspicuous non-reader was probably the late Deborah, Duchess of Devonshire, who died in 2014. According to nearly every obituary, she always professed that she never read books. Had that been true, which not many believe, she filled the resultant vacuum admirably by writing quite a few books herself, and interesting ones at that.

Since nearly all members of the upper echelons of both sexes have a university education these days, reading has become more a sign of elevated status. As a mark of belonging, mastery of a certain literary canon is a must, as is a broad awareness of the contemporary book scene. Reading the *London Review of Books* is recommended. It follows that whether someone has shelves of books in their house or only racks of DVDs is another indicator of class.

NEWSPAPERS

England is the land not only of books, but also the daily press, having reportedly the highest newspaper readership per head after Japan. The dichotomy between the broadsheets or quality papers and the tabloids reflects the English liking for 'them and us'. The tabloids are subdivided into 'red tops' and 'compacts', the latter being considered more serious. The broadsheets include *The Times*, the *Guardian* (a compact since 2018), *Daily Telegraph*, *Independent* (digital edition only) and *Financial Times*. The biggest tabloids are the *Sun, Daily Mirror, Daily Mail* and *Daily Express*. Asking someone which paper they read is not a reliable way of determining their social rank, however, as many newspapers are read by people of every station (even if surreptitiously and in some cases in secret). But, as one might expect, there are still clear biases. The broadsheets are more often read by the upper classes, the tabloids by the others.[1] The paper you read not only signals your own class, but also highlights other traits of identity and likely political beliefs.

What applies to the daily papers also holds good for weekly magazines such as the *Economist* and the *Spectator*, as well as the Sunday papers, including the *Sunday Times, Observer, Sunday Telegraph, Sunday Express, Mail on Sunday, Sun on Sunday* and *Sunday Mirror*. As with the daily papers, someone who belongs to a certain class will take a specific paper. That is different from saying that someone who buys *The Times* or the *Sun* is therefore automatically a member of the class that enjoys reading these newspapers. All the same, someone wishing to change class is well advised to switch to the paper read by the class they aspire to join.

For their part the newspapers differ in their attitude to the English class system. Some appear indifferent, others mention it only ironically, but for many it is a preoccupation bordering on obsession. The favourite adjective of the *Sun* is 'posh', and it is not meant as a compliment.[2] David Cameron and the members of his cabinet, girls who attend boarding school, Oxford and Cambridge, the Royal Opera House and Selfridges – all are 'posh'. The *Guardian* seems to be in the grip of a kind of class neurosis. Many of its contributors set themselves up as vehement opponents of the English class system, demanding it be dismantled and calling for greater equality. Rather confusingly, the vast majority of the writers concerned are very clearly positioned in the upper half of the class construct, have been to good schools and universities, and are nearer the top than the bottom in the journalistic pecking order (see Chapter 7).

TELEVISION

Like the introduction of flat-pack furniture, labour-saving appliances such as the washing-machine and refrigerator, cheap clothes and good food accessible to all, the advent of television was expected to break down class differences. 'Night after night', wrote the Oxford professor and later Labour MP David Marquand in 1960, 'telly erodes what cultural barriers still remain to divide one class from another.'[3] His hypothesis was only partly correct. Certainly, television does exhibit elements of classlessness, or more accurately class neutrality. When it was originally launched and there was only one channel that people could watch, television had no class implications. Likewise today, when every Englishman has an almost unlimited choice of TV programmes in English or, if desired, in other languages too, television remains a great leveller.

Virtually all the English watch television at least once a day. A further unifying aspect is the way people of all classes tend to chat about their previous night's viewing or take something seen on TV as a cue for conversation. Some programmes are automatically assumed to have been seen by everyone. Then there are the broadcasts that are enjoyed by virtually all Englishmen, such as certain newscasts or coverage of major sporting events like the Olympic Games or the World Cup. A further favourite is *Gogglebox*, a format that features couples, friends and families watching TV and commenting on and discussing clips. Its viewers are a cross-section of society.[4]

Another initially surprising, class-busting aspect of television is advertising. Although the commercials are selected according to class-related criteria (the adverts for some products are aired mainly during shows popular with the working class), advertisers dare not offend class sensibilities. If the advert is too posh, it will upset the less affluent majority; too common, and it will annoy the cash-rich minority. The result is advertisements that are deliberately socially neutral.[5] When it comes to the television programmes themselves on the other hand, class differences fully kick in. Generally speaking, BBC Four is watched by different segments of society than the commercial channels. *I'm a Celebrity, Get Me Out of Here* will not have the same fans as a documentary on the BBC. The extent of television consumption is also heavily class-dependent. More than five hours per day are spent in front of the box by around one-third of working people, one-fifth of the middle class and just under one-tenth of the professional strata.[6]

CLUBS

The institution of the club splendidly mirrors the English desire both to belong to a group and at the same time exclude others (see Chapter 6). Although a bit at odds with the individualism of the English, it's this that sees England typically described as having more clubs and societies than any other country in the world. There are clubs for this and clubs against that, and reputedly even a club for the clubless. A club and society culture of this kind is ideal for making class-related distinctions: to each class its own club. And so it transpires, even down to the club name.

Alongside the trade unions, the working men's clubs were a pillar of the English labouring class, for many workers a kind of second home where they could turn up on their own several times a week and on certain occasions bring their families. They were the traditional place for workers to socialize and drink of an evening. As the blue-collar workforce as such has contracted, so working men's clubs have gone into decline. Whereas in the 1970s there were around 4,000 clubs with some six million members, only 2,200 clubs exist these days, with a membership of just under two million. The ban on smoking, popularity of television and rise in drinking at home have all had an impact.

On the other side of the class coin are the private clubs whose members are primarily upper and upper-middle class, as exemplified by the legendary gentlemen's clubs in London, such as White's, the Athenaeum, Boodle's, the Carlton, the Garrick, the Reform, the Travellers and the Turf.

Sports clubs reflect the class allegiances of the sport concerned. The membership of a darts club is rather different from that of the Guards Polo Club, and not only financially.

Modern private members' clubs such as Home House or Soho House are geared more to business and money than class. They are commercial enterprises which offer a place to people with money who prefer to stick with their kind.

SPECIAL OCCASIONS

Class is neither here nor there when it comes to the number of special occasions and the reasons behind them. Throughout England certain days and events are fittingly marked. Notable dates that apply to everyone are Christmas, New Year's Eve, Easter, May Day, Halloween, Guy Fawkes' Night, Valentine's Day, the spring and late summer bank holidays and Mothering Sunday. Individual rites of passage include engagements, weddings, the birth of a child, coming of age, graduation, silver or golden weddings, funerals, housewarmings, leaving dos and birthdays, as well as children's parties. All Englishmen and -women commemorate these occasions in some way or another. What differs in the extreme, however, is how they do so. The variety of ways is perhaps the clearest illustration that class is simply about difference. Christmas is held by the majority of Englishmen and -women, but with what observances? Most young people in England celebrate their coming of age, but how? Although marriage is less popular among the English these days, there is no shortage of weddings. How are the nuptials celebrated?

As a general rule, the various classes behave as follows on these occasions: the higher the status, the more straightforward, unfussy and relatively modest the proceedings. The lower the rank, the greater the effort, fuss and relative extravagance. The words general and relative are crucial here, for there is naturally nothing modest about a royal wedding, nor about the parties held to mark notable birthdays or graduations among offspring of the nobility or moneyed aristocracy. A case in point is the twenty-first birthday party held in honour of Hugh Grosvenor at a reported cost of £5 million. In the traditional upper class the heir's coming of age was a most significant event not just for the family, but for the whole estate: the birthday was celebrated by the tenants and staff, the neighbours and the county. The villages, gates and lodges of the whole estate were decorated, and feasting on a huge scale went on for days. But these exceptions apart, the upper echelons are less ostentatious with their celebrations than those of lower rank.

Weddings are a good example. Of course, many etiquette books are available on the subject, but these are usually of limited interest for class purposes since they represent only the *one* variant they see as correct. Kate Fox amusingly charted the class differences associated with weddings for four different social groups, providing a vivid summary in key words.[7]

Working-class wedding: a big do, modelled on the ideal of a lavish celebrity-style affair, sometimes themed; sit-down meal in a hotel, restaurant or pub function room; big fancy car or even a horse-drawn carriage; bridesmaids in tight, revealing dresses; everyone in glamorous, brand-new, Sunday-best outfits and matching accessories; generous food, a huge, three-tiered cake; a big noisy evening party with free-flowing booze; a honeymoon somewhere hot. No expense spared.

Lower-middle and middle-middle class: smaller and more prudent affair; careful attention to doing everything properly and tastefully; pride if hard work and thought going into the wedding are noticed; fairly traditional wedding along royal lines; no wacky themes or gimmicks; romantic location; dainty and effortlully elegant details; colour of flowers, serviettes and place cards all co-ordinated and matching bride's mother's outfit; food bland and safe; meals garnished with parsley and radishes carved into flower shapes; fine wines, but sometimes not enough; anxiety over relatives and guests who might get drunk or behave badly, or that the best man might make a smutty speech.

Upper-middle class: class-secure upper-middles aim for an air of effortless elegance, an appearance of casual, unfussy stylishness (which of course takes just as much thought and hard work to achieve, as seen elsewhere with their gardens); traditional locations, ceremonies and vows; overall a slight retro tendency. Class-anxious upper middles strive to distinguish themselves visibly from the middle-middles by choosing less traditional music, 'different' food that is not necessarily pleasant to eat, clothes are quirky but not way-out.

Upper class: fairly traditional, often a quiet, muted, simple affair; clothes worn by guests have not been bought specially as they attend so many similar functions; no desire to be distinctively different or stand out, so usually take the most basic standard vows. If a religious wedding is planned, a church with some special meaning in London is picked or an ancient village church in the shires.

It is quite astonishing how little this description differs from that of Jilly Cooper, who was writing 35 and 15 years respectively before Kate Fox.[8] Class habits die hard.

Part III

Always and Forever?

29

A Classless Society

We all rail against class-distinctions, but very few people seriously want to abolish them.

George Orwell, *The Road to Wigan Pier* (1937)

There is no method by which men can be both free and equal.

Journalist and constitutionalist Walter Bagehot,
Economist (1863)

A classless society has long been coveted, called for or predicted as inevitable by thinkers, poets, politicians and activists too numerous to count. Even today, not a day goes by without someone claiming that class barriers have been broken down or calls for this to happen. But comparatively few have ventured to suggest what shape a classless society should take. Their visions rarely go beyond vague indications of ending man's dominion over man, all people living in harmony, and everyone being cared for according to their needs in a world where justice and equality reign.

HARD CLASSLESSNESS

Even Karl Marx, the most famous champion of the classless society as the historically inevitable end phase of human society, was none too specific, preferring instead to express himself in figurative and idyllic terms. In capitalist society, he foresaw,

> each man has a particular, exclusive sphere of activity, which is forced upon him and from which he cannot escape. He is a hunter, a fisherman, a herdsman, or a critical critic, and must remain so if he does not want to lose his means of livelihood; while in communist society, where nobody has one exclusive sphere of activity but each can become accomplished in any branch he wishes, society regulates the general production and thus makes it possible for me to do one thing today and another tomorrow: to hunt in the morning, fish in the afternoon, rear cattle in the evening, criticize after dinner, just as I have a mind, without ever becoming hunter, fisherman, herdsman or critic.
>
> If everybody must work, if the opposition between those who do work and those who don't disappears . . . and moreover, one takes count of the development of the productive forces engendered by capital, society will produce forces engendered by capital, society will produce in six hours the necessary surplus, even more than now in 12 hours; at the same time everybody will have six hours of 'time at his disposition', the true richness; time which will not be absorbed in direct productive labour, but will be available for enjoyment, for leisure, thus giving scope for free activity and development.

Leon Trotsky hoped for a 'new man'.

> Socialism, if it is worthy of the name, means human relations without greed, friendship without envy and intrigue, love without base calculation.
> Communist man . . . will develop all the vital elements of contemporary art to the highest point. Man will become immeasurably stronger, wiser and subtler; his body will become more harmonized, his movements more rhythmic, his voice more musical. The forms of life will become dynamically dramatic. The average

human type will rise to the heights of an Aristotle, a Goethe, or a Marx. And above this ridge new peaks will rise.

In *Culture and Anarchy* (1869), Matthew Arnold pinned his hopes on culture:

> It seeks to do away with classes; to make the best that has been thought and known in the world current everywhere; to make all men live in an atmosphere of sweetness and light, where they may use ideas, as it uses them itself, freely-nourished and not bound by them.

In the closing pages of *The Road to Wigan Pier* (1937), George Orwell concluded that class distinctions will not be abolished by the bourgeoisie embracing its proletarian brothers or the proletariat giving up its contempt of the 'old school tie'. In rather woolly terms, Orwell hoped for a Socialist party, in which the 'widely separate classes fight side by side against the plutocracy' and consequently gain a new understanding of one another. 'And then perhaps this misery of class-prejudice will fade away.' Ten years later he thought three measures 'obviously necessary' for a (more) classless society. First, 'Above a certain point all incomes should be taxed out of existence.' Secondly, a uniform educational system for all children up to the age of twelve or at least ten, whereafter it 'becomes necessary to separate the more gifted children from the less gifted'. Thirdly, to remove the class labels from the English language by creating a 'national accent – a modification of cockney, perhaps, or of one of the northern accents – [that] should be taught as a matter of course to all children alike'.[1] As we know today, these wishes were unrealistic.

In his essay *The Rise of the Meritocracy*, written in 1956, Michael Young boldly delivered a prophetic view of 2009. In it, a local group of the Technicians' Party (as the workers' party had been rebranded) issued the 'Chelsea Manifesto'. The group's goal was the classless society.

They oppose inequality. They deny that one man is in any fundamental way the superior of another. They seek the equality of man in the sense that they want every man to be respected for the good that is in him. Every man is a genius at something, even every woman, they say: it is the function of society to discover and honour it, whether it is genius at making pots, growing daisies, ringing bells, caring for babies, or even (to show their tolerance) genius at inventing radio telescopes.

The Manifesto summarizes the classless society:

The classless society would be one which both possessed and acted upon plural values. Were we to evaluate people, not only according to their intelligence and their education, their occupation, and their power, but according to their kindliness and their courage, their imagination and sensitivity, their sympathy and generosity, there could be no classes. Who would be able to say that the scientist was superior to the porter with admirable qualities as a father, the civil servant with unusual skill at gaining prizes superior to the lorry-driver with unusual skill at growing roses? The classless society would also be the tolerant society, in which individual differences were actively encouraged as well as passively tolerated, in which full meaning was at last given to the dignity of man. Every human being would then have equal opportunity, not to rise up in the world in the light of any mathematical measure, but to develop his own special capacities for leading a rich life.

Modern politicians who have made a classless society their goal, such as John Major, have experienced similar difficulties attempting to define their objective. Shortly before becoming prime minister, Major famously said:

In the next ten years we will have to continue to make changes which will make the whole of this country a genuinely classless society in which people can rise to whatever level their own abilities and their own good fortune may take them from wherever they started.

Six-and-a-half years later, in his last press conference as prime minister, he returned to this theme, saying that he wanted 'the chance to take forward my belief in a classless society, where more of the have-nots are able to join the haves'. When in power, however, he did nothing notable to translate his idea into action.

The failure to design a credible classless society comes as no surprise, given that no-one has ever seen a human society that is truly free from class strictures. Even the USA and Australia, which both arose as a kind of counter-model to their class-ridden English mother-country, are no exception. They differ from England in that they measure class in other ways: that is, not according to titles, ancestry, accent and terminology, but by money and power. When it came to the USA, Somerset Maugham was under no illusion: 'Of all the hokum with which America is riddled the most odd is the common notion that it is free of class distinctions.'[2] In his book *Class: A Guide through the American Class System* (1983), Paul Fussell examines the American class system in detail. According to Gallup in 2000, 33 per cent of Americans described themselves as 'working class', a term that had seemingly been redundant for a long time. By 2015 that number had risen to 48 per cent, almost half of America.

The new (and more troubling) phenomenon in the USA concerns the children of the rich and mighty: successful men marry clever and successful women (assortative mating). They conceive bright children and bring them up in stable homes, unlike the mothers of high-school drop-outs, most of whom are unmarried. They stimulate them relentlessly: children of professionals hear three million more words by the age of four than those of parents on benefits. They move to pricey neighbourhoods with good schools, spend a packet on flute lessons and pull strings to get their children into a top-notch college.[3] In short: brains have become hereditary, and the result is a hereditary meritocracy. And those who have made it, regardless of how egalitarian their public discourse, do all they can to protect their children's interests. The journalist-turned-politician Chrystia Freeland tells of an illuminating encounter:

> At Davos in 2012, I spoke about access to the Ivy League and social mobility with Ruth Simmons, then the president of Brown University. She is a widely respected pioneering member of the super-elite – the first African American to lead an Ivy League university. Simmons spoke enthusiastically about helping poor children get to Brown, and supporting them financially after they got there. But when I asked her whether the legacy system, which explicitly favours the children of alumni, should be abolished, the conversation turned personal. 'No, I have a grand-daughter. It's not time yet', she said with a laugh.[4]

Just because Australia has never had the historical class structure of its English mother country and, apart from a small number of governors early on, has never had a nobility, this does not mean that classes do not exist. Those with sufficient money and power belong to the upper class. However, accent and terminology play a less important role than in England. Indeed, being able to claim descent from the people who arrived in Australia in a bygone age on the convict ships from England can provide a kind of social superiority.

The communist states likewise failed to create a society free from class distinctions. In the Soviet Union pre-1989 and today's communist China in particular, things are anything but class-free. Before the collapse of Communism in 1989, the division of classes into 'them' and 'us' in the Soviet Union was especially crass. On the one hand, there were the ordinary people, on the other the members of the Communist Party and the elite known as the *nomenklatura*. These were the 'comrades' who held nearly all the key positions in government, industry, agriculture, science and education, the army and the police, and who enjoyed many privileges and advantages such as dachas, travel to the West and access to shops selling Western goods the common people could only dream of. The same holds true for today's China, but with one important addition. The ruling political class in China is the Communist Party (CPC) – which governs without opposition in the absence of any other parties, which are banned. What makes China stand out is that the CPC, having recognized that a centrally-planned economy makes the population poorer rather than richer, decided to permit and encourage a capitalist approach. Within a relatively short space of time, this resulted in the formation of a super-rich upper class and a fairly large, prosperous middle class: a more unequal distribution of incomes and wealth than in practically any other country, and the very opposite of a classless society.[5]

Even in societies in which the starting conditions are the same for everyone or for the majority, upper, middle and lower classes very quickly crystallize if people have sufficient freedom of development. Here, too, the USA provides the best example. Although the first settlers who arrived there in droves from Europe at the beginning of the seventeenth century essentially started out under the same conditions, by the time of the American Revolution in 1776 the cities were dominated by wealthy merchants who owned stately houses, fine furniture, carriages and half the wealth. Below them, in a finely-graded hierarchy, came artisans, subdivided into master craftsmen and wage-earning journeymen, followed by indentured servants, apprentices, black slaves, sailors, dockworkers and unskilled labourers – all in a city such as Philadelphia of not much more than 30,000 people.[6] Likewise in the country there were major landowners with many workers (including slaves) vying with a large number of smaller farmers.

A more modern example is provided by the slaves who came to America from Africa. They all had the same (unfavourable) starting conditions, and this continued until they obtained the same rights as white Americans. Once this barrier had been lifted and black Americans had access to the opportunities offered by meritocratic America, the black population fairly quickly evolved into upper, middle and lower classes. The most striking change in fortunes came with the rise of the 'new black overclass' or 'Newbos', as the American journalist Lee Hawkins calls them.[7] Newbos are young African Americans who rely on working-class values, a capitalistic philosophy and entrepreneurial instincts to create wealth unimaginable to their forebears. Largely male, they use entertainment, professional sports and media as foundations upon which to build diversified enterprises, some already worth hundreds of millions of dollars. Droves of other young blacks are building businesses and careers in industries that have sprung up around these sports, entertainment and media figures. Names that spring to mind are the basketball star LeBron James, football quarterback Michael Vick, golf star Tiger Woods, the late singers Michael Jackson and Prince, as well as TV presenter Oprah Winfrey. For the most part, hardly any of this was attributable to adapting to 'white society', but these young moguls and their retinues found economic power in refusing to assimilate and by embracing and commercializing their interpretations and versions of black style and culture. Nowadays a classic career in corporate America is also up for grabs: take American Express Chairman Ken Chenault, Merrill Lynch's E. Stanley O'Neal, and Time Warner's Dick Parsons. It was not their privileged background, including an elite education, that took them to the top, but intelligence, talent, hard work, practice and of course a smidgen of good luck, which no-one can do without. The American dream came true, but at the cost of inequality.

Notwithstanding this, not only does a classless society remain the ideal for many thinkers and politicians, but every few years it is also claimed to have arrived or be imminent. On its launch in 1964 the *Sun* newspaper boldly stated:

'Steaks, cars, houses, refrigerators, washing machines are no longer the prerogative of the "upper crust" but the right of all. People believe, and the *Sun* believes with them, that the division of Britain into social classes is happily out of date.'[8] Similar comments followed the mass arrival of television.

Another development that led to declarations of a society free from class divisions was the availability of affordable travel to anywhere in the world through budget airlines such as Ryanair and easyJet. It was a similar story with mass-produced clothing, which allowed the checkout girl to dress just as fashionably as a duchess – this too was heralded as the dawn of a new, class-free era. Fast food and pop music were hailed as steps to a society of equals. That remains nonsense. Just because all households have cars and refrigerators and washing machines, anyone can fly anywhere, and everyone can buy smart clothes does not mean classes have disappeared: on the contrary, the very differences in individuals' choices of home furnishing, travel destination and clothing are exactly what defines their social class.[9]

The dreams of bringing about classless society by building brand new housing estates or new towns – the brainchild of Aneurin Bevan – also fell flat. As housing minister in the Attlee cabinet, Bevan's idea of a place 'where the doctor, the grocer, the butcher and the farm labourer all lived in the same street' became the vision of many, including politicians, town planners, architects, sociologists and economists, and was shared by many tenants who became the first occupants of the new council houses.[10] These hopes completely backfired. There was no mixing of classes in the council estates because virtually everyone not working-class refused to live there, and the last thing many members of the working class wanted was middle-class neighbours. Within a few years, the council estates came to symbolize virtually pure-blood concentrations of working-class people strongly demarcated from other sections of the population. To have your home there became a badge of working-class identity. Something intended to create class neutrality or even classlessness instead generated a one-sided society. The objective of many aspiring individuals living there was to get out, as exemplified by the biography of Lynsey Hanley in her now famous *Estates – An Intimate History* (2007).

SOFT CLASSLESSNESS

The vast majority of those advocating a classless society have defined it in economic terms of greater equality of wealth and income, and more equal opportunity to achieve higher incomes and greater wealth. In this respect, the soft class markers have played little or no role. It is a lot harder to overcome the barriers posed by soft class markers than the economic constraints of class. In fact it may be impossible. George Orwell tried it in 1936. He had the advantage, although educated, of being just as poor as the working-class people he frequented:

> For some months I lived entirely in coal miners' houses. I ate my meals with the family, I washed at the kitchen sink, I shared bedrooms with miners, drank beer with them, played darts with them, talked to them by the hour together. But though I was among them, and I hope and trust they did not find me a nuisance, I was not one of them, and they knew it even better than I did. However much you like them, however interesting you find their conversation, there is always that accursed itch of class-difference, like the pea under the princess's mattress. It is not a question of dislike or distaste, only of *difference*, but it is enough to make real intimacy impossible. Even with miners who described themselves as Communists I found that it needed tactful manoeuvrings to prevent them from calling me 'sir'; and all of them, except on moments of great animation, softened their northern accents for my benefit. I liked them and hoped they liked me; but I went among them as a foreigner, and both of us were aware of it. Whichever way you turn this curse of class-difference confronts you like a wall of stone. Or rather it is not so much like a stone wall as the plate-glass pane of an aquarium; it is so easy to pretend that it isn't there, and so impossible to get through it.[11]

The soft class markers are a barrier to equal opportunity. Let us consider language, a key factor in the definition of class, and start with accent. Children cannot learn a different accent from the one spoken by their parents, and they are therefore linguistically 'branded' from birth. They may be able to discard this accent and pick up a different one at a later date, but this calls for a huge effort and is not easy to pull off. Or take terminology and the eloquence associated with it: in a child's early years these are assimilated entirely from the family, whose influence remains dominant for as long as the child still lives at home, during which time school plays only a supporting role. Compensating for these differences is no easy task. Early-years teaching prior to starting school was launched in 1998 through the Sure Start programme, but its effectiveness still divides opinion. Even where such pre-school education is offered, many other soft class markers affected by disparities at family level, such as good manners and taste, remain unchanged (see Chapter 31).

THE CLASS PYRAMID

In short, there is no such thing as a classless society. And to be honest, this is out of the question anyway, given the extreme divergence in human attributes such as intelligence, diligence, talent, character and appearance. No matter how assiduous their efforts, not everyone can write plays like William Shakespeare, discover laws of nature like Newton or Einstein, write songs like the Beatles or serve aces like Roger Federer. The very reason why artistic or creative accomplishments are so admired is because so few people have this ability. If even just 1,000 people could have painted and drawn like Picasso, his works would cease to be masterpieces of humanity, but would become examples of the painter's craft – solid and skilful, but not world-class. If Thomas Edison had been just one in 1,000 people having the same ideas for innovations, his name would have simply passed into history. Progress is created not by Mr Average, but by unique individuals. To quote Michael Young again: 'Civilization does not depend upon the stolid mass, the homme moyen sensual, but upon the creative minority, the innovator who with one stroke can save the labour of 10,000, the brilliant few who cannot look without wonder, the restless elite who have made mutation a social, as well as a biological fact.'[12]

All known human societies are structured like a pyramid, although the shape does not have to be broadest at its base, but can taper to a point again, more like a diamond. However, the top part of the pyramid is pure in form, insofar as the number of people decreases steadily towards the apex. Accordingly, there is one prime minister, but twenty ministers, sixty secretaries of state and so on. Companies have one CEO, five board members, twenty managers at division level and so forth. Among sportsmen and -women, there is usually one top earner, closely succeeded by a small number of near rivals, and the many who just scrape a living. If we take the professions, such as lawyers, a select few are paid millions, but many eke out only a modest living, with a large group between the two.

Not only the nation as a whole, but also all its branches are formed of pyramids of this kind. If everyone had the same schooling or even the same university degrees, the pyramids of power, wealth and status would still exist. This mechanism is comparable with the rising level of performance in sport. Since 1969, tennis players have improved a lot in absolute terms, yet this is of no benefit to today's players who leave in the first round. They remain unknown and impoverished. Only those at the top of the pyramid – that is to say the winner and perhaps the runner-up and semi-finalists – become famous and rich.

The same effect occurs when more and more people go to university. The twentieth century and present day are characterized by an explosive increase in the number of school leavers benefiting from higher education. Over a 100-year period, English universities have seen student registrations rise from some 30,000 in 1910 to around 200,000 in 1960, and around 2.5 million in 2010. By the age of 30, just under half of young Englishmen and -women have received some form of higher education. What effect has this expansion had on equality? None. On the contrary, inequality appears rather to have increased in recent decades of burgeoning student numbers. Just about every relevant study ultimately finds that the expansion in higher education has benefited those from a richer background far more than poorer young people.

The obvious conclusion is that more education may even cause greater inequality, as this is the inevitable corollary of meritocracy. Anyone not convinced by the maths need only take a taxi driven by a university graduate. Having a degree no longer means automatic access to a better job. The call to education does not pave the way to equality, but invites parents to outdo and beat the child next door – the rat race in a more pleasant form. What would happen if, for the sake of argument, the number of law students rose to such an extent that millions were graduating from the law schools? This would not by any means result in more law graduates becoming judges, as the number of judicial positions would remain the same. The sole consequence is more candidates vying for the same jobs, in other words a stiffer competition. Education becomes a race. What's the value in a degree when practically everyone has one? Suddenly only a first-class degree from a top university is good enough. But with all those elite graduates around, you then need to get at least a doctorate, or preferably a PhD. So that's what you do – but then so does the rest of the crowd. Now you need proficiency in an exotic language, too: Hindi, Chinese or Russian, perhaps. To put it another way: When you're in a crowd, you stand on tiptoe to see better. In the end, it's simply the tallest person who gets the best view.

Some twenty years ago the American Ivy League universities were accepting just over a quarter of applications. These days, Harvard takes just 5 per cent of hopefuls. This is not because the number of available places has gone down, but because the volume of applicants has risen exponentially. Therefore the number of candidates who lose out on a university place has increased as well. Twenty years ago, it was 75 per cent, now it is 95. For the majority, failure is inevitable. Depression and other mental health problems loom. The law of meritocracy kicks in: few winners, many losers. Accordingly, the fight for university places involves not only the prospective students, but also their parents.

University pays. People with college degrees earn more than those without them. Graduates from elite universities earn more than those who have attended lesser institutions. Parents know that. They therefore map out their children's lives in that direction. Even before they are born, some put their child's name down at a top school that provides a pipeline to a further prestigious establishment offering university preparation, to ensure they pass the entrance exam. Reportedly, some parents get their children up extra early in the morning so they can practise reading and arithmetic before going to school. This is not an isolated, American problem, but a global phenomenon. Lamentably, those who propel youngsters into this 'rug rat race' delude them into believing that the only possible outcome is success, while keeping quiet the much greater likelihood of failure. They have good reasons for doing so. Electors' votes and sales figures are secured by the vision of success, not defeat. However, this approach generates many more disappointments than feelings of satisfaction and is, incidentally, one of the reasons why so many young people despise politicians: they realize they are being lied to. The same holds true for the idea of lifelong learning propagated among others by the Commission on Social Justice set up by the former Labour leader John Smith and maintained by Gordon Brown. Far from guaranteeing upward mobility, having access to lifelong learning is merely a ticket to join the race to the top from which most people emerge as losers.

Many people, particularly politicians wishing to achieve popularity among voters, promote the idea that every pupil should receive the highest possible grades regardless of academic performance. In a congratulatory culture, everyone's a winner. The reasoning is that to do otherwise would be to lessen or even ruin a young person's life chances. But what is the result? If all the applicants for a position have equally good grades, those recruiting must then base their selection on other criteria, including those the proponents of inflated grades hoped to rule out, such as family background, accent, polish, etc.: a classic example of unforeseen consequences!

The overall effect of raising the level of education for as many people as possible is naturally positive for a country, indeed indispensable to avoid falling behind in the world of globalization. And it is equally obvious that individuals should try for the best possible education (and that their parents should encourage them). While a university degree is no longer a golden ticket, those without a good education are immediately out of the race. Yet it is mistaken to believe that a good education for all will also bring about greater equality: it only raises the standard of the competition.

Inverting the pyramid is no more likely to succeed than a society with more chiefs than Indians. Majorities are always led or controlled by minorities. The famous words uttered by Abraham Lincoln in his Gettysburg address in 1863 extolling 'government of the people, by the people, and for the people' made for wonderful rhetoric, but a people as a whole cannot govern itself: it can only determine those (the few) it wishes to be governed by. Likewise, the call contained in clause IV of the Labour Party constitution as amended in 1995 'to create for all of us a community, in which power, wealth and opportunity are in the hands of the many, not the few' is perhaps attractive to voters but unrealistic when it comes to power. The general issues orders to his soldiers, which they obey. The CEO and his fellow board members give instructions to the workers, which they follow. The English novelist Ian McEwan put it like this:

'No human society, from the hunter-gatherer to the post-industrial, has come to the attention of anthropologists that did not have its leaders and the led.'[13]

The vociferous and persistent repression of the fact that only a very small number of people can make it to the top is a woeful failing of the modern debate. Virtually every politician calls for everyone to have the same opportunities, regardless of their background, and promises to make this happen. Take the comments of Sadiq Khan in his mayoral victory speech in May 2016:

I have a burning ambition for London. I want every single Londoner to get the opportunities that our city gave to me and my family. The opportunities not just to survive, but to thrive. The opportunities to build a better future for you and your family . . . the opportunities for all Londoners to fulfil their potential.

What he omitted to say was how few people have sufficient potential to accomplish his hopes for everyone or do what he had done, and that even then, only one person can become Mayor of London. Similar comments are forthcoming from many others who have made it to the top. In a recent interview the singer Adele, for example, delivered a message to all the ten-year-old girls of this world: 'If I can do it, then you can too.' Unfortunately this is total nonsense.

One of those ten-year-old girls (maybe) might make it, but not all of them.

One need only consider the careers of a few famous individuals from different professions who fit the bill. The Mayor of London Sadiq Khan, a practising Muslim, is the son of a Pakistani bus driver and a seamstress ('I grew up on a council estate'). The actress and former MP Glenda Jackson is the daughter of a bricklayer and a cleaning lady. The baroness, ex-lingerie queen and multimillionaire Michelle Mone is the daughter of a printer in Glasgow's East End and a mother with three jobs. The journalist and author Lynsey Hanley grew up in a working-class family on the biggest council estate in England. These are just a few examples. What they all have in common is a rejection of the way of life of their class of origin. They have cast off the markers of their class and learned new behaviours. It was not by retaining their working-class markers that their rise was propelled, but by giving them up. Sadiq Khan did not become Mayor of London because he stayed exactly as his parents were or even as he had been as a boy, but because he moved on. This is a difficult process, and only people of quite exceptional intelligence, diligence and staying power can attempt it, let alone make a success of it. That this can only ever be a minority is clear. And it stands to reason that only one of them in turn can become Mayor of London. To act as if everyone has the same opportunity or that the same chance is offered to everyone is unfortunately pure fiction. When the pyramid of opportunity on all levels stops growing, the only way to have more people climb up is to let other people slide down.

The race for the top exposes two conflicting aspects of human behaviour. One is the ability to recognize a shared interest, to co-operate and work in partnership in order to realize the common goal – a belief that together we are stronger. Alongside his intelligence, the act of co-operating is undoubtedly man's greatest strength. But there is another key feature: that of rivalry, confrontation and struggle, the desire to assert one's own interests over the interests of others. Both are peculiar to man and inherent in human society,[14] culminating in violent struggles, especially in wars. There was surely no day in the discernible history of mankind without smaller or bigger struggles somewhere on Earth. That (unfortunately) holds true for the present too. Well over 90 per cent of articles in the newspapers or of TV news reports include an aspect of opposing positions or battles to gain the upper hand: Labour versus Conservatives, employers versus employees, the 99 per cent versus the 1 per cent, UK versus EU, Apple versus Samsung, the Bank of England versus the market, separatists versus central government, North Korea versus South Korea, terrorists versus civilization – a vast array of opposing positions fighting to prevail.

This is played out in the macrocosm and microcosm of society. Open the local newspaper, and most of the reporting has conflict at its heart: in favour of new roads being built or against them; for a new supermarket or against it. Compromises do of course come about if no single side has the upper hand. But the aim is always to come out on top. Struggle is just as much a facet of humanity as co-operation and partnership. Someone who should know more about this than most is Tony Blair's former head of communications Alastair Campbell: 'I don't think I've ever fundamentally seen life as being a pursuit of happiness. I think it's a bit of a struggle.'[15] To talk about this in such terms is currently prohibited by political correctness: opponents are not adversaries but partners, just as rivals are hopefuls, and we are all in this together. Only in a select number of spheres are we allowed to acknowledge freely that winners and losers exist and name them as such, for instance in sport or elections or wars.

WHO WANTS A CLASSLESS SOCIETY?

There is a massive contradiction between what people say in public and what they actually think (and say in private, if at all). In the same way as no-one refers to themselves openly as upper-class, classlessness is treated with similar reticence. Under the public gaze, no-one would reject the idea out of hand, although a certain scepticism is allowed ('I don't think it's realistic'). In reality, people don't want to be the same as everyone else. They want to be different. They have no wish to associate with people from another class, but want to stick to their own kind. Professionals have no desire to spend their evenings and weekends with labourers, just as manual workers would rather not spend their time off in the company of intellectuals (apart from in contexts where class differences are temporarily suspended – see Chapter 30). The groups not only decline to socialize, but are also disinclined to inhabit the same houses or live in the same part of town. Anyone with sufficient money wants a different house and furnishings from people who are poor. As so often, George Orwell is once more our guide:

> Many people, however, imagine that they can abolish class-distinctions without making any uncomfortable change in their own habits and 'ideology'. Hence the eager class-breaking activities which one can see in progress on all sides. Everywhere there are people of good will who quite honestly believe that they are working for the overthrow of class-distinctions. The middle-class Socialist enthuses over the proletariat and runs 'summer schools' where the proletarian and the repentant bourgeois are supposed to fall upon one another's necks and be brothers for ever; and the bourgeois visitors come away saying how wonderful and inspiring it has all been (the proletarian ones come away saying something different). And then there is the outer-suburban creeping Jesus, a hangover from the William Morris period, but still surprisingly common, who goes about saying 'Why must we level *down*? Why not level up?' and proposes to level the working class 'up' (up to his own standard) by means of hygiene, fruit juice, birth control, poetry, etc. Even the Duke of York (now King George VI) runs a yearly camp where public schoolboys and boys from the slums are supposed to mix on exactly equal terms, and do mix for the time being, rather like the animals in one of those 'Happy Family' cages where a dog, a cat, two ferrets, a rabbit and three canaries preserve an armed truce while the showman's eye is on them.

All such deliberate, conscious efforts at class-breaking are, I am convinced, a very serious mistake. Sometimes they are merely futile, but where they do show a definite result it is usually to *intensify* class-prejudice.[16]

The best modern illustration is the phenomenon of gentrification in Great Britain since the 1960s in major cities such as Manchester, Birmingham and Edinburgh, and most noticeably in London. Gentrification is the buying and renovation of houses and stores in urban neighbourhoods that have come down in the world by middle- or upper-income families or individuals, improving property values but at the same time displacing the original inhabitants of low-income families and small businesses. It is also called urban renewal or revival. The term was coined in 1963 by the sociologist Ruth Glass:

> One by one, many of the working-class neighbourhoods of London have been invaded by the middle-classes – upper and lower. Shabby, modest mews and cottages – two rooms up and two down – have been taken over, when their leases have expired, and have become elegant, expensive residences . . . Once this process of 'gentrification' starts in a district it goes on rapidly, until all or most of the original working-class occupiers are displaced and the whole social character of the district is changed.[17]

Gentrification does not usually occur overnight, but in stages. What is initially a neighbourhood populated by homes and shops for the working classes, the unemployed and immigrants is 'discovered' by intellectuals, teachers, journalists, artists, architects, social workers and so on as an attractive and still affordable place to live if the properties are upgraded. Those in the lower half of this group even do a lot of the work themselves. Thereafter the upper half moves in, calling to an increasing extent upon the services of architects, interior designers and stylists. In the final wave the rich and beautiful, powerful and famous arrive with their entourage of advisers and associates. Two prime examples of gentrification in London are Notting Hill and Islington, the latter a stronghold of the Labour elite, home of the 'super-gentry' and to such political heavyweights as the Blairs (until

1997), Neil Kinnock, Margaret Hodge and Jeremy Corbyn, and later also Conservatives like Boris Johnson. These days, the apartments and houses here sell for anything from £1 million to £3 million.[18]

Nowhere is the incompatibility of the classes more blatantly revealed. While it might have been assumed that the left-wing intelligentsia and subsequent party of power would seek to live in harmony with the original working-class residents, the opposite was the case. The incomers did everything in their power to rid themselves of the remaining grass-roots population, who were confronted with increased rents, higher property prices, expensive shops and plans for luxury homes. The working-class residents could not keep up financially and felt uncomfortable, inferior and out of place in their changed surroundings. They moved out willy-nilly to more affordable neighbourhoods that had remained working class, amid allegations of being snubbed, treated as second-class citizens and isolated socially. The newcomers passed their own comments: 'We would love the contact, but it's tricky, what with our work and family taking up so much time,' 'We don't know if we're welcome. We tried everything' or 'The children don't get on. The gap is just too big.' If this sounds forced and rather dishonest, that's because it is.

It was a similar story of displacement when the super-rich got the idea of 'taking over' Islington: the red Porsche replaced the Volvo estate as the gentrifiers were succeeded by the super-gentrifiers.[19] The second wave's comments about the super-rich were pretty much identical to those of the original residents about the first incomers: no solidarity, a lack of community spirit, etc. The remarks from those on high sound even more false, especially when they express regret when 'such first-class neighbours' decide to leave. Given the political pedigree of the middle classes moving to Islington, the prospects for the working and middle classes to live together in harmony could scarcely have been better. Although the new residents might not have been able to create a class-free society, a socially-mixed community might have been on the cards at least. But they had no appetite for it and chose class segregation instead.

London is also affected by the 'poor doors' phenomenon.[20] For some upmarket apartment blocks planning permission is only given if the plans include affordable housing. There are luxury homes for which buyers pay high prices and more modest flats occupied by social housing tenants in the same building. Since the rich don't want to mix with the poor, the planners design separate entrances with very different looks (the 'posh' doors and the 'poor' doors); mail delivery and bins are kept apart, there are separate lifts, affordable tenants have no access to car or cycle parking. The cheaper flats are confined to a separate block or all on separate floors. The aim is for the upmarket buyers to have little or no contact with those occupying the social housing in the building. If such designs are not permitted, the more expensive apartments become unsaleable or drop in value. How did George Orwell put it?

> The middle-class ILP'er and the bearded fruit juice drinker are all for a classless society so long as they see the proletariat through the wrong end of the telescope; force them into any real contact with a proletarian – let them get into a fight with a drunken fish-porter on Saturday night, for instance – and they are capable of swinging back to the most ordinary middle-class snobbishness.[21]

EQUALITY VERSUS FREEDOM

Based on the modern understanding of freedom in Western countries including England, a classless society is not even desirable. It could be achieved only if everybody were entirely equal. However, complete equality is the destroyer of freedom. If, regardless of income, everyone is taxed in such a way that all ultimately have the same amount of money, the most intelligent and hard-working individuals will stop trying. We will all go back to living in caves. On the other hand, complete freedom leads to out-and-out inequality. If two dogs have to catch their dinner and there is only sufficient food for one, then the slower of the two will starve. Unadulterated freedom and equality cannot exist without forfeit, as Isaiah Berlin expounded in his famous lecture *Two Concepts of Liberty* (1958):[22]

... nothing is gained by a confusion of terms. To avoid glaring inequality or widespread misery I am ready to sacrifice some, or all, of my freedom: I may do so willingly and freely: but it is freedom that I am giving up for the sake of justice or equality or the love of my fellow men. I should be guilt stricken, and rightly so, if I were not, in some circumstance, ready to make this sacrifice. But a sacrifice is not an increase in what is being sacrificed, namely freedom, however great the moral need or the compensation for it. Everything is what it is: liberty is liberty, not equality or fairness or justice or human happiness or a quiet conscience.

The soundness of Berlin's argument becomes clear when people get serious about creating equality. Certainly, economic equality between individuals could be achieved, and the means of doing so are no secret. The rich could be dispossessed (and even murdered), as actually happened during the French Revolution of 1789 and following the Russian Revolution in 1917. Private property could be banned and only the state allowed to continue owning assets. The state could decree that all people earn the same wage for their work or that earnings be capped at a certain level. The former is believed to have been implemented in the early days of the Israeli kibbutz movement. The latter found expression in the 1970s in Germany when the Young Socialists (the youth organization of the Social Democratic Party) called for no-one to be allowed to earn more than 5,000 deutschmarks a month (a limit naturally ignored by those who had demanded it once they themselves started to earn more than that amount).

Nowadays people are calling for a cap on executive pay. If wage inequality could not be eradicated, then some money could be taken away from those with more and given to those with less until everyone had the same amount. This could be achieved by appropriate taxation, something demanded by virtually all opponents of inequality, most recently Thomas Piketty, but also by supranational organizations like the OECD.[23] It would also be possible to do away with private inheritance law so that, when someone died, their estate passed to the state, which could then redistribute it to the 'populace', something frequently demanded in the past that was indeed introduced in communist Russia in 1918 (but deleted again in 1922).

Finally, everybody could also be compelled to live in accommodation of a specific size, and ghettos inhabited exclusively by the rich or poor could be banned in favour of mandatory mixing. To prevent rich and poor districts from being created, the state could order people to rotate houses every few years by drawing lots, as the great British humanist and statesman Thomas More proposed in the second part of his world-famous book *Utopia* (1515). There can be no doubt that, while such measures would promote equality, they would also curtail freedom.

Even the influence of family background could be at least partly neutralized. To stop people speaking with different accents and terminologies in future, a radical solution would be to remove the children from their parents and have them educated exclusively in uniform state institutions, as was occasionally mooted in Russia following the Communist takeover of power in 1917. Under this scheme, upper-class accents and terminology could be eradicated by making access to schools, universities and jobs in the public and private sectors conditional on non-posh comportment. Lastly, the abolition of public schools could be considered, something long demanded by various parties.

Should people be banned from certain professions or assigned to them depending on their background? Apparently quite serious suggestions have been made by politicians, among them Harriet Harman and the Labour Shadow Equalities Minister Gloria De Piero, that applicants from humble backgrounds should be considered above those from a relatively privileged (i.e. middle-class) one, and recently Matt Hancock, the Health Secretary, suggested that companies should ask job applicants whether they went to private schools, seemingly with the aim of sidelining them in favour of other applicants during recruitment to the Civil Service, for instance. In a January 2017 report titled *The Class Ceiling*, the all-party parliamentary group on social mobility stated that bosses should give jobs to applicants from poorer backgrounds ahead of candidates who are better qualified. Even doctors should be chosen using social factors instead of their level of skill and knowledge, said the MPs (although they would never opt to be treated by them themselves, but only the most skilled practitioner they could find). Much the same line is taken by the policy of 'affirmative action' familiar from the USA and the recent suggestion by an English university that, where two applicants have equal qualifications, preference should be given to the one from the less privileged family. Should a special tax be introduced for particularly gifted or attractive people in order to negate their competitive advantage? Should less intelligent and lazy people be supported more than their clever and diligent counterparts? Here too, freedom would be the casualty. Maximum equality would be achieved if there were a single autocratic ruler, and everyone else were his slaves. Forced equality destroys freedom.

In England, too, the battle between equality and class exists. As so often, the campaigners on both sides have waived their claim to an absolute victory and settled for a kind of co-existence, with rules that are unwritten, difficult to identify and frequently changing. People muddle through. Part of this compromise is that, in the absence of a classless society, there are at least some class-free zones or specific areas in which the barriers of class are temporarily lifted.

30

Class-free Zones

If there is no such thing as a classless society, are there at least some spheres in which class is immaterial? A number of activities and areas of life do seem to be. However, on closer inspection, such appearances are deceptive: the barriers of class are not removed, but rather circumvented or lifted temporarily.

HUMOUR

English humour is often regarded as a class-free zone. This is correct, insofar as all classes share the general English tendency to see the funny side of things and not take themselves too seriously, expressed through self-deprecation, understatement and irony. Another feature common to all classes is their tendency to ridicule the class system itself. The 1966 class sketch with John Cleese, Ronnie Barker and Ronnie Corbett has become famous. They stand in class, height and clothing order.

> Cleese: 'I look down on him [Barker] because I am upper-class.'
> Barker: 'I look up to him [Cleese] because he is upper-class. But
> I look down on him [Corbett] because he is lower-class.'
> Corbett: 'I know my place.'

However, there are differences in who laughs at what. Then class kicks in yet again. Some jokes and satires are amusing to one class and not to another, or at least go down better in some circles than in others. In this respect, English humour is connected to class.

PUBS

In the age-old English institution of the public house, it is often claimed that class and social distinctions have no place. All classes frequent pubs, with uniform consistency. Three out of ten Englishmen go to a pub at least once a week. The pub is a bastion of egalitarian culture. The guests treat the publican and the staff with the same respect as their companions, as demonstrated by the offer to buy the landlord a drink. The patrons show one another the kind of consideration reserved for equals. In this light, the pub is a great leveller. However, generally speaking, people tend to socialize with their own kind in the pub, although people from different classes with a shared interest can mix more easily there. This is particularly true of sport, with disparate individuals coming together to watch the football, for instance. And once the visit to the pub is over, things go back to how they were beforehand anyway.

A COMMON INTEREST

A similar mechanism takes effect if people from quite different classes have a shared hobby, such as riding. Horses are a common denominator. Horsey talk and riding chat bring people together, posh and unposh. A young female trainee hairdresser tells of how on a train she saw a girl opposite her reading *Your Horse* magazine. Though generally never talking to people on the train she said: 'Oh, is that the November one?' 'Oh, yes', the girl replied. 'Do you ride as well?' and they chatted away like best friends. Asked if the girl looked like the kind of person she might want to talk to and be friends with apart from the magazine, she answered:

> To be honest, no. She looked quite posh, and quite a bit older than me, um, wearing a smart business suit – you know, like knee-length skirt, tights, smart shoes, and a posh briefcase and all. No, now I think about it, I'd have thought she was probably a bit snobby

333

and, um, boring. But she wasn't, she was a good laugh, really nice – even though she's into poncy dressage and I like jumping. It's all horses, isn't it?[1]

People who are not horse owners or riders may well enjoy horse racing. Like the pub, the racecourse is a meeting place for all the social classes. The shared interest in the racing, the discussions beforehand about the horses' chances and the dissection afterwards of why they won, or more likely, why they lost when they were 'dead certs', masks all social disparities. Every Englishman's enjoyment of a flutter also breaks down class differences.

SPORT

Active sportsmen and -women also inhabit a class-free zone. In cricket, the distinction between gentlemen (amateurs) and players (professionals) was abandoned in 1963. The clubs and associations want to win and need the best players, regardless of which class they come from. The shared experience of sport – the training, the victories and the defeats – supersedes the relationships formed at school or university and even family ties. This bond is further strengthened if playing for the same school or university team. Anyone who has rowed in the Oxford or Cambridge eight generally remains friends with their fellow rowers for the rest of their life, regardless of family background or how rich their parents are. Of course, different sports are more or less closely associated with a specific social class, but that's another story (see Chapter 25).

FOOTBALL

The nearest thing to a class-free zone in sport is football, not so much on the part of the active players, most of whom are working-class, but among the spectators. By the time Nick Hornby's memoir *Fever Pitch* was published in 1992, football had been embraced by polite society. The interest in the football played at the highest level and by the national teams is likely to be around 100 per cent across all classes. Many footballers, such as Paul Gascoigne in his heyday, are able to induce an 'all-consuming, irrational and totally childlike happiness'[2] among spectators. It is just as natural for a member of the upper class like the Archbishop of Canterbury to be a fan of a football team as it is for a leading London lawyer, a farmer or a call-centre worker. This applies to women as well as men. In the case of politicians, we face the familiar problem of wondering whether or not they are sincere. Football's enormous popularity compels them to be equally enthusiastic about the game, support a club and in particular cheer on the national side during the nail-biting highs and lows of international fixtures. When John Major declared his admiration for Chelsea and Tony Blair said he backed Newcastle United, this seemed entirely plausible. If, in a speech in South London in April 2015, David Cameron said he supported West Ham, when he is really an Aston Villa fan, this can be put down to a 'brain fade'; his joy when his team or the English national side wins should not be doubted. As what was traditionally a working-class phenomenon found its way onto the fashionable broadsheets, the distinction between white- and blue-collar fans became blurred. One can say that football, shaped (although not invented) by public schoolboys in the nineteenth century and subsequently the preserve of the working class, has transcended the English class structure.[3] There are very few occasions on which the sense of community of all classes is more fully engaged and expressed than when watching an England match together in the pub.

SCHOOL

To create schools free from the strictures of class has been the dream of politicians and educationists down through the years. Small children are not conscious of social differences. But as soon as their awareness develops, school is anything but a class-free zone. Since the children are able to perceive class but not influence it themselves, they simply perpetuate what they know from home and their surroundings – without self-correction because they are not sufficiently advanced in their development. The nationwide obsession of English parents with choosing the 'right' school for their child and the differentiation between different types of schools, particularly between the state sector and the public (private or independent) schools attended by around 7 per cent of all pupils, reinforces this. When the majority of grammar schools were disbanded in 1975, this eliminated the 'discrimination' against those who did not pass the eleven-plus examination and thereby removed a great deal of unfairness, desperation and misery.[4] On the other hand, it deprived ordinary people's children of an opportunity for upward mobility and further cemented the predominance of public schools for the upper classes, with their obvious class bias – quite contrary to the intentions of those who abolished the grammar schools. Schools perpetuate rather than alleviate the English class system. If any schools have a certain levelling effect on class differences for their pupils, then it is the private boarding institutions. When everyone is in view of everyone else and away from the differing influences of home, is taught the same curriculum and receives not only the same school uniform but also a more or less uniform education, class differences shrink.

UNIVERSITY

So school, with its private and state sectors, is not a class-free zone, but the great divider. Is university any different? When students are just beginning their degree it is for many their first opportunity to meet people of different classes. The tasks and challenges facing all newcomers transcend social differences: away from home for the first time, in a strange environment with unfamiliar classmates and limited finances, having to cope with academic demands and college rules. The knowledge that others are in the same situation strengthens mutual solidarity, a feeling bolstered by the rite of passage that is freshers' week, with its endless partying. At university, friendships that often last a lifetime are formed beyond class boundaries. But far from exclusively: as students reach the latter stages of their studies, there is a growing tendency for birds of a feather to flock together, as the social classes gravitate towards their own kind once more. Same-class friendships both between people of the same sex and between men and women are disproportionately high in number. In this respect, the class differences observed at school are perpetuated at university. The poet Louis MacNeice described his experience:

There were many undergraduates like myself who theoretically conceded that all men were equal, but who, in practice, while only too willing to converse, or attempt to, with say Normandy peasants or shopkeepers, would wince away in their own college halls from those old grammar school boys who with impure vowels kept admiring Bernard Shaw or Noël Coward while grabbing their knives and forks like dumb-bells.[5]

The tragically murdered Labour MP Jo Cox, the first member of her family to attend university, put her class experience at Cambridge without using the word 'class' thus:

I never really grew up being political or Labour. It kind of came at Cambridge where it was just a realization that where you were born mattered, that how you spoke mattered . . . who you knew mattered. I didn't really speak right or know the right people . . . To be honest, my experience at Cambridge really knocked me for about five years.[6]

OCCUPATION

The job one does is a hard class marker par excellence – indeed, according to most official classifications, the only one (see Chapters 3 and 4). The road sweeper is in a different class from the university professor. The situation changes within individual professions. If two people from quite different social backgrounds take up the same occupation, class differences play only a very small role and often cease to matter. This applies most strongly to occupations calling for a high level of professional expertise, especially of a technical or scientific nature, and includes engineers, pilots, doctors, as well as schoolteachers and university lecturers. The university professor whose origins are working-class has the same social status within the university as the university professor from an upper-middle class background, and the same would apply to two senior civil servants or judges, say. Naturally differences exist between them, but these are measured principally by their subject expertise. A person may change social class depending on their chosen profession. A child from humble origins who, through excellence, grows up to become a university professor or judge is no longer working-class, but belongs to the middle or upper-middle class instead.

WAR

Everyone, reputedly, is equal in death. Hence it seems fair to assume that the part of life that brings us closest to death, namely war, is also the greatest social equalizer. In actual fact, the two world wars of the twentieth century are repeatedly credited with furthering the demise of the English class system, as men from all classes responded to the call to arms with a willingness to risk life and limb for king and country. The First World War undoubtedly kindled an understanding between the haves and have-nots and also created common bonds. Despite the discrediting of leading military figures who without exception came from the aristocracy (much later, mainly after the Second World War, popularized as 'lions led by donkeys'), the troops recognized and acknowledged that their officers were far from being mere haughty dimwits, but cared for them, loved them even, and also died for them. The English upper-class officer was no shirker, but the first to go over the top. And the officers recognized and acknowledged that the troops were far from being mere stupid, brutish and illiterate subordinates, but were loyal, feeling beings, often of outstanding courage. The shared victory, only achieved by a united push at every level, was a further tie. This mood was captured by King George V in his address to the first post-war parliament, when he raised the prospect of 'a better social order', as it had been by Prime Minister Lloyd George in November 1918 when he asked: 'What is our task? To make Britain a fit country for heroes to live in.' In the Second World War, too, British officers and enlisted men were distinguished by their high moral values. The motion passed by students of the Oxford Union in 1933 that 'This house will under no circumstances fight for its king and country' – which was carried by 275 votes to 153 and subsequently attained world notoriety – was emphatically not borne out by reality. The Second World War was regarded as the People's War, and seen by many as the end of all classes. 'There is one thing and one only, about this war – it is an instant and complete leveller of classes.'[7] Even Winston Churchill, grandson of a duke, told the boys of Harrow School in December 1940 that there is 'no change which is more marked in our country than the continual and rapid effacement of class differences.' 'This war', prophesied George Orwell, 'unless we are defeated, will wipe out most of the existing class privileges. There are every day fewer people who wish them to continue.'[8] The programme of the Labour government under Clement Attlee from 1945 onwards, with its nationalization of key industries and creation of the National Health Service and the welfare state, could only strengthen this feeling. Deep down, however, it was only an impression, not reality. 'The belief that the British class system dissolved or was basically modified during the war is a total myth.'[9] The armed forces are not class-free today either. This is ruled out by definition by the hierarchical rank structure. All things considered, members of the upper classes are more likely than the man in the street to become officers, even if the path to such status is open to anyone with sufficient drive and intelligence.

CHURCH

All men are equal before God; God is class-free. Perhaps. The church has preached its classlessness from the very beginning. But who believes that it does not hold bishops in higher esteem than simple members of the congregation? There are even different ranks among believers, including at church services. In Paul Thompson's *The Edwardians: The Remaking of British Society* (1975), an Essex farm-worker's boy tells how around 1900 his mother, who was poor, sat at the back; in the middle were 'the local shopkeepers and people who were considered to be a little bit superior to the others'; at the front were 'the local farmers, the local bigwigs, . . . posh people'. A century later J. R. Daeschner in *True Brits* describes a Sunday service in which the Vicar Davis reads a passage from the Bible: 'Hasn't God chosen the poor in this world to the rich in faith? Aren't they the ones who will inherit the Kingdom he promised to those who love Him? And yet, you insult the poor man! If you pay special attention to the rich, you are committing a sin.' In other words, the Reverend Davis explains, God doesn't make distinctions between the rich and the poor; it's man who creates the barriers. And then he exhorts the audience to disregard rank and riches: 'If you meet the binman, the *dustbin*man, treat him as if he were Prince Charles. And if you meet Prince Charles, treat him as if he were the dustbinman.' The listeners are the parishioners and Lady Bagot is sitting in the family pew in the chancel, near the altar and tombs, cut off from the congregation and the vicar by one of the few rood screens to survive England's Civil War. Asked why she sat in the chancel rather than out in the nave Lady Bagot answered: 'Because these are our seats.'[10]

ANY MORE EXAMPLES?

There are even more 'nooks and crannies' of life in which people are all in the same boat and treated in the same way and can therefore be described as class-free zones. You see it in the underground or when queuing to board a flight with Ryanair or another no-frills airline, or when, once on board, you either get nothing to eat at all, or the same soggy, tasteless sandwich as everyone else. This is classlessness at its most achievable – where as many people as possible all have it equally bad.

England does not have any zones that are entirely free from class constraints. Some spheres get close, but largely only when people from different social backgrounds come together in the same place, and then for a limited time. It is therefore important for an Englishman – as mentioned before (Chapter 6) – to know which class he belongs to by birth, and if and how he can change his class.

31

Class of Origin

Wealth and power are much more likely the result of breeding than of reading.

Fran Lebowitz, *Social Studies* (1981)

Those who are born poor are more likely to stay poor and those who inherit privilege are more likely to pass on privilege in England than in any other comparable country.

Conservative Education Secretary
Michael Gove (2012)

Family is the reproductive cell of class.

A. C. Halsey, *Change in British Society* (1995)

To forecast from birth how a person's life might turn out, two determinants would be paramount: on one hand, the individual child's intelligence and character, according to the binary distinctions smart or stupid, hard-working or lazy, the genetic starting point;[1] on the other, the home, sorted by educated or uneducated, rich or poor. A child's chances of success could be rated as follows:

- A smart, hard-working child of educated, rich parents has the best prospects
- A stupid, lazy child of uneducated, poor parents has the worst prospects.

There are many stages in between: the slow, indolent child of wealthy, cultured parents still has a chance. The clever, industrious child of poorly educated, disadvantaged parents also has a chance, although they must work for it. Cultivated parents who are hard-up provide their children with quite different possibilities from those who are moneyed but lack schooling. The not-very-bright and inactive child of well-off but uncultured parents may still (using their parents' wealth) lead a comfortable, perhaps even luxurious, existence. The bright but undiligent child of erudite but less wealthy parents is likely to struggle. And of course there is a large group whose circumstances are less extreme, but who fall somewhere in the middle, of average intelligence and prepared to work hard, but not all the time. The nature/nurture combination also determines a person's class.

The prime factor that determines an Englishman's class and generally lasts a lifetime is the family into which he is born (see Chapter 4). This is his class of origin. Through parents and their social circle, and through siblings and friends, birth and breeding shape the soft class markers of appearance, clothing, pronunciation, terminology, taste, manners, leisure activities, interests, ideas and political affinities. Generally the manners and traditions learned in childhood persist from birth to death. Hard class markers too are predicated by one's family. A decisive role is played by the practice, firmly rooted in all Western societies, of bequest: when someone dies, their private property is bequeathed, in most cases to their own descendants. As a consequence, the hard class markers of wealth in the form of land, houses, businesses and financial assets, together with the associated earnings, fall to the heirs without any effort on the latter's part (albeit only after the state has taken its share in the form of inheritance tax). In England there is the further hard class marker of hereditary title, for one child at least. Those siblings who lose out on the substantive title may receive a courtesy title instead, together with the undiminished social cachet of being the progeny of such a family.

The children of high-income parents usually find it easier to enter a well-paid profession too. Naturally, a degree or academic qualification cannot be inherited, but must be achieved by individual effort.

But to be set on the 'right track' by one's parents and automatically provided with the right approach without having to work for it is a clear advantage. A child growing up in a home with thousands of books and sophisticated conversation has better educational prospects than a youngster of similar intelligence in households without reading and discourse, but awash with trash TV; even with a lower IQ, the first child will probably end up with better results. In educated families children hear around 30 million more words from their parents in the first four years of their lives through being talked to, read to and from conversation than in working-class households where parents speak much less to their children.

And that is not all. Children from families with a lower social status are exposed to the latter's limited vocabulary of around 12,000 English words, whereas the offspring of educated families learn a much greater word-stock of maybe 25,000 words – which is why some children start school knowing 500, others 5,000 words. Small children go through a phase of asking questions: why is the sky blue, why is daddy daddy and not mummy? Why? Why? Why? In some families, these enquiries are answered indulgently and with a patience that only wears thin when the same query is repeated for the tenth time. In others the replies are more likely to be along the lines of: what are you asking that stupid question for? Or, leave me in peace, will you! When children of similar intelligence from two such families start primary school at five, the youngster from the educated home is already streets ahead, while the child from the proletarian family is lagging behind. As the Sutton Trust found, by the age of five children from the poorest fifth of families are almost a year behind middle-income families in their vocabulary abilities.[2] Making good this deficit, not to mention overtaking their classmate, is a feat achievable only by a huge effort on the part of the working-class child.

In class terms, being born into an upper-echelon family is a major advantage. The child of well-to-do parents can effortlessly accumulate numerous skills confirming or enhancing their social status that can be acquired by the son or daughter of poorer parents only by supreme endeavour, if at all. A youngster of upper-class stock learns how to hold a knife and fork and picks up pronunciation, terminology and manners automatically and with ease. The child of more lowly origin may have spent two decades learning to do things the 'wrong' way before struggling to assimilate the 'right way', a process that can take years and hardly ever succeeds completely.

Affluent parents can have their offspring educated at the best schools, or send them abroad to acquire foreign languages and experience other cultures. They can bring them into contact with people and expose them to influences that will enable them to compete with the very best in later life. Uneducated and poor parents can do little or none of this, because they lack the necessary know-how; even with it, they have insufficient financial resources. With the knowledge, manners and connections provided by his family and private education, the upper-crust scion, however dim and lazy, can unquestionably enjoy much more success in life than the smart, hard-working kid of modest means who has attended a state school. Taken to extremes, the stupid, idle child of wealthy parents is usually educated and honed in such a way as to reach a social level that would demand an immense effort on the part of a bright and diligent child from a humble home.

This is not only true of capitalist countries. The son of a high-ranking communist official in communist states naturally possesses far greater chances of advancement than the son of an agricultural worker who is not a party member. Nearly half the members of the present Politburo of the Communist Party of China are the children of former Politburo members.[3] On the whole, parents pass on superior opportunities to their children. This is most clearly reflected in the choice of school, as the journalist Robert Shrimsley recently described with honesty:

> I was privately educated and am now sending my own children to private schools. But I pay precisely because it offers them the very advantages discussed. People aren't stupid: you don't spend that kind of cash to teach them to play hockey. I don't feel guilty about this. I can think of no better use of my money than maximizing my children's prospects.[4]

The class of origin is also responsible for a number of other factors that influence professional advancement and social esteem, e.g. that leg-up a young person may receive from immediate family, close relatives and friends because of their connections, especially if the parents are prominent people. One often hears of the children of celebrated and/or wealthy individuals how much they suffer because of their famous name, how hard it is to cut the parental cord and fly free, what a great burden their family represents. They congratulate themselves on making it on their own against painful odds. This may sometimes be the case, but generally it is otherwise. These children, dubbed the 'Sads' – Sons and Daughters – by Julie Burchill, as if by magic achieve the same or similarly agreeable and well-paid jobs as their parents, relatives or close friends. Examples appear weekly in every glossy magazine:[5] Take the columnist and author Pippa Middleton (younger sister of Kate Middleton, Duchess of Cambridge), the models Lottie Moss (half-sister of Kate Moss) and Rafferty Law (son of Jude Law and Sadie Frost), the model, singer and socialite Pixie Geldof (daughter of Bob Geldof and Paula Yates), the actor Freddie Fox (son of actor Edward Fox and actress Joanna David), the actor Max Irons (son of actor Jeremy Irons and actress Sinead Cusack), the actress Rebecca Hall (daughter of theatre director Peter Hall and opera singer Maria Ewing), or the 19-year-old actor and model Damian Hurley (son of actress and model Elizabeth Hurley).

But when it comes to the careers of children of the rich and famous, the Beckhams provide the ultimate role model. David and Victoria Beckham have a fortune estimated by the media to be around £500 million. They are therefore not only famous but also super-rich, and excellently connected within the English upper class. Their four children range in age from 20 to eight. Brooklyn, the eldest (godfather Elton John, godmother Elizabeth Hurley), models for a teen fashion brand and urges people to 'jump barriers' – easy to say on an income of £6 million. Romeo began his modelling career at Burberry and appeared alongside Naomi Campbell. Cruz started with YouTube videos, posted by his parents, singing along to Justin Bieber songs. Eight-year-old Harper has her own fashion blog featuring her current wardrobe – handily complete with links to the relevant manufacturers. Based on statistical probability, none of them would have had any chance of getting these jobs. It was the connections of their relatives and friends that helped them on their way. Rebecca Hall was honest about it. Asked if she owed her career to her father, she answered: 'It's an arrogance to complain about that sort of thing. And it's true. Of course I've had connections. Of course I've had a charmed life in terms of what I want to do.'[6]

As well as by their parents, children are moulded – often particularly so – by other youngsters. Children and young people famously want to be the same as their contemporaries, and therefore copy the behaviour of others, especially the peer-group leader. Naturally, it becomes rather important who the other children are with whom your offspring play, attend school, play sport, travel, etc. Here, too, a clear group behaviour can be identified: upper-class children tend to associate with others from the same background rather than working-class youngsters, for instance. When cross-mixing does occasionally occur, especially among the very young, it is more or less coincidental. The newspapers are full of reports about the progeny of the rich and famous (the *jeunesse dorée*): they always stick together, taking their holidays in the same places, frequenting the same fun spots, doing the same sports, networking with each other (and only with each other) on social media, reading the same books and idolizing the same stars. The isolation of upper-class children from the man in the street is not only a form of snobbery but also has rational reasons, e.g. a fear of criminality. Who can blame someone like Bill Gates for taking care that his children do not fall in with 'the wrong crowd'? Soft class markers are consolidated by the peer group as well as by parents and usually cemented for life. They are certainly sustained if the young people remain in the social circles in which they have grown up. Children from other classes may be included, and lifelong friendships can of course be forged between working-class youngsters and the sons or daughters of nobility. However, these are stand-out exceptions that serve primarily to confirm the rule of social concentration.

The influence of the parental home on reaching high office also has a bearing in an unexpected quarter, where the top positions are assigned not by individuals or a small group, but by mass selection involving people not personally known to the candidate: politics. It is striking how many members of parliament, even in recent times, are connected by family ties[7]. The most common combination among MPs is parent and child: Winston and Randolph Churchill, Harold and Maurice Macmillan, William Wedgwood Benn and Tony and Hilary Benn, Neil and Stephen Kinnock, Charles and Estelle Morris; or the grandfather-grandson relationship, as in the case of Herbert Morrison and Peter Mandelson. Siblings also feature – Boris and Jo Johnson, David and Ed Miliband – as well as couples: Aneurin Bevan and Jennie Lee, Harriet Harman and Jack Dromey, Victoria and Peter Bottomley. Estelle Morris followed in the footsteps of an uncle as well as her father. Here too the context is clear: the statistical probability of such political successions is approaching zero.

The practice of passing on advantages to the next generation is far from restricted to old-established families. It is often those who have made it to the top from lowly beginnings through their own endeavours who do everything to provide their children with the head start in life they themselves did not have (because they appreciate how hard it is). Neil Kinnock is a case in point. As a miner's son, he had to fight his way to the top from the very bottom (see Chapter 5). He was able to give his son Stephen all the early advantages befitting the family of a top politician, EU Commissioner and well-heeled member of the English peerage. Consequently, Stephen Kinnock enjoyed an education at prestigious universities (Cambridge and Bruges) and, at first attempt, was chosen as the candidate for a safe Labour seat in preference to a working-class contender. If a young Neil Kinnock – intelligent, hard-working and a man of integrity – had stood against his son Stephen in 2015 he would have hardly stood a chance.

There is a simple explanation: the parents of the 'Sads' (privileged sons and daughters) know the right people, the movers and shakers, who and what counts. 'All things being equal, friends buy from friends. All things being not so equal, friends still buy from friends.' This maxim applies to much more than just commercial life.

As in the USA (see Chapter 29), the phenomenon of 'hereditary meritocracy' exists in England. The children of the rich and powerful are far from all stupid and lazy, but are in many cases superior to the kids of 'ordinary' people. The reasons may be hereditary, or lie in the parents' education and money. At any rate, the upshot is that, even when objective criteria are applied, these children often appear to achieve better results than youngsters from lower-class backgrounds. The classic manifestation is in school attainment. Those who attend public schools on average get better results than those from state schools, with the consequence that the top universities, and Oxbridge in particular, accept a disproportionately high number of students from the private sector. Is this unfair? It certainly provokes pangs of conscience, as David Cannadine has related:

> In the days when I was director of studies in history at Cambridge in my college, one of the things I always used to find most diffi-cult was interviewing for admissions the people who had been to the appropriate public schools and had read all the books, were hugely confident, wrote well, and were incredibly articulate on one side; and on the other side, people who came from inner city comprehensives, who had not been well taught, who had very few textbooks, who did not read much because they were not encour-aged to do so, and who might have been filled with unrecognized talent but it was very hard to tell. What do you do under those circumstances? I never found it easy to decide.[8]

All the above can be illustrated by countless examples. Imagine two people with the same set of genes – identical twins, say – intelligent and hard-working, one born and bred on an east London council estate, the other born and bred at Blenheim Palace. Would the two still be identical at the end of their lives? Of course not. It's very likely they would have different jobs, and virtually all their soft class mark-ers would differ. Even if the two had by chance trained and worked

in the same profession, as a university don, for instance – something which, although rather unlikely, is nevertheless theoretically
possible – would they end up as similar people? The answer would
again be negative. In respect of many soft class markers they would
differ because of their family of birth and their upbringing. One
has achieved this success relatively easily; the other has had to fight
to get there. The East End youngster has had to overcome massive
resistance and push himself to the limit to become a university don,
whereas his Blenheim brother has probably taken things in his stride
with the effortless superiority a boy from the East End can only
dream of. These things take their toll. And what would happen if
the twins, instead of being intelligent and hard-working, were stupid
and lazy? The East Ender would have practically no chance of social
mobility; he would stay in the class he was born in. The Blenheim
scion would not become a university don, if indeed he got a degree,
but even as an idle dolt, he would belong to the cream of English society, be treated accordingly and showered with invitations, honorary
positions, etc. English literature abounds with descriptions of daft,
thick and dim members of the nobility who nevertheless lead an
extremely good life.

There is no shortage of examples. We have already mentioned
the Kinnock family several times. The class of origin of the father,
Neil Kinnock, was working-class, his son Stephen is upper-class
(see Chapter 5). Or take the family of Tony Blair. He was originally
middle-class, but his children are upper-class by origin. The Blairs
are a model case because the facts are largely known. Tony Blair and
his wife Cherie are intelligent and rich (see Chapter 8). They are
famous and probably have the best connections available in the UK
and worldwide; they are educated and comfortable using the accent
and vocabulary of the upper echelons. All the other class markers
likewise signal an upward trend. The couple have four children.
Euan Blair, born 1984, did not attend the local comprehensive but
went to the Roman Catholic London Oratory School. After missing out on a place at Oxford, he graduated from Bristol University
and also studied at Yale in the US. His wife, Suzanne Ashman, was

educated at St Paul's, a private school for girls in London, and Oxford University. After working for the investment bank Morgan Stanley, he is rumoured to aspire to a political career. He lives in a £3 million house in London. Nicholas Blair, born 1986, also attended the London Oratory School rather than the local comprehensive. After reading history at Oxford and following a couple of years teaching at a comprehensive, he became a football agent.[9] He is married to divorce lawyer Alexandra Blair, who was educated at University College London and Université Paul Cézanne Aix-Marseille. Kathryn Blair, born 1988, also did not attend the local school but went to the Sacred Heart High School, a high-scoring Roman Catholic school in Hammersmith, and studied law at King's College London, afterwards becoming a barrister at Lincoln's Inn and New Court Chambers aged 24. Leo Blair, born 2000, does not attend the local school but goes to a Roman Catholic school (a fact long kept secret by his parents). These four children were clearly in the top tier if not from the outset, then at the latest when Tony Blair became prime minister in 1997. There is no guarantee that they will remain there forever. As is well known, the offspring of famous politicians have had both impressive and very modest careers. But one thing is certain: their chances of high status were a hundred times greater than those of a child of similar intelligence born at the same time but into a working- or middle-class family.

An even crasser instance attracted much media attention in 2016. This time both the father and the son were upper-class. In August 2016 Gerald Grosvenor Duke of Westminster died at the age of 64. The heir to the dukedom and his fortune of around £9 billion was his 25-year-old son Hugh Grosvenor, now 7th Duke of Westminster. Hugh Grosvenor studied countryside management in Newcastle and later at Oxford. He is close to the Royal Family: one of his sisters is married to a good friend of Prince William's, and he himself is friendly with Prince William and his wife Kate and a godfather to Prince William's first child, Prince George. When he celebrated his 21st birthday with a party at the family seat of Eaton Hall in Cheshire that reportedly cost around £5 million, Prince Harry was among the guests. He has access to the crème de la crème of the United Kingdom, especially since he came into his inheritance.

What if Hugh Grosvenor had been switched at birth with the child of a working-class family? Although Hugh Grosvenor would look exactly as he does now (apart from his clothes), and his genetic endowment would be the same, what would he have in common with the present Hugh Grosvenor? Practically nothing. It is already far from certain that he would have had the same education. At any rate, he would speak a different language and behave in another way. He would be without title and wealth. He would not be personally acquainted with royalty, far less a godfather to the third in line to the throne. The junior, working-class Hugh Grosvenor would have nothing in common with Hugh Grosvenor the duke's son – for the sole and simple reason that the two had different parents. And what of the child born to the working-class couple? Naturally his basic genetic make-up would be different from Hugh Grosvenor's. But his entire outer personality would resemble that of the grown-up Hugh Grosvenor, including his accent, behaviour, mode of dressing, etc. – and above all he would now be the Duke of Westminster and exceedingly rich.

Who can doubt the influence of the family on class? How many working-class children from a council estate have the opportunities afforded from birth to the offspring of Tony Blair or Neil Kinnock? How many council estate youngsters are given the start in life enjoyed by the children of David and Victoria Beckham, or receive the starting chances of the Duke of Westminster Hugh Grosvenor? None. As R. H. Tawney recognized, 'The existence of opportunities [to rise] depends not only on an open road, but upon an equal start.'[10] This is true, but is there such a thing as an 'equal start'?

A child's class of origin bestows the three factors that (although not exclusively) play a determining role in its future life chances:

- Parents pass on their genes: children are born with a varied genetic make-up, diverse physical characteristics and different intellectual attributes such as intelligence and talent.

- Parents 'bequeath' their language and culture and their peer group: children are brought up by their parents and for a long time share their surrounding world.
- Parents hand down their wealth: the children of the rich also become rich.

To paraphrase a quote from Cecil Rhodes, who said that being born an Englishman is to have 'won first prize in the lottery of life', the jackpot in the lottery of English social life is to be born into a well-to-do and cultivated family; those from an uneducated and impoverished background have a much harder lot in life. Although the exact figures are not known, it seems reasonable to assume that birth and breeding have a 60 to 70 per cent bearing on the class one ultimately belongs to.

These findings are not at all new or original, of course, but known the world over. Something peculiar to Britain is the profusion of related studies, newspaper articles and television and radio programmes. For decades, one scientific study after another has been revealing the truth of these relationships. Without exception the research comes from reputable institutions, including the Sutton Trust, the Social Mobility Commission and the Joseph Rowntree Foundation. The authors are usually academics with an excellent educational background. The following list shows recent publications:

Social Mobility Commission: *Social inequalities and post 16-choices* (December 2016)

Joseph Rowntree Foundation: *Monitoring poverty and social exclusion 2016* (December 2016)

London School of Economics: *Entry to elite positions and the stratification of higher education in Britain* (2015)

Centre for Social Investigation, Nuffield College: *CSI 21 Social class mobility in Britain* by John Goldthorpe (June 2016)

The All-Party Parliamentary Group (APPG) on social mobility: *Class Ceiling* (2017)

Social Mobility Commission: *The class-pay-gap in British professions* (2017)

To an onlooker, what is fascinating is that for decades these studies have been reaching the following conclusions:

1. Before starting school, children from educated homes already have a greater vocabulary than youngsters from less well-educated households.
2. At the age of five, children from poor and uneducated families are less ready for school than youngsters from wealthy and educated families.
3. Rich parents can buy their children a better education than poor ones.
4. The elite universities are attended by 20 per cent of children of the top 1 per cent of the income scale.
5. Only 7 per cent of all children attend private schools, but these account for 40 per cent of students at Oxford and Cambridge and go on to make up 40-50 per cent of the high-class professions.
6. Children whose parents are in senior roles in business, the public sector or academic professions have a better chance of attaining similar positions than youngsters from families whose parents do not hold such posts.
7. Only 4 per cent of doctors, 6 per cent of barristers, 11 per cent of journalists and 12 per cent of solicitors are of working-class origin.
8. In the same profession and a similar position, children from poor families earn less than youngsters from rich families.
9. Families who own their own homes are better off than those that rent.

And specifically concerning public schools:

1. A third of MPs are privately educated.
2. A third of FTSE chief executives are privately educated.
3. Three-quarters of the senior judiciary are privately educated.

4. More than two-thirds of British Oscar winners are privately educated.
5. Most of the top 100 news journalists are privately educated.

What is new about these discoveries? Nothing, absolutely nothing. The bottom line is always the same. So why do these pronouncements still keep coming? In reality, this is less about science and more about a political call to action. This is no bad thing – on the contrary, but it should be stated loud and clear. Such deception can even undermine the cause. For every right-minded person, including the targeted politicians, knows that the 'new' findings are just the same old trope, and their fate is consequently similar to that of all their predecessors, to be filed away more or less graciously in a drawer. There may also be another explanation: the authors and publishers are without exception not members of the working class, but belong to the upper echelons and almost always to the Establishment (although they usually vehemently deny this: see Chapter 7). Could it be that they are using this debate to stage a huge soap opera, in which the poor and powerless can continue to dream of justice and equality among mankind?

The indisputable advantage held by children from education and/ or wealthy homes is anathema to modern politicians, irrespective of their political leaning. In speech after speech they underline that their party doesn't care where you come from, but only where you are going, is not interested in your birth and breeding but in your potential. But how to level out this advantage in practice? You could do to the public schools what the Labour government did to the grammar schools, what Labour politician Anthony Crosland undertook in 1965 with the now famous words: 'If it's the last thing I do, I'm going to destroy every fucking grammar school in England. And Wales, and Northern Ireland.'[11]

But to what avail? In non-selective schools the offspring of educated and/or rich parents naturally again fare best. The politically correct answer to this problem from modern-day politicians is to back parents who want and do the best for their children, but to explain their own desire to bring all children up to a high level. As David Cameron said in 2012: 'To all those people who say "He wants children to have the kind of education he had at his posh school," I say: "Yes – you are absolutely right!"' In his speech to mark 100 days of the new Conservative government in August 2015 he reiterated: 'We want everyone to have a chance to succeed and education is the best way of ensuring that.' This is of course not possible, but goes down well with the voters and so they get to hear it. The promise of equal opportunity let alone equal outcomes is at best well-intentioned, at worst an outright lie.

In any discussion of class of origin, there is one paradox that must not be forgotten. People's roots often have quite different effects on their motivation. Many who are born on top become apathetic and lazy ('Why should I make an effort?'). And many who begin life at the bottom are consequently ambitious and hard-working ('I want to get out of here.'). Far from everyone who grows up in a privileged background takes advantage of the opportunity this represents, whether their good fortune consists of having parents who are rich or (only) highly intelligent and well-educated. We all know kids from rich families who get nowhere professionally and never earn a penny, but are already fretting by the age of 25 about how to spend the money they already have as well as their future inheritance. Far from simply leading a dissolute life or indulging in luxury, many of these offspring sense or understand that people who enjoy spending money are highly popular wherever they go, so they contemplate philanthropy. Not unusually, and driven by similar motives, they develop a penchant for collecting art with the further aim of diverting attention from their own inadequacies. It is one of the great achievements of capitalism to find the blood, sweat and tears of miners and steelworkers transformed into world-famous art collections within just one or two generations of great industrialists' entrepreneurial achievements, such as the Thyssen Bornemisza gallery in Madrid. Unless they are entirely stupid, these unemployable children usually remain at the top end of society in financial terms.

The same cannot be said of children who have grown up in a family that is (only) educated and intellectual. It is not unusual for a couple who have spent their lives in academic professions as university researchers or professors and have achieved a very high educational level to one day realize with a heavy heart that their children are unlikely to make the grade to get into university, let alone obtain a degree. Despite all the opportunities afforded by an educated home, these offspring have lacked the talent or willingness to convert their chances. Without a financial cushion, they slide down the professional and social ladder. Unfortunately, no books have been written about such financial and intellectual drop-outs, either by the protagonists themselves or by others, although it would be interesting to follow these downward life paths and trace the impact on the souls of those concerned. On the other hand, for many who grow up in humble circumstances this in itself propels them on to great things as a means of social advancement. They might not have reached their ultimate status had they been brought up in a more privileged background, been more spoilt and enjoyed greater comforts, and therefore not tried so hard.

However, by no means everyone is bound to remain immutably in the class to which they belong by birth. Changing class is also a possibility.

32

Change of Class

Changing class is like emigrating from one side of the world to the other.

Lynsey Hanley, *Respectable* (2016)

Few thought he was even a starter
There were many who thought themselves smarter
But he ended PM
CH and OM
An earl and a knight of the garter.

Clement Attlee (1956)

Tomorrow every Duchess in London will be wanting to kiss me.

Prime Minister Ramsay MacDonald, after
forming the National Government in August 1931

Changing class is a big deal, down as well as up. Most people don't do it. Those who do often retain the wounds and scars. There is no single empirical model or set of rules, nor can there be, since class is determined by such disparate criteria. A critical difference is whether the shift (be it upward or downward) applies solely to financial circumstances or intellectual and cultural standing, or both. A worker who wins the lottery advances financially, but not intellectually or culturally. The child of a high-earning plumber or electrician who becomes a university professor achieves intellectual advancement, but does not necessarily also move up the financial ladder. The child from a working-class home who becomes a barrister and highly paid Queen's Counsel rises in the world both intellectually and financially. The offspring of the academic couple or barrister who do not go to university lose status intellectually, but not always financially.

DOWN

A downward change from upper to lower class, either economic or cultural, is relatively rare. It is astonishing how many families can retain their economic level for long periods, even without any particular merit on the part of ensuing generations. The 'law', whereby the first generation creates the fortune, the second holds onto it, and the third and fourth lose it – as epitomized by the decline of a family in Thomas Mann's novel *Buddenbrooks* (1901) – by no means applies to everyone. Studies have found that the same families as 600 years ago commonly remain on top, e.g. in Italy. There seems to be a glass floor or a net that stops the upper classes from sliding to the bottom. In the UK the effect seems to last about six generations. Philip Beresford and William D. Rubinstein's *The Richest of the Rich, The Wealthiest 250 People in Britain since 1066* (2007) highlights the 'conservative' nature of top fortunes, with land-owning and inherited wealth forming the basis of a very large share of these fortunes into the twentieth century'. However, there are plenty of cases of economic demise, classic among them those befalling the second and third sons of peers, not to mention the daughters. Under English primogeniture, the eldest son is the sole inheritor: he receives the title, the land and country estate, the other assets and the seat in the House of Lords (insofar as it is still available to hereditary peers). If the family fortune was insufficient to offer the second son too a carefree life, or he didn't marry into money (as Winston Churchill's father Randolph did), the non-heir had to seek employment and thus very often became economically middle-class. In bygone days some protection from too harsh a decline was afforded by the standard second-son professions of military officer or clergyman or a posting to the colonies, but by the Second World War at the latest this escape route had been closed off.

But even rich heirs have not been, and are not, immune to impoverishment. Changing peripheral conditions, such as industrialization, falling land rents (especially in the nineteenth century), high inheritance and income taxes and/or personal circumstances such as incapacity or illness caused many substantial fortunes to be depleted and often wiped out. Even venerable and exalted aristocratic titles are by no means always protected against the descent into criminality, addiction, illness and poverty, as the public has witnessed in recent years in the fates of John Hervey 7th Marquess of Bristol, Jamie Blandford 12th Duke of Marlborough and Alexander Montagu 13th Duke of Manchester. Nevertheless, as a general rule, the working class is populated by very few individuals with upper- or upper-middle-class origins.

Even if someone has fallen on hard times economically, they can still belong to their previous class by dint of their soft class markers. Just because a member of the upper classes has a more lowly occupation does not mean they have changed class. Alexander, Viscount Lascelles, the son and heir apparent of David Lascelles 8th Earl of Harewood, is employed as a chef in London. He is upper-class. Likewise, the son of an impoverished peer who, lacking an inheritance and talent, works as a bookkeeper and lives in a terraced house in the suburbs, will not automatically become working-class, provided he retains the soft class markers of his family, losing which is well-nigh impossible. George Orwell described the actual difference it makes to someone from the upper echelons who embraces socialism or perhaps even joins the Communist Party:

Look at any bourgeois Socialist. Look at Comrade X, member of the CPGB[1] and author of *Marxism for Infants*. Comrade X, it so happens, is an old Etonian. He would be ready to die on the barricades, in theory anyway, but you notice that he still leaves his bottom waistcoat button undone. He idealizes the proletariat, but it is remarkable how little his habits resemble theirs. Perhaps once, out of sheer bravado, he has smoked a cigar with the band on, but it would be almost physically impossible for him to put pieces of cheese into his mouth on the point of his knife, or to sit indoors with his cap on, or even to drink his tea out of the saucer. Perhaps table manners are not a bad test of sincerity. I have known numbers of bourgeois socialists, I have listened by the hour to their tirades against their own class, and yet never, not even once, have I met one who had picked up proletarian table-manners.[2]

Qualifying himself as lower-upper-middle-class, Orwell also related his own personal experience in this respect:

The fact that has got to be faced is that to abolish class distinctions means abolishing a part of yourself. Here am I, a typical member of the middle class. It is easy for me to say that I want to get rid of class distinctions, but nearly everything I think and do is a result of class distinctions. All my notions – notions of good and evil, of pleasant and unpleasant, of funny and serious, of ugly and beautiful – are essentially *middle-class* notions; my taste in books and food and clothes, my sense of honour, my table manners, my turns of speech, my accent, even the characteristic movements of my body, are the products of a special kind of upbringing and a special niche about halfway up the social hierarchy.[3]

The Labour politician Tony Benn discovered for himself how difficult it is to shed being upper-class. Born as Anthony Wedgwood Benn, he became the 2nd Viscount Stansgate after the death of his father, but spent years pushing through the Peerage Act of 1963, which allowed the renunciation of peerages, and became the first peer to renounce his title. Though he attempted to get details of his education (Westminster, Oxford New College and President of the Oxford Union) removed from *Who's Who*, became a Labour MP for Bristol South-east and announced that he wanted to be known simply as Mr Tony Benn and was always a left winger in his party, proposing the abolition of the monarchy in 1991, it was very difficult not to see in him a member of the upper classes.

Those whose economic status has been downgraded, e.g. as a result of business misfortune, family quarrels or, equally, through ineptitude, cleave most despairingly to the markers of their class. The public school man whose income drops to benefits level 'immediately becomes twenty times more Public School than before and clings to the Old School Tie as to a life-line' (George Orwell). The upper-class person, who has lost his house and estates will, says Julian Fellowes, explain

> to some American visitor that money is not important in England, that people can stay in society without a bean, that land is 'more of a liability, these days', but in his heart, he does not believe any of these things. He knows that the family that has lost everything but its coronet, those duchesses in small houses near Cheyne Walk, those viscounts with little flats in Ebury Street, lined as they may be with portraits and pictures of the old place ('It's some sort of farmers' training college, nowadays'), these people are all déclassé to their own kind. Hence they will do everything to keep at least some requisite acquaintance and props of their former class.[4]

'I always think it rather pathetic', wrote an Irish earl in the thirties of the last century,

> when I see people who have been turned out of their country houses by taxation stick up their family portraits in small London flats. They are clinging to the past and will not realize that an old family only remains such as long as it continues to own the family home and landed property.[5]

Intellectual demotion occurs more frequently than one might imagine. Statistically speaking, it is almost bound to happen in the course of a family's history, the name for this being 'reversion to the mean'. We are all familiar with the ineluctable law that the more illustrious the ancestor, the more difficult it is to surpass or even simply match their greatness, and the more likely the descendants are to fall short of the mark. This is equally true of the intellect. The greater the intellectual prowess of the parents, the less likely that their progeny will reach the same heights. In the case of geniuses or exceptional minds this stands to reason: no-one expects the children of Isaac Newton, Charles Darwin and co. to replicate their fathers' intellectual or artistic brilliance. Naturally, smart parents often have smart kids. But smart parents can have stupid or unwilling kids too. The son or daughter of the famous lawyer who 'doesn't fancy' law or a profession can sometimes be found working in a warehouse or driving a truck. If they are lucky and their parents have earned money with their intelligence, they will remain reasonably well-off financially. Otherwise, they must start again from scratch. Here we see the major difference: material wealth can be easily passed on, brains only up to a point.

UP

Moving to a higher class has always been possible in England, and still is. Its permeability has been a particular feature of the English class system. A number of English historians consider the most remarkable 'event' of more recent English history to be the non-occurrence of a revolution of the kind seen in France, Russia and Germany (apart from a few insurgencies).[6] One of the reasons might be that in England the ruling class always accepted newcomers, be they people of merit, or merely outsiders and troublemakers it was unable to suppress, often making of them disciples who pursued the cause with the zeal of the converted. 'Suitable' marriages also played a major role in elevating women in particular to the social standing of their spouse. Kate Middleton, Duchess of Cambridge, is the modern epitome. As Alexis de Tocqueville already observed: the resilience of the British class system is due to this marriage of new money and old style. The British upper class acts as a sponge for talent and ambition, and snobbery can act as a spur to personal achievement.

How did people rise to the top in the past? Every family, without exception, that made it to the upper class in the course of its history started with someone from the lower orders. This is of course true the world over, and not possible any other way. Many of the families that later became England's richest and most distinguished began with fathers and mothers who were ordinary soldiers (maybe as long as a thousand years ago alongside William the Conqueror), agricultural workers, servants, simple peasants, and sometimes even criminals who founded their dynasty by illegal means. Social elevation was primarily granted on the basis of military conduct, or civil deeds in the service of the king, or the acquisition of wealth, rather than scientific or artistic achievement. In recent centuries, the process of moving up in the world on the strength of the hard class markers money and assets has rarely been accomplished in a single generation, but has generally been in three stages.[7]

To begin with, a successful artisan or merchant developed his trade, built a mill or works and accumulated some capital. During the second generation the company expanded and an even bigger factory was built. The third generation transformed it into a joint stock company with its head office in London and global business contacts. In parallel, the family's education became more sophisticated. While the founder still attended the village school, his children were educated at the local grammar schools, his grandsons at a major public school and an Oxford or Cambridge college. Parallel to this, the family title rose through the ranks of the honours system, from knight via baronetcy to a peerage as a baron or viscount or sometimes an earl. Not unusually, this was accompanied by a fourth, political transformation, as the new grandees switched their voting allegiances from Liberal to Conservative and progressed from the Commons to the Lords.

No family illustrates this ascent better than that of Harold Macmillan. His paternal great-grandfather was a Scottish crofter from the Isle of Arran. His grandfather founded the Macmillan publishing house (1843). His father managed the company until 1936 and became rich. Harold Macmillan married the daughter of the Duke of Devonshire, held virtually every important political office in the UK, served as prime minister from 1957 to 1963 and, in 1984, became 1st Earl of Stockton, the last prime minister to receive a hereditary peerage.

Apart from war, business and wealth, political office and public service as well as the professions were a track to success in gaining nobility. Take the astronomical rise of Frederick Edwin (F. E.) Smith, who was born in 1872 and was one of Winston Churchill's best and most enduring friends. He didn't exactly come from humble beginnings, but neither were they grand. His father was a local councillor and solicitor. Smith studied jurisprudence on a scholarship in Oxford, where he became president of the Union. After serving an appointment as a lecturer in law as a fellow of Merton College, he became one of the best known and most highly paid barristers in the country, 'taking silk' as a king's counsel in 1908. From 1906 he was a Conservative MP. At the age of 43 he became Solicitor General, after that Attorney General, at 48 Lord High Chancellor and Secretary of State for India before his untimely death in 1930. He accumulated honours with equally breathtaking speed: after a baronetcy in 1915, he became Baron Birkenhead in 1919, Viscount Birkenhead 1921, Earl of Birkenhead and simultaneously Viscount Furneaux (from the name of his wife) in 1922. All this resulted not from his ancestry, however, but was down to his outstanding personality, brimming with intelligence, eloquence, oratory and wit.[8]

Although there have always been individuals who have risen prodigiously to the top in terms of almost all the class markers – that is to say money, power, title and culture – such class changes seem easier today than before. Present-day figures who have made it thanks to money include the self-made businessmen Philip Green (fashion), Mike Ashley (retail sports equipment), Richard Branson (tourism, finance, media), Peter Hargreaves (finance) and John Caudwell (telecoms), the CEOs of major enterprises and institutions Stephen Hester (CEO of Royal Sun Alliance), Stuart Gulliver (HSBC) and Mervyn King (Bank of England), and rich celebrities such as the Beckham family. When it comes to power, former prime minister John Major stands out, his father having been a trapeze artist in the music halls turned garden gnome businessman; an example of spectacular advancement based on culture is the former Archbishop of

Canterbury George Carey, a man who had failed the 11+ exam and left school at the age of 15.

These days, moving up the class ladder is usually measured by whether the next generation reaches a higher level on the seven-class version of the Official National Statistics Socio-Economic Classification (NS-SEC) than their parents. Numerous scientific studies'[9] general thrust is that upward and downward mobility have existed in the past and still persist. However, while movement to a higher class clearly outweighed the decline to a lower status in the four decades following the Second World War (the era of 'More Room at the Top'), since then the trend has been reversed. Nevertheless, measured in this way, class membership remains extremely stable, particularly in the higher echelons. The chances of a child with a higher professional or managerial father ending up in a similar position rather than in a wage-earning, working-class position are up to 20 times greater than the corresponding chances for a child with a working-class father.[10]

This approach to social mobility relates only to the professional and financial aspects of changing class. However, simply acquiring the hard class markers is by no means enough to secure membership of a higher social class, as the lottery winner awash with cash but devoid of manners serves to illustrate. Michael Carroll, a part-time binman and repeat offender, won £9.7 million in the National Lottery in 2002 aged 19. Within eight years he had spent almost his entire winnings on new homes, cars, drugs, jewellery, parties, relatives and friends and a lavish lifestyle. He was proud to be nicknamed 'Lotto lout' and affixed a 'King of Chavs' banner on his Mercedes, which he called his 'Loutmobile'. Apart from that, he continued his career of 42 previous convictions, was banned from driving, shot out shop and car windows while driving through town and was jailed for affray. It takes more than money to make a 'success' of changing class. As with admission to the aristocracy in days of yore, 'those who want to get in have to know where the importance of money stops and where the importance of manners begins.'[11] Can one change the soft class markers as well?

This question is something of a classic theme of English literature, made famous with George Bernard Shaw's play *Pygmalion* (later adapted as the musical and film *My Fair Lady*). In it, the phoneticist Professor Henry Higgins says of the flower girl Eliza Doolittle, with her working-class Cockney accent: 'You see this creature with her kerbstone English. The English that will keep her in the gutter to the end of her days . . . Well, Sir, in three months I could pass that girl off as a Duchess at an ambassador's garden party.' And he actually pulls it off. Shaw's *Pygmalion* has its modern equivalent in television makeover shows such as *What Not to Wear* (WNTW) or *From Ladette to Lady*, in which people from more modest backgrounds are transformed by acquiring the behaviour and accessories of the upper echelons, almost always under the guidance of individuals who for their part have distinctively upper-class pedigrees. The makeover is essentially 'the transformation of self with the help of experts in the hope or expectation of improvement of status and life chances through the acquisition of forms of cultural and social capital',[12] meaning more or less the soft class markers.

Such transformations or attempts at them are not restricted to stage or screen. Until not too long ago, many regarded elocution lessons as an essential precondition of social advancement, a means of throwing off a working-class accent in favour of socially superior speech. It is extremely difficult, however, to eradicate any trace of the pronunciation learned as child. A word or stress out of place, and the game is over. Although a BBC accent or received pronunciation (RP) is no longer absolutely essential for an upward career trajectory, and regional and other accents are also accepted in many professions, especially in popular television and radio programmes, becoming a member of the upper classes with your working-class accent still intact is likely to prove rather difficult.

Although easier to learn than the accent, assimilating the terminology of a different class calls for lengthy practice and the utmost control bordering on enforced indifference, as Margaret Thatcher found out to her cost when, in 1983, she accused Denis Healey in the House of Commons of being 'frit' (a word meaning 'frightened' that betrayed her

East Midlands origins) of an election. Terminology has become more relaxed, and many words that were previously taboo have become respectable in polite society, with the upper echelons absorbing much of the language of the working classes – and using it not merely for irony. Yet the 'wrong' terminology can be a barrier to crossing class divides that even substantial sums and/or power cannot remove.

Changing the other soft class markers is simpler. Whatever the subject, guides can be purchased. Better still, you can hire a private tutor. Information is available on the correct furnishings, the right leisure activities and the most appropriate pets, suitable modes of dress, the right hairstyles, de rigueur holiday locations, required reading, table manners and much more besides. Some members of the aristocracy earn a living teaching such lessons. But beware! Knowing is one thing, doing another. For many of these soft class markers it takes prolonged practice to internalize them to the same extent as someone who has picked them up automatically through breeding. Take table manners: someone who has only learned the 'right way' later in life will need years for it to become second nature so they no longer notice that they are behaving correctly.

It is exactly this predicament that makes it so incredibly difficult to move from simply knowing another class's rules, to living them out in practice. For anyone who has not picked them up at home, they are 'alien', and above all they are rules. For those born into that class, these are not rules. It is rather like the acquisition of language by children. When learning their mother tongue, they are oblivious to the fact that they are also learning rules. Native speakers, with their perfect knowledge of English, German or French, are neither aware that their language has rules nor indeed that they are using them. They use the accusative case or the perfect participle or future tense, choose the appropriate words and pronounce them correctly with not the slightest inkling that they are at the same time applying rules. By contrast, the non-native speaker immediately recognizes the rules and tries to learn them. If he or she gets them wrong, this is noticed by the native speaker straight away. Exactly the same is true of class behaviour. Children born into a specific class behave in the way they have learned from their family. They are likewise unaware that they are following rules when they say 'loo' instead of 'toilet' or 'what' rather than 'pardon', or hold their cutlery in a certain way. They have not been drilled or schooled to keep these rules. It is more like breathing in and out or riding a bike: stopping to think about what they are doing would quickly disrupt their rhythm. This makes it so unbelievably difficult for the upper-class newcomer not to be immediately identified as such. A slip-up by someone who has just moved up a class marks him as an outsider.

Moving from lower to upper strata is not always an easy journey emotionally and can be painful. It hurts to leave one's existing environment, relatives, friends and complete social circle behind. The word 'uprooted' best sums up this experience, as many who have followed this path have described. Examples include the recent autobiographical account by Lynsey Hanley[13] and the book from which she quotes extensively, *The Uses of Literacy* (1957) by Richard Hoggart, or the remark made by the actress and writer Eleanor Bron, who studied in Cambridge: 'My three years . . . certainly made me unfit to live with my family any more. I was too clever, my new friends were too clever.'[14]

Most of these reports are unfortunately rather one-sided: while they freely portray the loss of their former world and how sad this is, very few indicate that they nevertheless prefer their old class to the new one. As far as we can tell, no-one has ever tried to go back. And few are honest enough to admit that, apart from with their closest relatives, they simply no longer feel at ease in the company of their former peers, indeed often cannot fully understand them any more, because the things that trouble the middle classes are generally quite different from the concerns of working-class people. Lynsey Hanley's parents did not think about or discuss her school. She automatically went to the local state secondary. Hanley herself will probably ponder very carefully which school her son will attend – state, selective or private – and this will be very much a talking point for her and her husband. Someone who changes class must realize that you can't have your cake and eat it.

For all their regrets about leaving their old class behind, however, a certain pride prevails among those who have made the grade to a higher level. As is to be expected, this is carefully glossed over, for to say so would be derided – both by members of their previous class ('She thinks she's better than us') and by denizens of the higher echelons ('He is a naff social climber'). A more frequent line, and one particularly favoured by intellectual upward movers, is to combine criticism of the class system in general with an indication that the critic's own mobility has been secured thanks to their personal strength and resources. This approach satisfies public morality while at the same time allowing the author to take pride in their own achievement. Many impressive memoirs of social climbers follow this pattern. This stance is more honest and more appealing than that of those who, having climbed the social ladder, attempt to wipe out all trace of their past, acting as if they have always belonged to their new class, an affectation not uncommon among the upwardly mobile from trade and industry (see Chapter 4).

A change of class is all-pervading. The person who makes this transition usually endeavours to adapt to their new class in every respect, which is precisely the nature of class change. Another possibility of course is to change class 'partially', in other words to abandon only specific class rules. Breaking the rules is almost as much an English peculiarity as keeping them – albeit as ever, only up to a point.

33

Breaking the Rules

To break the rules you must first master them.

Proverb

Manners are especially the need of the plain. The pretty can get away with anything.

Evelyn Waugh, *Observer* (1962)

Quod licet jovi, non licet bovi.

Latin saying: What is permissible for
Jove is not permissible for an ox.

England is the paradise of individuality, eccentricity, heresy, anomalies, hobbies and humours.

George Santayana, *Soliloquies in England* (1922)

Someone whose class is firmly established can break that class's rules almost at will without their social status changing either up or down. It therefore follows that the rule-breakers are usually members of the highest and lowest classes, since their rank is more secure than that of the middle classes. The established upper class can do as it likes anyway; the working class does not mind if one of its number dallies with the jet set – they are still one of its own. The middle class goes to great lengths to keep its own rules and often those of a higher caste too, so as to dispel any doubts about its standing. A middle-class

Englishman who is afraid of appearing working- or lower-middle class would never place his knife and fork at the end of a course anywhere but in the middle of the plate, the knife being on the right, the fork on the left and the prongs towards the centre of the table. Someone certain of his acceptance in society would do just as he pleases, for he would be unconcerned by what was 'done' or 'not done'.

Conversely, breaking the rules can even be evidence of class. If a top person defies the accepted mores, they may be setting a new standard which from then on becomes the yardstick. History is full of kings and other worthies who have behaved badly but thereby rendered such transgressions acceptable. One example is the bottom button of a waistcoat. Traditionally the bottom button was done up. The rule of leaving it unfastened is said to have begun with King Edward VII, whose expanding waistline prevented him from closing it. His court copied his style to make him feel less self-conscious. Today, leaving the bottom button unfastened is de rigueur while buttoning it is still seen as a fashion faux pas.

FAUX PAS

All the soft class markers have their rights and wrongs. 'Wrong' can apply to your hairstyle, dress, and accent; you can use the wrong words; your table manners can be wrong, as can your car, the flowers in your garden or your choice of pet. You can take your vacation in the wrong place and read the wrong newspaper. Each class has a different idea of what is 'wrong', and it varies from class to class.

The most outlandish 'faux pas' are naturally those committed by the upper classes, and the subject of hundreds of (genuine and invented) anecdotes. Dukes and their offspring as well as the other members of the peerage provide a rich seam of material. In *Class*, Jilly Cooper tells of walking through the streets of Oxford with a boy from the upper echelons when, after breaking a bar of chocolate in half, her companion gave her one piece and ate the other himself. "'But you can't eat sweets in the street!" I gasped, shocked. "I', he answered with centuries of disdain in his voice, "can do anything I like". Cooper recounts how, when she went shooting in Northumberland, she

371

noticed a handsome blond young man in a red sweater at the next butt, and asked why he didn't have to wear camouflage like the rest of the people present. "'Because he is a duke's son," said the host. "He can do what he likes.'" Or she recalls a lunch party in a middle-class house where some Americans had been invited to meet a duke's daughter. The daughter of the house wore a tweed coat and skirt, flat shoes, a pale blue cashmere jersey and pearls. The duke's daughter roared up on a motorbike, wearing a leather skirt, fishnet stockings, a tight black sweater and punk eye make-up. Another anecdote concerns

> a stag party in a private room at a London club where the men had just finished dinner when the bridegroom's father, an aged earl, suddenly beckoned to a waiter and said, 'Pot'.
> 'We're not allowed to supply it, sir,' said the waiter, nervously.
> 'Don't be bloody silly,' roared the earl. 'I mean pisspot.'
> Whereupon a huge chamber pot was brought down from one of the bedrooms and the Earl proceeded to use it in full view of the other guests.[1]

Dress provides a field day for rule-breakers. Generally, the higher social ranks dress inconspicuously and unobtrusively (see Chapter 11). But there are exceptions reserved for special occasions, such as the dandyish striped blazers worn at regattas and garden parties and the flashy waistcoats worn by members of exclusive university dining clubs. Even in everyday settings some upper-class males wear brightly-coloured trousers, red in particular, to the extent that 'toffs in red trousers' have become a bit of a national joke. But there are limits! The red has to be matte, not shiny, and the trousers always have to be loose-fitting, not tight. Some reds are more equal than others. Raspberry reds are OK, orangey shades less so.[2] Julian Fellowes explains how the commoner Edith dressed in the country, selecting her outfit with care.

> Casual country clothes, well-bred and unshowy. A duke's daughter might get away with wearing some streetwalker's outfit from

Voyage at a dinner in Shropshire, indeed she would be praised for her aristocratic eccentricity, but she, Edith, would never be given the same licence. Had she dared to wear London clothes in the country, to Charles's circle it would only have been a confirmation of her ill-breeding.[3]

For an article on his Scone Project (named after Scone Palace, the family seat in Scotland), which offers ultra-rich heirs a leadership programme in a 'safe space', William Murray, Viscount Stormont, heir to the Earl of Mansfield, had no problem being photographed in his palace wearing striped socks and a waistcoat without a jacket – against all the sartorial rules.[4] When Prince Harry chose to wear an SS uniform for a fancy-dress party, his rule-breaking may have overstepped the unspoken boundaries of the permissible, but this by no means damaged him long term and may have even increased his popularity, hinting at eccentricity.

Those whose social station is secure are also allowed to flout terminology rules. The 12th Duke of Devonshire, son of Deborah Duchess of Devonshire, the younger sister of Nancy of U and Non-U notoriety, had no problem welcoming a female television reporter and replying with an American 'I'm good' when asked 'How are you?'[5] Everything is in any case allowed for the sake of irony – even the word 'toilet'. With someone whose class is not at issue, the use of taboo words is automatically regarded as humorous. The phenomenon of the upper and lower classes having something in common occurs with bad language (see Chapter 15). Both use obscenities much more than the middle classes, who take care to avoid swearing for fear of 'getting something wrong' (see Chapter 5). A survey revealed that people belonging to social classes A and B actually say 'fuck' more often than those in class C1.[6] In several professions that tend to be counted as upper-class, 'fuck' has become an everyday expression, used by people in particular to mock individuals and behaviours that are different from their own, the most obvious being the political class and the media. In Alwyn Turner's *A Classless Society*, on Britain in the 1990s, the word 'fuck' comes up in quotations myriad times. Whether this is driven by a sense of superiority or sheer rudeness is unclear.

Eating also presents an open invitation to rule-breakers. Many aristocrats, typically male, are notorious for their lamentable table manners, be it that they start before everyone has been served ('I'm ravenous'), or gulp down their food or drink too much. To display every gift you have ever received in your front room, however, is definitely working-class. If Princess Anne does this in her house, Gatcombe Park, including tacky dolls and cheap African carvings, this is regarded as harmless eccentricity.[7] The same holds true for gardens: once a garden owner has acquired a prestigious reputation, it is quite permissible for him to express a tenderness for the unfashionable, the plebeian and the downright naff.[8] Even a garden gnome could be accepted. Ferdinand Mount tells a charming story:

> When the doyen of gardening writers, Christopher Lloyd, in his old age decided to abandon the tasteful muted efforts he had been achieving all his life at his famous garden, Great Dixter, in Kent, and go for the brightest scarlet and orange flowers he could think of, there was a sharp intake of breath among his fellow gardeners. He had, so to speak, gone over to the other side. But he was soon forgiven for what was identifiable as a classic high camp gesture in which bad taste is, at the whim of the insider, decreed to be good.[9]

Rule-breaking is another manifestation of the paradox whereby the exact same behaviour is viewed differently depending on people's class. If a member of the proletariat does not remove his sunglasses when talking to someone else, this counts as bad manners. Yet if a member of the upper echelons behaves in exactly the same way, he is clearly doing it for medical reasons. By extension, the host of a gathering in a historic house can very well depart from the cast-iron rule of passing the port clockwise and slide the port decanter across the table to the person opposite without this being frowned upon. Only the uninitiated newcomer would be offended. But if the latter were to act in the same fashion, the whole crowd would ostracize him as uncouth.

This points to a rule for middle-class rule-breakers that upper-class offenders need not follow. The latter's class being evident, their status will not be damaged by (pretty much) any breach of rules. The same applies to the working class. By contrast, the socially insecure members of the middle class must be careful. If they slip up on a minor matter, those around them could easily think that they are unaware of the rule and are therefore lower-class. If the code is blatantly flaunted, as by the earl with his chamber pot (see above), the breach is evaluated quite differently: 'It really cannot be that he does not know that such things are simply not done.' A flagrant gaffe can be smarter than a slight misdemeanour in class terms.

Breaking the rules is not restricted to the upper echelons. The working-class girl who has a passion for the upper-class equestrian sport of eventing and keeps a horse (free in return for mucking-out) and festoons her council-house kitchen with rosettes and photographs of herself competing in local hunt trials and one-day events is, notwithstanding her 'posh' horsey doings and decorations, accepted by her working-class friends and neighbours as their peer. The innocuous quirk of having a somewhat eccentric hobby in no way affects her status as their social equal.[10]

The 'misdemeanours' of the upper classes are not to be confused with the class denial (see Chapter 7) to which they are also most prone. In both instances the transgressor is very familiar with the rules and knows what he is doing. When deviating from accepted standards, the culprit remains authentic, in the knowledge that his aberration will not be judged as such and that he will continue to be counted as a member of his class. The aim of the class denier is to conceal his status.

LIMITS

Nevertheless, unfettered rule-breaking is not permitted, and infringements must not exceed certain unwritten and unseen but very real limits. The bounds of acceptability are defined not by the rule-breakers but by their social equals, and beyond that society as a whole. What's more, they vary from person to person. Behaviour that might be tolerated from a duke may be unacceptable from a politi-cian. Politicians may be forgiven things that would be unpardonable when done by a duke. It is rather like our attitude to highly gifted artists or scientists: conduct towards other people that would other-wise be inexcusable – mistreatment of their fellow human beings for instance – is sometimes overlooked. We know or sense the emotional strain those with exceptional gifts may be under when producing brilliance. Moral reprehensibility is cancelled out by the high value of their scientific or artistic achievements for the common good. But only to a certain extent. Even the greatest genius is not allowed to break all the rules, for example by torturing or even killing another person for artistic or scientific purposes. Here, too, the true maestro knows where the limits are.

That there are rules that cannot be broken by even the highest-ranking person in the land was experienced by King Edward VIII, who was probably the most prominent upper-class rule-breaker of the last century. His mistresses and dubious friends, his sympathies for Germany, his accent (perceived by many as 'non-U' – although that phrase had not yet been coined) did not undermine his social standing. As the Prince of Wales, he was first in line to the throne and later became king. Only when he insisted on marrying the twice-divorced American Wallis Simpson did he overstep the mark, committing an act for which not even the King could be forgiven and which famously led to his abdication in 1936. Had he been alive 70 years later, marrying a divorcee would either have ceased to constitute a breach of protocol or been within the bounds of acceptability, as in the case of Prince Charles and his wife Camilla.

A relatively recent curb on rule-breaking has been imposed by political correctness. The basic elements of this phenomenon have of course always existed in the form of good manners: respect for people who are intrinsically different from oneself (in gender, race, sexuality, etc.) without demeaning them. Modern-day sanctions for infringing political correctness appear, however, to be harsher and more severe than those imposed for failed social graces in earlier times. Anyone using taboo words such as 'Paki' or the N-word risks not only social condemnation, but also criminal prosecution, dismissal from work and other similar, very tangible penalties. Curiously, these sanctions are imposed not only by those who truly find such remarks objectionable, but also by people who (naturally behind closed doors) hold the same views as the culprit. They feel obliged to comply with what is politically correct, even if a large majority of people take a different view. Political correctness comes and goes with fashion. Homosexuality, as we know, was a crime in England until 1966, and homosexual men were often the object of ridicule and derision. To say anything disparaging about gays today is to put paid to one's civil career (even though statistically more than 95 per cent of the population are not homosexual). What an extraordinary turnaround!

Some of the rules of political correctness are very complicated. What you can and can't do often depends on who you are. A black man can use the N-word with reference to himself and other black people without objection (though often with a different spelling for ironic effect), and indeed the term has been used more recently with a certain pride. Likewise, some young Asians employ the word Paki as a term of endearment, some gay men have proudly appropriated the term queer as an identity, and many chavs have no problem using the word themselves.[11] Coming from anyone else outside these groups, however, these terms are deemed offensive and unacceptable.

Meanwhile, a counter movement has also emerged. 'Inverted political correctness' indicates strength of character in defiance of the PC meme. When Tony Blair chose not to send his sons Euan and Nicholas to the school in whose catchment area they lived but to have them transported half across London to a 'better' school (see Chapter 31) – extremely politically incorrect, given the Labour stance on selective education – Blair defended his decision by saying that he 'refused to impose political correctness on his children.'[12] Here was a member of the upper classes flouting the rules of PCness. It may have cost Blair sympathies in the Labour Party, but not in the wider electorate, as he went on to win the two subsequent elections with a large majority.

THE ENGLISH ECCENTRIC

The words 'English' and 'eccentric' belong together like Great and Britain.[13] The English eccentric has certain similarities with the rule-breaker who can flout the conventions of his class without suffering any loss of status. The eccentric goes a step further, disregarding the entire code of normal human interaction. Seen in this way, the eccentric is the apotheosis of the class rule-breaker.

In England it seems that eccentrics were predominantly found in the upper echelons and frequently in the aristocracy. These individuals enjoyed a life of comparative ease, unlike the working population which, after eight or ten hours at work each day, did not have the same energy for the kind of japes favoured by someone who could indulge their fantasies all day long. The majority of members of the Eccentric Club in London, founded in 1781, came from the upper classes, and it is perhaps no coincidence that its most recent patron was Prince Philip, Duke of Edinburgh. The 'exploits' that have made them eligible for membership naturally defy categorization. They include the construction of extravagant buildings of predictably striking design. Known as follies or architectural follies, these were designed exclusively or primarily for decoration or aesthetic pleasure, to astonish or impress. The gardens at Stowe, for instance, feature among other things pavilions by Gibbs, a menagerie, Dido's Cave, Vanbrugh's Rotondo and temples to Venus, to Ancient and to Modern Virtue, to Friendship and to British Worthies.[14] Further famous examples are Broadway Tower in Worcestershire, Wimpole's Folly in Cambridgeshire and White Nancy in Cheshire. Less durable but equally bizarre were designs for absurd contraptions such as a pistol for shooting flies, or strange notions such as calling one's horse as a witness in court, trying to teach a dog to fly by throwing it out of a tower window, dyeing pigeons all colours of the rainbow, or riding to a party on a bear's back. Some of the more famous examples of eccentric behaviour include staying almost exclusively alone in one's castle and underground passageways for fear of being seen by one's servants, spending decades in the same room through fear of inhaling air, sitting on the motorway reading a newspaper in order to stop the traffic because of an aversion to cars, changing one's name to King Arthur and running around with a crown, coat of chain mail and the sword Excalibur, or creating a kind of harem with 70 wifelets surrounded by paintings from the *Kama Sutra*. This last wheeze was performed by the 7th Marquess of Bath (who incidentally remained married to the same woman for 45 years) at his Longleat seat, earning him the nickname the Loins of Longleat.

As with the breaker of class rules, the eccentric is also bound by unspoken limits that he exceeds at his peril. However, the scope is wide because the eccentric himself acts as the boundary marker. Unless a taboo is broken, or seen to be broken, it does not exist. Only when society's (ever fluid and changing) morality is actually tested by the eccentric is it possible to discover how far you can go.

HOW TO GET ON IN SOCIETY

In his famous poem of the same name, John Betjeman describes rule-breaking at perhaps its most delightful:

> Phone for the fish-knives, Norman,
> As Cook is a little unnerved;
> You kiddies have crumpled the serviettes
> And I must have things daintily served.
> Are the requisites all in the toilet?
> The frills round the cutlets can wait
> Till the girl has replenished the cruets
> And switched on the logs in the grate.

The instances of rule-breaking we have described here are those of Englishmen. They are deeply characteristic not only of class, but also of Englishness. Foreigners do not know these rules. What appears at first glance to be a disadvantage emerges on closer examination as the opposite.

34

Foreigners

*We cannot bring ourselves to believe it possible that a
foreigner should in any respect be wiser than ourselves.*

Anthony Trollope, *Orley Farm* (1862)

*England is so great that an Englishman cares little what
others think of her, or how they talk of her.*

Thomas B. Macaulay, diary (1849)

Abroad is unutterably bloody and foreigners are fiends.

Uncle Matthew, in Nancy Mitford,
The Pursuit of Love (1945)

The relationship between the English and foreigners is not equal.
Many foreigners have for centuries admired England and the English:
they travel to England, settle there and write books about England,
virtually all of them appreciative and positive.[1] Like many Englishmen
themselves (see Chapter 1), foreigners too have compiled lists encap-
sulating Englishness, for example the American Bill Bryson:

> Marmite, village fêtes, country lanes, people saying 'mustn't grum-
> ble' and 'I'm terribly sorry but', people apologizing to *me* when I
> cronk them with a careless elbow, milk in bottles, beans on toast,
> haymaking in June, stinging nettles, seaside piers, Ordnance Survey
> maps, crumpets, hot-water bottles as a necessity, drizzly Sundays.

... this is still the best place in the world for most things – to post a letter, go for a walk, watch television, buy a book, venture out for a drink, go to a museum, use the bank, get lost, seek help, or stand on a hillside and take in a view.[2]

One such list is particularly charming. Prospective visitors from 25 countries were asked to name six characteristic virtues or symbols that epitomized England for them. In the view of these citizens of the world there were 50 'quintessences of Englishness': the Royal Family, Big Ben/the Houses of Parliament, Manchester United Football Club, the class system, pubs, a robin in the snow, Robin Hood and his Merrie Men, cricket, the White Cliffs of Dover, imperialism, the Union Jack, snobbery, 'God Save the King'/the Queen, the BBC, the West End, *The Times*, Shakespeare, thatched cottages, a cup of tea/ Devonshire cream tea, Stonehenge, phlegm/a stiff upper lip, shopping, marmalade, Beefeaters/the Tower of London, London taxis, a bowler hat, classic TV serials, Oxford/Cambridge, Harrods, double-decker buses/red buses, hypocrisy, gardening, perfidy/untrustworthiness, half-timbering, homosexuality, *Alice in Wonderland*, Winston Churchill, Marks & Spencer, the Battle of Britain, Francis Drake, Trooping the Colour, whingeing, Queen Victoria, breakfast, beer/ warm beer, emotional frigidity, Wembley Stadium, flagellation/ public schools, not washing/bad underwear, the Magna Carta.

This inventory is not in fact based on a real survey of foreigners, but is the brainchild of the English author Julian Barnes, who came up with it for a novel.[3] But actual foreigners would have scarcely said anything else. Interestingly, following three external icons, the class system is listed in fourth place as the first character-related feature.

Yet this feeling is not reciprocated. The English find foreigners suspicious, different – best given a wide berth. Rather than xeno-phobic, they are more pitying towards foreigners who have the misfortune not to be English and therefore not among Cecil Rhodes' winners of the first prize in the lottery of life. This benign superior-ity is probably best epitomized in the legendary newspaper headline: 'Fog in Channel – Continent Cut Off'. Nor can foreigners ever become English from the English point of view: once a foreigner, always a foreigner. They may become British, but never English. Even the English royal family, which, after Queen Victoria reigned over England as the house of Saxe-Coburg and Gotha, was not renamed Windsor until 1917 when anti-German sentiment was running high, is still referred to by a section of the press as 'the Germans'.

Perhaps this is also why the English have such difficulty in accepting that they are no longer exclusively in control of their own destiny, which has been extensively determined by international organizations, foremost among them the European Union (EU) including the European Court of Justice (ECJ) and the European Court of Human Rights (ECHR), the G7 and G20 states, the United Nations (UN), the North Atlantic Treaty Organization (NATO), the International Monetary Fund (IMF), the Organization for Economic Co-operation and Development (OECD) and the World Health Organization (WHO). The acronyms alone appear threatening. If globalization has not greatly changed this English attitude, it may have tempered it slightly. This is hardly surprising considering that, in the heyday of the Empire prior to the Second World War, England had already inhabited a world of equally global reach, then as top nation, today as one of many. Having once stood supreme, that recollection does not easily fade. The English upper class could be very reserved towards foreigners, sometimes blatantly hostile, an outlook immortalized by Nancy Mitford in Uncle Matthew, a thinly disguised portrait of her father. And for the working class, Johnny Foreigner is no darling, any more than are the Krauts (Germans), Frogs (French) or Dagos and Wops (southern Europeans). Historically speaking, the decision to leave the European Union is therefore no surprise, but the return to a traditional position ('Wogs begin at Calais').

THE ENGLISHMAN'S VIEW

At the bottom of his heart, even the lowliest English Lord
considers himself superior to the King of France.

Fürst Hermann von Pückler-Muskau,
Letters of a Dead Man, Letter 30, 31 August 1828

Unsurprisingly, the scepticism towards foreigners permeates the social classes. The call of Marx and Engels for workers of the world to unite – an exhortation also repeated by modern political activists on the left[4] – never resonated particularly with the English labouring classes, which is why the associated endeavours of the English Communist Party were wholly ineffectual. Patriotism and loyalty to their ruling classes were more important to English workers than the interests they shared with other nations' proletarians.

At the top end of society, by contrast, an international coterie including the English had existed for some time, particularly among the nobility. Connections through marriage and kinship were a major factor. Before the First World War the great royal dynasties had been at the apex of an interconnected European hierarchy, as exemplified by Queen Victoria's nine children, who married into royal and noble families across Europe. Foreign gentry were never quite regarded by the English as their equals, however. When, in the early nineteenth century, England was inundated with foreign aristocrats, particularly from France and Italy, seeking a wealthy bride ('cash for class'), in 1826 the diarist Clarissa Trant voiced the widespread view that 'Italian counts and German barons are a suspicious, or at best suspected race,' as were Frenchmen of rank.

The German prince and famous garden designer Fürst Pückler-Muskau was immortalized for an English audience through his *Briefe eines Verstorbenen*, a series of letters written to his (divorced) wife about his two years in England, which came out in 1830 and in English translation in 1832, under the title *The Tour of a German Prince*, in which he described the manners, character and behaviour of all English classes.[5] He was also caricatured in Charles Dickens's *Pickwick Papers*, serving as the model for Count Smorltork, a German aristocrat who is gathering material 'for his great work on England' despite a poor understanding and command of English.

Regardless of his prestigious rank in Prussia and Germany, Pückler-Muskau was never entirely accepted by the English upper classes, who dubbed him 'Prince Pickle and Mustard'. Pückler commented that, in England, foreign noblemen 'rank 50 per cent lower than the native-born variety.[6] Foreign upper-class women had it easier, especially if they were rich. At the end of the nineteenth century a host of impoverished English aristocrats married wealthy, mainly American, heiresses with the aim (among other things) of restoring their financial position in a trade-off of money for class. The more famous marriages included Consuelo Vanderbilt to the Duke of Marlborough, Jennie Jerome to Winston Churchill's father Lord Randolph Churchill, and Mary Leiter and Grace Hinds to George, Marquess Curzon.[7] After some teething problems, they generally won the acceptance of the class to which their husbands belonged, especially if their marriage produced children and heirs.

In the modern era the English attitude to upper-crust foreigners is typified by how the 'Euro Sloanes', who hit London after the Big Bang in 1986, are regarded. Despite their breeding, palaces, share portfolios, perfect manners, impeccable English, London residence, international connections and access to sections of the English upper class, as well as their popularity among the English upper-middle class, they are still at risk of being classified (behind their backs) as 'Euro trash'.[8]

As always in England, there are exceptions. Some foreigners become members of the English upper class, at least after several generations. Names like Baring and Rothschild from Germany come to mind. Gaining acceptance at that level in one generation on the other hand is unusual for a foreigner. The late Lord George Weidenfeld became part of the English upper-class establishment. Likewise, a number of Greeks have formed a certain exception, notably the shipowners Stavros Niarchos and Aristotle Onassis. As George Mikes stated, the most sought-after people are Greeks, as there is a notion afloat that every Greek is a millionaire.[9] In the case of Niarchos and Onassis this was true, and at least one of the reasons for their acceptance by the English (and French) upper classes. It was good to be asked to holiday on their yachts. Even Churchill favoured Onassis's yacht *Christina* for eight cruises after his premiership. The owner's character, education and wit would probably not have been sufficient.

The very select group of the 'international super-rich' can arrange their lives regardless of national borders or financial constraints. They hail from all corners of the Earth, coming until recently predominantly from the USA and Western Europe as well as Central and South America, and latterly also from Russia and Asia, in particular the Middle East, China and India. Many have chosen London or rural England as their main or second residence. Their privileged fiscal status (non-domiciled, or taxation on a remittance basis) is debated and pilloried, but changes are seldom made. They bring in much more in taxes than they cost. Names that spring to mind include the steel magnate Lakshmi Mittal, the Russian oligarch and owner of Chelsea Football Club Roman Abramovich, the pop star Madonna and some Arabian princes. However, they too essentially remain outside the English class system, accepted as neighbours, but still not a part of England, let alone the upper class. Though perhaps Prince Harry's marriage to Meghan Markle may signal a new trend.[10]

England's globalism, first in the British Empire and later in the Commonwealth, always involved the English in ranking foreigners according to social class, e.g. Indian princes in the British Raj. This led to a sometimes strange contradiction: on the one hand, foreign ranks were formally accepted, an example being the visit to England of King Kalakaua of Hawaii in 1881. He was a guest at a party also attended by the Prince of Wales, who would eventually become King Edward VII, and the German crown prince, who was Edward's brother-in-law and the future Kaiser. The Prince of Wales insisted that the king should take precedence over the crown prince. To the objection of the German crown prince, he explained: 'Either the brute is a king, or he's a commoner or garden n-----. And if the latter, what's he doing here?'[11] At the time this was not a racist remark, but simply a recognition of the king's high rank. On the other hand, the English colonial rulers clearly always ranked a notch above the colonies' highest indigenous representatives. Even God had to step aside. 'The Aga Khan', declared the London-based College of Heralds (College of Arms), 'is held by his followers to be a direct descendant of God. English Dukes take precedence.'[12]

In class terms the undeniable advantage for foreigners is that they are less confined by class barriers and class rules than Englishmen 'for they know not what they do'. Allowances can and therefore must be made for them. For this reason, foreigners are well advised to speak English with a slight accent and make the occasional slip, even if they could pass for a native with never a mistake. The English will immediately leap to their defence and forgive all their class transgressions.

THE FOREIGNER'S VIEW

The froth at the top, dregs at bottom, but the middle excellent.

> Voltaire comparing the English to their
> own beer, *Edinburgh Magazine* (1786)

The French way of thinking is that they do not wish to have superiors. The English wish to have inferiors. The Frenchman constantly raises his eyes above himself in anxiety. The Englishman lowers them beneath him in satisfaction.

> Alexis de Tocqueville, *Voyage en Angleterre* (1835)

As long as you maintain that damned class-ridden society of yours you will never get out of the mess.

> German Chancellor Helmut Schmidt to
> Prime Minister James Callaghan (1975)

Social class has naturally not gone unnoticed by foreign visitors and observers of the English, and virtually all who have commented on England have also turned their attention to the class system.[13] The English class system is a minefield for foreigners, especially all the denying, evading, camouflaging and rationally inexplicable features which no foreigner has any chance of understanding, let alone mastering. On the other hand, foreigners confronted with the class system have not been blinded to its peculiarities by centuries of education and inculcation. Nor are they prevented by the system's conventions from openly discussing it. Outsiders sometimes see more than insiders.

Long ago, the German Fürst Pückler-Muskau described the characteristics of the English class system (without calling it that) in letters to his wife written from 1826 to 1828. Nearly 200 years later, some of these traits, while not so crass and obvious, would still be instantly recognizable: 'It is a nearly universal weakness of the non-noble English,' he wrote, 'to boast about their distinguished acquaintances,'[14] and, 'Just like English fields, every type of society is separated from the next by thorny hedges. Each has its own manners and expressions, its "cant", as one calls it here, and above all an utter contempt for everyone ranked lower.'[15] His definition of the word 'gentleman', although outdated because the old-fashioned gentleman no longer exists (see Chapter 3), still makes amusing reading.

A gentleman is neither a nobleman nor a noble man but, strictly speaking, nothing more than a man whose wealth and meticulous knowledge of the customs of good society renders him independent. Any man who serves or works for the public in some way or other – with the exception of higher public servants and, for instance, writers and artists of the first rank – is not a gentleman, or at best half a one . . .

A truly poor man, who is not in a position to incur any debts, can in no circumstances be a gentleman, because he is the most dependent of all. A rich scoundrel, on the other hand, if he has been properly brought up and knows how to manage his reputation reasonably well, can pass for a perfect gentleman. Still-finer nuances are evident in the exclusive society of London. There, for instance, anyone who behaves with ladies in a timid and courteous way, instead of acting familiar and treating them with a certain nonchalance and little deference, will arouse the suspicion that he is not a gentleman. But should that unlucky man ask for a second helping of soup at a *dîner* or appear in evening dress at a large breakfast that begins at three in the afternoon and ends at midnight, though he may be a prince and a millionaire, he is definitely not a gentleman.[16]

To some foreigners, class distinctions even epitomize the good old days. 'Well, well', lamented the German-born British peer Lord Dahrendorf, who had himself written a book on class,[17] 'What one admired about this country, was the aristocracy and the working class. Now that Britain has become a middle-class nation, it's no longer any different from anywhere else in Europe. Well, well.'[18]

One of the English foibles that can throw foreigners is English schools and their class associations. The names themselves are confusingly diverse, there being grammar, public (major or minor), fee-paying, independent, private, selective, prep, boarding, academy, state, primary, specialist, grant-maintained, foundation, high, secondary, comprehensive, day, community, free-foundation, sink, faith and day schools. This kaleidoscope is further enriched by the English obsession with obtaining a classy education for their children. The wife of the German ambassador in London in 2006, Jutta Falke-Ischinger, recalls almost disbelievingly how she tried to find somewhere suitable for her daughter Josie, who was two at the time, to spend time with other children of the same age.

> After our first attempts to check out the English educational landscape, our emotions wavered from incredulous to bewildered. There was no doubt that we were living in a divided country. But, with the exception of those who were not interested in anything at all, they all had just one thing in mind: finding the best possible school for their children. On the one hand, there were the less wealthy parents, who became embroiled in a ferocious fight for places at the limited number of good state-run nurseries and schools or ran up debts to finance private schooling after all. On the other hand were the well-to-do parents, who sang the praises of achievement, discipline and the elite the whole day long and were prepared to pay whatever it took to get it.[19]

Foreigners do not understand lots of things about the English class system. Many reject the parts of it they do (or think they do) understand as old-fashioned or undemocratic or unfair. But at the same time they are fascinated by it, visiting the stately homes of the upper classes in droves, boasting that they have seen a real lord in the flesh, enthusiastically watching TV series such as *Downton Abbey* which are based on that very same class system. And if they can afford it, they buy a house in London and do their utmost to get their children into exactly those public schools and universities that are considered the mainstay of the class system.

PERSONAL MEMORIES

I first visited England in summer 1961 at the age of 16 during the school holidays. It was quite common at the time for English families, ideally with children, to take in German and other youngsters from abroad for a few weeks as paying guests. My host family comprised a vicar and his wife, together with their young daughter, who was coming up for five. They lived in an idyllic village in the Cotswolds. The four weeks I spent there enriched my life. Not only did I improve my schoolboy English and become more fluent, but the family also took me with them on their shopping trips in their plush Morris Minor, usually to Chipping Norton. On Sundays we attended the village church together. We went to watch the motor racing at Silverstone, picnicked in the country, and the vicar showed me Oxford University and explained about its colleges.

But what impressed me most was the many conversations that the Reverend Hubert, to call him by his first name, who was then in his mid-40s, carried on with a rather wet-behind-the-ears 16-year-old. The vicar, as folk in the village referred to him, was a good-hearted soul: clever, educated, helpful and gentle, yet quite clear about his moral and ethical principles. Perhaps this was also partly due to his slight stoop which, as he himself put it, had focused his concentration more on the spiritual than on the physical. Emanating from the parishioners who visited us or whom we visited, and from the congregation in church, was always an aura of love and devotion, but also respect for their vicar. I still admire him today for how he and his wife managed the not-so-easy duties of an English country clergyman. During my stay I also learned something about Englishness and even about the English class system, although this knowledge was more sensed and intuited than consciously understood.

It started on my journey there, which was rather complicated: by train from Bonn to Ostend, ferry to Dover and then train to London Victoria, taxi to Paddington and train to Oxford, where I was to be met by the family. At Paddington Station I experienced for the first time an English character trait singled out by many foreigners and described by the English themselves in the mantra 'Keep calm and carry on'. I was sitting there on a bench for some time, on my right an Englishman who was clearly enjoying reading his newspaper from cover to cover. High above me, in the metal girders of the station roof, a host of pigeons were whirring, regularly descending onto the platform to search for food and swooping rather gracefully past travellers' heads. Suddenly there was a loud splat on my right shoulder, where a whitish-grey pile of pigeon shit had started to spread – to my not inconsiderable dismay. No such emotion was evident from the Englishman sitting next to me, even though he had narrowly escaped the same fate. Without raising his eyes from his newspaper, he said, 'It's not safe here, is it?' and continued to read unperturbed. I was of course too shy to talk to him about my misfortune, but the impression I formed explained what is meant by the expression 'as cool as a cucumber'.

The next milestone to Englishness related to the Test match being played at the time between England and Australia, which the family was closely following on a new television set. Since their German guest clearly did not have a clue about cricket, the host explained the rules with a touching display of patience, including such enduring mysteries as LBW (leg before wicket) and others described famously and in inimitably English style by A. G. Macdonell in *England, Their England* (1933). The cricket novice listened intently as his host gave a skilful commentary on the game and straightforwardly concluded that the Australians would win as they were bowling and batting better than the English, an assessment with which the youngster dutifully concurred. This proved to be a mistake. My host took me to one side: 'You are quite right, Detlev. Australia are playing better than England. But perhaps I can give you a piece of advice. As a foreigner, you would do well not to say so. Leave it to us.' In a few words the vicar had borne out a rule of English interaction with foreigners, summarized succinctly as so often by George Orwell: 'We spend our lives in abusing England but grow very angry when we hear a foreigner saying exactly the same things.'[20]

Fortunately, comments in the opposite direction are allowed. If a foreigner praises certain features of England, the English are pleased, although they will immediately play down the merits of what has been admired and claim that it is actually not so great. If a foreigner is lucky enough to be in England when the weather is beautiful (not at all unusual) and shares their joy with an Englishman, the latter will almost certainly warn the visitor that such sunshine is rare and they should prepare for rain. The English happily moan about anything and everything, including the things they are actually rather proud and fond of. Thank goodness for the knowledge that this should be taken with a pinch of salt! Hopefully this book does not contain too many breaches of these rules.

One of the insights into the English class system during these four weeks I gained on the last Sunday of my stay, when the bishop came to visit. I still remember being impressed by his black cassock and the large amethyst ring on his finger. The day before, my host parents gave me a lesson in good manners, something they had never previously done. One was the two-cup rule of tea-drinking: a single cup was deemed impolite as not enough; three cups were considered impolite as too many. I was also kindly counselled not to engage the bishop in conversation myself, but to wait until he spoke to me, and to address him as Bishop rather than Mr Johnson or whatever his name was. When the tea came it tasted quite different, and I did not enjoy it at all. I repressed the urge to ask if there was something wrong with it, but posed the question of the strange taste once the bishop had left. 'It was China tea,' the hostess explained. When I asked why it was different from the tea we usually drank, I heard for the first time in my life that it was 'because of the bishop'.

The second time was when my host family called on a landowner who lived in the area, the parish's most esteemed personage. Sir John, as we shall call him, was an imposing man just approaching 70. At the time I was very interested in ships and sea battles, as boys sometimes are. I could reel off the order of battle and course of events at the Battle of Trafalgar. When we arrived in the hall of the large and rather grand residence, I spotted on the opposite wall a painting of a scene from the Battle of Jutland. Without thinking, I stopped in front of it and said, 'Oh, the famous manoeuvre of crossing the T by Admiral Jellicoe!'[21] There was the briefest of silences before we proceeded to take tea and scones.

Afterwards, Sir John asked me how I recognized the scene in the picture, and I told him about my interest in the Royal Navy. He signalled me to follow him, and we entered a room full of British naval memorabilia. It transpired that Sir John had actually fought in the Battle of Jutland. He talked about it to me, and his role in it, for almost an hour. I was eager to know whether he had known admirals Jellicoe and Beatty. It was an hour suffused with mutual affection between old and young, with never a word out of place and certainly no nationalistic undertones, and I remember it vividly to this day.

On the way home, the mother complained about Sir John's unconventional behaviour, having neglected the adult guests and spent so much time with a youngster. 'Well, it may be years since he had such an admirer,' replied her husband, 'let alone such a young one – and by the way, he can do whatever he thinks fit.' I do not recall the word 'class' being spoken on these occasions, but somehow they left me with the indelible impression that, beyond the vicar's family and villagers, other spheres existed where different habits and standards applied. I had caught a whiff of class.

These summer holidays were the beginning of a life-long fascination and affection for England that has led to many visits, many, many books and finally to my own place there, not far from the spot where my English 'career' began.

In summer 2015 my wife and I were travelling through Gloucestershire and Oxfordshire. By chance, our route took us through the small village where my old host family had lived. Past memories came flooding back, so it was an easy decision to visit the village and its vicarage and church. The couple would probably no longer be alive, but perhaps someone would remember them. Standing outside the vicarage, I felt too shy to ring and ask the new occupants about the fate of their predecessors. But in the church someone showed us a roll of past vicars, and there indeed was the name of 'my' vicar and his dates in office from 1959 to 1971. And that was the end of that – until mid-2016, that is, and the Brexit referendum, David Cameron's resignation as prime minister and the process of choosing a successor. The candidacy of Theresa May spawned widespread reporting about her background and early life.

And that is when it became clear how small the world really can be. For the idyllic village in the Cotswolds was Church Enstone, the vicar and his wife were Hubert and Mary Brasier, and their small daughter was called Theresa, today known to every Englishman as former Prime Minister Theresa May. Sadly, I then also learned that Mr Brasier had been killed in a car accident in 1981, and his wife had died of an illness the following year.

Part IV

Beyond Class

35

This Happy Breed of Men

I love my home and country with a fierce protectiveness.

Labour politician Barbara Castle,
The Castle Diaries 1974–76, 2 July 1975

It was the nation and the race dwelling all round the globe that had the lion's heart.

Winston Churchill (1940)

After so many class distinctions, so many nuances of status setting people apart from one another, one wonders if there is such a thing as Englishness beyond class. Is there something that Englishmen of every social hue can happily endorse or recognize and acknowledge as intrinsic to people of all levels? Thanks be to God (or rather St George), there is. In fact, two important traits common to all classes spring to mind almost instantly. Both are impervious to accent, language usage, education, title, ancestry, income, wealth, hobbies, bookcases or table manners. Both are English traditions and characterize England today as much as ever.

The first of these is that Englishmen love their country – maybe not all of them, all of the time, but when things get serious and it counts, all Englishmen do. Class does not matter. No-one has found greater words to express their enthusiasm for England than William Shakespeare. Admittedly, reading and understanding – let alone enjoying – the Bard's works is not given to everyone and not without its own class implications. But if there is one description of England that unites Englishmen of all classes, then it is that evoked by the Duke of Lancaster, John of Gaunt, in the play *Richard II* written by Shakespeare in 1595:

> This royal throne of kings, this scepter'd isle,
> This earth of majesty, this seat of Mars,
> This other Eden, demi-paradise,
> This fortress built by Nature for herself
> Against infection and the hand of war,
> This happy breed of men, this little world,
> This precious stone set in the silver sea,
> Which serves it in the office of a wall,
> Or as a moat defensive to a house,
> Against the envy of less happier lands,
> This blessed plot, this earth, this realm, this England.

Ask any Englishman and he will say: 'That's how it is' (and the author happily agrees).

The second thing common to all Englishmen is courage. They are without fear of the unknown. Class does not matter. Can a people that is afraid of the unknown and only does things that it has planned out precisely in advance sail the seas, settle in distant lands, evolve the idea of democracy, make ground-breaking scientific discoveries and experiment with just about everything that exists, as the English have done? I think not. In 1913 the following advertisement appeared in *The Times*:

> MEN WANTED for hazardous journey. Low wages, bitter cold, long hours of complete darkness. Safe return doubtful. Honour and recognition in event of success.
>
> Ernest Shackleton
> 4 Burlington St

It is uncertain whether this advertisement was actually ever placed by Ernest Shackleton. If not, it is the greatest myth ever created about the English and their courage. Certainly, that quality was needed by those on the expedition. In fact, the party failed to achieve its goal of being the first to cross the Antarctic from coast to coast because its ship, the *Endurance*, became trapped early on in the pack ice of the Weddell Sea and subsequently sank. The crew only narrowly escaped death thanks to an audacious rescue mission that involved sailing 800 nautical miles (1,500 km) in a small lifeboat, an exploit for which Shackleton rightly became world famous. The response to the advertisement was, allegedly, overwhelming. More than 5,000 men are said to have replied, although only around 1 per cent of them would have been needed.

In Germany (as in many other countries), change is often accompanied by warnings from politicians and the media that the consequences are unforeseeable. This nearly always results in the new idea being rejected by the majority, for fear the unforeseeable consequences will be detrimental. The idea of entering unfamiliar or uncharted territory has rather negative, fear-inducing associations in many languages and cultures. Not so in English or in wider English society. Here, consequences that are unforeseeable are simply unknown; the outcome may even be better than the present. For the English, an unknown future harbours more opportunity than risk. Andrew Marr has characterized Britain as

> a country that has always been on the edge. We moved from being on the edge of defeat, to the edge of bankruptcy, to the edge of nuclear annihilation and the edge of the American empire, and came out on the other side to find ourselves on the cutting edge of the modern condition, a post-industrial and multi-ethnic island.[1]

The Labour MP Angela Rayner chips in that 'all of Britain's great advancements in the past have been because we've had the gumption to take a risk.'[2] One might add that only when they are really up against it are the English at their best. It is no coincidence that almost all of England's celebrated events and hallowed places are connected with periods of history in which the country faced danger or was undergoing radical change: Alfred the Great, the Norman Conquest, Magna Carta, the Battle of Agincourt, the Reformation, the fall of the Spanish Armada, Oliver Cromwell and the Civil War, the Glorious Revolution of 1688, Nelson and the Battle of Trafalgar, the Duke of Wellington and Waterloo, the Indian Mutiny, the Western Front, Dunkirk and the Battle of Britain. Perhaps one day Brexit will be mentioned in the same breath.

It is hard in these Brexit times to write a book about England that does not deal with the decision to leave the EU. Linking the Brexit decision to class, however, is easy. The class-savvy English media identified the 'ordinary people' as the supporters of Leave and the upper classes as the Remainers. Of the English (as opposed to the British as a whole), a fairly clear majority voted to leave the EU, not only from one class, but from across all strata. Could this be the resurrected spirit of those who applied to join Shackleton's expedition? The Remain campaigners who argued their case with warnings of unforeseeable consequences if people voted to leave struck the wrong note with the English. They forgot the Englishman's love of his country and his courage.

If the author may be allowed to venture a prediction: by deciding in favour of Brexit, the English are taking a big step into the unknown. They genuinely don't know where the road will lead – no-one does. They will be put through the mill, they will waver, be tormented, feel defeated and maybe even once more endure Churchill's blood, toil, tears and sweat (metaphorically speaking, of course). But at the end of the process, they will look pretty good, and the scars they retain will suit them rather well. Fittingly, several different meanings are ascribed in English to the word class. And so, having opened with it, this book can close with it too. Beyond class boundaries, England remains in a class of its own.

Bibliography and Further Reading

This book is by no means the first book about class in England. As noted in the introduction, a great deal of excellent work has been produced on the subject. The English class system can be observed and described from many angles: historians, sociologists, economists, politicians, philosophers, novelists, playwrights, humourists, journalists, travellers, biographers, autobiographers and diarists have all written on it from their own perspectives. Of the books listed below, those marked with an asterisk (*) take a comprehensive look at Englishness and class in England and are particularly recommended. Some are out of date and today seem like caricatures. But, like all good caricatures, they contain a kernel of truth, especially in tradition-conscious England. The reading list, like the rest of the book, is a cheerful mix of the serious and playful, scholarly articles and feature sections. The sources of the epigraphs preceding the chapters and sections, and newspaper articles, are not repeated here.

Claire Ainsley, *The New Working Class*, Bristol, Polypress, 2018
Matthew Arnold, *Culture and Anarchy*, London, Smith Elder, 1869
Clive Aslet, *Anyone for England? A Search for British Identity*, London, Little Brown, 1997
Will Atkinson, *Class*, Cambridge, Polity Press, 2015
Will Atkinson, *Class in the New Millennium: The Structure, Homologies and Experience of the British Social Space*, Abingdon, Routledge, 2017*
Julian Baggini, *Welcome to Everytown – A Journey into the English Mind*, London, Granta Books, 2007
Ernest Barker, *The Character of England*, Oxford, Oxford University Press, 1947
Julian Barnes, *England, England*, New York, Vintage Books, 1998
Stephen Bayley, *Taste: The Secret Meaning of Things*, London, Circa Press, 2017
Ann Barr and Peter York, *The Official Sloane Ranger Handbook*, London, Ebury Press, 1983*
John Duke of Bedford, in collaboration with George Mikes, *Book of Snobs*, London, Peter Owen, 1965*
John Duke of Bedford, *A Silver-Plated Spoon*, London, Pan Books, 1966

Mark Bence-Jones and Hugh Montgomery-Massingberd, *The British Aristocracy*, London, Constable, 1979

Philip Beresford and W. D. Rubinstein, *The Richest of the Rich: The Wealthiest 250 People in Britain since 1066*, Petersfield, Harriman House, 2011

Isaiah Berlin, *Two Concepts of Liberty*, Oxford, Oxford University Press, 1958

Tom Bingham, *The Rule of Law*, London, Penguin, 2010

Anita Biressi and Heather Nunn, *Class and Contemporary British Culture*, Basingstoke, Palgrave Macmillan, 2013*

Jeremy Black, *The British Abroad – The Grand Tour in the Eighteenth Century*, Cheltenham, The History Press, 1993

James Bloodworth, *The Myth of Meritocracy*, London, Biteback Publishing, 2016

Alain de Botton, *Status Anxiety*, London, Hamish Hamilton, 2004

Peter James Bowman, *The Fortune Hunter*, Oxford, Signal Books, 2010

Melvyn Bragg, *The Adventure of English – The Biography of a Language*, London, Sceptre, 2003

Chris Bryant, *Entitled: A Critical History of the British Aristocracy*, London, Transworld Publishers, 2017

Bill Bryson, *Notes from a Small Island*, New York, William Morrow, 1996

Bill Bryson, *The Road to Little Dribbling*, London, Black Swan, 2016

Edmund Burke, *Reflections on the Revolution in France*, London, J. Dodsley, Pall Mall, 1790

Ian Buruma, *Voltaire's Coconuts – Anglomania in Europe*, New York, Vintage Books, 1998, US title: *Anglomania – A European Love Affair*

David Cannadine, *Class in Britain*, London, Penguin, 2000*

David Cannadine, *The Decline and Fall of the British Aristocracy*, New York, Vintage Books, ed. 1999

David Cannadine, *Ornamentalism – How the British Saw their Empire*, Oxford, Oxford University Press, 2001

Karel Capek, *Letters from England*, London, Continuum, 1924

Miranda Carter, *Anthony Blunt: His Lives*, London, Macmillan, 2002

Charles Clarke (ed.), *The Too Difficult Box: The Big Issues Politicians Can't Crack*, London, Biteback Publishing, 2014

Price Collier, *England and the English*, New York, Duckworth, 1909

Robert Colls, *Identity of England*, Oxford, Oxford University Press, 2004

Nathan Connolly (ed.), *Know Your Place: Essays on the Working Class by the Working Class*, Liverpool, Dead Ink, 2017

Anne de Courcy, *The Husband Hunters: Social Climbing in London and New York*, London, Weidenfeld & Nicolson, 2017

Jilly Cooper, *Class – An Exposé of the English Class System*, London, Corgi Books, 1999*

Susan Crosland, *Tony Crosland*, London, Hodder & Stoughton, 1982

David Crystal, *The Stories of English*, London, Penguin, 2004

Tom Cullen, *Maundy Gregory – Purveyor of Honours*, London, The Bodley Head, 1974

J. R. Daeschner, *True Brits*, London, Arrow, 2004

Ralf Dahrendorf, *Class Conflict in Industrial Society*, Stanford, Stanford University Press, 1959

Philippe Daudy, *Les Anglais: Portrait of a People*, London, Barrie & Jenkins, 1991

Debrett's New Guide to Etiquette & Modern Manners, New York, Thomas Dunne Books, 1996

Debrett's A-Z of Modern Manners, London, Debrett's Limited, 2015

Debrett's and Richard Buckle (ed.), *U and Non-U Revisited*, London, Debrett's Peerage, 1978*

Deborah Devonshire, *Wait for Me*, New York, Farrar, Straus & Giroux, 2010

Wilhelm Dibelius, *England*, 1922 German, Stuttgart, Deutsche Verlagsanstalt, 1930 English

Charles Dickens, *The Chimes*, London, Chapman & Hall, 1844

William Doyle, *Aristocracy*, Oxford, Oxford University Press, 2010

Mark Easton, *Britain Etc. – The Way We Live and How We Got There*, London, Simon & Schuster, 2012

George Eliot, *Middlemarch*, Edinburgh and London, William Blackwood and Sons, 1871

T. S. Eliot, *Notes Towards the Definition of Culture*, London, Faber & Faber, 1948

Geoffrey Evans and James Tilley, *The New Politics of Class: The Political Exclusion of the British Working Class*, Oxford, Oxford University Press, 2017

Fabian Review, The Class Issue, London, Fabian Society, Summer 2008

Jutta Falke-Ischinger, *Wo bitte geht's zur Queen?*, Munich, Collection Rolf Heyne, 2010

Julian Fellowes, *Snobs*, London, Phoenix, 2005*

Kate Fox, *Watching the English*, 2nd ed., London, Hodder & Stoughton, 2014*

Robert H. Frank and Philip J. Cook, The Winner-Take-all Society, London, Virgin Books, 1995

Chrystia Freeland, *Plutocrats – The Rise of the New Global Super-Rich*, London, Penguin, 2013

Sam Friedmann and Daniel Laurison, *The Class Ceiling*, Bristol, Policy Press, 2019

P. N. Furbank, *Unholy Pleasure or The Idea of Social Class*, Oxford, Oxford University Press, 1986

Hans-Dieter Gelfert, *Typisch englisch*, Munich, C. H. Beck, 2011

Anthony Giddens and Philip W. Sutton, *Sociology*, 7th ed., Cambridge, Polity Press, 2013

Ruth Glass, *London: Aspects of Change*, London, MacGibbon & Kee, 1964

Tim Glencross, *Barbarians*, London, John Murray, 2014

A. C. Grayling, *The Challenge of Things*, London, Bloomsbury, 2015

A. H. Halsey, *Change in British Society*, 4th ed., Oxford, Oxford University Press, 1995

Lynsey Hanley, *Respectable – The Experience of Class*, London, Allen Lane, 2016

William Hanson, *The Bluffer's Guide to Etiquette*, 2014, London, Thomas Drewry, 2015

Michael Hartmann, *Die globale Wirtschaftselite*, Frankfurt, Campus Verlag, 2016

Ronald Hayman (ed), *My Cambridge*, London, Robson Books, 1977

Henry Hemming, *In Search of the English Eccentric*, London, John Murray, 2008

Peter Hennessy, *Establishment and Meritocracy*, London, Haus Publishing, 2014

Alexander Herzen, *My Past and Thoughts*, New York (1968), Knopf, 1870

Henry Hitchings, *Sorry! The English and their Manners*, London, John Murray, 2013

Douglas Hurd and Edward Young, *Disraeli or the Two Lives*, London, Weidenfeld & Nicolson, 2013

Lawrence James, *The Middle Class – A History*, London, Little Brown, 2006*

Lawrence James, *Aristocrats – Power, Grace and Decadence: Britain´s Great Ruling Class from 1966 to the Present*, New York, St. Martin's Griffin, 2009

Simon Jenkins, *England's Thousand Best Houses*, London, Penguin, 2003

Charles Jennings, *Them and Us – The American Invasion of British High Society*, Cheltenham, The History Press, 2007

Owen Jones, *Chavs – The Demonization of the Working Class*, London, Verso, 2012*

Owen Jones (ed.), *The Establishment – And How They Get Away With It*, London, Penguin Books, 2015

Braj B. Kachru, *World Englishes and Culture Wars*, Cambridge, Cambridge University Press, 2017

Alfred Kerr, *Ich kam nach England, Tagebuch 1936–40*, Trier, Wissenschaftlicher Verlag Trier, 1984

Anthony King, *Who Governs Britain?*, London, Pelican Books, 2015

Krishan Kumar, *The Idea of Englishness: English Culture, National Identity and Social Thought*, Abingdon, Routledge, 2015

Raymond Lamont-Brown, *A Book of English Eccentrics*, Exeter, David & Charles, 1984

Harold Laski, *The Danger of Being a Gentleman*, London, Routledge, 1932

James Lees-Milne, *Diaries 1993–97*, London, John Murray, 2005

John Lloyd, *What the Media are Doing to our Politics*, London, Constable, 2004

Marion Löhndorf, *England*, Zürich, Vontobel Stiftung, 2015

Sarah Lyall, *A Field Guide to the British*, London, Quercus Books, 2008

Archibald Gordon Macdonell, *England, Their England*, London, Macmillan, 1933

Harold Macmillan, *Cabinet Years Diaries 1950–57*, London, Macmillan, 2012

Louis MacNeice, *The Saturday Book*, London, Hutchinson, 1961

Peter Mandler, *The English National Character – The History of an Idea from Edmund Burke to Tony Blair*, New Haven, Yale University Press, 2006

Andrew Marr, *The History of Modern Britain*, London, Pan Books, 2016

Arthur Marwick, *Class: Image and Reality in Britain, France and the USA since 1930*, London, Fontana/Collins, 1990

Karl Marx and Friedrich Engels, *The Communist Manifesto*, London, Workers Educational Association, 1848

W. Somerset Maugham, *A Writer's Notebook*, London, 1951, Readers Union, 1941

Ian McEwan, *Enduring Love*, London, Jonathan Cape, 1987

Lisa McKenzie, *Getting By – Estates, Class and Culture in Austerity Britain*, Bristol, Policy Press, 2015

Anthony Miall and David Milsted, *Xenophobe's Guide to the English*, London, Oval Books, 2013

George Mikes, *How to be a Brit*, 1984 (*How to be an Alien*, 1946; *How to be Inimitable*, 1960; *How to be Decadent*, London, Penguin, 1977)*

Nancy Mitford (ed.), *Noblesse Oblige*, London, Hamish Hamilton, 1956 (with contributions by Alan S. C. Ross, Nancy Mitford, Evelyn Waugh, Strix, Christopher Sykes, John Betjeman)*

Ferdinand Mount, *Mind the Gap – The New Class Divide in Britain*, London, Short Books, 2005*

Ferdinand Mount, *The New Few or A Very British Oligarchy*, London, Simon & Schuster, 2012

Harry Mount, *How England Made the English*, London, Penguin, 2013

Cardinal Newman, *The Idea of a University*, San Francisco, Ignatius Press, 1852

Adam Nicolson, *The Gentry – Stories of the English*, New York, Harper Press, 2011

Not Actual Size, *The Art of Being Middle Class*, London, Constable, 2012*

George Orwell, *The Road to Wigan Pier*, London, Left Book Club, 1937*

George Orwell, *The Lion and the Unicorn*, London, Secker & Warburg, 1941*

George Orwell, *The English People*, London, Collins, 1947*

Stanislaw Ossowski, *Class Structure in the Social Consciousness*, London, Routledge, 1963

Thomas Paine, *The Rights of Man*, London, J. S. Jordan, 1791

Jeremy Paxman, *Friends in High Places – Who Runs Britain?* London, Penguin, 1991*

Jeremy Paxman, *The English – A Portrait of a People*, London, Michael Joseph, 1998*

Jeremy Paxman, *The Political Animal – An Anatomy*, London, Penguin, 2007

Jeremy Paxman, *On Royalty*, London, Penguin, 2006

Hesketh Pearson, *The Pilgrim Daughters*, London, Heinemann, 1961

Harry Pearson, *The Far Corner*, London, Little Brown, 1994

Minxin Pei, *China's Crony Capitalism*, Harvard, Harvard University Press, 2016

Roy Perrott, *The Aristocrats*, London, Littlehampton Book Service, 1968

Nikolaus Pevsner, *The Englishness of English Art*, London, London BBC, 1956

Roger Powell and Peter Beauclerk, *Royal Bastards: Illegitimate Children of the British Royal Family*, Cheltenham, The History Press, 2008

J. B. Priestley, *The English*, New York, The Viking Press, 1973

Hermann Fürst von Pückler-Muskau, *Briefe eines Verstorbenen*, 1830; English trans. Linda B. Parshall as *Letters of a Dead Man*, Harvard, Harvard University Press, 2016

Charles Quest-Ritson, *The English Garden – a Social History*, New York, Viking, 2001

Simon Raven, *The English Gentleman*, London, Blond & Briggs, 1961

Ivan Reid, *Class in Britain*, Cambridge, Polity Press, 1998*

Gustaaf Johannes Renier, *The English: Are they Human?*, London, Williams & Norgate, 1931

Stuart Ritchie, *Intelligence*, London, John Murray Learning, 2015

Ken Roberts, *Class in Contemporary Britain*, 2nd ed., Basingstoke, Palgrave Macmillan, 2011*

Robert Roberts, *The Classic Slum*, Manchester, Manchester University Press, 1971

Edward Royle, Modern Britain – A Social History 1750–2011, 3rd ed., London, Bloomsbury, 2012

David Runciman, *Political Hypocrisy: The Mask of Power, from Hobbes to Orwell and Beyond*, Princeton, Princeton University Press, 2010

Alan Rusbridger, *Play it Again*, New York, Vintage, 2013

Vita Sackville-West, *English Country Houses*, London, Collins, 1944

Anthony Sampson, *Anatomy of Britain*, London, Hodder & Stoughton, 1962

Anthony Sampson, *Who Runs this Place? The Anatomy of Britain in the 21st Century*, London, John Murray, 2004

George Santayana, *Soliloquies in England*, New York, C. Scribner's Sons, 1922

Mike Savage, *Social Class in the 21st Century*, London, Pelican Books, 2015*

Kenneth Scheve and David Stasavage, *Taxing the Rich*, Princeton, Princeton University Press, 2016

Roger Scruton, *England: An Elegy*, London, Bloomsbury Continuum, 2000

John Seeley, *The Expansion of England*, Cambridge, Cambridge University Press, 1883

Edith Sitwell, *The English Eccentrics*, London, Faber & Faber, 1933

Adam Smith, *Wealth of Nations*, London, W. Strahan & Cadell, 1776

Godfrey Smith, *The English Companion, An Idiosyncratic A to Z of England and Englishness*, Botley, Old House Books, 1996*

Jessie Streib, *The Power of the Past: Understanding Cross-Class Marriages*, Oxford, Oxford University Press, 2015

Florence Sutcliffe-Braithwaite, *Class, Politics, and the Decline of Deference in England*, Oxford, Oxford University Press, 1968–2000, 2018

Douglas Sutherland, *The English Gentleman*, London, Debrett's Peerage, 1978

David Tang, *Rules for Modern Life*, London, Portfolio Penguin, 2016

R. H. Tawney, *Equality*, London, Allen & Unwin, 1931

Hugh Thomas, *The Establishment – A Symposium*, London, A. Blond, 1959

Mark Thompson, *Enough Said: What's Gone Wrong with the Language of Politics?*, London, The Bodley Head, 2016

E. P. Thompson, *The Making of the English Working Class*, London, Gollancz, 1963

Alexis de Toqueville, *Democracy in America*, London, Saunders & Ottley, 1835

Anne Thwaite (ed.), *My Oxford*, London, Robson Books, 1977

John Timpson, *Timpson's English Eccentrics*, Norwich, Jarrold Publishing, 1991

Adrian Tinniswood, *The Long Weekend: Life in the English Country House Between the Wars*, London, Jonathan Cape, 2016

Selina Todd, *The People*, London, John Murray, 2014

Robert Tombs, *The English and Their History*, London, Penguin, 2014

Anthony Trollope, *Can You Forgive Her?*, London, Chapman & Hall, 1865

Peter Trudgill, *Sociolinguistics: An Introduction to Language and Society*, London, Penguin, 1984

Alwyn W. Turner, *A Classless Society – Britain in the 1990s*, London, Aurum Press, 2014

Edward Vallance, *A Radical History of Britain*, London, Little Brown, 2009

Laura Wade, *Posh*, London, Oberon Books, 2010 (play)

George Walden, *The New Elites – Making a Career in the Masses*, London, Penguin, 2001*

Harry Wallop, *Consumed – How We Buy Class in Modern Britain*, London, William Collins, 2014*

Ellis Wasson, *Born to Rule – British Political Elites*, Stroud, Sutton Publishing Ltd., 2000

Ellis Wasson, *Aristocracy and the Modern World*, London, Red Globe Press, 2006

David Weeks, *The Gifts of Eccentrics*, CreateSpace Independent Publishing Platform, 2015

John Welshman, *Underclass: A History of the Excluded 1880–2000*, London, Continuum, 2006

Francesca M. Wilson (ed.), *Strange Island: Britain Through Foreign Eyes 1395– 1940*, London, Longmans Green, 1955

Richard Wilson and Alan Mackley, *Creating Paradise*, London, Continuum, 2000

Robert Winder, *The Last Wolf: The Hidden Springs of Englishness*, London, Apacus, 2017

Peregrine Worsthorne, *In Defence of Aristocracy*, New York, Harper Collins Publishers, 2004

Tony Wright, *Doing Politics*, London, Biteback Publishing, 2012

R. J. Yeatman and W. C. Sellar, *1066 and All That*, New York, E. P. Dutton & Co., 1930

Peter York, *Authenticity is a Con*, London, Biteback Publishing, 2014

Peter York and Olivia Stewart-Liberty, *Cooler, Faster, More Expensive – The Return of the Sloane Ranger*, London, Atlantic Books, 2007*

Michael Young, *The Rise of the Meritocracy*, London, Thames & Hudson, 1958

R. G. von Zugbach, *Power and Prestige in the British Army*, Aldershot, Avebury, 1988

Notes

CHAPTER 1

1 George Orwell, *The Lion and the Unicorn*.
2 George Mikes, *How to be an Alien*.
3 Most of them are listed in Robert Winder, *The Last Wolf*; Krishan Kumar, *The Idea of Englishness*; and in Peter Mandler, *The English National Character*. A selection up to the present day can be found in the notes and the appendix to this book.
4 *The Lion and the Unicorn*, op. cit.
5 Ibid.
6 Letters, vol. 1, 1926–1951, quoted in Jeremy Paxman, *The English People*, p. 151.
7 T. S. Eliot, *Notes Towards the Definition of Culture*.
8 Mandell Creighton, *The English National Character*.
9 In his books *Friends in High Places*, *The English – A Portrait of a People*, *The Political Animal*, *On Royalty*, *Empire*, and many items for television and essays.
10 Paxman, *The English*, op. cit.
11 Millennium New Year message 29 December 1999.
12 Kate Fox, *Watching the English*.
13 A. H. Halsey, *Change in British Society*, p. 3.
14 John Seeley, *The Expansion of England*.
15 George Orwell, *The Road to Wigan Pier*.

CHAPTER 2

1 Trevor Phillips, 'Equality', in Charles Clarke (ed), *The Too Difficult Box*.
2 *Economist*, 5 November 2016.
3 Anthony Atkinson, *Britain in Inequality: What Can be Done?*; Branko Milanovic, *Global Inequality: A New Approach for the Age of Globalization*; François Bourguignon, *The Globalisation of Inequality*; Walter Schiedel, *The Great Leveller: Violence and the History of Inequality from the Stone Age to the Twenty-First Century*.
4 Ferdinand Mount, *The New Few or A Very British Oligarchy: Power and Inequality in Britain Now*.

5   Alain de Botton, *Status Anxiety*. p. 91.
6   Chrystia Freeland, *Financial Times*, 31 April 2007.
7   Robert H. Frank and Philip J. Cook, *The Winner-Take-all Society*.
8   Owen Jones, *Chavs*, p. 96.
9   *Economist*, 4 June 2016.
10 In its report *Elitist Britain?*. A more recent study from the Sutton Trust by Philip Kirby, *Leading People 2016, The educational background of the UK Professional Elite*, comes to conclusions along the same lines.
11 Michael Hartmann, *Die globale Wirtschaftselite*.
12 *The Establishment*, op. cit., p. 99.
13 Owen Jones, *Guardian*, 15 December 2014.
14 *Guardian*, 16 January 2017.
15 Tom Bingham, *The Rule of Law*.
16 George Mikes, *How to be Inimitable*.
17 George Walden, *The New Elites*, p. 195.
18 Ibid, p. 200.

CHAPTER 3

1   Traced from Biblical Legends to the present day by Stanislaw Ossowski in *Class Structure in the Social Consciousness*.
2   David Cannadine, *Class in Britain*, on which this chapter draws and from which the quotations from Burke, Cobbett, etc. have been taken; Edward Royle, *Modern Britain – A Social History 1750–2011*.
3   Cecil Frances Alexander, 'All Things Bright and Beautiful'.
4   Charles Dickens, *The Chimes*.
5   Matthew Arnold, *Culture and Anarchy*.
6   Lawrence James, *The Middle Class*, p. 376.
7   *Sunday Mirror*, 7 September 1980.
8   Described and explained in detail in Mike Savage, *Social Class in the 21st Century*.
9   Jilly Cooper, *Class*, p. 127.
10 Harry Wallop, *Consumed*, p. 8; Evans and Tilley, *The New Politics of Class*.
11 Halsey, op. cit., p. 57 ff.
12 de Botton, op. cit.
13 Paxman, *Friends in High Places*, op. cit..
14 Mike Savage, *Social Class in the 21st Century*, p. 308.
15 Anthony Sampson, *Anatomy of Britain* (1962 and later editions until 2004); Paxman, *Friends in High Places*; Mount, *The New Few*; Peter Hennessy, *Establishment and Meritocracy*; Owen Jones, *The Establishment*.
16 *Establishment and Meritocracy*.
17 In his books *Friends in High Places, The English, The Political Animal, On Royalty, Empire*.

18 *Economist*, 17 December 2016.
19 Anita Biressi and Heather Nunn, in *Class and Contemporary British Culture*, p. 94, call them 'the ones who got away'; Andrew Marr, *The History of Modern Britain*, p. 274, 514.
20 For example, Bence-Jones and Montgomery-Massingberd, *The British Aristocracy*.
21 Douglas Sutherland, *The English Gentleman*.
22 Cardinal Newman, *The Idea of a University*.
23 Ernest Barker, *The Character of England*.
24 David Tang, *Rules for Modern Life*, p. 209.
25 Roger Scruton, *England: An Elegy*.
26 *The English Gentleman*.

CHAPTER 4

1 E.g. Biressi and Nunn, *Class and Contemporary British Culture*; Roberts, *Class in Contemporary Britain*; Will Atkinson, *Class*.
2 Julian Fellowes, *Snobs*, p. 121.
3 David McKie, *Guardian*, 30 October 2013.
4 Roger Powell and Peter Beauclerk, *Royal Bastards: Illegitimate Children of the British Royal Family*.
5 Bruce Anderson, *Spectator*, 29 July 2017.
6 Nicolson, *The Gentry*, p. 221.
7 David Cannadine, *The Decline and Fall of the British Aristocracy*, p. 308.
8 Tom Cullen, *Maundy Gregory*, p. 110.
9 Wallop, p. 227.
10 Ibid, p. 109.
11 *Daily Mail*, 1 November 2014.
12 Tony Wright, *Doing Politics*, p. 239.
13 *Financial Times*, 27/28 August 2016.
14 Mikes, *How to be Inimitable*.
15 Russell Group: Universities of Birmingham, Bristol, Cambridge, Cardiff, Durham, Edinburgh, Exeter, Glasgow, in London: Imperial College, King's College, London School of Economics and Political Science, Queen Mary University, University College, then Leeds, Liverpool, Manchester, Newcastle, Nottingham, Oxford, Belfast, Sheffield, Southampton, Warwick, York.
16 Alexanderv Herzen, *My Past and Thoughts*.
17 Harry Mount, *How England made the English*, p. 139.
18 Simon Jenkins, *England's Thousand Best Houses*.
19 Paxman, *Friends in High Places*, p. 37.
20 Anthony Trollope, *Can You Forgive Her?*
21 Benjamin Barber, *Consumed*, p. 312.
22 *Independent*, 18 January 1994.

23 R. G. von Zugbach, *Power and Prestige in the British Army*.
24 Blake Morrison, *Guardian*, 3 April 2003.
25 Bingham, *The Rule of Law*.
26 Cooper, *Class*, p. 129.
27 Charles Jennings, *Them and US*; Anne de Courcy, *The Husband Hunters*.
28 A comprehensive list is available on Wikipedia under 'List of Country Houses in the United Kingdom'.
29 Vita Sackville-West, *English Country Houses*, p. 7.
30 Richard Wilson and Alan Mackley, *Creating Paradise*.
31 George Orwell, *The English People*.
32 Nikolaus Pevsner, *The Englishness of English Art*.

CHAPTER 5

1 E. P. Thompson, *The Making of the Working Class*; Eric Hobsbawm, *The Making of the Working Class 1870–1914*.
2 Debrett's, *U and Non-U Revisited*.
3 Cf. Royle, *Modern Britain*, p. 178; Atkinson, *Class*, p. 80; Evans and Tilley, *The New Politics of Class*.
4 *Financial Times*, 22 December 2015.
5 *New Statesman*, 8-14 July 2016.
6 *New Statesman*, 25 January 2016.
7 Biressi and Nunn, *Class and Contemporary British Culture*, p. 155.
8 Jones, *Chavs*, p. 40.
9 See quotations in Mount, *Mind the Gap*, p. 133.
10 Julian Baggini, *Welcome to Everytown*, p. 12.
11 Mount, *Mind the Gap*, p. 89.
12 Jones, *Chavs*.
13 Ibid, p. 116.
14 *Respectable*; see also Gena-mour Barrett, 'Living on an Estate', in Connolly, *Know Your Place*, p. 156.
15 Lisa McKenzie, *Getting By*, p. 198.
16 Mount, *Mind the Gap*, p. 264.
17 Sutton Trust, Philip Kirby, *Leading People 2016*.
18 Sutton Trust, *Leading People 2016*; Bloodworth, *The Myth of Meritocracy*, p. 53.
19 John Duke of Bedford, *A Silver-Plated Spoon*.
20 Orwell, *The Lion and the Unicorn*.
21 *Spectator*, 7 August 2010.
22 Cannadine, *The Decline and Fall of the British Aristocracy*, p. 8.
23 e.g. Anthony King, *Who Governs Britain?*
24 *New Statesman*, 11 February 2016.
25 William Doyle, *Aristocracy*.
26 Chris Bryant, *Entitled*.

27 Cf. the annual Rich List of the *Sunday Times* as well as Beresford und Rubinstein, *The Richest of the Rich*.

28 Cf. Biressi and Nunn, p. 124.

29 Laski, *The Danger of Being a Gentleman*.

30 Hesketh Pearson, *The Pilgrim Daughters* (1961).

31 *Spectator*, 22 July 2017.

32 *Spectator*, 9 December 2017.

33 Mikes, *How to Be Decadent*.

34 BBC headlines, 5 May 2006.

35 *Not Actual Size, The Art of Being Middle Class*.

36 Laurence James, *The Middle Class*, p. 506.

37 Baggini, p. 13.

38 Paxman, *Friends in High Places*, p. 121.

39 James, op. cit., p. 585.

40 Ibid, p. 593.

41 Ibid.

42 Ibid, p. 591.

43 Lewis and Maude, *The English Middle Classes* (1949), quoted by Robert Colls, *The Identity of England*, p. 81.

44 David Cannadine, *The Decline and Fall of the English Aristocracy*.

45 Welshman, *Underclass*; Biressi and Nunn, *Class and Contemporary British Culture*, p. 44; Roberts, *Class in Contemporary Britain*, p. 97; Jones, *Chavs*, p. 18; Savage, *Social Class in the 21st Century*, p. 355.

46 Quotes taken from Biressi and Nunn, *Class and Contemporary British Culture*, p. 44 ff.

CHAPTER 6

1 Mike Savage, *Class in the 21st Century*, p. 6.

2 *Times Literary Supplement*, 24 January 1997.

3 Fellowes, *Snobs*, p. 14

4 Fellowes, *Snobs*, p. 14

5 Ian Buruma, *Anglomania*, p. 264.

6 In Nancy Mitford, *Noblesse Oblige*.

7 Mikes, *How to Be an Alien*.

8 John Duke of Bedford, *Book of Snobs*, p. 27.

9 Institute for Public Policy Research.

10 Jessie Streib, *The Power of the Past*.

11 Mount, *Mind the Gap*, p. 16.

12 Zoe Williams, *Across the Barricades: Love Over the Class Divide*, Guardian, 19 October 2012; letter to Dear Mary, *Spectator*, 28 March 2020.

13 *Financial Times* 14/15 January 2017.

14 Alan Rusbridger, *Play it Again*, p. 3.

CHAPTER 7

1 Jones, *Chavs*.
2 With exceptions, e.g. William Hanson, *The Bluffer's Guide to Etiquette*.
3 Ann Thwaite (ed), *My Oxford*.
4 *U and Non-U Revisited*, p. 30.
5 Fox, p. 344.
6 Jones, *Chavs*, p. 169.
7 Paxman, *On Royalty*, p. 245.
8 *Vanity Fair*, January 2010.
9 *Financial Times*, 11 August 2016.
10 Walden, *The New Elites*, p. 93.
11 Ibid, p. 89; Julie Burchill, *Spectator*, 29 July 2017; Andrew Marr, Introduction to the 2017 edition of Tina Brown, *The Diana Chronicles*.
12 Adrian Tinniswood, *The Long Weekend*, p. 340.
13 Turner, *A Classless Society*, p. 516.
14 Fellowes, p. 60.
15 *Financial Times*, 13/14 August 2016.
16 Fellowes, p. 281.
17 Walden, op. cit.
18 Reid, *Class in Britain*, p. 32.

CHAPTER 8

1 *Financial Times*, 25/26 June 2016.
2 Ibid.
3 Ibid.
4 Jones, *Chavs*, p. 101.
5 John Lloyd, *What the Media are Doing to Our Politics*, p. 17.
6 Mark Thompson, *Enough Said*, p. 100.
7 Douglas Hurd and Edward Young, *Disraeli or the Two Lives*.
8 Cannadine, *Class in Britain*, p. 138.
9 Reid, op. cit., p. 235.
10 Wright, op. cit., p. 4.
11 Jones, *Chavs*, p. 98.
12 Mount, *Mind the Gap*, p. 13.
13 Reid, op. cit., p. 235.
14 Mount, *Mind the Gap*; Jones, *Chavs*, wants 'to end the conspiracy of silence over class'.
15 Anthony King, *Who Governs Britain?*, p. 49.
16 Paxman, *The Political Animal*, p. 22.
17 *Telegraph*, 2 April 2013.
18 Wallop, p. 31.

19   *Guardian*, 3 January 2014.
20   King, *Who Governs Britain?*, p. 238.
21   *Guardian*, 13 May 1999.
22   Jones, *Chavs*, p. 251; Atkinson, *Class*, p. 80.
23   *Sun*, 16 January 2016; *Guardian*, 14 March 2014.
24   See Owen Jones, *The Establishment*, p. 69.
25   *Financial Times*, 22 July 2016.

CHAPTER 9

1   Debrett's, *U and Non-U Revisited*, p. 84.
2   Fox, p. 58.
3   *Prospect*, 19 February 2015.
4   James, *The Middle Class*, p. 558.
5   Grayson Perry, *Daily Telegraph*, 15 June 2013.
6   Grant Feller, *Telegraph*, 22 August 2014.
7   Lara Prendergast, 'Snobbery in the Age of Social Media', *Spectator*, 12 August 2017.

CHAPTER 10

1   Brian Unwin, *With Respect, Minister* (2017).

CHAPTER 11

1   *Letters of a Dead Man*, Letter of 8 July 1828.
2   Letter of 3 January 1829.
3   Mikes, *How to be Decadent*.
4   'Equality', in Charles Clarke (ed.), *The Too Difficult Box*.
5   Fox, *Watching the English*, p. 403; Cooper, *Class*, p. 273; Wallop, *Consumed*, p. 144; David Tang, *Rules for Modern Life* and, until August 2017, in his weekly columns in the Weekend edition of the *Financial Times*.
6   Jemima Lewis, *Telegraph*, 2 September 2016.
7   Wallop, p. 5.

CHAPTER 13

1   Ibid, p. 63.
2   Michael Kerr, 'A chav-free break? No, thanks', *Daily Telegraph*, 21 January 2009.
3   Jones, *Chavs*, p. 5.
4   Savage, *Class in the 21st Century*, p. 363 and 387.
5   Wallop, p. 61.

6   Hanson, *Etiquette*, p. 72.
7   *Spectator*, 1 July 2017.
8   Fellowes, p. 57.
9   Deborah Devonshire, *Wait for Me*, preface.

CHAPTER 14

1   Alan S. C. Ross in Mitford, *Noblesse Oblige*, p. 34.
2   Kate Fox, 'The Wrong Frequency', in Connolly (ed.), *Know Your Place*, p. 189.
3   Halsey, *Change in British Society*, p. 12; see also Rym Kechacha, 'What Colour is a Chameleon', in Connolly (ed.), p. 226.
4   Stewart-Liberty and York, *Cooler, Faster, More Expensive*.
5   In Mitford, *Noblesse Oblige*.
6   Thwaite (ed.), *My Oxford*, p. 194.
7   *Class*, p. 92.
8   Ibid, p. 295.
9   Debrett's, *U and Non-U Revisited*.
10 Mount, *Mind the Gap*, p. 100.
11 Ruth Gledhill, *The Times*, 7 April 2014; Peter York, *Authenticity is a Con*, p. 29.
12 Fellowes, p. 55.
13 Cooper, p. 93.

CHAPTER 15

1   Fox, p. 105.
2   David Crystal, *The Stories of English*; Braj B. Kachru, *World Englishes and Culture Wars*; Simon Horobin, *The English Language*.
3   See e.g. Trudgill, *Sociolinguistics*.
4   Mark Easton, *Britain Etc*.
5   Bence-Jones and Montgomery-Massingberd, *The British Aristocracy*, p. 205.
6   Easton, p. 257.
7   Ibid, p. 264.
8   Interview 26 November 2015 with Hattie Collins.
9   *Spectator*, 3 March 2018.

CHAPTER 17

1   John, Duke of Bedford, *A Silver-Plated Spoon*, p. 112.
2   John, Duke of Bedford, *The Book of Snobs*, p. 61.

CHAPTER 18

1   Sarah Lyall, *A Field Guide to the British*, p. 2.

2 Not Actual Size, *The Art of Being Middle Class* p. 187; *Debrett's New Guide to Etiquette and Modern Manners*, p. 219.

CHAPTER 19

1 *Book of Snobs*, p. 59.

CHAPTER 20

1 Wallop, p. 25.
2 Fox, p. 429; Cooper, p. 262, 269.
3 *Guardian*, 12 March 2004.
4 *Telegraph*, 18 January 2014.
5 *Guardian*, 12 March 2004.

CHAPTER 21

1 Short version in *Telegraph*, 18 January 2013.
2 *Telegraph*, 18 January 2013.
3 Fox, p. 345.
4 Harry Wallop, *Telegraph*, 18 January 2013.

CHAPTER 22

1 Fox, p. 189; Cooper, p. 205.
2 Fox, p. 330.
3 Wallop, p. 123.

CHAPTER 23

1 Charles Quest-Ritson, *The English Garden*; Cooper, p. 243; Fox, p. 208.
2 Harry Mount, *How England Made the English*, p. 182.
3 See Cooper and Fox, ibid.

CHAPTER 24

1 Easton, p. 33.
2 Perrott, *The Aristocrats*, p. 235.

CHAPTER 25

1 The highest handicap is 10, which is held by only around 10 players in the world, all of them Argentinians.
2 *Observer*, August 1999.

CHAPTER 26

1 Jeremy Black, *The British Abroad*.
2 Cannadine, *The Decline and Fall of the British Aristocracy*, p. 370.
3 Edward Royle, *Modern Britain*, p. 300.

CHAPTER 27

1 Cooper, p. 303.
2 de Botton, p. 137.
3 Paxman, *Friends in High Places*, p. 288.
4 Ibid, p. 294.
5 Miranda Carter, *Anthony Blunt: His Lives*.
6 Cooper, *Class* p. 312.

CHAPTER 28

1 Fox, p. 332.
2 Wallop, p. 252.
3 *Guardian*, 9 December 1960.
4 *Economist*, 12 March 2016.
5 Cooper, p. 323.
6 Atkinson, p. 57.
7 Fox, p. 539.
8 In the 1979 and 1999 editions of her book *Class*.

CHAPTER 29

1 Orwell, *The English People*.
2 W. Somerset Maugham, *A Writer's Notebook*.
3 *Economist*, 24 January 2015 and 21 March 2015 and 28 January 2017.
4 Chrystia Freeland, *Plutocrats: The Rise of the New Global Super-Rich and the Fall of Everyone*.
5 Minxin Pei, *China's Crony Capitalism: The Dynamics of Regime Decay*.
6 Mount, *Mind the Gap*, p. 129.
7 Lee Hawkins, 'Newbos: The Rise of America´s new black overclass', CNBC 26 February 2009.
8 Wallop, p. 252.
9 Wallop, *Consumed*, Introduction.
10 Ibid, p. 84.
11 Orwell, *The Road to Wigan Pier*.
12 Michael Young, *The Rise of the Meritocracy*.
13 Ian McEwan, *Enduring Love*.

14 In Charles Darwin's words the struggle for life and the survival of the fittest. Modern authors prefer conflict as Edmund Fawcett in *Liberalism: The Life of an Idea* (2018): 'Conflict is inescapable.'

15 *FT Wealth*, March 2017.

16 Orwell, *The Road to Wigan Pier*.

17 Glass, *London: Aspects of Change*; see also Atkinson, *Class*, p. 118 for Bristol.

18 Carole Cadwalladr, 'From Blair to Corbyn: the changing face of Islington, Labour's London heartland', *Guardian*, 9 August 2015.

19 Wallop, p. 98.

20 Hilary Osborne, *Guardian*, 25 July 2014.

21 Orwell, *The Road to Wigan Pier*.

22 In response to R. H. Tawney, *Equality*.

23 Scheve and Stasavage, *Taxing the Rich*; OECD, Key Issues Paper (June 2017).

CHAPTER 30

1 Fox, p. 179.

2 Harry Pearson, *The Far Corner*, p. 48.

3 Turner, *A Classless Society*, p. 78; Royle, *Modern Britain*, p. 297, 306.

4 James Bloodworth, *The Myth of Meritocracy*, p. 79.

5 *The Saturday Book*.

6 *Yorkshire Post*, December 2015.

7 Vivien Hall in 1939, see Arthur Marwick, *Class*, p. 215.

8 Orwell, *The Lion and the Unicorn*.

9 Kenneth O. Morgan, quoted by Cannadine, *Class in Britain*, p. 146.

10 J. R. Daeschner, *True Brits*.

CHAPTER 31

1 The nature versus nurture debate surrounding intelligence continues unabated. Studies of twins seem to support the former: monozygotic twins have roughly the same intelligence, even if raised apart. The intelligence of dizygotic twins very often differs greatly, even if they grow up together. Supporters of the nurture theory cite biographies of people who reach very high levels of achievement, including in intellect, as a result of exceptional circumstances such as the loss of their parents or other major strokes of fate. Intelligence is at any rate at least partly inherited. No-one claims that all people are born equally intelligent. Cf. Stuart Ritchie, *Intelligence*.

2 Sutton Trust, 1 February 2010.

3 A. C. Grayling, *The Challenge of Things*.

4 *Financial Times*, 3 June 2016.

5 James Bloodworth, *The Myth of Meritocracy*, p. 51.

6 *Guardian*, 21 July 2016.

7 Paxman, *The Political Animal*, p. 28.
8 *Fabian Review*, The Class Issue (Summer 2008).
9 *Sun*, 16 January 2016.
10 Tawney, *Equality*.
11 Susan Crosland, *Tony Crosland*.

CHAPTER 32

1 Communist Party of Great Britain.
2 Orwell, *The Road to Wigan Pier*.
3 Ibid.
4 Fellowes, p. 121.
5 Ellis Wasson, *Aristocracy and the Modern World*, p. 210.
6 Edward Vallance, *A Radical History of Britain*.
7 Ellis Wasson, *Born to Rule*, p. 65.
8 David Freeman, *The Churchill Centre Finest Hour*, 139.
9 Cf. for many details Savage, *Social Class in the 21st Century*, p. 189; Bukodi/ Goldthorpe/Waller/Kuha, 'The Mobility Problem in Britain: New findings from the Analysis of Birth Cohort Data', *British Journal of Sociology* 66: 93–117; the Social Mobility Commission and Sutton Trust publish regularly on this subject.
10 Bukodi et al.
11 Robert Colls, *Identity of England*, p. 76.
12 McRobbie (2004), quoted in Biressi and Nunn, *Class and Contemporary British Culture*, p. 135.
13 *Respectable*.
14 Ronald Hayman (ed.), *My Cambridge*.

CHAPTER 33

1 Cooper, *Class*, p. 176.
2 Fox, p. 416.
3 Fellowes, p. 307.
4 *FT* Wealth, May 2017.
5 *Telegraph*, 6 May 2012.
6 Lyall, *A Field Guide to the English*, p. 123.
7 Fox, p. 194.
8 Ibid, p. 209.
9 Mount, *Mind the Gap*, p. 40.
10 Fox, p. 194.
11 Jones, *Chavs*, p. 9.
12 Walden, *The New Elites*, p. 200.
13 Edith Sitwell, *The English Eccentrics* (1933); Raymond Lamont-Brown, *A Book of English Eccentrics* (1984); John Timpson, *Timpson's English*

Eccentrics; Henry Hemming, *In Search of the English Eccentric*; David Weeks, *The Gifts of Eccentrics*.

14 Harry Mount, *How England Made the English*, p 156.

CHAPTER 34

1 For many see Price Collier, *England and the English*; Wilhelm Dibelius, *England* (1922 German, 1930 English); Karel Capek, *Letters from England* (1924); George Santayana, *Soliloquies in England*; Gustaaf Johannes Renier, *The English: Are They Human?*; Alfred Kerr, *Ich kam nach England, Tagebuch 1936–40*; Philippe Daudy, *Les Anglais. Portrait of a People*; Bill Bryson, *Notes from a Small Island* and *The Road to Little Dribbling*; Sarah Lyall, *A Field Guide to the British*; Hans-Dieter Gelfert, *Typisch englisch*; most are named in Ian Buruma, *Voltaire's Coconuts – Anglomania in Europa*; Bibliography up until 1940 in Francesca M. Wilson (ed.), *Strange Island: Britain Through Foreign Eyes 1395–1940*.

2 Bryson, *Notes from a Small Island*, p. 378.

3 Julian Barnes, *England, England*, p. 83.

4 Jones, *Chavs*, p. 268.

5 New translation by Linda B. Parshall, *Letters of a Dead Man* (2016), from which the Pückler quotations in English have been taken.

6 Letter of 19 October 1826; Bowman, *The Fortune Hunter*, p. 91.

7 Jennings, *Them and US*; de Courcy, *The Husband Hunters*; Cannadine, *The Decline and Fall of the British Aristocracy*, p. 397.

8 York and Stewart-Liberty, *Cooler, Faster, More Expensive*.

9 Mikes, *How to be Inimitable*.

10 Harry Mount, *Spectator*, 9 December 2017.

11 Cannadine, *Ornamentalism*, p. 8.

12 James Morris, *Farewell the Trumpets* (1978).

13 e.g. Lyall, *A Field Guide to the British*, p. 111; Buruma, *Voltaire's Coconuts*.

14 Letter of 19 October 1826.

15 Letter of 8 July 1828.

16 Letter of 23 August 1828.

17 Ralf Dahrendorf, *Class Conflict in Industrial Society*.

18 Buruma, *Voltaire's Coconuts*.

19 Jutta Falke-Ischinger, *Wo bitte geht's zur Queen?*.

20 Orwell, *The Road to Wigan Pier*.

21 When a line of warships crosses in front of a line of enemy ships at right angles.

CHAPTER 35

1 Marr, *A History of Modern Britain*, Prologue.

2 *Spectator*, 6 January 2018.

Picture Credits and Permissions

The following images are reproduced by kind permission of the copyright holders.

1. Women workers circa 1940 taking their lunch break. (Thinkstock/ Getty Images)
2. All dressed up in evening wear. (George Marks/Getty Images)
3. Couples at dinner, with the maid pouring the soup. (George Marks/ Getty Images)
4. Supping wine in the living room. (George Marks/Getty Images)
5. Businessman reading a newspaper. (George Marks/Getty Images)
6. Eton College pupils cycling to their 'posts' during rifle-shooting practice. A parashooter's detachment to patrol Eton was formed and it includes 50 Eton College boys, all members of the Officer Training Corps and all aged 17. (Hulton-Deutsch Collection/CORBIS/Corbis via Getty Images)
7. Worker in the 1950s holding a wrench and looking delightedly at his paycheck. (George Marks/Getty Images)
8. Bank Holiday Cheese Rolling Festival. This annual tradition which is thought to date back to Roman times, draws competitors from far afield to race the cheese 200 yards down a near-vertical slope in pursuit of a seven-pound Double Gloucester cheese. Injuries are commonplace, and have forced the cancellation of the event in the past. (Peter Macdiarmid/Getty Images)
9. Spectators pose for a portrait at the Henley Royal Regatta in July 2019. An important part of the English social season, it is held annually over five days on the River Thames. (Gareth Cattermole/Getty Images)
10. England captain Joe Root reacts during day five of the second Test Match between England and India at Lord's Cricket Ground in August 2021. (Stu Forster/Getty Images)
11. Participants in the Eton Wall Game ruck for the ball during the traditional St Andrew's Day match, November 1936. (J. A. Hampton/ Topical Press Agency/Getty Images)

12. Awaiting the arrival of Queen Elizabeth II at the Royal Enclosure at Royal Ascot in June 2002. The traditional annual horseracing event, attended by the Queen and other members of the Royal Family, is one of the highlights of the social season for Britain's upper classes. (Sion Touhig/Getty Images)
13. Row of brick 1950s detached houses. (Sean Gladwell/Getty Images)
14. Filming of *Quadrophenia* in Brighton, based on the Mods and Rockers battles of the mid-1960s, starring Phil Daniels and with British rock group The Who providing the music. (Geoffrey Day/ Mirrorpix/Getty Images)
15. 'I look down on him because I am upper class...' (L-R) John Cleese, Ronnie Barker and Ronnie Corbett in the class sketch from the television series *The Frost Report*, in 1966. (Don Smith/Radio Times/ Getty Images)
16. The audience waves flags and sings along during the climax of the Last Night of The Proms at The Royal Albert Hall in London, on 8 September 2012. (Nicky J. Sims/Redferns via Getty Images)
17. The Prince of Wales refuses to give an autograph to local builder, Hedley Venning, during his visit to north Cornwall on 2 February 2005. (Colin Shepherd/Getty Images)

The following extracts are reproduced by kind permission of the copyright holders:

Index of Names